Languages of Belonging

LANGUAGES OF BELONGING

Islam, Regional Identity, and the Making of Kashmir

CHITRALEKHA ZUTSHI

HURST & COMPANY, LONDON

First published in the United Kingdom by
C. Hurst & Co. (Publishers) Ltd,
38 King Street, London WC2E 8JZ
by arrangement with Permanent Black, Delhi
Copyright © 2004 Permanent Black
Printed in England

The right of Chitralekha Zutshi to be identified as the author
of this publication is asserted by her in accordance with
the Copyright, Designs and Patents Act, 1988.

A Cataloguing-in-Publication data record for this book
is available from the British Library.

ISBNs
1-85065-694-0 *casebound*
1-85065-700-9 *paperback*

For my parents
Lalita and Bal Krishan Zutshi

Contents

PLATES

Maps

Acknowledgments

A lthough a solitary journey, researching and writing this book has been enriched by a number of people, places, and incidents. The debts I have incurred along the way, especially to the people and institutions involved, are countless. The book was conceived of as a dissertation project at Tufts University and most of the research for the study, which spanned archives and individuals in three continents, would not have been possible without a 1997–8 dissertation fellowship from the American Institute of Indian Studies. A grant from the Taraknath Das Foundation at Columbia University aided in follow-up research over the summer of 1999. Tufts University provided a generous writing fellowship in 1999–2000, which allowed me to complete the dissertation. The dissertation was reincarnated as a book in the stimulating atmosphere of the history departments at the University of South Alabama and the College of William and Mary, both of which were generous with financial and intellectual support for a historian at the start of her career. Specifically, the College of Arts and Sciences at the University of South Alabama provided funds for research trips in 2000, while the College of Arts and Sciences at the College of William and Mary funded several research and publication trips in 2001.

Since this project is about, and involved research in, a region plagued by civil strife, I would especially like to acknowledge the contribution of several people in Kashmir who made it possible for me to conduct research in comfort, and, more importantly, safety. Mufti Maqbool Ahmed, at the risk of his own life, very effectively introduced me into Kashmiri society, so that I could access priceless private collections. His wife, Maqsooda Maqbool Ahmed, provided undying optimism, and a safe haven, where I was taken care of regardless of political conditions. At all times, Peerzada Mohammad Ashraf was generous beyond the call of duty with his time, knowledge, and his family's private collections. The other individuals who provided access to their private collections, despite the war raging outside their doors, include Sayyid Iftekar Jalali, Fidah Hassnain, A.R. Wafai, Moulvi Mohammad Shafi Qari, Bahar Kashmiri, Professor Nooruddin Zahid, Abdul Rahman Kondoo and Bhushan Bazaz. Moulvi Omar Farooq generously provided access to his family library for my perusal. I would particularly like to mention Mr S.N. Bhatt Haleem, who spent hours laboring over obscure and barely legible Persian and Kashmiri manuscripts with me in an effort to decipher and translate them.

I also owe much to those librarians and archivists of the Srinagar State Archives, the Research and Publications Department of the University of Kashmir, and the Jammu State Archives, who helped me locate valuable and rare documents for this study. Individuals who deserve special mention in this regard are Ghulam Mohiuddin, director of the Jammu and Kashmir State Archives, and Shakeela Shawl, head librarian at the Government Press Department, Srinagar, both of whom made sure that I had access to crucial archival documents and newspaper clippings. The Interlibrary Loan staff at the University Library, University of South Alabama and the Earl Gregg Swem Library, the College of William and Mary, was critical in ensuring the uninterrupted progress of this book. I would particularly like to thank Hope Yelich and Alan Zoellner at the Swem Library for being so willing to help out in any way possible. In addition, the staff of the history departments at the University of South Alabama and the College of William and Mary—Martha Hunn, Betty Flanigan and Roz Stearns—was helpful in more ways than one.

I have had the honor of interacting with a peerless group of scholars through my academic career, all of whom have influenced my intellectual development in significant ways. In this regard, I owe the greatest debt to my dissertation adviser, Sugata Bose, who has been a unique combination of mentor, critic, staunch supporter, and friend. Ayesha Jalal, who encouraged this project since its conception, has been an inspiration as teacher and intellectual. John Rogers perhaps read more drafts of this project than anyone else and contributed hours of patient advice. C.A. Bayly managed to comment on and encourage this book from across the Atlantic over several years. Leila Fawaz took time off her duties as dean to act as an invaluable mentor through my years at Tufts. I would also like to thank Lynda Shaffer for always being there and encouraging me to look beyond the confines of my own region.

Although some readers of this work remain anonymous, that this book benefited immensely from their comments at key stages of its development, is without a doubt. I have been extremely fortunate in my publishers and editors, Rukun Advani at Permanent Black and Dedi Felman at Oxford University Press, New York, who provided a vision for this book that has transformed it beyond all measure. Michael Dwyer at Hurst & Co. provided crucial support during the publication process. I have presented component parts of this book at a variety of conferences and received excellent comments from several individuals, too numerous to name. Needless to say, the faults that remain are all mine.

My colleagues and friends have over the years sustained me through the ups and downs of writing this book. I could not have asked for a better first chairperson than Clarence Mohr at the University of South Alabama, with whom I had many spirited discussions about nationalism, religious identity and conflict, and who helped shape this book in more ways than he will ever know. I would also like to mention Prachi Deshpande, Mridu Rai, Mahesh Rangarajan, Madhavi Menon, Semanti Ghosh, Martha-Jane Brazy, Satadru Sen, Frank Conlon, Douglas Haynes, Jim McCord, Laurie Koloski, Cindy Hahamovitch, Scott Nelson, Leisa Meyer, Craig Canning, Judy Ewell, Ed Pratt, Abdul-Karim Rafeq, and Chandos Brown, among many others, each of whom, in their individual ways, cheered me on as I grappled with various stages of the writing and publication process.

Annette Lazzara, Marina Diaz-Cristobal, Asja Mandic, Samer Kassab and Janie Bess were always there to remind me that there was life beyond this book. In Jammu, Raj Dulari and Dr R.K. Zutshi provided the comfort of home and encouraged me to continue in the face of severe odds. In Delhi, Ashima and V.K. Kaul readily opened the doors to their home, where I always had a place to stay and unwind on the way to and from numerous research trips. In Boston, Louis Allegro regaled me with stories when the process got too overwhelming, and Jim Allegro, Corrinne Mandrafino, Andrew Allegro, and Julie and Brian Sim provided encouragement and support.

My family has been the most significant factor in determining the course of my scholarly development. To my parents, Lalita and Bal Krishan Zutshi, I would simply like to say thank you, thank you for it all, but especially for letting me go, letting me go to places where most parents would not dream of sending their daughters. Without their unflinching faith and love, I would not have had the courage to take on or complete this daunting assignment. They have given me a strength that is seldom shaken. And to them, I dedicate this book. I can safely say that my sister, Urvashi Zutshi, provided a sense of perspective and humor rarely found in people; her ceaseless confidence and love for me have been a source of much comfort through this process. And finally, my husband, James J. Allegro, has been an unfaltering intellectual and emotional presence in my life. He not only challenged me at every step of this process, from its conception to its birth, he also managed to be my greatest and most dogged champion. I dare say that without him the process of writing this book, as the study itself, if at all possible, would have been decidedly less inspiring.

Williamsburg, Virginia   Chitralekha Zutshi

Glossary

anjuman	An association or society
assami	A tenant of the state who possessed permanent hereditary occupancy rights to his/her portion of the land
begar	Forced labor, usually without recompense, performed by Kashmiri peasants when called upon by the state to render services such as road building or carrying loads and rations for officials and tourists
biddat	Innovations in the religious realm
chak	Fallow land assigned by the state to individuals called *chakdars* to encourage cultivation; the *chakdar* was entitled to produce from this land as long as he remained loyal to the state and paid his dues on time
darbar	Royal court
fatwa	Opinion or verdict on a particular issue articulated by a Muslim leader
galladar	Grain dealer
hadith	Tradition of the Prophet Muhammad, which includes a compilation of his sayings and actions
hak milkiyat	Proprietary right
jagir	A land grant given by the state to an individual, called a *jagirdar*, for a limited time period; the individual held the right to assess and collect land revenue and other taxes from this land
kafir	Non-believer
karkandar	An owner of a shawl manufactory
khadim	A low-level administrator in a shrine's hierarchy

khalisa	Land owned and utilized by the state
khanqah	A mosque, devotional retreat, or residence of a saint
Kharif	Autumnal crops
kharwar	Unit of weight used for revenue assessment in Kashmir; one *kharwar* is roughly 192 pounds or 87 kg
madrasa	A school run by *moulvis;* also referred to as a *makhtab*
millat	Religious community
miras	Hereditary right to land occupancy and use enforced by custom
Mirwaiz	Title given to the head preacher of a mosque, city, or region
mohalla	A locality or neighborhood
moulvi	Title given to Muslim religious teacher learned in religious texts; also referred to as a *mullah*
muafi	A land grant exempt from payment of land revenue, given by the state to an individual, shrine, mosque, temple or other institution; the holder was known as a *muafidar*
mulk	Homeland or country
mutawalli	The custodian of a shrine
pandit	Title given to a Brahman learned in Hindu texts; also teacher or expert
pathshala	A school run by *pandits*
pir	A Muslim religious elder associated with shrines; could be a mendicant roving the countryside and performing religious rituals for the peasantry, a *mullah* of small means, or a manager/head of a particular shrine; this group of figures also referred to as *pirzadas*
qaum	Depending on context, can refer to a community, clan, sect, or nation
Rabi	Spring crops
sabha	An association or society
sajjadanashin	The spiritual head of a particular shrine

Sayyid	A Muslim claiming descent from the Prophet Muhammad
shali	Unhusked rice
sharia	The set of rules and legal injunctions that guide all realms of a Muslim's life; defined variously based on four major schools of Islamic jurisprudence
shaal baf	A weaver of shawls
Sheikh	In the Kashmiri context, a descendant of a Hindu convert to Islam
shirk	Assigning partners to Allah by going against the principle of *tawhid*; those who commit *shirk* are referred to as *mushriks*
tawhid	The unity of all creation under Islam; the monotheistic principle of the existence of one God
ulema (sg. *alim*)	Muslim religious elite learned in Islamic texts and jurisprudence
umma/ummat	The worldwide community of Muslims
wazkhaani	The act of preaching a sermon at a mosque, shrine, or other location
wadhdar	Moneylender
waiz	A preacher at a mosque or shrine
waqf	An endowment, usually made in the name of a shrine or mosque, by the state or wealthy patron; the endowment deed is referred to as a *waqfnama*
watan	Homeland or nation
zamindar	In the Kashmiri context, a cultivator of land or peasant
ziarat	A devotional retreat, grave, or tomb of a saint

Introduction

Let us all offer thanksgiving,
For Freedom has come to us;
It's after ages that she has beamed
Her radiance on us.

In western climes Freedom comes
With a shower of light and grace,
But dry, sterile thunder is all
She has for our soil.

Poverty and starvation,
Lawlessness and repression—
It's with these blessings
That she has come to us.

Freedom, being of heavenly birth,
Can't move from door to door;
You'll find her camping in the homes
Of a chosen few alone.

There's restlessness in every heart,
But no one dare speak out—
Afraid that with their free expression
Freedom may be annoyed.

"Azadi," Ghulam Ahmad Mahjoor[1]

Alternately reviled as a traitor and glorified as a patriot, the Kashmiri poet Ghulam Ahmad Mahjoor perhaps best captures the ironies inherent in the Kashmiri historical experience. Written at the dawn of the independence of India, the creation of Pakistan,

[1] Ghulam Ahmad Mahjoor, "Azadi," [Freedom] in Trilokinath Raina, ed. and trans., *An Anthology of Modern Kashmiri Verse* (*1930–1960*) (Poona: Sangam Press, 1972), 74–7. These are selections from the poem, which has not been quoted here in its entirety.

and the partition of Kashmir, "Azadi," one of Mahjoor's lesser known poems, reflects Kashmiris' ongoing engagement with, and deeply ambiguous relationship to, the bywords of the postcolonial era— independence, nationalism, citizenship, and rights. Interestingly, however, it is Mahjoor's poetry that has been appropriated as the un- likely symbol of the immutable, unquestioned, and state-endorsed Kashmiri nationalist identity, *Kashmiriyat*.[2]

Nationalist discourse, particularly of the state-sponsored variety, is characterized by a unified and cohesive vision of the nation's past, aim- ed at papering over internal differences, conflicts, and contradictions in not only the nation's history, but also the history of the nationalist movement that brings its corollary—the nation-state—into existence.[3] In the case of Kashmir, Indian and Kashmiri nationalist discourses have both converged to define Kashmiri history and cultural identity in terms of a concept widely known as *Kashmiriyat*. Akin to its Indian cousin, Kashmiri nationalism's memory of the past is refracted through rose-tinted glasses, in which Kashmir appears as a unique region where religious communities lived in harmony since time immemorial and differences in religion did not translate into acrimonious conflict until external intervention.

[2] Sheikh Mohammad Abdullah's National Conference regime in Jammu and Kashmir (1948–1953) adopted Ghulam Ahmad Mahjoor (1885–1952) as the main spokesperson of its secular mantra, *Kashmiriyat*. It is deeply ironic that the same regime had imprisoned Mahjoor not long before, in 1947, when he wrote: "Though I would like to sacrifice my life and body for India, yet my heart is in Pakistan." Subsequently released after recanting this statement, Mahjoor was re- surrected by the National Conference as a votary of *Kashmiriyat*, and given the title of National Poet of Kashmir for the body of his work. See Prem Nath Bazaz, *The History of the Struggle for Freedom in Kashmir, Cultural and Political, From the Earliest Times to the Present Day* (New Delhi: Kashmir Publishing Company, 1954), 296–9.

[3] For an insightful discussion on Indian nationalist discourse and its engagement with Indian history, see Amartya Sen, "On Interpreting India's Past," in Sugata Bose and Ayesha Jalal, eds., *Nationalism, Democracy and Development: State and Politics in India* (Delhi: Oxford University Press, 1997), 10–35.

The Subaltern Studies group has also attempted to disclose the singularity of Indian nationalism as well as its complicity with colonial discourse. For a concise overview of the Subaltern Studies project, see Gyan Prakash, "Subaltern Studies as Postcolonial Criticism," *American Historical Review* (December 1994): 1475– 90.

The wholesale acceptance of *Kashmiriyat* in public discourse on Kashmir is absolutely central to two interlinked political projects, which alternately overlap, diverge, and clash: first, the discourse of a unified Indian nation-state based on a unitary nationalism; and second, a highly federalized nationalism based on regionalized and plural identities. Scholarship on Kashmir, particularly on accession and recent political upheavals, broadly falls under these two categories.[4] As such, it unquestioningly accepts the concept of *Kashmiriyat*, offers no critical engagement with its origin, its definition, and its historically contingent nature, and as a result remains oblivious to the critical relationship between history, identities, and nationalism. This book, instead, locates and interrogates *Kashmiriyat* as a historical entity, asserting that Kashmiri regional identities have been far more ambiguous, and certainly more complex than the term *Kashmiriyat* would lead one to believe. Kashmiri-ness was, and continues to be, a series of dynamic identities that have emerged in interaction with, and at times been overshadowed by, other forms of belonging, particularly the religious and national.

It is significant to point out at the outset that the idea of *Kashmiriyat* is not the original product of nationalist minds, since it draws on a colonial discourse on Kashmir that far pre-dates the emergence of nationalism. As early as the seventeenth century, European travelers to the Valley were writing about the absence of religious discord in the region, presenting it as a place where Hindus were uncaring of caste rules and Muslims did not make the pilgrimage to Mecca,[5] since they lived in what eventually came to be described as the "Happy Valley."[6]

---

[4] For instance, M.J. Akbar, *India: The Siege Within* (England: Penguin Books, 1985) and Verinder Grover, ed., *The Story of Kashmir, Yesterday and Today*, vols 1–3 (Delhi: Deep and Deep Publications, 1995), fall in the first category. Sumit Ganguly, *The Crisis in Kashmir: Portents of War, Hopes of Peace* (Cambridge: Cambridge University Press and Woodrow Wilson Center Press, 1997) and Sumantra Bose, *The Challenge in Kashmir: Democracy, Self-Determination and a Just Peace* (New Delhi: Sage, 1997), fall in the second category.

[5] See Francois Bernier, *Travels in the Mogul Empire AD 1656–1668* (London: W. Pickering, 1826; repr., New Delhi: Atlantic Publishers, 1989).

[6] Kashmir was first described as "the Happy Valley" by W. Wakefield, who visited Kashmir in 1875, in his book entitled *History of Kashmir and the Kashmiris: The Happy Valley* (London: S. Low, Marston, Searle & Rivington, 1879; repr., Delhi: Seema Publications, 1975).

The "happiness" of the Kashmir Valley, particularly for India's colonial masters, perhaps had more to do with its geographical attributes, which rendered it a cool haven for the heat-weary British, than with any peculiarities of the people in the region.[7] By the mid-nineteenth century, however, colonial discourse on Kashmir was deeply imbricated with the creation and maintenance of Kashmir as a princely state within the British Indian Empire, and the exigencies of indirect colonialism. Either way, it was in the interests of the colonial state, even as it began to intervene in the political and economic affairs of the princely state, to perpetuate the myth of the distinctiveness of the historical trajectory of Kashmir and its inhabitants from British India.

Indeed, it is the historical narrative on Kashmir, drawing to a significant extent on colonial histories and travelogues, that has most often bandied about the term *Kashmiriyat*, attempting to locate this anachronistic identity in the history of the region.[8] This narrative paints all Kashmiris, from mystic poets in medieval times to common folk in the Dogra period, with the brush of a unique, syncretic Kashmiri identity. The focus on discovering *Kashmiriyat* throughout Kashmiri history is responsible, in no small measure, for the significant lacunae in the region's historiography, a historiography that refuses to acknowledge the parallels between Kashmiri history and that of the rest of pre-colonial and colonial India.

The centrality of Kashmir to contemporary global politics makes it all the more timely and imperative to contest this narrative of secular culture, religious syncretism, and a primordial Kashmiri identity by

[7] The British reinvented Kashmir into a combination of picnic spot and sportsman's paradise, away from the dusty plains, where the mundane business of ruling British India could be discussed over hiking, trout-fishing, and hunting expeditions. See Vasant Saberwal, Mahesh Rangarajan, and Ashish Kothari, *People, Parks, and Wildlife: Towards Coexistence* (New Delhi: Orient Longman, 2001), 35, and Mahesh Rangarajan, *India's Wildlife History: An Introduction* (Delhi: Permanent Black, 2001), 35–45.

[8] To mention only a couple, see Bazaz, *The History of the Struggle for Freedom in Kashmir* and G.M.D. Sufi, *Kashir: Being a History of Kashmir From the Earliest Times to Our Own*, 2 vols (New Delhi: Light and Life Publishers, 1974). A recent exception is Mridu Rai, *Hindu Rulers, Muslim Subjects: Islam, Rights, and the History of Kashmir* (New Delhi: Permanent Black, and Princeton: Princeton University Press, forthcoming 2004).

outlining an alternative trajectory of Kashmiri history. This book examines the regional history of Kashmir in the *longue duree* to illustrate the shifting nature of Kashmiri identities over the course of the late eighteenth to twentieth centuries, with a brief look at the medieval period. While rescuing Kashmir from blatant attempts at re-inventing its past, it also returns Kashmir to the regional historiography of South Asia. The discourse and antecedents of nationalism, particularly with reference to Bengal, have been debated at length in South Asian historiography. Expressions of regional belonging from other parts of the subcontinent and their relationship to nationalism, however, have been ignored until very recently.[9] Furthermore, discourses of regional affiliation in the pre-colonial period seem to have garnered even less attention. The present book fills both lacunae in South Asian historiography by examining Kashmiri narratives of regional belonging in dialogue with other affiliations, including religion, locality, and the nation, across the pre-colonial and colonial periods.

Further, through a study of Kashmiri public discourse in the *longue duree*, I hope to dispel the notion that colonialism was a historical rupture that politicized religious and regional identities in late-nineteenth-century Kashmir. It is undeniable that the establishment of the British Residency and the centralization of the Dogra state under the British at the turn of the twentieth century provided the context for an emphasis on "community," variously defined, as the reference point for identities. However, it would be a gross oversight to ignore the different, yet significant, Kashmiri expressions of regional and religious belonging in the pre-colonial period. After all, neither the writing of history, nor discourses on good government, nor even a poetic tradition, was alien to the Valley prior to the late nineteenth century.[10]

This book thus charts a middle course between a primordial and instrumentalist reading of Kashmiri political culture. While the

---

[9] Several recent studies have introduced new regional perspectives into the equation. See, for instance, Prachi Deshpande, "Narratives of Pride: History and Regional Identity in Maharashtra, India, *c.* 1870–1960" (Ph.D. dissertation, Tufts University, 2002), and Farina Mir, "The Social Space of Language: Punjabi Popular Narratives in Colonial India,*c.*1850–1900" (Ph.D. dissertation, Columbia University, 2002).

[10] The *Rajatarangini*, or the *History of Kings*, dating from twelfth-century Kashmir, and considered the first recorded history from the Indian subcontinent

narrative on Kashmiri regional and religious identities was no doubt transformed in the social and political context of indirect colonialism, the historical discourse, literary forms, and religious idioms and symbols from the pre-colonial period were easily identifiable in nineteenth- and twentieth-century Kashmiri public discourse. For instance, poetic and other narratives expressing longing for a homeland with just rulers, first identifiable at the turn of the nineteenth century, formed an important aspect of Kashmiri public discourse well into the twentieth century.

However, when one considers the engagement between regional and religious identities in the Valley's political culture, it becomes clear that the transition from the pre-colonial to the colonial was far from seamless. While the discourse on belonging in the pre-colonial period transcended but did not erase religious differences, the discourse on regional identities in the early twentieth century specifically denigrated religious affiliations in favor of an all-encompassing regional nationalism. Clearly, religious identities did not become more politicized in the colonial period than they were earlier, but their articulation certainly operated in a dramatically changed context, which in turn endowed them with a different set of meanings.

In other words, although the terms I employ here to identify various forms of belonging—religion, region, nation—remain the same through the pre-colonial and colonial periods, their content and modes of operation change with the changing social, economic and political scenario of early colonialism, which, in the case of Kashmir, did not take place until the last two decades of the nineteenth century. I thus place Kashmiri discourses on identity and culture in the context of the Valley's political and economic formations. Transformations in the political economy of the Kashmir Valley over the period of study shifted the relationships and consequently the modes of interaction between the state, economic imperatives, and the needs and demands of Kashmiris. The perceived and actual impact of these changes, in

---

by the British, articulates a theory of orthodox statecraft and ethical government. According to this theory, an ideal king maintained firm control over unruly elements in his kingdom, while also upholding a benevolent attitude toward his subjects. See Madhavi Yasin, "Kalhana and his *Rajatarangini*," in K.N. Kalla, ed., *The Literary Heritage of Kashmir* (Delhi: Mittal Publications, 1985).

turn, played a crucial role in determining whether the Valley's political culture focused on and glorified regional, religious, or national affiliations.

Finally, this book adds, I believe, something of importance to the vibrant body of scholarship on Islam in South Asia.[11] A study of Islam in Kashmir is especially significant in the current political scenario, for the religion of the majority of the Kashmiri population is often held responsible for the insurgency in the region. Moreover, Islam in Kashmir is often described, at times in the same breath, as tolerant and syncretic as well as militant and separatist. In its examination of Islam and Kashmiri Muslims in the Valley, this book transcends the revival/ reform, folk/elite, syncretic/separatist or communal categories that have defined scholarship on Islam in other parts of the Indian subcontinent. It argues that Islam proved to be a significant site for the unfolding discourse on identities in Kashmiri political culture, not only as a marker of community identities, but equally significantly as a cornerstone of faith for individual Kashmiris as they wrestled with the various monumental changes of their time.

The discourse and practice of Islam in Kashmir, thus, was more than simply a set of symbols presented to an unsuspecting public by groups of elites seeking power or protecting themselves from running afoul of the state.[12] On a similar note, religion was not simply an "ideological smokescreen" for clashes between social groups and entities in their ultimate quest for power.[13] Islam did indeed prove to be a powerful symbol for emergent leaders in Kashmir across the colonial divide; however, its ideological and normative meanings for the leadership,

[11] For a brilliant survey of developments in the historical scholarship on Islam in South Asia, see Francis Robinson, *Islam and Muslim History in South Asia* (New Delhi: Oxford University Press, 2000), especially the Introduction.

[12] Sandria Freitag, for instance, argues that communal conflict in the urban areas of north India was generated by competing elites attempting to consolidate their position within the Muslim community by portraying themselves as defenders of the faith. See Sandria B. Freitag, *Collective Action and Community: Public Arenas and the Emergence of Communalism in North India* (Berkeley: University of California Press, 1989).

[13] Peter van der Veer, for instance, has argued against treating religious discourse and practice simply as "ideological smokescreens that hide the real clash of material interests and social classes." See Peter van der Veer, *Religious Nationalism: Hindus and Muslims in India* (Berkeley: University of California Press, 1994), ix.

and Kashmiri Muslims in general, remained central to debates on defining the boundaries of their regional or religious communities as well as their individual positions in society.

This book also introduces a number of individual Kashmiri Muslim leaders to the scholarship on Islam in South Asia. These individuals, such as Hamidullah Shahabadi, Mirwaiz Rasool Shah, and Moulvi Mohammad Nooruddin Qari Kashmiri, among others, were at all times able to mediate their individual faith in Islam with public presentation of their religion as a panacea for Kashmiri Muslims and Kashmir in general. At the same time, they were able to reconcile their religious and regional identities effortlessly. There was no necessary contradiction between the religious, regional, and even the national in the writings of these individuals. Furthermore, while these individuals and the movements they represented were unique to the Kashmiri social and political context, they reflected concerns similar to those among Muslim leaders of British India—such as, for instance, Altaf Husain Hali, Sayyid Ahmed Khan and Mohammad Iqbal—and were aware of, and drew from, Muslim movements in other parts of South Asia.

Clearly, Kashmir was neither isolated from, nor unique in, the rest of the Indian subcontinent from the late-eighteenth to the midtwentieth centuries. At the same time, its study as a geographically strategic and politically distinct region in British India does provide a unique perspective on the interactions between state ideologies, class formation, and the development of political culture from the peripheries of South Asia. Most significantly, Kashmir's regional specificities illuminate manifestations of and interactions between alternative languages of belonging within the subcontinent, whether in the form of regional identification, religiosity, or nationalism.

Kashmir: Land and Geography

The state of Jammu and Kashmir lies on the northern fringes of the Indian subcontinent and exhibits a varied geography. In 1947, before 45 per cent of its territory became the northernmost state of the Indian Union, the area of this largest princely state in British India was 222,797 sq. km.[14] The relief of the territories that form Jammu and

[14] A.N. Raina, *Geography of Jammu and Kashmir*, 3rd rev. ed. (New Delhi: National Book Trust, 1981), 9.

Kashmir presents three distinct physiographic divisions: the province of Jammu with the Siwaliks and Outer Hills, largely an extension of the Punjab plains; the Valley of Kashmir, a structural basin that lies between the Pir Panjal and the Himadri, defined by the river Jhelum that flows out of Baramulla, meanders the vale, enters the Wular lake, leaves it near Sopore, and flows into a narrow gorge across the Pir Panjal to Muzaffarabad, where it turns sharply toward the south; and the region of the greater Himalayas beyond the Kashmir Valley to the north and east where Ladakh and Gilgit form habitable areas at very high altitudes.[15]

The three main administrative entities within the princely state of Jammu and Kashmir roughly corresponded to these geographical divisions: the province of Jammu, which had been the heartland of Dogra control in the Punjab; the province of Kashmir, purchased from the British in 1846; and the provinces of Ladakh and Baltistan, the former conquered by the Dogras in 1834 and the latter in 1840. There were other distinct political entities at the British Indian frontier, which as a result of their geographical location had to formulate some type of political relationship with the princely state. The most significant of these was the Gilgit Agency, which the British attached to Jammu and Kashmir for political convenience in 1889, and which the Dogra state leased back to them in 1935. Poonch, another important border area, came under the formal control of Jammu and Kashmir state in 1936 (see Map 1). The governor of Kashmir was the executive head of Kashmir province as well as the Gilgit Agency, while the governor of Jammu was responsible for Jammu province as well as Ladakh and Baltistan.

Although this book examines the entire state of Jammu and Kashmir, its primary focus is on the Valley of Kashmir, roughly congruent with Kashmir province, with Srinagar as its political and economic center, its Kashmiri-speaking inhabitants, and the socio-economic and religious developments within this geographically and administratively distinct entity. The Valley has a distinct climate, located as it is among the Himalayas 6000 feet above sea level, with cold winters and precipitation in the form of snow, rainy springs, and hot summer months. This climate has severely restricted the Valley's sowing season and crop yields, which have been considerably smaller than those of Jammu province. The people of the Kashmir Valley spoke Kashmiri,

---

[15] Ibid., 9–10.

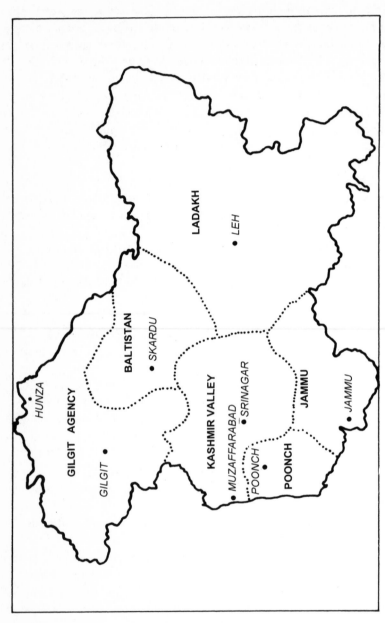

Map 1: Princely State of Jammu and Kashmir and its Main Administrative Divisions, *c.* 1846-1947.

and consisted mainly of Kashmiri Muslims, who formed the majority of the population, with a small but significant minority of Kashmiri Hindus, or Pandits.

There were genealogical and occupational divisions within these two communities. However, since most sources on this subject are British colonial sources, one has to view them with a certain degree of skepticism, particularly since the lines of division that appeared within the communities in the late-nineteenth and early-twentieth centuries did not neatly spring from these particular genealogical divisions. Nevertheless, it is important to recognize that Kashmiri Muslims and Kashmiri Pandits were not monolithic groups. Kashmiri Muslims were divided into Sheikhs, descendants of Hindu converts to Islam; Sayyids, who claimed a direct line of descent from the Prophet's family; Mughals, with Central Asian origins; and Pathans, the descendants of Afghans. These groups practised a variety of occupations, with agriculture and related occupations being the single most important. Sayyids and Mughals were more likely to be landholders and administrators of shrines. Several occupational groups also came under the category of Kashmiri Muslim, such as Doms, usually village watchmen; Watals, entrusted with janitorial tasks; Galawans, the horse-keepers; and Gujjars and Bakarwals, nomadic pastoral tribes that herded goats and sheep for their livelihood.

Kashmiri Pandits were divided into the astrologer class (Jotish), the priests (Guru or Bachbhat), and followers of secular occupations (Karkun). The vast majority of Kashmiri Pandits, particularly from the Karkun category, were salaried state employees in the lower rungs of the administration, while some practised cultivation and related occupations. A small minority, primarily from the first two categories, was involved in strictly religious occupations, such as astrology and the performance of Pandit rites and ceremonies.[16]

Sources and Contents

Most histories of Kashmir are based on a reading of British and Dogra government documents, presenting a version of Kashmiri history mediated through the state. I have attempted to transcend this limitation

---

[16] Walter R. Lawrence, *The Valley of Kashmir* (London: H. Frowde, 1895; repr., Jammu: Kashmir Kitab Ghar, 1996), chapter XII. See also T.N. Madan,

by tapping into an eclectic variety of sources, mainly drawn from Kashmiris themselves. This book is based on sources in the Kashmiri language, both oral and written, which have hitherto been ignored in historical writing on the region. Sources in other languages, including Urdu, Persian, and English have also been used in creating this palimpsest of Kashmiri history. Much of the source material for the study, besides material available in the archives, was mined from the private collections of individuals in Srinagar, Jammu, and Delhi.

The sources that have been used include private diaries, letters, unpublished manuscripts of poetry and polemical writings, published political and social pamphlets, newspapers, folk narratives, oral histories, and interviews. Most of these sources were penned, published, and narrated by the Kashmiri elite, a class that evolved through the hundred-odd years this work covers, but was always defined by its access to wealth and social resources, such as education. However, this does not imply that the Kashmiri masses remained aloof from the public discourse being generated by the elite. In fact, Kashmiri society, although illiterate, was characterized by literacy-awareness, a term that has been used by C.A. Bayly to describe Indian society in the precolonial period.[17]

Although they may not have been able to wield much influence until the early twentieth century, ordinary Kashmiris were an integral part of the political culture of the Valley, mostly as consumers, but sometimes also as actors, through the actions of peripatetic personages of various kinds, such as folk minstrels, self-proclaimed saints, and religious figures, all of whom orally transmitted political, social, and religious ideas to people in the countryside. It is simply fallacious to dismiss these figures as the producers of a "folk culture" divorced from the larger political culture, since it is amply evident—from attempts by the religious elite to malign them in the early twentieth century—that they acted as social and political mediators between urban centers and rural areas.

Family and Kinship: A Study of the Pandits of Rural Kashmir (Delhi: Oxford University Press, 1989), chapter II.

[17] Bayly suggests that although pre-colonial societies may not have been very literate, they did possess sophisticated regional and even interregional systems of communication. See C.A. Bayly, *Empire and Information: Intelligence Gathering and Social Communication in India 1780–1870* (Cambridge: Cambridge University Press, 1996), 10–44.

The chapters of this book are broadly chronological and thematic. Chapter one traces the development of Kashmiri political culture in the pre-colonial period, not only to highlight its transformation in the face of colonial intervention, but equally to illustrate and trace the pre-colonial origins of this discourse. It explores the articulation of a regional culture by Kashmiris, a culture that transcended but did not obscure religious affiliations, and which was defined in the universal language of Islam. Kashmiri regional narratives of the mid-eighteenth to the late-nineteenth centuries, furthermore, sketched the contours of a Kashmiri homeland that had to be rescued from the oppressive rule of outsiders through an appeal to the religious identities of the people.

Chapters two and three consider transformations in Kashmir's political economy in the late-nineteenth and early-twentieth centuries and their impact on the public discourse of the period. Specifically, chapter two explores the nature and impact of the colonial intervention on class formation in the Kashmir Valley, in the process delineating the changing relationships between Kashmiri social groups, the emergent Dogra state, and the British Residency. It assesses the nature of changes in the Valley's economic structures and social interactions in the context of a radically altered late-nineteenth-century political milieu, in the process drawing a bridge between the Valley's economic and socio-cultural institutions.

Chapter three examines the writings of a variety of Kashmiri Muslim individuals to outline the changing relationship between religion and community in the period between 1880 and 1930 against the backdrop of transformations in the Valley's political economy. A key question raised and addressed in this chapter is whether one can interpret the increased focus on religious community among Kashmiri Muslims as the rise of "communal" identities in the Valley. It argues that the salience of religion to the discourse on identities in this period was a direct result of the overtly Hindu nature of the Dogra state's apparatus of legitimacy, and, as significantly, social and economic changes ushered into Kashmir through the state's contact with British India.

The evolving relationship between the nature and agenda of the Dogra state and the discourse on Kashmiri Muslim identities is elaborated on in chapter four. Through a study of Kashmiri Muslim educational reform movements and the rhetoric on education in general, the chapter reveals that while the Dogra state was not the only reference point for the articulation of Kashmiri Muslim identities, it was both shaped by and played a key role in determining the contours of Kashmiri Muslim communitarian identities in the early twentieth century. Although the Muslim leadership of this period was unable to unify Kashmiri Muslims or even appeal to a cross-section of the community, their efforts on the educational front did lead to the recognition of Muslims as a distinguishable community with distinct interests in the state structures of the Valley.

Chapter five traces the emergence of a new Kashmiri Muslim leadership on the Valley's political landscape in the 1930s, which developed a belligerent discourse on rights and freedoms for Kashmiri Muslims based on an Islamic vision of a just, equitable society. It explores the content, and ultimately the effectiveness, of the political ideology articulated by this leadership and its organization, the All Jammu and Kashmir Muslim Conference, in an effort to include all Kashmiris in its ultimate goal of securing self-government by the Kashmiris for the Kashmiris. One of the key issues the chapter raises is the extent to which the leadership was able to reconcile its support base, rooted among certain groups of the Valley's Muslims, with its claim to be the sole representative of all residents of the state, regardless of their regional and religious backgrounds.

The final chapter examines the period between 1940 and 1953 from the perspective of the informal arenas of Kashmiri politics, to transcend the trend to analyse the period solely in terms of the de facto partition of Kashmir in 1948. It assesses the Kashmiri "nationalist" leadership's agenda in light of the varied critiques launched against its ideology and politics by a wide variety of Kashmiri political organizations and individuals in the 1940s. The alternative political visions for Kashmir's future, articulated by Kashmiris against the leadership of the National Conference in the pre-independence and immediate post-independence history of the region, it argues, are key to understanding the disjunction between regional aspirations, nationalist imperatives, and religious affiliations that ultimately lie at the root of the present imbroglio in the region.

The book ends with a brief conclusion that considers the continued significance of themes of regionalism, nationality, citizenship, and religious affiliation in the post-1953 Kashmiri context. Those who claim to represent Kashmiris, at the regional or national levels, have failed to resolve the uneasy historic relationship between religion, region, nation, and more recently nation-states, which informed and continues to inform, the political culture of the Kashmir Valley. While independence was an ambivalent experience for several groups in South Asia, it was profoundly so for Kashmiri Muslims, who became citizens of India and Pakistan without acquiring the concomitant social, economic and political rights on either side of the border. A lasting solution to the Kashmir problem is not possible until policy makers, scholars, and intellectuals on both sides of the border and abroad deconstruct Indian and Pakistani nationalist narratives and agendas in relation to Kashmir and examine contemporary Kashmiri political culture in the broader context of its articulation in the pre-colonial and colonial periods.

CHAPTER 1

Mulk-i-Kashmir

History, Memory, and Representation

E ven a cursory examination of the political culture of pre-colonial Kashmir highlights the bankruptcy of the concept of an immutable Kashmiri identity, particularly its inability to engage with various forms of belonging. We need to trace the main themes in the political culture of the Valley from the fourteenth to the mid-nineteenth century in an attempt to disentangle representations of Kashmir in popular and scholarly discourse from historical fact. While being far from the last word on pre-colonial Kashmiri history, such tracing does provide an initial thematic framework for a foray into this particularly understudied period.

I suggest here that the political culture of pre-colonial Kashmir was defined by its creative interaction between a variety of languages of belonging. The narrative on regional belonging in this period certainly transcended religious affiliations in expressing a vision of Kashmir as a homeland that had to be saved from destruction by outsiders. At the same time, it allowed for an accommodation, not an erasure, of religious difference. Kashmiris were quite aware of belonging to religious groups with a certain set of rules that set them apart from those outside the bounds of those rules. But they recognized larger affiliations, such as those with the land they lived in and the people who belonged to the region. Pre-colonial Kashmiri public discourse exhibited a comfortable coexistence of regional specificity and religious universality.

Contrary to popular belief, it was not the isolation of the Kashmir Valley that produced narratives of regional and religious belonging; rather, it was the Valley's links with the world outside that helped reinforce the poetic discourse on identities in the mid-eighteenth to early-nineteenth centuries. Instead of seeing the Valley and its inhabitants as being fettered by the mountains that surround them into

1. View of the Kashmir Valley. Chitralekha Zutshi's collection.

articulating an immutable, insular identity,[1] the use of another geographic metaphor, that of the river, is more apt in discussing the political culture and discourse on identities in the region. The river Jhelum, which has carved the Kashmir Valley out of the mountains and defines its geographic boundaries, is in constant motion, changing its course through the rough and tumble of the Valley's landscape, even as it continues to transform it. The articulation of identities by inhabitants of the Valley is a similar process of interaction—in this instance between socio-political factors, religious affiliations, and shifting geographic contexts.

The Immortalized Mystics of Kashmir: Lal Ded and Nund Rishi

Scholarship on religious identities in various regional settings of pre-colonial India is pervaded with the notion of religious syncretism, a term which, apart from being inadequately defined, does not satisfactorily address the issue of religious difference. By implying the existence of an amalgamated religious culture drawing from various religious traditions, the term not only erases the possibility of the formal appearance of confessional difference, but in the process creates further dichotomies, such as elite and folk religion and orthodox and mystical religion. Thus, it relies on normative understandings of religion, particularly Islam, judging the articulations of religious identity on the basis of their conformity to an unchanging body of religious thought, defined for instance by the *sharia*.[2] Scholarship on pre-colonial Kashmir suffers from similar limitations, since historians of Kashmir are particularly insistent on defining the period in terms of a fluidity of religious boundaries and the presence of a syncretic religious culture, both integral aspects of *Kashmiriyat*.[3]

[1] Pandit Anand Koul, for instance, described Kashmir as "a fairy land of peace and contentment, removed from the terrors and turmoils of the world and wrapped around the devotional silence of the Himalayas." See Anand Koul, *Lalla Yogishwari: Her Life and Sayings* (Lahore: Mercantile Press, 1900), 7.

[2] See, for instance, Asim Roy, *The Islamic Syncretistic Tradition in Bengal* (Princeton: Princeton University Press, 1983); Richard Eaton, *The Rise of Islam and the Bengal Frontier, 1201–1760* (Berkeley: California University Press, 1993); and Susan Bayly, *Saints, Goddesses, and Kings: Muslims and Christians in South Indian Society 1700–1900* (Cambridge: Cambridge University Press, 1989).

[3] Even scholarship that has attempted to transcend the concept of syncretism,

To this end, scholars present the mystic tradition in Kashmiri poetry as an example of "exemplary tolerance between different sects professing various religions."[4] Moreover, they view it as a transcendental experience that was somehow far removed from everyday reality: "In this happy and tolerant climate the fertile mind of Kashmiris geared its intellect to unravel the unknown—beyond speech and mind. Mysticism is an exercise in the quest of the spirit. It is the identification of the self with the super-self."[5] The collective memory of two historical figures, both mystic poets from the fourteenth and fifteenth centuries, is critical to these arguments for a uniquely Kashmiri syncretic culture. Both figures invariably make their appearance divorced from the historical context.

Scholars and lay persons alike recognize Lala Arifa—or Lal Ded, as she is commonly known—as the first mystic poet of the Kashmir Valley. She is credited with having introduced and given substance to the idea of *Kashmiriyat* through her verses, which have formed the cultural repertoire of generations of Kashmiris.[6] The potent symbolism

---

such as Mohammad Ishaq Khan's work in the case of medieval Kashmir, has only succeeded in emphasizing the uniqueness of the Kashmiri Muslim identity. Khan argues against the portrayal of Kashmiri Islam as syncretic, since in his view the syncretic tradition has been a necessary concomitant of the process of Islamization rather than its culmination. Thus, for Khan, the exaggerated emphasis on "folk Islam" is liable to create the impression that the followers of the so-called folk Islam are not eventually moving in the direction of sharia-oriented Islam. As Khan correctly points out, it would be fallacious to assume that Kashmiris were unaware of the normative ideal of Islam and were not striving to attain it. However, it is clear that Khan's argument rests on the teleological assumption of the existence of a singular Muslim identity, encompassed by the sharia, which although defining itself through the local culture, ultimately dispenses with these local cultural elements over time in pursuit of true Islamization. See Mohammad Ishaq Khan, *Kashmir's Transition to Islam: The Role of Muslim Rishis (Fifteenth to Eighteenth Century)* (Delhi: Manohar Publications, 1994).

[4] K.N. Dhar, "Mysticism in Kashmiri Poetry," in M. Amin Pandit, ed., *Alamdar-i-Kashmir: Standard Bearer, Patron-Saint of Kashmir* (Srinagar: Gulshan Publishers, 1997), 44.

[5] Ibid.

[6] Lal Ded's verses grace most sites on the world-wide web dedicated to the advancement of Kashmiri self-determination. See, for instance, *http://www. homestead.com/kasheer/kashmir.html*, entitled "The Rape of Kashmir," which puts forth the following verse by Lal Ded: "I could disperse the southern clouds/I could

of the figure of Lal Ded is evident from the intense debate generated around the question of her religious affiliation. Kashmiri Pandits claim she was a Shaivite and a member of their community, while Kashmiri Muslims argue that though she was born in a Kashmiri Pandit family, Lal Ded accepted Islam later in her life.[7] Despite presenting a complicated picture of the mystic poetess in his pioneering work on the transition of Kashmir to Islam, Ishaq Khan falls into arguing that Lal Ded was more influenced by Islam, which she adopted, than by Kashmiri Pandit Shaivism, into which she was born. To this end he states that "the presumption that she wanted to reform the Hindu society flounders on the bedrock of her seminal historical role which speaks more of her association with Islam than with Saivism."[8]

Herein lies the irony and contradiction: the poet who represents the uniquely Kashmiri culture that transcends religious boundaries has herself become the center of contentious debate over those very boundaries between the two communities of the region. Rather than engaging in this debate, one is better served by examining Lal Ded's verses in the context of the social and political landscape of fourteenth-century Kashmir. Lal Ded was born when Kashmir was undergoing plunder and pillage by a Tartar warrior named Dalchu in the early part of the fourteenth century. She witnessed the conversion of the Tibetan Buddhist ruler of Kashmir, Richen, to Islam and the establishment of the Sultanate in Kashmir under Sultan Shamasuddin, who took over the throne after marrying Richen's widow, Kota Rani, in 1339.[9] Lal Ded came of age in a society within which Islam had just begun to be introduced through the activities of the Sayyids of Persia. Without going into the intricacies of Kashmir's transition to Islam, suffice it to say that this was a period of social and political turmoil as a new dynasty was established and a new religion came to be propagated with much fervor, particularly among the ruling classes.

---

empty the waters of the ocean/I could cure the affliction of Leprosy/But I could not make an idiot understand the truth."

[7] Madhu Kishwar, "Kashmir and Kashmiriyat: The Politics of Language, Religion and Region," in Kishwar, *Religion at the Service of Nationalism and Other Essays* (Delhi: Oxford University Press, 1998), 280.

[8] Khan, *Kashmir's Transition to Islam*, 73.

[9] For a detailed description of the political history of this period, see R.K. Parmu, *A History of Muslim Rule in Kashmir, 1320–1819* (New Delhi: People's Publishing House, 1969) and Sufi, *Kashir*.

Lal Ded, far from a passive spectator to these changes, played a significant role in setting the course for the integration of these changes into the historical memory of the Kashmir Valley. Far removed from the preoccupations of courtly writers, she was able to capture the changes occurring in the social landscape of the Kashmir Valley via her simple Kashmiri verse. That Lal Ded was aware of the changes in her surroundings—which were leading to a redefinition of state, society and religious affiliations—and capable of questioning them—is amply clear from her verses. For instance, she sang:

> Behold a wise man dying of hunger,
> As an autumnal leaf shed from the bough;
> And behold the oaf lashing the cook,
> I languish to break the fetters of my delusion.
>
> The fans, the canopy, the chariot, the throne,
> The revelry, dancing, and the cushioned beds;
> Have everything and yet you are not safe,
> It cannot allay your dread of death.[10]

Although heavily influenced by Sanskrit, her poems constitute the earliest extant literature in Kashmiri either in oral tradition or manuscript form.[11] For this reason scholars have called her the forerunner of medieval Hindu reformers, such as Kabir and Nanak, who were part of the Bhakti movement and made significant contributions to the development of regional languages in other parts of the Indian subcontinent.[12]

The reason Lal Ded's poetry is so essential for votaries of *Kashmiriyat* is self-evident from an examination of her verses. These are suffused with a sense of the fluidity of religious boundaries, and this has been interpreted as a manifestation of the Kashmiri ethos of tolerance. In the following verse, for instance, she seems unable to decide between being a follower of Allah or of Shiva:

---

[10] Naji Munawwar and Shafi Shauq, *Kashur Adabuk Tawarikh* [History of Kashmiri Literature] (Srinagar: Department of Kashmiri, University of Kashmir, 1992), 20.

[11] G.L. Tikku, *Persian Poetry in Kashmir 1339–1846: An Introduction* (Los Angeles: University of California Press, 1971), 27.

[12] See G.L. Tikku, "Mysticism in Kashmir: In the Fourteenth and Fifteenth Centuries," *Muslim World*, LIII (July 1963): 226–33.

I said la illah il Allah
I destroyed my Self in it
I left my own entity and caught him who is all-encompassing
Lalla then found God
I went to look for Shiva
I saw Shiva and Shaitan (devil) together
Then I saw the devil on the stage
I was surprised at that moment
I adore Shiva and Shiva's house
When I die, what then?[13]

In the following famous verses, she openly questions the Brahmanical orthodoxy of the period:

Shiva abides in all that is, everywhere
Then do not distinguish between a Hindu and Mussalman.
If thou art wise, know thyself
That is true knowledge of the Lord.[14]
I gave up falsehood, deceit, untruth,
I saw the one in all fellow beings, and
Preached the same doctrine to the mind.
What then is the inhibition in eating
The food offered by a fellow human being?[15]

Lal Ded was undoubtedly against organized religion, particularly as represented by Brahmanism, and probably laid the groundwork for the propagation of Islam among the Kashmiri populace by the Rishis. Furthermore, her verses illustrate the union of the streams of Shaivite philosophy and Sufism in fourteenth-century Kashmir. However, it is significant that her poetry does not attempt to present the vision of a land where religious affiliations do not matter. Instead it presents society in a state of flux, with religious and regional affiliations in the process of redefinition. To identify an "ethos of tolerance" in Lal Ded's verse is an anachronistic reading of the Kashmiri mystic tradition, which was revived and popularized, significantly, in the 1930s and 1940s by proponents of an emergent Kashmiri nationalism.

[13] Hafiz Mohammad Inayatullah, *Lalla Arifa barzabane Kashmiri* [Lalla Arifa in Kashmiri] (Lahore: Din Mohammad Electric Press, undated), 14–15.

[14] Koul, *Lalla Yogishwari*, 61.

[15] Nil Kanth Kotru, *Lal Ded: Her Life and Sayings* (Srinagar: Utpal Publications, 1989), 29.

Considered Lal Ded's spiritual successor, Sheikh Nooruddin or Nund Rishi (b. 1378), is another figure central to the memory and meaning of *Kashmiriyat*. Again, both Kashmiri Pandits and Kashmiri Muslims claim him as their spiritual guide, the former referring to him as *Shazanand* (one who has attained ultimate truth) and the latter calling his verses the *Koshur Quran* (Kashmiri *Quran*).[16] Since Sheikh Nooruddin is more squarely placed in the Islamic tradition, his writings have had a significant impact on the discourse on Kashmiri Muslim identities. Mohammad Ishaq Khan, in the only English full-length study of the Rishi movement—of which Nooruddin was the founder—points out that the mystic's religious career and the development of Kashmiri Muslim society are integrally connected: "An understanding of Islam's historical manifestation in Kashmir, therefore, requires a prior understanding of the man who influenced the Kashmiri mind more than any other religious leader."[17] Thus Khan sets about to discover not only the mystic Nooruddin but also the maker of what he calls the "Kashmiri Muslim identity." The potency of Nooruddin to proponents of *Kashmiriyat* lies in the fact that not only was he a Muslim, but, according to them, he practised a kind of Islam that blurred religious boundaries. As Khan puts it: "Nooruddin's poetry expresses the cultural style of the Islamic civilization in a regional setting . . ."[18] By effectively bridging the gap between religious thought and its regional backdrop, Nooruddin's poetry provides a ready vehicle for Kashmiri nationalists.

A more fruitful means of analysing the poetry and social significance of the two Kashmiri mystics, particularly Nooruddin, is to place them in the context of what Sheldon Pollock has referred to as "vernacularization," a process occurring in the early centuries of the second millennium in South Asia and other parts of the world, through which "the universalistic orders, formations, and practices of the preceding millennium were supplemented and gradually replaced by localized forms."[19] It was during the course of the vernacular millenium that,

[16] This title refers to the fact that the bulk of Nooruddin's poetry is a Kashmiri rendition of the *Quran* and *Hadith*. G.N. Gauhar, *Sheikh Noor-ud-Din Wali (Nund Rishi)* (New Delhi: Sahitya Akademi, 1988), 54.

[17] Khan, *Kashmir's Transition to Islam*, 95.

[18] Ibid., 107.

[19] Sheldon Pollock, "India in the Vernacular Millennium: Literary Culture and Polity, 1000–1500," *Daedalus* 127 (2) (Summer 1998): 41.

2. View of Chrar Sharif, Sheikh Nooruddin's shrine. Chitralekha Zutshi's collection.

according to Pollock, "cultures and communities were ideationally and discursively invented,"[20] leading to the creation of new regional worlds. The emergence of regional languages as the languages of literary culture played a significant role in the development of these regional cultures. It is clear that the activities of Lal Ded and Nund Rishi fit in with Pollock's general theory, since these individuals began to compose texts in a language "that did not travel," perhaps even with the knowledge that it did not travel as far as Sanskrit or Persian, ultimately leading to the creation of a regional ecumene in late medieval Kashmir.

Sheikh Nooruddin's poetry was composed in the diction used by common Kashmiris, and although dominated by the message of escape from this life of illusion, is redolent with a sense of place. Regarding Nooruddin's influence on Kashmiris and their language, Khan writes: "As such, Kashmiri owes a great deal to Nooruddin since it is through his compositions that it articulated the expanding complex of impulses and responses, and orchestrated the music of consciousness. Kashmiri, in the ultimate analysis, is the verbal correlative of people's genius; it symbolises . . . a way of life."[21] Regardless of whether one can view Nund Rishi's poetry in terms of a self-conscious articulation of a break with the earlier more global and transregional culture in order to produce a regional alternative, it is undeniable that his poetry did indeed contribute to the development of the Kashmiri language, and later to the articulation of a self-consciously Kashmiri culture.

However, there were distinctive features in the process of vernacularization in Kashmir, particularly when compared to the kingdoms of southern India. Foremost, in Kashmir, the primary site for the production of vernacular culture at the outset was not the royal court, as was the case with vernacularization elsewhere in the subcontinent. In fact, it was not the courtly elite that sponsored vernacularization, but religious leaders such as Nooruddin, who specifically separated themselves from the court, which continued to operate in a classical, universal language, namely Persian. Nooruddin was able to create a framework for a regional culture through his use of the Kashmiri language to propagate a devotional religion, which was, significantly,

[20] Ibid., 42.
[21] Khan, *Kashmir's Transition to Islam*, 107.

outside the purview of the state. In fact, the reigning Sultan of Kashmir, Ali Shah (1413–20), ordered him arrested for preaching rebellious
ideas to the people.

Second, religious and regional cultures were being articulated in
tandem with one another in Kashmir so that the process of Kashmir's
transition to Islam is integrally linked with the process of vernacularization in the region. Sheikh Nooruddin's poetry contributed to the production of a regional culture on the site of the development of a new
religious culture. As Pollock points out, in southern India vernacular
writings themselves became new scriptures, thus obviating the need
for the translation of Sanskrit holy texts into the vernacular.[22] In
Kashmir, while Rishi writings did indeed become sacred in a sense,
Sheikh Nooruddin's object was first and foremost to bring the message
of Islam to the people of Kashmir, whom he exhorted to embrace Islam
as encapsulated in the *Quran* and *Hadith*. Contrary to presentations
of Nooruddin as a Rishi who was neither Hindu nor Muslim but one
who followed a syncretic religion, he was clearly a Muslim. As he himself said, "I uttered the Kalima, experienced the Kalima/Converted
myself into the Kalima/Kalima permeated into every fiber of my
being/I reached the abode of the abodeless with Kalima."[23] In fact one
of his poems, dedicated to explaining the meaning of being Muslim,
could easily be placed in the early twentieth century, when Kashmiri
Muslims were redefining the boundaries of their community. A couple of verses from his poem suffice to illustrate the point:

> One who does not neglect one's daily duties,
> Who longs to live by the sweat of one's brow,
> Who controls the bestial anger of one's mind,
> Who shows fortitude in provocation,
> May be truly called a Muslim.

> He will be among the people of paradise
> Who shares meals with the hungry,
> (Who) is obsessed with the idea of removing hunger,
> Who humbly bows (in prayer) in all sincerity,

[22] Pollock, "India in the Vernacular Millennium," 63.
[23] G.R. Malik, "Sheikh Noor-ud-Din Noorani—The Mystic Poet of Kashmir,"
in Kalla, ed., *Literary Heritage of Kashmir*, 146.

Who scorns anger, greed, illusion, arrogance, and self-conceit,
May truly be called a Muslim.[24]

Third, to make a sharp distinction between regional and universalistic cultures in the Kashmir case would be to overstate the point. While in other parts of the subcontinent, particularly southern India, votaries of regional cultures were attempting to self-consciously break away from the universal ecumene, their Kashmiri counterparts, writing in a vernacular medium, nevertheless expressed a universal humanism, as reflected in the above verse. After all, the regional culture of the Valley was being articulated in the universal language of Islam. And although Nooruddin's Islam was clearly affected by its Kashmiri context, it was quite as much a part of the universal Islamic faith as an expression of the particulars of Kashmiri Islam. If asked, Nooruddin would most definitely have contradicted the notion that the Islam he preached was a version peculiar to the Kashmir Valley.

Finally, it would be fallacious to argue that the classical language, Persian, which was part of a larger—one can argue Islamic—cultural space, declined as a literary language in this period. It would also be misplaced to create a dichotomy between Persian as the language of non-Kashmiri rulers and Kashmiri as the language of the people of Kashmir, since elite Kashmiris adopted Persian as their literary language and some of the most potent expressions of regional belonging from the late-eighteenth and early-nineteenth centuries are, in fact, in Persian. Sayyid Muhhamd Amin Uvaysi, popularly known as Baba Mir Uvays, was a mystic from the Sultanate period who had ties to the ruling dynasty and wrote primarily in Persian. Uvaysi's verse illuminates the interaction between region and religion as well as the particular and the universal:

The whole creation belongs to me:
Beyond the void is my abode.

O supplicants of Time, listen attentively:
My banquet spreads from Qaf to Qaf.[25]

[24] Khan, *Kashmir's Transition to Islam*, 124.

[25] Qaf or Jabl al-Qaf in Islamic cosmology is the name of the mountains surrounding the terrestrial world; the expression Qaf ta Qaf implies the whole terrestrial world. See Tikku, *Persian Poetry in Kashmir*, 24.

Know that this world of being is naught;
The true world, be sure, belongs to me.

He whom you find to be without any trace
Is watchman at my gate.

I chose solitude in Kashmir,
For this universe is my garden.[26]

As a Muslim, the poet accepts the whole world as his abode and, at the same time, recognizes that his chosen place of belonging is Kashmir. Since he is a Muslim, the whole world belongs to him; as a Kashmiri, he belongs to Kashmir; and yet this poet's chosen language of expression is Persian, not Kashmiri.

The mystic tradition, for self-evident reasons, has been central to expressions of *Kashmiriyat*. The mystic poets of Kashmir, perhaps unintentionally, laid down the framework for a regional culture defined by the emergence of a vernacular, which coexisted with the emergence of a religious culture defined by a universal religious faith. However, the image of Kashmir as a place where Islam and religious culture were somehow different, and more accepting, needs to be qualified. Medieval Kashmir was a society in transition where social, political and religious affiliations were in a process of redefinition. Mystic poets, on the site of poetry and religious debate, were able to capture this fluidity most evocatively, providing Kashmiri nationalists with rich ammunition for the propagation of *Kashmiriyat*.[27]

A Threat to *Kashmiriyat?* The Mughals in Kashmir

P.N. Bazaz laments in his book: "Meanwhile, as a last flicker of the dying Kashmiri Nationalism, the patriotic nobles put Usuf's son Yaqub Khan on the throne and fought vigorously against the Mughal

---

[26] Tikku, *Persian Poetry in Kashmir*, 23–4.

[27] So strong is the association between Nooruddin and the vision of this uniquely Kashmiri cultural identity that while most shrines became centers of dispute between rival factions of Kashmiri Muslim religious leaders, and between Kashmiri Pandits and Muslims in the twentieth century, the shrine dedicated to the memory of Nooruddin at Chrar-Sharif remained the only uncontested sacred space in the Kashmir Valley. When the shrine burnt down in 1995, Kashmiri political groups

armies . . . But Yaqub Khan proved unfit as a ruler," and patriotic Kashmiris had no alternative but to seek the Mughal emperor's help to liberate the Valley from his tyrannical rule.[28] According to G.M.D. Sufi, the Mughals weakened the courage of the hitherto martial Kashmiris and broke their independent spirit.[29] Almost all works on the history of Kashmir consistently portray the incorporation of the Kashmir Valley into Mughal India after Chak rule as the beginning of the end of Kashmiri independence, when *Kashmiriyat* came under threat from outsiders. In Bazaz's view, Mughal governors proved to be "tyrannical, barbarous and uncultured," and encouraged Hindu–Muslim and Shia–Sunni factionalism among the tolerant and peace-loving Kashmiris.[30] While these scholars lament the decline of Kashmiri cultural identity in the Mughal period (1586–1758), I would argue that it was precisely in the Mughal period that Kashmiri poets first began to self-consciously articulate a sense of regional belonging.

Kashmir occupied a special place in the psyche of the Mughal emperors. Even as it was administratively integrated into the larger empire and began to share in the prosperity enjoyed by other Mughal provinces, Kashmir was different in that the Mughal emperors took keen personal interest in its affairs. In fact, the axiom of Kashmir as the paradise on earth, which even then belied the reality of the condition of the Valley and its inhabitants, was coined by the Mughal emperor Jehangir.[31] Jehangir's obsession with the beauty of the Valley led to an alteration of its landscape, since some of the more scenic architectural marvels of the region, such as the Mughal Gardens and the Pari Mahal, were built during his reign.[32] The emperor was so enamored of the Valley that he took an uncommon interest in the concerns and complaints of its people. He dismissed one of his high-ranking officers, Qulich Khan, then governor of the Valley (1606–9), on receipt of complaints against him: "O protector of administration! your

---

alleged that it was an act of arson by the Indian state, and a direct attack on *Kashmiriyat*.

[28] Bazaz, *Struggle for Freedom in Kashmir*, 70.

[29] Sufi, *Kashir*, vol. II, 675.

[30] Bazaz, *Struggle for Freedom in Kashmir*, 71.

[31] Sufi, *Kashir*, vol. I, 295.

[32] Francis Younghusband, *Kashmir* (London: Adam and Charles Black, 1911), 157.

complainants are many, your thanksgivers few/Pour cloud water on the lips of the thirsty or get away from the administration."[33]

Undoubtedly, the Mughals epitomized the tradition, as Mridu Rai states, of effacing Kashmiris from depictions of Kashmir: "Therefore, in Mughal miniatures, Kashmir put in an appearance either in the form of humanly manicured gardens or of scenery glimpsed incidentally through a window in what was otherwise predominantly the architecture of the Mughal city. The Kashmiris were barely deemed worth the wastage in paint."[34] Nevertheless, the argument needs some qualification, since it forecloses the possibility of the ability of Kashmiris to reinsert themselves in artistic or poetic renditions of their beautiful Valley. Kashmiris might have been absent from the paintings, but they were capable of both creating as well as integrating the newly emerging vision of their land into a discourse on belonging.

The Mughal era was one of intense cultural regeneration in Kashmir, when Kashmiri poets and ideologues built on existing cultural forms through contact with poets from the Delhi court and the court of Persia. Persian became the medium of literary expression, not only for those who migrated to Kashmir, but also for native Kashmiris. Kashmir became the center of intellectual convergence for Iranian poets such as Saib, Kalim and Qudsi; for poets from the Mughal court such as Faydi and Urfi, who came on short visits to the Valley; and for native poets, even as the ghazal became the primary form of literary expression.[35] Kashmiri poets composed numerous *masnavis* (narrative poems) in this period for presentation to the Mughal emperors. This descriptive poetry was dedicated to glorifying the beauty of the Valley, establishing its geographical contours, and describing the gardens and buildings constructed by order of the Mughals. This was the period in which the lush meadows of the Valley, its snow-capped peaks and calm lakes, were immortalized in beautiful verse.

The uniqueness of the landscape found further expression in the works of Kashmiri painters who produced miniatures in a style known

[33] Tikku, *Persian Poetry in Kashmir*, 84.

[34] Mridu Rai, "The Question of Religion in Kashmir: Sovereignty, Legitimacy and Rights, *c.* 1846–1947" (Ph.D. dissertation, Columbia University, 2000), 2–3.

[35] Tikku, *Persian Poetry in Kashmir*, 94–7.

as Kashmiri Qalam.[36] To dismiss this art and poetry as simply further evidence of the invention of a landscape devoid of its people would be to overlook its incorporation into the cultural repertoire of the Valley, the symbols of which were created and manipulated by Kashmiris themselves. This was the period when the Valley was first likened to a garden, a work of natural beauty that stood out as unique from the rest of its surroundings. The image of Kashmir as a garden became increasingly important in the works of poets from the late eighteenth century. In fact, the image continued to inform nationalist writings of the 1940s, when Mahjoor composed his famous poem, "My Country is my Garden."

Even as the poets of the Mughal period glorified the beauties of the Valley, their poetry did not obscure the realities of the land and the lives of its people. Although clothed in philosophical terms, the following verse articulates poignantly the curse of the Valley and its inhabitants:

> The path of poverty [faqr] is evident from the road leading to Kashmir:
> Its very first step means the renunciation [*tark*] of the world.
>
> How can one pass this path with ease:
> For the very first condition means relinquishing life?
>
> How can a traveler escape this calamity,
> Except that a slip of the foot may become a cause of his rescue?[37]

The land of Kashmir, as articulated in the works of Kashmiri poets of the Mughal period, may have existed for the most part only in the imagination of the Mughal emperors and their court poets, but it is undeniable that its cultural expression informed later articulations of Kashmiri identities.

The Mughal period saw the continuation of the Kashmiri tradition of mystical poetry, although in a new form and medium of expression. Prominent Kashmiri mystical poets of this period were instrumental in expressing the interaction between religious traditions, even as the Kashmiri regional identity was being formulated. A representative

---

[36] P.N.K. Bamzai, *A History of Kashmir, Political, Social, Cultural, from Earliest Times to the Present Day* (New Delhi: Metropolitan Book Company, 1973), 576.

[37] Tikku, *Persian Poetry in Kashmir*, 98.

mystic poet is Habibullah Ghanai, or Hubbi (1556–1617), who was born to a grocer in the Valley and became a famous dervish recognized by Emperor Jehangir. Although he composed in Persian, common people recognized his ghazals, since they were sung in musical assemblies in order to create an atmosphere of ecstasy. One of his verses attempts to understand the nature of religious differences:

> Tell, O Heart, the why of the diversity in religions:
> Why is one a disbeliever, the other a believer?

> This diversity arose out of the contradiction of names:
> One is opposed to the other, and that opposed to the next.

> With these two sects only the two Gods are pleased,
> But this is not worthy of the Supreme Lord's wish.

> The diversity of religions is not his making,
> For in that exists neither disbelief nor belief, neither doubt nor certainty.

> O Habib, your sayings he alone shall comprehend
> Who in Self sees His visage and gains his knowledge.[38]

Although Hubbi's answer to his queries is an escape from Self, the significance of his verse lies in its illumination of religious affiliations as sites of debate, rather than as strictly defined and divinely ordained entities. At the same time, the very fact that he was plagued by these questions implies that religious difference did exist in the Valley.

C.A. Bayly argues that "it was often the binding force of unevenly developing and differently expressed regional patriotisms and the political discourse of good government rather than the policies of supposedly secular pre-colonial rulers that provided the main resistance to those forces in pre-colonial India which stressed the exclusive bonds of religious community."[39] If viewed from this perspective, and placed in the context of the development of regional identities, the existence of religious affiliations that were not antithetical to a sense of belonging to a land becomes easier to understand. (Later, I discuss this point in greater detail.) During the Mughal period, Kashmiris were not only incorporated into the culture of the Mughal court, but by extension

[38] Ibid., 100–4.

[39] C.A. Bayly, *Origins of Nationality in South Asia: Patriotism and Ethical Government in the Making of Modern India* (Delhi: Oxford University Press, 1998), 45.

became integral parts of the discourse and principles of ethical government that were developed in this era. Successive governors of the province introduced the institutions of Mughal government to Kashmir. Generally solicitous of the welfare of Kashmiris, the Mughal emperors established a tradition among Kashmiris of complaint to the central government in cases where the governors were subjecting people to oppressions and mistreatment.[40] As noted earlier, Jehangir expelled one of his governors from the Valley because of complaints against him.

Most significant to later articulations of regional identities, however, was the establishment of the tradition of Kashmiri historiography in Persian. Akbar ordered the translation of the *Rajatarangini* into Persian, a task allotted to Mulla Ahmad Shahabadi. During Jehangir's time, Malik Haider and Narayan Kaul Aziz—one a Kashmiri Muslim and the other a Kashmiri Pandit—wrote detailed histories of the Valley in Persian.[41] It is also significant that one of the more prominent historians of the late Mughal period, Khwaja Azam Dyadmari, was the first historian to revive the memory of Lal Ded in his famous *Tawarikh-i-Kashmir* (History of Kashmir), written in 1730.[42] By the early eighteenth century, local Kashmiri historians had begun to play an important role in articulating a sense of belonging to Kashmir by carrying forward the tradition of complaint to its logical conclusion, evident in the following verse by Khwaja Mohammad Azam:[43]

So great is the distress of the people of Kashmir,
That it escapes even their own comprehension.

When the people were weakened by famine,
Chaos sprang up from town to desert.

No rice or grain can be found anywhere,
Except in the wheaty-complexioned beauty of the beloved.

Bellies like ovens are heated to the grilling point,
Yearning for a piece of bread.[44]

[40] Bamzai, *A History of Kashmir*, 386.

[41] Ibid., 556.

[42] J.L. Kaul, "Kashmiri Poetry: Some Forms and Themes," in Kalla, ed., *Literary Heritage of Kashmir*, 92.

[43] Khwaja Mohammad Azam authored a history of the Valley entitled *Waqiat-i-Kashmir*. See Sufi, *Kashir*, vol. II, 373.

[44] Tikku, *Persian Poetry in Kashmir*, 86.

Written after the famine that hit the Valley in 1733, this verse clearly makes a plea for restitution to the Mughal court. However, at this time the Mughal central administration was in no position to redress the grievances of even its Kashmiri subjects. Provincial governors had become independent and assertive in other parts of Mughal India, leading to the rise of independent successor states. The same process unfolded in Kashmir, with the significant difference that, instead of becoming an independent kingdom, Kashmir succumbed to the Afghans in 1752.

Although Kashmir was in a sense objectified in the poetry, painting and imagination of the Mughal emperors, it would be historically inaccurate to assume that Kashmiris themselves had no role to play in this process. It would also be a gross oversimplification to suggest that Kashmiris bought into the image of their land created by the Mughals. Not only were Kashmiris instrumental in shaping an image of their land, they also utilized, by the eighteenth century, these expressions to articulate a sense of being Kashmiri. Additionally, neither the sense of regional identity developing in this period, nor its later expressions, would exclude religious affiliations from their purview. The rhetoric of regional identities would at times include and at other times transcend religious identities. At no point, however, would it deny their existence.

Bagh-i-Suleiman: The Articulation of Kashmiri Regional Belonging during Afghan and Sikh Rule

God wanted that this blue-colored land
Should tire of wailing like the reed's heart.

He gave its control to the Afghan,
He gave Jamshid's garden to the demons.[45]

Articulations of Kashmiri regional belonging that included and transcended religious, tribal and other local affiliations became particularly insistent during Afghan rule (1753–1819). From a beautiful garden that was the envy of the entire world, Kashmir now became a garden left to the mercy of cruel Afghans bent on its annihilation: "I

[45] Ibid., 159. Tikku states that the above verses were on the lips of Kashmiris during the Afghan period.

inquired of the gardener the cause of the destruction of the garden/ drawing a deep sigh he replied, 'it is the Afghans who did it.'"[46] Relegated to a subservient position and severely oppressed by the Afghans, Kashmiris increasingly turned to poetry as a means of expressing their opposition to the rulers and a sense of belonging to their homeland. Despite the lack of patronage, Kashmiri Muslims and Pandits alike wrote prolifically, recording the mood of the times and their deep sense of resentment toward the new rulers, attempting to invoke ideas of good government during the chaotic rule of both Afghans and, later, Sikhs.

If the Mughal period is seen as the beginning of the end of Kashmiri independence by Kashmiri historians, the Afghan period is seen as its end. Most historians of Kashmir agree on the rapacity of the Afghan governors, a period unrelieved by even brief respite devoted to good work and welfare for the people of Kashmir. According to these histories, the Afghans were brutally repressive with all Kashmiris, regardless of class or religion. Merchants and noblemen of all communities were assembled and asked to surrender their wealth to the first Afghan governor, on pain of death. Kashmiri peasants, jagirdars, nobles and merchants alike were buried under the burden of heavy taxation. The *jazia*, or the poll tax on Hindus, was revived and many Kashmiri merchant families fled the Valley for the plains during this period. With the departure of merchants and with the peasantry avoiding cultivating the land for fear of exactions, the Kashmiri economy was effectively ruined.[47]

Without detailing the oppressions of various Afghan governors, for there were many, suffice it to say that the Kashmir Valley underwent a period of immense political and economic crisis over sixty-seven years of Afghan rule. Despite its near accuracy, this tale of plunder and woe needs to be qualified through mention of Kashmir's position at the crossroads of trade routes from the north, north-west and east during the Afghan period. The axis of the Mughal empire—the Grand Trunk Road—was completely redirected by the Afghans. The new route, in the eighteenth century, circumvented the Punjab and Delhi

---

[46] According to Bamzai, a local poet wrote these lines during the Afghan period. See Bamzai, *A History of Kashmir*, 424.

[47] Lawrence, *The Valley of Kashmir*, 197–8, and Bamzai, *A History of Kashmir*, 424–37.

and from Durrani Kashmir the caravans could now reach Peshawar and Kabul without touching Sikh territory.[48] Furthermore, the economic and cultural links between Kashmir and Central Asia continued uninterrupted in this period, as did Kashmiri literary activities, which continued to flourish through contact with Central Asia and Persia.

Interestingly, it was in the Afghan period that Kashmiri Pandits attained proficiency in Persian and not only began to form part of the administration of the land,[49] but, more significantly, became an integral voice in the expression of a sense of longing for and belonging to the Kashmiri homeland. One such Kashmiri Pandit poet, Dayaram Kachru (1743–1811), came from a family known for its scholarship in Persian and Sanskrit and for service as civil officials to the Afghans. Even as Kachru held a number of civil positions with the Afghans, both in Srinagar and Kabul, he wrote prolifically in Persian, composing verses on Kashmir, his homeland, and introducing Hindu devotional themes to Persian poetry in Kashmir. Not only did Kachru translate the *Bhagvadgita* into Persian, he also composed the *Masnavi-i-Kashmir*, which he wrote in praise of his homeland while stationed in Kabul:

> O Lord, blossom the bird of my hopes,
> And show me spring in the garden of Kashmir.
> I pine in separation from my home,
> Not knowing why destiny cast me away.
>
> Where is the fervor of those fountains,
> Whose sighs, O Lord, are lifted to the heavens by the wind?
>
> I cannot describe the state of my separation.
> Fortitude is better, fortitude is better.[50]

Although not always in such positive and glowing terms, Pandit and Muslim voices articulated a sense of belonging to Kashmir while remaining faithful to their religious affiliations. Most writing from

---

[48] Jos J.L. Gommans, *The Rise of the Indo-Afghan Empire c. 1710–1780* (Leiden: E. J. Brill, 1994), 41–2.

[49] Tikku, *Persian Poetry in Kashmir*, 166, and Jia Lal Kilam, *A History of Kashmiri Pandits* (Srinagar: Gandhi Memorial College Managing Committee, 1955), 242–5.

[50] Tikku, *Persian Poetry in Kashmir*, 197–8.

this period, whether of a historical nature or lamenting the condition of the city and the land of Kashmir, began with a benediction to God, Shiva or Ganesh in the case of Pandits, and Allah and the Prophet Mohammad in the case of Muslims. In fact, several authors called on their religious identity by invoking their particular God to come to the aid of Kashmir—the focus of their regional affiliation. In the early part of the nineteenth century, Sanaullah Kriri (1796–1873), a devotional poet who wrote *naats* (songs eulogizing the Prophet Mohammad) composed the following verse:

> Will you not go there,
> Where the Prophet lies asleep?
> You will tell him my condition,
> He is the medicine for our illnesses.
> He is the beautiful one,
> He is our well-wisher.
> Will you not tell him,
> That the Kashmiris have fallen?
> They are helpless, useless, and unskilled
> Without friends or helpers.[51]

To view this verse simply as a eulogy to the Prophet Mohammad and a glorification of the poet's Muslim identity would be to ignore the regional affiliation to which the verse so poignantly draws attention.

Bayly has illustrated the definitions and development of old patriotisms in pre-colonial (particularly western) India, at great length. He presents the sixteenth-century Maratha state as a "paradigmatic example of pre-colonial Indian patriotism," where all three conditions for the emergence of old patriotism were in evidence. These conditions, according to him, include the presence of "active social and ideological movements binding together people of a perceived region and coming to communicate in a common language;" a locally based political power that institutes "a conscious and sustained attempt to foster an active sense of common identity;" and a series of conflicts with external Others, to which ideological meaning is endowed and crystallized in cultural discourse for future generations.[52]

It is interesting to note that Kashmir does not yield most of these

---

[51] Munawwar and Shauq, *Kashur Adabuk Tawarikh*, 174.
[52] Bayly, *Origins of Nationality in South Asia*, 21.

conditions for the existence of a pre-colonial patriotism in that region. Although the Kashmiri mystic tradition can be classified as an ideological and social movement that bound people together through the common language of Kashmiri, Persian was as important in expressing a local identity. The locally based political power in Kashmir, the Afghans, were not interested in fostering a sense of common identity among the people and, ironically, came to represent the greatest "Others" in the memories of Kashmiris. And yet, Kashmir from the mid-eighteenth to the mid-nineteenth centuries presents a clear case for the existence and articulation of a sense of belonging to a homeland, or *mulk*, which, although uttered in muffled tones for fear of persecution, was hardly weak or incoherent. Instead, despite all odds, it was able to bring together people of various religious affiliations into expressing despair over alien rulers who were bent on destroying the homeland without insisting on an erasure of religious affiliations.

Through the chaos created by the Afghans emerged *Mulk-i-Kashmir*, the homeland of the Kashmiris, the memory of which would be immortalized by histories written during this period. The author of a history of Kashmir entitled *Bagh-i-Suleiman* (Solomon's Garden), Saiduddin Shahabadi, wrote in scathing terms of the tyrannies of the Afghans:

> The garden of Kashmir became a wound of pain,
> The master's pleasure became the people's indigence.
> They fell upon the soul of Kashmir,
> As voracious dogs set loose.
> The doors, walls, roofs and streets,
> And every soul complained like a doleful flute.
> The hearts of the tyrants were as hard as stone,
> They were too implacable to feel the people's pain.[53]

The historians of Kashmir did not stop at criticizing Afghan rule. They brought to notice examples of good government from their past. Drawing inspiration from the theory of good government outlined in the *Rajatarangini* and examples of just kings in history, these writers put their stock in a strong ruler who nevertheless kept the welfare of his subjects at heart. One such historian, Mulla Mohammad "Taufiq" (d.1765), wrote a versified history of Kashmir entitled the *Shahanama*.

[53] Munawwar and Shauq, *Kashur Adbuk Tawarikh*, 200.

In the section called *Ahval-i-Mulk-i-Kashmir*, which examines the political history of the Valley, he describes the reign of Yusuf Shah Chak[54] in terms of its justice and generosity:

> That when Kashmir for the second time
> Came under the command of the famous king Yusuf,
>
> He endeared himself in the hearts of the urban and village dwellers
> With generosity, with gifts, justice and fairness.
>
> With laudable conduct and prudent course,
> With policy of generosity and justice:
>
> When he captivated the hearts of people,
> With composed mind he set his heart on pleasure.[55]

This lament for the just rulers of their land continued through a more explicit Kashmiri discourse on regional belonging during the rule of the Sikhs, who followed the Afghans in 1819.[56] The Sikh governors deputed to administer Kashmir on behalf of Maharaja Ranjit Singh were "hard and rough masters,"[57] particularly as Kashmir was a considerable distance from Lahore. More significantly, they consistently followed anti-Muslim policies in Kashmir, thus subjecting the majority of the population of the Kashmir Valley to severe hardship in relation to the practice of their religion. The second Sikh governor, Deewan Moti Ram, ordered the closure of the Jama Masjid in Srinagar to public prayer and forbade Muslims from saying the *azan* (call to prayer) from mosques in the Valley. He also declared cow-slaughter a crime

---

[54] Historians of Kashmir regard the Chak period (1530–86) as the final years of Kashmiri independence. Yusuf Shah Chak was the last ruler of the Chak dynasty (1579–86) before the Mughal advent.

[55] Tikku, *Persian Poetry in Kashmir*, 189.

[56] The ruler of the Sikhs, Maharaja Ranjit Singh, entered into a treaty with the British in 1809 whereby the British agreed to abstain from interference in territories north of the Sutlej, if he gave up claim on territories south of the river. After the conclusion of the treaty, Ranjit Singh began his campaigns to conquer principalities north of the Sutlej, and expelled the Afghans from Multan, Dejarat and Kashmir. He valued the Kashmir province not only for its revenues, but also for its strategic position which facilitated his numerous military campaigns. See Bamzai, *History of Kashmir*, 601–2.

[57] Younghusband, *Kashmir*, 159.

punishable by death.[58] Lands attached to several shrines were resumed on order of the state. Sikh governors began the policy of declaring mosques, such as the Pathar Masjid, as the property of the state. The continuation of this policy under the Dogras in the late nineteenth century would provide the fuel for the organization of Kashmiri Muslims as their leadership took up as a cause the return of state-owned mosques to the community. The Sikhs thus established a specifically "Hindu" tone to their rule, setting the stage for the Dogra dynasty which began ruling Kashmir in 1846. The Sikh rulers did not formulate these "Hindu" policies specifically for the Kashmir Valley to harass Kashmiri Muslims; they tried hard to ban the slaughter of sacred cattle in all the lands they conquered. Their emphasis on asserting Hindu and Sikh beliefs was part of an attempt to articulate a Sikh identity separate and distinct from that of the Mughals.[59]

Kashmiri histories emphasize the wretchedness of life for the common Kashmiri during Sikh rule. According to these, the peasantry became mired in poverty and migrations of Kashmiri peasants to the plains of the Punjab reached high proportions. Several European travelers' accounts from the period testify to and provide evidence for such assertions. Explaining the reasons for Maharaja Ranjit Singh's neglect of the Valley, G.T. Vigne, who visited the Valley in the 1840s, says: "Ranjit assuredly well knew that the greater the prosperity of Kashmir, the greater would be the inducement to invasion by the East India Company . . . and most assuredly its [Kashmir's] ruin has been accelerated, not less by his rapacity than by his political jealousy, which suggested to him, at any cost, the merciless removal of its wealth."[60]

While there is clear evidence for oppressive conditions under Sikh rule, it is also important to remember that historians of Kashmir and European travelers had their own reasons for presenting Sikh rule in a negative light. Historical evidence points to the fact that, despite its anti-Muslim overtones, Sikh rule stabilized the economy of the

[58] Sufi, *Kashir*, vol. II, 726.

[59] C.A. Bayly, *The New Cambridge History of India, II. 1, Indian Society and the Making of the British Empire* (Cambridge: Cambridge University Press, 1990), 22.

[60] G.T. Vigne, *Travels in Kashmir, Ladak, Iskardo, the countries adjoining the mountain-course of the Indus, and the Himalaya, north of the Panjab*, vol. 2 (London: Henry Colburn, 1842), 318.

Kashmir Valley. After the famine of 1832, the governors realized the folly of heavy taxes and thereafter "revenue divisions were made, and the villages were either farmed out to contractors or leased on the principle that the state took half the produce in kind. Agricultural advances were made free of interest, proper weights were introduced and fraudulent middlemen were punished."[61] The Kashmiri shawl trade reached its apogee during this period, for Kashmiri shawls had by this time become prized articles of fashion in Europe and units of royal exchange in the Mughal successor regimes. One cannot ignore the fact that Kashmir was the second richest province of the Sikh kingdom in terms of revenue receipts, next only to Multan.[62]

Furthermore, far from retreating into oblivion in the twenty-seven years of Sikh rule, Kashmiri voices articulated a sense of belonging for their land, a land that now required the loyalty of its inhabitants to rise from the depths of suffering and tribulations. Mulla Hamidullah Shahabadi (1783–1848), who lived through the Afghan and Sikh regimes during his lifetime, is the best exemplar of the deep sense of regional identification that pervaded Kashmiri discourse in this period. A schoolteacher and theologian, Shahabadi wrote prolifically and is considered the foremost epic poet of his age. His deeply satirical poetry dealt with a number of topics, but almost all of it conveys his rancor at the poor state of Kashmir and its inhabitants.

Shahabadi began the tradition of writing elegies on Kashmir's devastation. In the tradition of *shahr-i-ashob* poetry in other parts of the Indian subcontinent, his verses celebrate his attachment to the Kashmir Valley—which is identified as a city—and mourn its moral and social degeneration under Afghan and Sikh rule. Shahabadi wrote several elegiac poems and treatises, such as *Shahr-i-Ashob* (The City of Tumult), *Babujnama* (A History of Injustice), and *Napursan Nama* (Story of Lawlessness), all of which strongly condemn the rulers and people for allowing the beautiful Valley to slide into chaos and ugliness. In *Napursan Nama*, he declares: "When Kour (blind) Singh, the governor appointed by Ranjit Singh [who had only one eye], is the

---

[61] Lawrence, *The Valley of Kashmir*, 200. See also Bamzai, *A History of Kashmir*, 636.

[62] D.C. Sharma, *Kashmir Agriculture and Land Revenue System under Sikh Rule* (*1819–1846*) (Delhi: Rima Publishing House, 1986), 1.

King [of Kashmir], one should not complain of tyranny since the administration is run by the blind."[63] Shahabadi was aware of the consequences of writing such dissenting works, and admitted to cloaking them in fictional characters and locales to avoid persecution.[64]

However, he was not merely interested in recounting the vices of the ruling classes, for in his view the moral decay of Kashmiri society from within was partially responsible for the reprehensible condition of the land. At his satirical best in *Napursan Nama*, he describes the complicity of Kashmiri intellectuals and the religious elite with the corrupt aristocracy in bringing about the moral degeneration of society:

> The scholars and philosophers and physicians of the day were assembled to give their verdict. Father Corruption, the Judge, while discussing the case with a plaintiff, stated:
>
> "Scholarship and art should be learnt from me; the principles of religious behavior should be heard from me; I remember the treasure of traduction by heart; I am the first teacher and the master of the essence of stupidity . . .
>
> Ablution is defiled by four things: wearing of dress, drinking of water, eating of food, and drawing of breath . . .
>
> Faith dwells in two things: filling the belly from navel to throat, and resting the body from evening to midday.
>
> Purity, piety and good deeds have totally vanished from the earth; what remains thereof is the name; that too shall not remain henceforth."[65]

Babujnama describes the utter moral chaos into which Kashmiri society has fallen, where rules of conduct and decorous behavior seem to have disappeared. According to Shahabadi, the condition of the land has become almost bizarre, with owls preaching in mosques, traders selling off turmeric as saffron to hapless customers, and petitioners being fined for questioning their behavior.[66] Similar themes pervade

---

[63] Tikku, *Persian Poetry in Kashmir*, 203.

[64] Zubeida Jaan, *Mullah Hamidullah Shahabadi: Hayat aur Karname* [Mullah Hamidullah Shahabadi: Life and Works] (Srinagar: Maqdomi Press, 1996), 90–100.

[65] Tikku, *Persian Poetry in Kashmir*, 202–3.

[66] Mullah Hamidullah Shahabadi, "Babujnama" [A History of Injustice], unpublished manuscript in Persian, Acc # 866. Persian and Arabic Manuscript Section, Research and Publications Department, University of Kashmir, Srinagar. Translated by Chitralekha Zutshi and S.N. Bhatt Haleem. All Persian and

the poetry of Mirza Asadullah Khan Ghalib, Mirza Rafu Sauda, Khwaja Mir Dard, Akbar Allahabadi, Nazir Akbarabadi—among other Muslim poets—all of whom lament the decline of Mughal central authority and the consequent strife and social upheaval in various urban centers of the subcontinent in the eighteenth century.[67] Their lamentations, as Shahabadi's, are not about the decline of Islam but are concerned primarily with the decay of their city, their home, their *mulk*. As Ayesha Jalal points out, in the period prior to 1850 "the religious identity of individual Muslims was closely intermeshed with the territorial contours of the cities in which they lived."[68]

It was clear to Shahabadi that Kashmiris themselves, now a clearly identifiable people distinct from the rulers and the religious elite, had to take responsibility for their homeland if its conditions were to undergo any improvement. The rulers were not interested in justice for the people, nor were religious leaders interested in the moral reformation of society. To this end, he wrote a narrative poem entitled *Akbarnama*, which describes the defeat of the Sikhs by the Afghan Prince Akbar Khan. Although the *Akbarnama* is not a "national" epic, since its heroes are not Kashmiris, the poem clearly upholds the bravery and patriotism of Prince Akbar Khan as an example to be followed by Kashmiris to rid their land of foreign rulers. Shahabadi exhorted Kashmiris to give up their cowardice and take on their oppressors for their homeland: "*Rishta Abul Watan/Az Dile Burid/Raft Dighar Barkas/Roshan Nadid.*" (If the sentiment of love for the homeland rises from the heart/It will not prove a burden on the individual.[69])

Significantly, Shahabadi's call to Kashmiris' regional identity did not take place in a religious vacuum, since he recognized affiliations to the religious collectivity. However, he derided what he thought of as people's emphasis on their religious identity at this time, this having been encouraged by the anti-Muslim policies of the Sikh governors: "There is one thing on the lips of people/Rule of religion, destruction

---

Kashmiri sources used in this book have been translated by me, with the assistance of S.N. Bhatt Haleem, unless otherwise noted.

[67] See Ayesha Jalal, *Self and Sovereignty: Individual and Community in South Asian Islam since 1850* (London and New York: Routledge, 2000), particularly chapter one, for a detailed discussion of their poetry and the themes therein.

[68] Ibid., 13–14.

[69] Jaan, *Mullah Hamidullah Shahabadi*, 91–114.

of Mulk."[70] Himself a mullah, to him religious affiliation was obviously important; however, it could not override the sense of regional belonging. In Shahabadi's view, Kashmir was in the throes of anarchy precisely because the religious elite did not have a larger sense of belonging to a homeland and unabashedly went about furthering their narrow personal interests.

The poetry from this period criticized Muslim religious leaders, not so much because Islam was in danger (which would characterize the discourse of the late-nineteenth- and early-twentieth-century Kashmiri Muslim leadership), but because these leaders were corrupting what had now come to represent "Kashmiri" traditions, such as shrine worship. A theologian from the Kashmir Valley, Hajji Sayyid Nizamuddin Furahi (b.1773), for instance, wrote a lengthy treatise in 1833 condemning the decline of the institution of "pirism" in the Valley. The treatise, *Mulhemaat*, or that which is bogus or meaningless, did not question the nature of Kashmiri Islam as being impure or meaningless, but instead lamented its takeover by the pirs who had led Kashmiris, both Hindus and Muslims, down the path of decadence, lies and deceit.[71] There is an important distinction between Furahi's versified treatise and the innumerable anti-pir poems written and published at the turn of the twentieth century, since the latter condemned pirs, alongside the entire institution of shrine worship, as un-Islamic. This is not to deny that treatises such as the *Mulhemaat* were on the nature of Islam, but to suggest instead that they were not designed to define the boundaries of a religious community in singular terms, as was the case with later Kashmiri Muslim political tracts.

In Furahi's view, shrine worship was essential to the profession of Islam and indeed any religion in the Valley. Since it was a Kashmiri phenomenon, its original purity had to be maintained. It was precisely for this reason that the degeneration in pirism was having a severely unfavorable impact on Kashmiri society. As he wrote, "People who do not believe in shrines are not Muslim/Those who wish evil against shrines have no righteousness."[72] Pirs, he wrote, were to be found in droves in villages and the city, but not one among them was a visionary

---

[70] Shahabadi, "Babujnama," 6.

[71] Sayyid Nizamuddin Furahi, "Mulhemaat" [Bogus], unpublished manuscript in Persian, Private Collection of Peerzada Mohammad Ashraf, Bemina, Kashmir.

[72] Ibid., 30.

who would lead society out of its morass of immorality and decline. Instead, they were busy accumulating wealth at the expense of Kashmiris, who were dying because of famine and floods. Ultimately, *Mulhemaat* is a treatise against a particular class of people perceived as accumulating wealth at the expense of a society sunk in poverty and decline, not a treatise on the nature of religion in Kashmir. Religion was certainly important, not in and of itself, but as a means of benefiting society and people. To Furahi, as to Shahabadi, the pirs were not so much profaning Islam as betraying their homeland.

Thus, *Mulhemaat* presented pirs and sayyids as figures who not only fleeced the people, but also kept them from attaining their individual and collective potential. According to Furahi, these religious figures were complicit with rulers in driving Kashmiris into backwardness and ignorance.[73] They kept the truth of religion from the people, instead teaching them tolerance and patience: "They dress themselves as honest, Godly people/They misuse the name of Allah and the Prophets/They have hypnotized the people/As a snake charmer puts a spell on a snake."[74] Furahi wondered at the whereabouts of the spirits of the saints who had once inhabited the Valley and propagated the dedication of one's life to the service of others. Although he compared contemporary pirs to Muslim saints from Kashmir's past, Furahi's ululations were not about the decline of religion in general and certainly not about the decline of Islam in the Kashmir Valley. *Mulhemaat* was most significantly about a severing of the connection that had bound religious leaders to the society of which they were a part. Ultimately, the treatise viewed the deterioration of religion and religious leaders as part of the more general social, economic, and moral deracination of Kashmiris from their regional context.

Although religious affiliation, rulership, and patronage had been successfully linked during Sikh rule, community identities with a singularly defined religion as the sole reference point were far from being articulated in Kashmiri public discourse. Furthermore, the

[73] There was no code of law in place in the Valley during Sikh rule, cases being left to the discretion of the local religious figures, such as qazis, pirs and mullahs. As a result, Kashmiris felt that they had been abandoned to the mercy of these figures who usually dispensed cases based on the whims of their Sikh masters. See Bamzai, *History of Kashmir*, 626.

[74] Furahi, "Mulhemaat," 43.

evidence of *Kashmiriyat* and the blurring of religious boundaries cannot be located in either the Afghan or Sikh periods. However, the discourse on belonging to a homeland, a *mulk*, for the benefit of which
one's religious affiliation could and should be harnessed, had clearly
become part of Kashmiri political culture in the early nineteenth century.

The Period of Transition: Religious and Regional Identities during Early Dogra Rule

The Kashmir Valley came under Dogra rule (1846–1947) with the
ominous terms of the Treaty of Amritsar signed between Raja Gulab
Singh of Jammu and the British in 1846, whereby the British "transfer
and make over for ever in independent possession to Maharaja Gulab
Singh and the heirs male of his body all the hilly and mountainous
country with its dependencies situated to the eastward of the River
Ravi including the Chamba and excluding Lahul, being part of the
territories ceded to the British Government by the Lahore State . . ."[75]
In return for this transfer, Gulab Singh had to pay the British seventy-
five lakhs of rupees. On the face of it, this was yet another transfer of
the Kashmir Valley from one ruler to another, this time under the
auspices of the princely state of Jammu and Kashmir within the British Indian Empire. However, the early Dogra period is critical for an
understanding of the development of identities in the Kashmir Valley,
since it set the stage for a transformation within the public discourse
of the Valley, from an emphasis on regional identities to a privileging
of the religious component of identities.

Kashmiriyat rises to the fore most vociferously in the historical narrative of the Dogra period. Historians of Kashmir assert that despite
the utmost efforts of the Dogra regime to divide Kashmiris along religious lines, as their colonial masters so deftly and effectively did in
India, *Kashmiriyat* was victorious. Kashmiris, regardless of their religious affiliations, launched a national movement against the Dogras.
This narrative, of course, is prejudiced by its insistence on locating a
unified, cohesive Kashmiri nationalist movement, untarnished by

[75] C.U. Aitchison, *A Collection of Treaties, Engagements and Sanads relating to
India and Neighboring Countries (revised and continued up to 1929), vol.XII: Jammu
& Kashmir, Sikkim, Assam & Burma* (Calcutta: Government of India Central
Publications Branch, 1929; repr., Delhi: Mittal Publications, 1983), 21.

religious, regional, or class distinctions within the princely state of Jammu and Kashmir. Furthermore, it fails to point out that the Kashmiri national movement of the 1930s and 1940s was preceded by a Kashmiri discourse on identities that focused primarily on defining the religious community, not the Kashmiri nation. And finally, the narrative on *Kashmiriyat* ignores the contradiction that forms the substance of the Kashmiri nationalist movement: this movement, which supposedly rescued *Kashmiriyat* from the jaws of the Dogra regime, based its demands squarely on the socio-economic distinctions between the two main religious communities in Kashmir, Pandits and Muslims. This contradiction is rooted in the story of the political, social and economic transformations introduced on to the Kashmiri landscape during the Dogra period.

The Dogras ushered in a new stage in Kashmiri history for a number of reasons. Although recognizing its strategic and economic importance to their empires, the earlier rulers of Kashmir had ruled the region through proxy while remaining primarily engaged with the concerns of those larger empires. For the Dogras, however, Kashmir itself was the empire; as a result, the story of Kashmir under the Dogras is imbricated with the story of the fashioning of the Dogra dynasty itself. The fashioning of the Dogra dynasty, in its turn, was thoroughly intertwined with the project of British colonialism in mid-nineteenth-century India. Doubtful about their decision to hand over Kashmir—which occupied a strategically critical position—to a minor Hindu Raja from Jammu who also happened to be ruling a Muslim-majority population, the British began a policy regarding Kashmir which was geared toward endowing Gulab Singh's dynasty with the ideals of legitimate rule. While the Dogras would be subject to constant scrutiny, Kashmiris became the subjects of a twice-removed situation within colonial rule, with dual loyalties and no clear means of seeking redressal for their grievances. Although subjects of the greater British Indian Empire, Kashmiris formulated their identities under the rubric of the apparatus of legitimacy deployed by the Dogra state, which continually attempted to balance its definition in terms of the idioms and instruments of Hinduism and the ideal of non-interference with religions so dear to the British.[76]

[76] For an insightful discussion of the establishment of the Dogra dynasty and its structures of legitimacy and sovereignty in Kashmir, see chapter one in Rai, "The Question of Religion in Kashmir."

The first Dogra ruler of Kashmir, the now "Maharaja" Gulab Singh, perfected the concept of personal rule soon after taking over the Valley. In fact, he came to personify the state as he set about pacifying unruly elements in his newly acquired territories. He launched an extensive campaign against the nomadic tribe, the Galawans, capturing their leaders and having them summarily executed. He drove the jagirdars of Muzaffarabad district, the Khakas and the Bombas, out of the Valley and set up strong garrisons in the forts guarding the mountain passes.[77] Additionally, he laid down the economic structure of the Valley whereby the distribution of rice became a monopoly of the state. The government set the price of rice and other commodities and undertook their supply to the city population. Similarly, the Dagh-Shawl Department that controlled the taxation and production of shawls was reorganized and brought firmly under the control of the state.[78] Most significantly, however, Gulab Singh endowed his rule with a framework of legitimacy drawn from Hinduism, through, for instance, the revival of a law banning cow-slaughter that had been introduced and then rescinded during the Sikh regime; the construction of temples throughout the state; and the establishment of institutions such as the Dharmarth.[79]

The regulations for the Dharmarth, which functioned essentially like a trust, and included the private charities of Maharaja Gulab Singh and his successor Maharaja Ranbir Singh, were laid down during Ranbir Singh's rule. These regulations, or the *Ain-i-Dharmarth* in Persian, were drafted and signed in 1884 by the scions of the Dogra dynasty—Pratap Singh, Ram Singh and Amar Singh. In the *Irshad* (edict) issued by Maharaja Ranbir Singh that accompanied the *Ain-i-Dharmarth*, he stated that Maharaja Gulab Singh had laid the foundation for the trust in the name of the Hindu deity Lord Rama, the interest from which was to be utilized for strictly religious purposes, such as the repair of temples, the construction of *dharamsalas*, and so on. To this end, Ranbir Singh ordered the establishment of a Council for the supervision, management and protection of the fund.[80] The edict ordered the successors of Gulab Singh's dynasty and the employees

[77] Bamzai, *A History of Kashmir*, 657.

[78] For a detailed discussion of the economic policies of the early Dogra state, see chapter two of this book.

[79] Bamzai, *A History of Kashmir*, 665.

[80] General and Political Department 1890/18, Jammu State Archives.

of the state to work toward the management of the Dharmarth with a warning: "Whoever among the heirs of the Sarkar and the State servants and officials expended any money towards any other head was to incur the sin of having killed one crore of cows."[81] The regulations stipulated the maintenance of six hundred scholars in temple schools on behalf of the Maharaja, the management of *gaushalas* (cow-sheds) where cows and bullocks would be provided for, the construction of a residential house at Kashi, Benaras, for the housing of pilgrims during times of pilgrimage, and the appointment of ten men capable of translating Arabic, Persian and other languages into Sanskrit.[82]

Maharaja Ranbir Singh's rule (1857–85) in general reflected the overtly Hindu tenor of the emergent Dogra state. Soon after his accession, Ranbir Singh consecrated a shrine to the worship of Rama, from whom, according to Dogra tradition, the dynasty was descended. This shrine soon became a center of extensive religious establishments and a college and library were attached to it. In keeping with the regulations of the Dharmarth fund, several hundred Brahman pupils were housed and educated in Sanskrit learning in the college and a translation department was set up where the whole range of Hindu religious texts were translated into Persian. Additionally, the Maharaja commissioned a Kashmiri Pandit scholar, Sahib Ram, to prepare a descriptive survey of all ancient pilgrimage sites in Kashmir.[83] Ranbir Singh's patronage of Sanskrit learning extended beyond the boundaries of his state, as he donated a handsome sum of Rs 62,500 to the Punjab University for the furtherance of Sanskrit scholarship.[84] Several poetic and prose tracts dating from this period celebrated the Maharaja's piety. One claimed that Ranbir Singh had ordered the construction of 144,000 idols of the Lord Krishna for personal worship, since he believed that Krishna could assume hundreds of forms.[85]

It is undeniable that the Dogras brought Kashmir into closer contact with British India. The rulers displayed the princely state's fealty to the British in overt ways, with Maharaja Ranbir Singh

---

[81] Ibid., 4.

[82] Sufi, *Kashir*, vol. II, 792.

[83] Ibid., 790.

[84] Ibid., 791.

[85] Untitled anonymous unpublished manuscript in Persian, 1877, Acc. # 1376 (Arabic and Persian Manuscript Section, Research and Publications Department, University of Kashmir, Srinagar).

providing troops to quell the revolt of 1857 in British India and signing the Commercial Treaty of 1870 with the British, which provided
for the duty-free import of goods into the state through British India.[86]
The extent to which the Dogra rulers framed their right to govern the
state through their association with the British empire and the
significant position accorded to the Kashmir Valley within the state's
framework is clear from the commissioning of a shawl by Maharaja
Ranbir Singh for presentation to the Prince of Wales at the time of his
visit to the state in 1876. This masterpiece of Kashmiri shawl manufacture, which legend has it was twenty-odd years in the making, is
embroidered with an intricate street map of the city of Srinagar that
includes the river Jhelum, rivulets, forts, gardens, roads, localities, places of worship, bridges and even prominent buildings (which are
labeled in the Persian script).[87] More significantly, as its label indicates,
Maharaja Ranbir Singh considered the city of Srinagar as the center of
his kingdom, which to him was represented by the Kashmir Valley.[88]
By presenting this shawl to the Prince of Wales, moreover, he was
clearly recognizing the suzerainty of the British Crown, while at the
same time laying claim to the much-coveted Valley as the domain of
the Dogra dynasty. Despite these moves, the British were suspicious
of the Dogras, particularly as their interest in the affairs of Central Asia
increased in the 1870s.[89] British intervention would culminate in the
establishment of the British Residency and a State Council to run the
affairs of the state in 1889.

[86] Sufi, *Kashir*, vol. II, 794–6.
[87] "Pashmina Shawl with Map of Srinagar," Sri Pratap Singh Museum, Srinagar, Kashmir.
[88] The embroidered inscription behind the shawl reads, "The map of Kashmir,
produced at the orders of His Highness the Maharaja . . ."
[89] As early as August 1847, Col. Henry Montgomery Lawrence and George
Taylor had written to Gulab Singh complaining about the distress of the Kashmiris as a result of the high prices of shali and high-handedness of the officials of
the darbar; dispatch of forces by the Maharaja to Gilgit; occurrence of four cases
of sati in the state; and Dharmarth realizations made by the darbar from the Kashmiris, suggesting the deputation of a British Resident in the state. Maharaja Gulab
Singh, while accepting their criticisms, had refused to accept the establishment of
a British Residency in Kashmir. British intervention in Kashmir would become
more insistent during the reign of Ranbir Singh. See Bamzai, *A History of Kashmir*,
661–2.

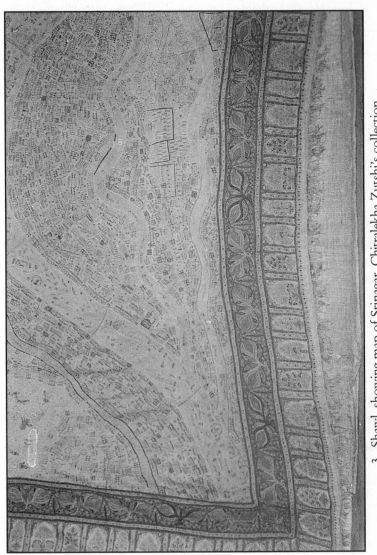

3. Shawl showing map of Srinagar. Chitralekha Zutshi's collection.
Source: Sri Pratap Singh Museum, Srinagar.

Far removed from British machinations and the scholarly pursuits of their rulers, Kashmiris continued to live under the yoke of heavy and arbitrary taxations and other oppressions of the administration. As we saw, Kashmiri Pandits had entered the administrative machinery of state during the Afghan period, and by the Dogra period they were firmly entrenched in the lower levels of the state bureaucracy. Although the Pandits were, like all Kashmiris, excluded from the upper echelons of the bureaucracy, they continued to exercise control in the countryside, away from the urban centers of power. The revenue structure of the early Dogra period placed the entire burden of revenue assessment and collection in the hands of local Pandits, not only because they were Hindu, but also because they were the traditional administrative and educated caste in Kashmir.[90] It is important to note that the alliance between Kashmiri Pandit elites and the Dogra state was at all times an uneasy one. Participation in the administrative structures of the Dogra state and belonging to the same religion as the rulers did not prevent the Kashmiri Pandit literati from participating in the rich tradition of Kashmiri poetry that glorified regional affiliation from the mid-nineteenth century.

It was in the mid-nineteenth century that, despite the lack of patronage to the Kashmiri language by the Dogras, poetry in Kashmiri began to be written alongside Persian compositions. One of the most prominent poets of this period, Parmanand (d.1880), a Kashmiri Pandit village accountant, devoted his writings to exhorting people to alleviate the distress within their lives. It would be easy to dismiss Parmanand as a Hindu poet with Hindu concerns, for much of his poetry is rooted in the *Bhagvadgita* and the love lore of Radha and Krishna. To do so, however, would be to simplify the project and meaning of Parmanand's writings, which were aimed at, and distinctly composed for, the uplift of the Kashmiri people. In his famous poem, *Karma Yoga*, Parmanand describes the journey of life and action within it through the imagery of cultivation:

In this land of action
The body will burn
With the strength of Dharma (duty);

[90] See chapter two for a detailed discussion of the administrative machinery of the state.

From the seed of contentment shall grow
The fruit of bliss.

With two breaths, the two oxen
Plough day and night;
With the rod of breath control
Hit the oxen hard.
Endeavor that no single piece of land
Be left unploughed.
From the seed of contentment shall grow
The fruit of bliss.

Spring is a three-day span
Of frenzied youth;
You should not waste
A single hour of this time.
Sow the seed, delay not, make haste;
From the seed of contentment shall grow
The fruit of bliss.

With weeding done through love
The field will become green;
The sprouts will appear
Through the ripe watering of Tapas [devotion]
Through disinterested devotion
Lilies will spring in the Dal Lake.
From the seed of contentment shall grow
The fruit of bliss.[91]

The imagery of the path of action to reach knowledge of the divine, taken from the *Bhagvadgita*, is clear in these excerpts. What is also visible is that the poem is addressed to Kashmiri peasants, most of whom were Muslim, and, far from recommending a mystical retreat into the self, it exhorts them to act to improve their condition. Writers have generally dismissed Parmanand as a predominantly Hindu poet, who wanted to bring Kashmiri Pandits closer to Hindu mysticism, by pointing out that his themes were Hindu and his Kashmiri too Sanskritized.[92] There is no doubt that Parmanand identified with his

[91] Tikku, *Persian Poetry in Kashmir*, 235.
[92] Ibid., and J.L. Kaul and Motilal Saqi, *Parmanand* (Srinagar: Cultural Academy, 1972).

religion; however, this did not render him incapable of also being a
Kashmiri who wanted to see his fellow Kashmiris take responsibility
for their lives. He was certainly not above criticizing Kashmiri Pandit
bureaucrats in his poetry:

> A line without a dot is Radhu Mal,
> A calamity on top of calamities;
> Encamped in Wular he fulminates,
> Blowing hornets from his mouth.
> "In Mattan he, our officer, intends
> to make at shradh a gift of patwaris,
> so many heads—than cattle cheaper far—
> whom will he be pleased to choose?" they trembling ask.
> Say, will the account of the patwaris
> Be ever reckoned right?[93]

The negotiation between Kashmiri discourses of regional and religious belonging was visible in most poetry composed during this
period. Even as Kashmiri Pandit writers translated major Hindu texts
into Kashmiri or Persian, they did so with an awareness of being Kashmiri and framed the translations in Kashmiri terms. Pandit Gopal
Kaul Gopal's translation of the *Bhagvadgita,* for instance, begins with
an appeal to Lord Krishna to alleviate the anguish of the Kashmiri
people:

> The hearts of the Kashmiris are heavy,
> They are downtrodden and poverty-stricken.
> In a land that is admired by all
> And is undoubtedly a paradise on earth.[94]

The discourse of regional belonging, which did not exclude religious
identities from its ambit, continued to be articulated during the early
Dogra regime, even as the distinction between the rulers and the ruled
emerged vociferously. In the poem *Darveshi,* Wahhab Pare (1845–
1914), for instance, spoke out clearly against the rulers on behalf of
Kashmiris:

---

[93] J.L. Kaul, "Parmanand: A Kashmiri Poet," in Kalla, ed., *Literary Heritage of
Kashmir,* 167.

[94] Abdul Qadir Sarvari, *Kashmir me Farsi Adab ki Tarikh* [History of Persian
Literature in Kashmir] (Srinagar: Majlis-i-Takhikat-e-Urdu, 1968), 266.

How many oppressions of the time can I count?
The authoritarian rulers have steeped the *Mulk* into chaos.
Anyone who is employed has to pay tax,
The plundering department is called *Nakdi Mahal* [cash only].
How many oppressions can I count on my fingers?
Every lion here has a hundred or more dogs with him to rip the people
apart.[95]

However, even as Kashmiri voices spoke out against the oppressions of the governing power, the religious component of identities was to become increasingly important toward the end of this period. By the 1880s the Kashmir Valley was in the throes of a major transformation in its polity, economy and society. No Kashmiri was immune from these changes, which threw communities into disarray with the reconstitution of social groups and the dismantling of the state structure as it came under the control of the British Residency. Preoccupation with their homeland continued as Kashmiris struggled to locate their identities within the changing political economy and society at this time. However, as the Dogra state became more interventionist, not only did its Hindu structures of legitimacy begin to reveal themselves, but more significantly, the state came to play an important role in defining the contours of the emergent discourse on community identities.

* * *

There is nothing exceptional about historical developments in Kashmir, despite what the historical narrative on the region has claimed throughout the past half century. To suggest that a Kashmiri identity, *Kashmiriyat*, defined as a harmonious blending of religious cultures, has somehow remained unchanged and an integral part of Kashmiri history over the centuries is a historical fallacy. Certainly, Kashmiri identities have followed a distinct trajectory depending on a host of factors, including state and economic structures, political culture, and the religious milieu at particular historical moments. One can even go so far as to say that Kashmiri political culture has been imbued with a sense of belonging, not only to the homeland, but also to religious

[95] Munawwar and Shauq, *Kashur Adabuk Tawarikh*, 247.

communities, sects, and localities. However, the content of these identities has changed over the centuries in response to historical circumstances. It is the story of this gradually unfurling narrative in dialogue with state, political economy, region and religion that the following pages seek to capture.

CHAPTER 2

Political Economy and Class Formation in Kashmir

The workings of economic and political formations in the Kashmir Valley played a significant role in determining the content of the discourse on identities in Kashmiri political culture. Here I offer an overview of the relationships between the rural economy, the market, urban areas, emergent social groups, and the state in the late pre-colonial period, while also tracing transformations in these relationships over the turn of the twentieth century. I argue that changing economic and political relationships created arenas for individuals to lay claim to leadership roles and definitions of "community," whether religious, political, or regional. We shall also see that while the colonial intervention doubtless had a significant role to play in these socio-economic transformations, in many instances it may have merely served to stimulate and shape processes that were already under way prior to the late nineteenth century.

Historians of South Asia have paid scant attention to the economic structures of the Kashmir Valley. Most economic histories of north India exclude Kashmir from their analyses of land revenue patterns in the pre-colonial period, the nature and impact of the colonial intervention, and the social composition of agrarian and urban landscapes during the two centuries of colonial rule. Perhaps this is because Jammu and Kashmir was a princely state on the fringes of British India, where the colonial impact was considered negligible, when considered at all. Another factor might be the paucity of sources on the political economy of the Valley. While there are reams of administrative and other documents on land revenue and economic systems from pre-colonial and colonial India, very few such documents are extant for the Kashmir Valley, rendering a thorough economic analysis extremely difficult. In so far as historians of Kashmir have attempted monographs on the subject of peasant economics or land structures, they have used the available sources, mostly colonial records, without considering them critically or placing economic developments in Kashmir in the larger context of similar processes in British India.[1] Even more egregiously, most historical monographs on Kashmir fail to make necessary and crucial links between the Valley's political economy and its political culture.

Although several parallels can be drawn between Kashmir and various regions of British India, it cannot be denied that Kashmiri economy and society responded in unique ways to the colonial intervention. The most significant difference begins with chronology, for the princely state came into existence in 1846 and the colonial authorities did not intercede directly in the region's political economy until the 1880s. However, even if colonial intervention and its impact came later in Kashmir, both were in many ways startlingly similar to these processes in British India. Another distinction that needs to be made is that the colonial impact in Kashmir was mediated through the Dogra state, the Dogras being direct rulers of the region. As a result, some colonial policies were resisted and transformed even before implementation; in other instances, particularly in the realm of administrative bureaucracy, the Dogra rulers sought to emulate their colonial masters.[2] These policies, whether initiated by the Dogras or the British, or as a compromise between the two, led to changes in the political economy of the Valley that had a far-reaching impact on not only

[1] See, for instance, R.L. Hangloo, *Agrarian System of Kashmir (1846–1889)* (New Delhi: Commonwealth Publishers, 1995); D.C. Sharma, *Kashmir Agriculture and Land Revenue System under the Sikh Rule (1819–46 AD)* (New Delhi: Rima Publishing House, 1986); and D.N. Dhar, *Socio-Economic History of the Kashmir Peasantry, From Ancient Times to the Present Day* (Srinagar: Centre for Kashmir Studies, 1989).

[2] This kind of mediation took place in many princely states, including Hyderabad and Baroda, particularly at the time of direct colonial intervention into their politics and economics. See Karen Leonard, "Hyderabad: The Mulki–Non-Mulki Conflict," and David Hardiman, "Baroda: The Structure of a 'Progressive' State," in Robin Jeffrey, ed., *People, Princes and Paramount Power: Society and Politics in Indian Princely States* (Delhi: Oxford University Press, 1978), 65–106, 107–35.

its political and economic structures, but also relationships within and between communities.

Peasants and Bureaucrats: The Rice Economy of the Kashmir Valley, 1846–87

What were the connections between the rural and urban economies of the Valley from the mid to the late nineteenth century? The answer to this question is key to uncovering the nature and composition of emergent social groups which played key roles in articulations of identity at the turn of the twentieth century. This endeavor is especially significant in order to rescue the historical narrative on Kashmir's political economy—much like the rest of its history—from statist/ colonial interpretations that ignore the involvement of indigenous groups and social entities in its economic formations as well as political discourses.

A historical analysis of the economic structures of the Kashmir Valley in the nineteenth century is considerably restricted by the extant sources on the subject and their accessibility. Most primary source materials on Kashmir's economy are colonial records, particularly settlement reports by British administrators, penned during their attempts to establish "order" within what they perceived as chaotic and fraudulent systems of land revenue administration prevalent in the state. While relying primarily on these sources, I attempt to disentangle colonial rhetoric and perception from the larger picture of socio-economic structures and land revenue patterns in the Kashmir Valley. However, colonial perceptions are significant because they played a considerable role in the formulation of land settlement policies, which in turn had an enormous impact on the political economy of the region. Peter Robb has pointed out that "ideas are important to agrarian history partly because they help explain what happened . . . often we have to enter the realm of ideas and discover how problems and solutions were perceived, in order to understand why particular actions were taken and their results."[3]

---

[3] Peter Robb, "Ideas in Agrarian History: Some Observations on the British and Nineteenth-Century Bihar," in David Arnold and Peter Robb, eds., *Institutions and Ideologies: A SOAS South Asia Reader* (Richmond, Surrey: Curzon Press, 1993), 213.

4. Rice fields in the Kashmir valley. Chitralekha Zutshi's collection.

Shali (unhusked rice) was the main crop cultivated in the Kashmir Valley, since the physical characteristics and climate of the Valley lent themselves to rice cultivation while preventing the intensive farming of most other crops.[4] There were two types of crops, Kharif or autumnal crops, which included rice, maize, pulses, cotton, saffron, millet and sesame, and Rabi, or spring crops, including wheat, barley, opium, rape, flax and beans. Since snow fell so soon after the Kharif crops were harvested, Rabi crops could only be planted in fields that had not been under Kharif cultivation. As a result, Kashmiri cultivators had to subsist on a one-crop economy, either Kharif or Rabi. Cultivators realized that their labor would not be repaid if they sowed crops other than rice and chose to concentrate on the Kharif production of rice, this being the main foodgrain of consumption, and the market for other crops was not really sufficient to make their cultivation profitable.[5]

Most importantly, rice had the greatest outturn per acre of any other crop in the Valley. While 27 seers of wheat sown per acre yielded only 2 kharwars of the crop per acre, 22–24 seers of shali yielded 15 kharwars of shali per acre.[6] As a result, rice accounted for three-fourths of the cultivable area during the Sikh period and was the most important crop among foodgrains in terms of value in the early Dogra period.[7] Walter Lawrence, Settlement Commissioner for the Jammu and Kashmir state, described the Kashmiri cultivator devoting all his energy to rice cultivation: "For rice he will terrace the fields, expend great labor in digging out irrigation channels, spend his nights out in the fields watching the flow of water, and will pass laborious days moving about like an amphibious animal in the wet deep mud."[8] Although other crops, such as maize, saffron, cotton, sesame and fruits were also grown and harvested, their importance to the agricultural economy remained marginal due to the absence of a substantial market for these products in mid-nineteenth-century Kashmir.

[4] Walter R. Lawrence, *Assessment Report of Baramulla Tehsil* (Jammu: 1905), 9.

[5] Lawrence, *The Valley of Kashmir*, 330.

[6] Charles Ellison Bates, *A Gazetteer of Kashmir and the Adjacent Districts of Kishtwar, Badrawar, Jamu, Naoshera, Punch, and the Valley of the Kishenganga* (Calcutta: Office of the Superintendent of Government Printing, 1873; repr., New Delhi: Light and Life, 1980), 55.

[7] Hangloo, *Agrarian System of Kashmir*, 17–26.

[8] Lawrence, *The Valley of Kashmir*, 330.

An intensive study of the available sources suggests that the land tenure system in the Kashmir Valley was akin to economic systems in other parts of the Indian subcontinent that came under the ryotwari settlement. A. Wingate, appointed Settlement Officer for the Kashmir Valley in 1887, described the revenue system there as "ryotwari in ruins."[9] According to Eric Stokes, the ryotwari village can be defined as one in which there were "a number of dominant office-holding families, one of which traditionally exercised political and revenue control as village head, subject to recognition by the ruling power."[10] The village elite were thus defined by their access to and control over offices, such as that of village headman, accountant, revenue collector and so forth, and the benefits they derived from the office were partly dues in cash and kind, and partly in revenue-exempt or revenue-privileged land.

In the case of the Kashmir Valley, the office holders were drawn from the ranks of the Hindu clerical caste of Kashmiri Pandits, and a few prominent Kashmiri Muslim Sayyid and Pir families. That Kashmiri Pandits were revenue administrators is hardly in doubt, given the vitriol poured on them by British land settlement officials. The earliest evidence of Kashmiri Pandits as office holders is from the Afghan period, when they became proficient in Persian and entered the ranks of the revenue administration.[11] As a social group, they were not dissimilar to one of the key groups in other successor states to the Mughal empire elsewhere in the subcontinent in the eighteenth century: the Muslim and Hindu clerical castes who had mastered the use of the pen and provided the crucial service of revenue management to these burgeoning regimes. Sayyid and Pir families performed similar functions for the Afghan, and later the Sikh and early Dogra, regimes. These three social classes were exempt from the regular revenue assessment and other taxes that the state levied on cultivators. Furthermore, they

[9] A. Wingate, *Preliminary Report of Settlement Operations in Kashmir and Jammu* (Lahore: W. Ball & Co., 1888), 34.

[10] Eric Stokes, *The Peasant and the Raj: Studies in Agrarian Society and Peasant Rebellion in Colonial India* (Cambridge: Cambridge University Press, 1978), 47.

[11] Anand Koul, *The Kashmiri Pandit* (originally published in 1924, repr. Delhi: Utpal Publication, 1991), 19, and Jia Lal Kilam, *A History of Kashmiri Pandits*, 242–5.

received revenue-free land grants from the rulers in return for services rendered to the state.[12]

The early Dogra regime under Gulab Singh (1846–53) and Ranbir Singh (1853–85) was eager to cultivate the loyalty of these classes to ensure Kashmir's smooth transition to a Dogra kingdom, in much the same way as the British needed either the adherence or quiescence of similar groups to ensure their emergence as colonial powers in late-eighteenth-century India. Once their rule had been established, however, and with the increasing intervention of the British in the late nineteenth century, Kashmiri revenue administrators had to increasingly share their positions with Dogras and other Hindus imported for the purpose from British India. Until the very end of the nineteenth century, however, the old class of local officials controlled the revenue administration, much to the chagrin of the British.

The revenue administration began with the patwari, or village accountant, over whom stood the tehsildar, and one or two naib-tehsildars, in charge of the fifteen tehsils. The tehsildar had the power to fix the yearly assessment on crops and he made the final decision on the amount of a village's crop to be collected by his subordinates. The list of his subordinates included the naib-tehsildar, thanedar, shakdar, kardar, and so on. These officials charged the peasants revenue at different rates, depending on the area and their needs at that particular moment.[13] The tehsils were divided into three districts or wazarats, presided over by officers known as wazir-wazarats. These wazirs were subordinate to the Hakim-i-Ala, or Governor of Kashmir, under whose orders the revenue establishment theoretically functioned. It is important to differentiate between the ranks of the bureaucracy, and the Pandit community in general, since the greatest beneficiaries of the system were the wazir-wazarats and the tehsildars. The lower ranks of the bureaucracy, including the patwaris, kardars and shakdars, most likely did not benefit as much from the system as British representations would have one believe. Furthermore, many Kashmiri Pandits in rural

---

[12] Wingate, *Report*, 18.

[13] Mirza Saifuddin, "Mirza Saifuddin Papers," vol. 1, 1848–62, unpublished manuscript in Persian, Acc. # 1420 (Persian and Arabic Manuscript Section, Research and Publications Department, University of Kashmir, Srinagar), 1, and Hangloo, *Agrarian System of Kashmir (1846–1889)*, 68–9.

areas were simply cultivators, with no connection to the revenue administration. Additionally, there was an important Kashmiri Muslim element in the revenue administration, drawn mostly from Sayyids and Pirs.

Maharaja Gulab Singh continued the revenue assessment of the Sikh period, under which the state took half the share of the Kharif crop and in addition four traks per kharwar. The Rabi crop was taxed at half-share of the produce, and three traks per kharwar,[14] in addition to various other cesses.[15] In practice, however, the cultivator had to pay much more than half the share of the total produce in the form of multifarious taxes to the state. These included the *nazarana*, levied four times a year, and the *tambol*, taken on occasions of marriages in the ruler's family.[16] In 1850, Mirza Saifuddin, a British spy in Maharaja Gulab Singh's court, classified the charges on the peasants into four categories: state share of the revenue, *rasum*,[17] additional state collections, and taxes freely paid by the cultivator himself.[18] Kashmiri Pandits, Sayyids, and Pirzadas were expected to pay only one trak per kharwar of the extra four traks levied by the state, in cases where they cultivated the land.[19]

The Kashmiri Muslim cultivator had to feed not only the darbar, but the whole contingent of middlemen between himself and the state, starting from the shakdar, the official in charge of watching the crops, to the kardar, the actual revenue collector. The peasant thus ended up paying out of every 32 traks of each Kharif crop, 21 traks and 11¾ seers as revenue in kind; and out of 32 traks of each Rabi crop, 20 traks and

[14] The government scale of weights used in collecting their proportion of grain was: 6 seers=1 trak, 16 traks=1 kharwar, while in selling the grain to the people the scale was changed as following: 6 seers=1 trak, 15 traks=1 kharwar. The extra trak gained by the government was to pay for the expense of transporting the grain from the villages to the city. See Robert Thorpe, "Kashmir Misgovernment," in S.N. Gadru, ed., *Kashmir Papers: British Intervention in Kashmir* (Srinagar: Freethought Literature Co., 1973), 53.

One kharwar amounts to roughly 192 lbs or 87 kg.

[15] Wingate, *Report*, 18–20.

[16] Ibid.

[17] Rasum was the revenue extracted by revenue officials from each village as their personal share.

[18] Saifuddin, "Mirza Saifuddin Papers," vol. 1, 2.

[19] Wingate, *Report*, 18.

6¾ seers as revenue in kind. The cultivator had also to concede a share of his fruit, ghee, fowls, honey, and sheep or goats to the government.[20] John B. Ireland, an American who visited Kashmir in the 1850s, exclaimed in wonder that, "on the birth of every lamb, the owner must pay a tax of one anna . . . the birth of a calf is four annas. For a marriage one rupee. A fishing boat four annas a day. Walnut trees ten annas a year for the oil, and if the crop fails, must be made up with ghee."[21]

The greater importance accorded to the city population in the economic system of the Valley—an important theme in the political economy of the pre-colonial subcontinent in general—put cultivators at a further disadvantage. King Lalitaditya, who ruled Kashmir in the eighth century, is quoted in the *Rajatarangini* as having said, "Cultivators must be repressed and their style of living must be lower than that of the city people or the latter will suffer."[22] Clearly, this system was not a product of the nineteenth century, although Kashmiri poetry from this century is rife with references to the evisceration of the countryside to provide for the inhabitants of urban areas. Undoubtedly, however, the policies undertaken by the early Dogra rulers entrenched this time-honored economic system, characterized by a one-sided flow of grains from villages to the city of Srinagar, in the late-nineteenth-century Kashmiri economy.

One of Maharaja Gulab Singh's first policies on assuming control of the Jammu and Kashmir state was to regulate the system of collecting shali in large government granaries in the city of Srinagar so that it could be sold by retail through government officials to the city population at a fixed price.[23] This was an integral aspect of the Maharaja's attempt at establishing control over his newly acquired territories, of which Srinagar, as the center of the lucrative shawl trade, formed the

[20] Thorpe, "Kashmir Misgovernment," 28–9.

[21] John B. Ireland, *From Wall Street to Cashmere, Five Years in Asia, Africa and Europe* (New York: Rollo, 1859), 397.

[22] *Grain Control in Kashmir* (Jammu and Kashmir State: Board of Grain Control, August 1923), 1.

[23] While the policy of controlling the grain market was not unique to Kashmir—many other rulers of princely states followed similar policies in their realms—it did set Kashmiri political economy apart from the political economy of British India in this period, for there the grain market was being released of its governmental fetters in the early nineteenth century.

epicenter. Furthermore, since Gulab Singh was in a precarious political position at the time of his accession in 1846, he did not want to risk the wrath of the Srinagar population, which was used to the Indo-Islamic system of state intervention in the grain market to ensure cheap grain to the city population. Gulab Singh's system, which remained in place with minor changes until the late nineteenth century, allowed each Kashmiri a fixed amount of rations; if an individual wanted more than the designated amount, he had to get permission from the officer-in-charge of the government storehouse.[24]

Higher-level revenue officials benefited greatly from this system of grain distribution and could make profits without much difficulty, since the state fixed commodity prices. While the prices of shali were kept lower than the market demand for the product would have warranted, the prices of commodities such as cotton and *mung* were hiked to much more than the demand warranted. For instance, Wingate noted that the state price of cotton was so high that it paid merchants to import cotton while tons of it was rotting at their doors. This gave the tehsildar the opportunity to make profits by taking less of the assessment in cheaply priced articles and more in cotton and mung, and other highly priced commodities, in spite of the fact that the state directed officials to take as little as possible of revenue in these highly priced articles.[25]

The officials additionally benefited from the sale of peasant labor to the state and foreign visitors. This system of forced labor, in which peasants could at any time be drafted into the service of the state, was known as *begar*. Begar entailed services such as carrying loads of rations and other supplies to Gilgit for the state, or for foreign visitors on their journeys around the Valley, or for royal processions from one part of the state to another. During the 1853 Gilgit campaign, each cultivator had to carry at the rate of 8 traks of load per head, consisting of rations and supplies for the soldiers in Gilgit.[26] Peasants were reduced to animals of burden, without any hope of payment for such services. Only in the case of requisition for begar being made by foreign visitors could the peasant expect a payment of 1¼ annas for every stage of carrying a load. The kardars, in charge of supplying such labor to the darbar, simply raided villages and conscripted men who could not come up

---

[24] Thorpe, "Kashmir Misgovernment," 32.

[25] Wingate, *Report*, 25.

[26] Thorpe, "Kashmir Misgovernment," 60–1.

with the bribes that would exempt them from this duty. In some cases, a village would have to pay as much as Rs 70 to Rs 90 to get an exemption from begar.[27] There are several pitiful accounts of Kashmiri peasants toiling under the burden of inhuman weights on their way to Gilgit.[28] Interestingly, the city population was automatically exempt from forced labor.

British settlement officials, introduced to the Valley in the 1880s, responded to the economic situation in Kashmir in much the same way as their counterparts had on encountering similar economic systems in British India. According to the British, Kashmir lacked a settled cultivator class, and even more significantly it lacked economic conditions under which these cultivators could be induced to extend cultivation in the hope of increased reward. Before such conditions could be created, it was necessary to eliminate flaws in the existing revenue system of the Dogra state. The settlement reports maligned revenue officials, particularly Kashmiri Pandits: "It is to be regretted that the interests of the State and of the people should have been entrusted to one class of men, and still more to be regretted that this class of men, the Pandits, should have systematically combined to defraud the State and to rob the people."[29]

The reports further lamented that Kashmir lacked a free and fair internal trading system in which cultivators could participate, since the state, and through it revenue officials, controlled the economy. Wingate described the system:

> The system has been sufficiently profitable to support a large body of the pandit population of the city in idleness, and the government has gradually become on the one side a farmer working with coolies under a management closely approximating forced labor, and of the other side, a gigantic bania's shop doling out food to the poor in exchange for their

[27] Dhar, *Socio-Economic History of the Kashmir Peasantry*, 127.

[28] According to Robert Thorpe, "The Kashmir authorities have been utterly careless of the comfort, and even of the lives, of unfortunate wretches who are dragged from their homes and families to trudge for months, over the wearisome marches of that arid country. They fall on the road to perish of hunger and thirst and, are destroyed in hundreds at a time, by the cold on the snowy passes." See Thorpe, "Kashmir Misgovernment," 61. Thorpe's entire treatise was designed to provoke British intervention in Kashmir, hence his description of begar is particularly maudlin.

[29] Lawrence, *The Valley of Kashmir*, 410.

coppers, and keeping with every cultivator an account showing what is taken from him whether in the way of grain, oil, wool, ponies, cows, etc. and what is given to him in the shape of seed, plough-cattle, cotton or wool to spin and weave . . . In Kashmir, the tehsildar is the bania, and he is a branch of the great official firm in Srinagar where the chief business is conducted.[30]

To the British, the Kashmiri peasant was no more than a "coolie cultivating at a subsistence allowance the State property."[31] Furthermore, the reports insisted that the urban artisan classes were also severely exploited under the state-controlled system of grain distribution. Through their contact with the state, influential individuals—these included the large proportion of the Pandit population of the city— were able to acquire rice at Rs 1¼ per kharwar, while poor artisans were left at the mercy of those who made huge profits off them during times of scarcity. Officials reported large sales at Rs 1¼ per kharwar to the treasury, and the profit made thereby was divided between officials who made over the shali and favored recipients. Shali was rarely sold at the low rate intended by the government. According to Wingate, "the places of sale were few, the days of sale fewer, the officers appointed insufficient. Every expedient was resorted to that admitted of the smallest public sale with the maintenance of the farce of selling freely."[32]

The picture that emerges from settlement reports is of an economic system in which the village was very much a tributary of the city. While there is probably some truth to this—successive rulers of Kashmir had attempted to keep the city population, especially those working in its shawl industry, supplied with cheap grain—the system was not in place at the expense of rural areas to the extent the British made it out to be. Certain rural groups, such as the Wani or Bakkal class of Muslim hucksters, were still able to engage in petty rural–urban trade and barter, as well as acting as local moneylenders. Since credit was usually supplied in kind, as in many parts of the subcontinent,[33] it also follows that the moneylenders were closely linked to the grain trade, implying

[30] Wingate, *Report*, 17.
[31] Ibid., 19.
[32] Ibid., 18.
[33] B.R. Tomlinson, *The New Cambridge History of India, III. 3, The Economy of Modern India, 1860–1970* (Cambridge: Cambridge University Press, 1993), 64.

that this local group did play a role in intra-rural as well as rural–urban trade. In the 1891 census, as many as 1,026 people in Srinagar identified themselves as grain dealers,[34] while their number in the entire Valley was as high as 3,336.[35] Much like the rest of British India, grain dealers and moneylenders drew ire from the British for allegedly robbing the peasantry by charging them exorbitant rates of interest.[36]

Undoubtedly, the revenue administration, composed mainly of Kashmiri Pandits and increasingly Dogras at the higher levels, profited from a system that placed them in a unique position to do so. However, it does not necessarily follow that these classes were particularly fraudulent in the conduct of their duties in Kashmir, as the British settlement officials would have one believe. The anti-Pandit, anti-middleman colonial rhetoric needs to be placed in its proper historical context. The 1870s and 1880s, when most of these British reports were penned, was a decade of increasing polarization in Britain and British India over the issue of Kashmir's status in the empire. On the one hand there were those who believed that it was the moral duty of the colonial state to rescue indigent Kashmiri Muslims from the tyrannical and rapacious rule of the Hindu Dogras and their Hindu compatriots, the Kashmiri Pandits.[37] Arrayed on the other side were those in favor of the Dogra dynasty's independence from colonial rule. The latter were clearly in a minority, since English public opinion as well as the position of the colonial government was overwhelmingly in favor of intervention.[38] Colonial documents from this period thus portrayed the general political and economic situation in the Valley in a wholly negative light, making British intervention appear desirable.

[34] Rai Bahadur Pandit Bhag Ram, *Census of India, 1891, Vol. XXVIII, The Kashmir State* (Lahore: Mufid-i-Am Press, 1893), cc.

[35] Ibid., 163.

[36] Walter Lawrence noted that the Wanis charged a 24–36 percent rate of interest. Lawrence, *The Valley of Kashmir*, 387.

[37] *The Times* of London, for instance, regularly ran stories in the 1870s and 1880s that criticized the Dogra state's policies toward its subjects, as well as the colonial government's complicity with an oriental despotism bent on ruining the "Happy Valley."

[38] The two leading texts against Dogra rule written during this period were Arthur Brinckman, "Wrongs of Cashmere," and Robert Thorpe, "Kashmir Misgovernment," while a text favoring the Dogra dynasty was William Digby, "Condemned Unheard." See Gadru, ed., *Kashmir Papers: British Intervention in Kashmir.*

Furthermore, colonial discourse on revenue administrators and middlemen in Kashmir is strikingly reminiscent of colonial discourse on similar social groups in British India throughout the nineteenth century. After all, these groups were considered one of the greatest hazards to the establishment of a colonial order defined by settled arable farming, homogeneous village communities, and, most significantly, "a well-to-do peasant class able to resist the vicissitudes of seasons and pay fair rent."[39] Simply because the colonial state did not encounter the "middleman" in Kashmir until the late nineteenth century does not mean that he had lost his potential to threaten the colonial state's drive to settle the land and ensure a steady flow of revenue to the state. Since Kashmir was a princely state ruled by the Dogras, colonial discourse on the political economy of Kashmir prior to direct colonial intervention was geared toward proving that the contingent of revenue middlemen was systematically defrauding the state and the cultivators, which could only be alleviated by a land settlement carried out under British auspices. The land settlement would establish a direct relationship between the state and the cultivator, thus rendering the middleman a cipher and deleting all manner of "illegal" revenue demands he had concocted to enrich himself at the expense of the cultivator and the state.

Apart from revenue officials, another class of individuals viewed with distrust by the colonial state and seen as profiting from the land were various types of land grantees. The Dogra darbar followed the policy of parceling out land to various individuals who had complete power over the peasantry cultivating those lands. This was clearly not an innovation on the rural, or for that matter urban, landscape of Kashmir or elsewhere in the subcontinent. The parceling out of land to grantees can be dated back to the Sultanate period in Kashmir, the practice becoming widespread under the Mughals, Afghans and Sikhs. However, it is interesting to explore the patterns of land dispensation under the Dogras. Beginning in 1862, the darbar began allotting fallow lands to non-cultivators to encourage the cultivation of such lands. These lands, called *chak zarniasi*, were granted for a period of ten years with a schedule of land revenue payable to the government.

[39] Robb, "Ideas in Agrarian History," 211.

The grantees, i.e. the *chakdars*, were entitled to the produce of their lands so long as they paid state dues on time, remained loyal to the state, and obeyed state rules regarding chak lands.

In 1866 and 1867, Maharaja Ranbir Singh granted *chak* lands to Hindus who were also members of his administration, on condition that they remain Hindus, accept service nowhere else, and pay at a low revenue assessment.[40] It is clear that the Dogra administration was attempting to create a class of men loyal to the state who, significantly, were not drawn from the ranks of Kashmiris; most were Punjabis or Dogras, alongside a few prominent Kashmiri Pandit bureaucrats. Various types of chaks granted by Ranbir Singh had multiplied by 1879–80, which ultimately led to the subverting of state rules and land-grabbing by officials of the state. Legally acquired chaks gradually swelled to include much larger tracts of land than were handed out in the original chak. Since the darbar was technically the "owner" of all land, the only way the use of the term *hak milkiyat* (proprietary rights) to describe the 5 percent remission of revenue to the chakdars can be explained was that the latter fostered ownership rights in such land assignments to put themselves in a position of power.[41] This was the source of much discomfort for British administrators and settlement officials in Kashmir, as is obvious from their constant maligning of such individuals.

The question of ownership rights was more evident in the lands parceled out by the state as jagirs. There were three types of jagirs granted by the state: jagir grants made as a reward for services rendered, or to be rendered, to the state; grants made for political exigencies; and religious grants mainly for the support of religious institutions. Every grant was made either as an equivalent of a certain annual sum of money, or in respect of a certain area of land, or in respect of whole villages.[42] The jagirdars had wide-ranging powers since they were required

[40] Wingate, *Report*, 27–9, and *Rules Regarding Grant of Waste Land for Cultivation as Sanctioned by His Highness the Maharaja Sahib Bahadur* (Jammu: 1917), Jammu State Archives.

[41] Wingate, *Report*, 28.

[42] H.L. Rivett, *Assessment Report on the Minor Jagir Villages situated in the Valley of Kashmir, 1896–97* (Lahore: Civil and Military Gazette Press, 1897), 6.

to "represent the Darbar in their jagirs."[43] They acted as the state in these villages, collecting revenue and imposing grazing fees, forest revenues, and other land taxes on cultivators who farmed in those villages. If a river passed through a jagirdar's lands, the peasants who fished in that river had to provide fish to the jagirdar.[44] The list of additional taxation imposed on the cultivators of jagir lands was formidable and included taxes on ponies, vegetable plots, fruits, honey, houses, persons whose main occupation was not agriculture, and so on.[45] Moreover, jagirdars could evict cultivators almost at whim since the latter had no occupancy rights on the land they cultivated. Jagirdars were mainly Dogra or Punjabi officials in high positions of government, or Pandits at the higher levels of the revenue administration, most residing in the city of Srinagar. The chief jagirdars rendering civil service to Maharaja Gulab Singh included Pandit Kamal Bhan, Chief Record Keeper; Munshi Trilok Chand, Chief Treasurer; Hakim Azim, Chief Physician; Lachman Pandit Dhar, Governor of Kashmir; Wazir Ratnu, Kotwal; and Ganesha, Chief Toshkhana. Other important jagirdars of the Maharaja included Wazir Punoo, Wazir Zorawoo, and Raja Kak Dhar, all in the service of the Dogra state.[46]

The institution of jagirdari, which was utilized by the Dogras in Kashmir in similar ways and for similar reasons as by the Mughals, Afghans, and Sikhs before them—to bolster the authority and prestige of the state while providing an efficient means of revenue collection—was regarded as not much more than a feudal institution by the British. Again, the primary reason they disliked the institution was that the jagirdars, who were meant to be merely assignees of a certain amount of revenue, ended up claiming ownership rights on their jagirs and additional wastelands surrounding the assigned lands. The case of Dewan Amar Nath, the governor of Kashmir, serves to illustrate the point. The original grant made to the Dewan as chak, which was later alienated in jagir, amounted to 2,965 acres of wet land and 2,850 acres of dry land. In 1896, the Dewan was in actual possession of 3,623 acres

[43] Private Records of His Highness, 1898/13, Jammu State Archives, 4.
[44] Political and General Department, 76/1876, Jammu State Archives, 2.
[45] Rivett, *Report*, 3–4.
[46] Saifuddin, "Mirza Saifuddin Papers," vol. 1, 3.

of wet land, 2,433 in dry land, 2,805 in culturable waste and 2,028 in unculturable wasteland. He was therefore in possession of 5,074 acres of land to which he had no right, according to British officials, thereby almost doubling his original grant.[47]

Moreover, Dewan Amar Nath raised a claim to *hak milkiyat* over these illegally acquired lands. The State Council rejected this claim in a resolution, stating he had no such right to his jagir lands and no such claim could be considered, since he only had *hak jajirdari*, or the right to collect the state share of revenue on certain lands.[48] By the time the State Council passed this resolution, the newly established British Residency tightly controlled governance in Kashmir. And it is worth pointing out that the ostensible fraudulence of Dewan Amar Nath's actions was part of the process of the emergence of a new urban land-holder class in Kashmir in the late nineteenth century, a class not dis-similar to the one that emerged out of the manipulation of muafi grants in late Mughal India.[49] To the British, however, this was the dreaded phenomenon of "steady and latterly increasing transference of land from the cultivating to the non-cultivating classes," giving rise to a "landlord element [that] is intruding itself between the cultivator and the State."[50]

More significant still to them was the fact that many jagirdars in the state had become absentee landlords who had handed over their jagirs to "unscrupulous" middlemen known as *mustajirs*, or revenue contract-ors, for years at a time. For instance, Dewan Amar Nath farmed out the collections of his jagir villages in the Kamraj district to Aziz Kakru from 1877 and Risk Kaul got the collection rights to his jagir villages in the Meraj district until 1891.[51] Colonial officials reported that these mustajirs not only exploited cultivators, but also jagirdars, resulting in heavy indebtedness among the jagirdar class. By the late nineteenth century, many jagir villages had passed from the hands of jagirdars to

[47] J.L. Kaye, *Note on the Assessment Report on the Minor Jagir Villages situated in the Valley of Kashmir* (Lahore: Civil and Military Gazette Press, 1897), 7.

[48] Ibid., 12.

[49] See Muzaffar Alam, *The Crisis of Empire in Mughal North India, Awadh and the Punjab, 1707–48* (Delhi: Oxford University Press, 1986), particularly chapter III.

[50] Wingate, *Report*, 27.

[51] Ibid., 15.

those of moneylenders.[52] The example of a jagir village in Rajwar amply demonstrates this trend. This village was farmed out to a certain Rasul Bat for three years, 1892–4, for which he paid the jagirdar a lump sum of Rs 360 per annum. In return, everything the village produced in the form of grain, fruit, and nuts was his property. In 1892, Rasul Bat extracted Rs 751 from the villagers, in 1893 he realized Rs 249 and in 1894 Rs 315, thus making Rs 236 on his bargain. Rasul Bat's activities led to the desertion of this village by 1894.[53] Not only was a new landowner class being created from the ranks of non-agricultural castes, to the even greater chagrin of the British, the dreaded revenue farmer, an alien intruder, was rearing his ugly head on the rural landscape of Kashmir.

Another type of land grant that continued into the Dogra period was the muafi, namely lands exempt from the payment of land revenue to the state. Muafi grants to Sayyid and Pandit families by previous regimes remained intact in the early Dogra period. There were two kinds of muafi grants in the Dogra period. The first was a religious muafi, under which one-third of the amount of land revenue was received by the muafidar in cash and the other two-thirds in kind. In 1848, land revenue of Rs 84, 375 was assigned to the free grants held by religious personages and other learned men in Persian, Arabic and Sanskrit languages. Religious muafi lands usually had religious institutions—such as mosques, shrines, temples and *mathas*—located on them, and were frequently hereditary, remaining within families for generations. Non-religious muafis were granted to persons for the construction of works for public use, such as bridges, wells, and so on.[54] In many cases, chakdars had their chak lands enlisted as muafis and made huge sums of money on them. The example of Dewan Badri Nath, Governor of Kashmir, is a case in point. The Dewan was granted a deserted government garden and with it was included some land he had bought from a woman, which he stated was assessment-free. He was to pay Rs 48 per annum on the lot and, although he bought some more land a few years later which he included with his earlier plot of land, he did not increase his revenue dues.[55]

---

[52] Rivett, *Report*, 6.

[53] Ibid., 8.

[54] Proceedings of the State Council of Jammu and Kashmir, 1898–1900, Jammu State Archives.

[55] Wingate, *Report*, 29.

Since the British assumed the Maharaja to be the sole proprietor of all land in Kashmir, they branded all attempts to acquire ownership titles to land as fraudulent. In reality, the emergence of a landholder class was a key feature of late-nineteenth-century Kashmir, much like eighteenth-century India, where a new landholder class had arisen out of the manipulation of muafi and other land grants handed out by the Mughal state.[56] The landholding element in Kashmir was intimately tied to the Dogra administration and probably acquired lands through tacit consent of the state. It was largely urban in nature, with landholders/administrators residing in the city of Srinagar while owning tracts of land in the surrounding villages. The transfer of land to "non-agricultural" castes was of particular concern to colonial officials in British India, where they were trying to halt similar trends through political and economic engineering in the early twentieth century.[57] The Dogra state undertook similar steps in the 1920s and 1930s (the effects of which will be discussed later in this book).

So what kind of picture of Kashmir's rural landscape can we sketch? If colonial sources, such as travelogues and settlement reports, as well as the Kashmiri nationalist narrative are to be believed, then it would appear that the Kashmiri peasantry was an undifferentiated mass of pauperized cultivators at the very bottom of the economic ladder, with a host of social groups living off their labor. A more subtle analysis of extant sources, however, prompts one to color this sketch a bit, especially since there is not only ample evidence of Kashmiri agency, but equally significantly because the rural–urban tributary relationship needs some qualification. If one heeds Tapan Raychaudhuri's astute observation that "the key to the actual position of the agriculturist is hence to be sought not in social or economic organization but the manner in which administrative and political power was distributed and deployed,"[58] it becomes possible to rethink the usually dismal descriptions of the Kashmiri rural landscape.

[56] Alam, *Crisis of Empire*, chapter III.

[57] The colonial state passed a series of legislative acts in British India to inhibit the sale of land to "non-agricultural castes" and urban interests, beginning with the Deccan Agriculturists Relief Act (1879) and ending with the Punjab Land Alienation Act (1900) and the Bundelkhand Act (1903). See Tomlinson, *The Economy of Modern India*, 64.

[58] Tapan Raychaudhuri, "The Agrarian System of Mughal India: A Review Essay," in Muzaffar Alam and Sanjay Subrahmanyam, eds., *The Mughal State, 1526–1750* (Delhi: Oxford University Press, 1998), 276.

Kashmir's agricultural landscape presented a bewildering variety in the latter half of the nineteenth century. Doubtless, peasant laborers were at the bottom of the economic ladder, cultivating for a small share of what they had produced from the soil, and with little bargaining power. These peasants typically migrated to the Punjab in search of labor during the winter months, saved some of their wages, and returned to Kashmir in early spring.[59] However, cultivators who claimed the hereditary right to cultivate certain plots of good and well-irrigated land within the boundaries of the village—a right referred to as *miras*—were in a somewhat better position to demand a greater share of the produce from revenue collectors. Lawrence declared, while conducting his land settlement in the late nineteenth century, that, "Changes of dynasty and changes of system, earthquakes, floods, and famines, have alike failed to obliterate the hereditary principle in land tenures in Kashmir, and while Mughals, Pathans, Sikhs, and Dogras have steadily ignored the existence of hereditary occupancy rights, these rights have been kept alive by the village."[60] It is important to note that miras was not a juridical occupancy right; rather it was a right enforced by custom.

Additionally, peasants working on chakdars' lands, jagirs, and other specially assigned villages were exempt from policies such as begar, and regularly transferred themselves from state property on to such lands.[61] British officials noted cases of entire villages acting in unison to dispute harsh revenue demands. Lawrence observed:

> The Kashmiri, in spite of his abject condition, is a very obstinate and determined person, and in cases where he considered that the assessment was too high he has steadily declined to pay the excess. An active and severe official has occasionally realized the revenue assessed in 1880 in full by selling up the sheep and cattle of a village, but the next year the village was fallow and the cultivators had emigrated to other villages more fairly assessed, or had taken service as farm laborers under some privileged landholder.[62]

[59] Wingate, *Report*, 16.
[60] Lawrence, *The Valley of Kashmir*, 428.
[61] Wingate, *Report*, 37, and Rivett, *Report*, 1.
[62] Lawrence, *The Valley of Kashmir*, 404.

Clearly, Kashmiri peasants did not hesitate to capitalize on opportunities that served their interests. One of these seems to have been cultivating specially assigned lands where the state and revenue administration was less intrusive. Even in state lands, moreover, the cultivators were able to negotiate with the administrative power and buy themselves off begar by bribing the officials in charge of conscription.[63] Unlike Raychaudhuri's argument for peasants in Mughal India—that the peasants in *Khalisa* or state lands were better off than those who farmed jagir lands[64]—in Kashmir the opposite seems to have been the case, with Kashmiri peasants in specially assigned lands having to deal with a less coercive administrative machinery than those who worked on state lands.

What of the cultivator's relationship to the market: this is important since his income was determined not simply by the revenue demand, but also by the price he could get for his produce on the market. Despite colonial assertions that the state controlled and defined the market, the Kashmiri peasantry did have the means to carry out various kinds of economic exchanges within and beyond the village. The composition, nature, and function of the social group of pirzadas forms an integral aspect of this story. The pirzadas were a loosely defined group—including mullahs, pirs, the petty ulema, preachers, religious mendicants and so forth—who made their living by roving the countryside and performing rituals for the peasantry, settling disputes among them, conducting marriages, and a host of other such functions in exchange for certain amounts of the peasantry's grain and produce. Some pirzada families owned land and orchards and were exempt from not only the extra land taxes levied by the state but also from begar.[65] At their most powerful, pirzadas were *mutawallis* (managers) of shrines, holding large tracts of revenue-free land grants along with access to the earnings of the shrine.

The importance of pirzadas lies in the fact that they formed an essential bridge between the village and the city, transferring goods and

[63] Wingate, *Report*, 38.

[64] Raychaudhuri, "Agrarian System of Mughal India," 275.

[65] S.N. Dhar, "Glimpses of Rural Kashmir," in Suresh K. Sharma and Usha Sharma, eds., *Kashmir through the Ages: Society, Economy and Culture*, vol. 3 (New Delhi: Deep and Deep Publications, 1998), 319.

ideas between the two areas—exchanges that could and did function independently of the state and its revenue administration. Through their organization of and participation in village and city fairs, usually under the auspices of a shrine, these itinerant figures created a space conducive to the dissemination of religious and political ideas from urban areas, as well as to the sale of grain and handicrafts by the peasantry.[66] Fairs were a time for interaction between rural and urban populations of the Valley, and, coupled with Friday congregations at the shrines, provided traders with a suitable outlet for their surplus products; in some instances these also gave rise to permanent bazaars.[67] As Lawrence pointed out, "The annual fairs held at the various shrines are red letter days in the dull lives of Kashmiri Muslims. Thousands crowd together and spend the day eating and buying fairings . . . Cobblers are hard at work . . . sweetmeat sellers drive a roaring trade, and alms flow into the shrine."[68] The relationship between peasants and pirzadas was by no means defined by an unnegotiated exercise of power on the part of the latter, a fact that would become increasingly significant at the turn of the twentieth century when struggles for the redefinition of Kashmiri Muslim identities required the inclusion of the peasantry.

While Kashmiris were able to negotiate within the Dogra economic system, they were still vulnerable to political changes as well as natural disasters. In 1877–8 Kashmir was hit by a famine linked to the Great Famine of British India that spread from South to North India in the years 1876–8. However, in the case of Kashmir it was not the failure of the monsoons, but instead an abundance of rains that destroyed the harvest, which was left to rot in the fields due to the rigid revenue mechanism that prevented peasants from harvesting grain until a revenue official was present at the site. By spring 1879 there was no seed left to sow during the autumn season. In the meantime, the prices of foodgrains shot up, since the state was unable to prevent revenue officials from hoarding state grain, mostly maize and barley. Thousands

---

[66] The relationship between pirzadas and peasants is recorded in detail by Maqbool Shah Kraalwari in the poem *Greeznama* [The Story of the Peasant] (Srinagar: Privately printed, 1912).

[67] Ghulam Hassan Mir, "Muslim Shrines of Srinagar (Kashmir) and their Role (1857–1925)," (M. Phil. thesis, University of Kashmir, 1986), 74–5.

[68] Lawrence, *The Valley of Kashmir*, 289.

5. Crowds thronging at a fair around Hazratbal mosque. Chitralekha Zutshi's collection.

of Kashmiris migrated to the Punjab, where relief measures installed by the colonial state were insufficient to meet the needs of the local and immigrant populations. The famine resulted from harvest failure, compounded by the failure of entitlements.[69]

Nevertheless, the picture of a desolate rural Kashmir, where peasants had no rights to either land or produce, and where the power of officials was beyond challenge, is a bit overstated. The economy of Kashmir, and the colonial rhetoric it produced, had more in common than not with conditions in British India. One must turn to economic and political conditions in the Valley's main urban center, however, to fully appreciate the ways in which relationships between the countryside and the city had an impact upon the Valley's political culture.

City on a Shawl: The Srinagar Shawl Trade,
1846–1883

The intricate representation of the city of Srinagar on a shawl dating from 1870 illustrates the centrality of the trade to the economy of the Valley in the nineteenth century. The pale blue shawl, with a map of Srinagar embroidered in various colors on it, was as we saw commissioned by Maharaja Ranbir Singh as a present to the Prince of Wales. As the embroidered inscription behind the shawl indicates—"The map of Kashmir, produced at the orders of His Highness the Maharaja . . . ,"[70] for the Dogra Maharaja Srinagar was, in fact, synonymous with "Kashmir." The shawl, as also the city in which it was manufactured, were and continue to be one of the most important material representations of Kashmir to the outside world, including Persia, Turkey, Europe and America.[71] The importance of the city of Srinagar

[69] See B.M. Bhatia, *Famines in India: A Study in Some Aspects of the Economic History of India (1860–1965)* (New Delhi: Asia Publishing House, 1967); Ajit Kumar Ghose, "Food Supply and Starvation: A Study of Famines with Reference to the Indian Sub-continent," *Oxford Economic Papers* 34 (2) (July 1982): 368–89; and Lawrence, *The Valley of Kashmir*, 214–18.

[70] "Kashmiri Shawl with Map of Srinagar," Sri Pratap Singh Museum, Srinagar, Kashmir.

[71] Of the Kashmiri shawls exported to the Western world in the 1860s, France imported about 80 percent, the United States followed with 10 percent, Italy 5 percent, Russia 2 percent, Germany 1 percent and Great Britain 1 percent. Of the above, about two-thirds were purchased in Kashmir directly by French agents and

to the economy of the state of Jammu and Kashmir can hardly be denied, particularly since the shawl trade of the Valley was concentrated in Srinagar.[72] Equally important to the story are individual shawl traders, who claimed leadership of the Kashmiri Muslim community through their positions as managers of local shrines, particularly in the wake of the decline of the shawl trade. Here we need to trace the vagaries in the shawl trade and the fortunes of those involved in it, for this offers a window into narratives of identity articulated in late-nineteenth-century Kashmiri political culture.

The origin of the shawl industry may lie in the fifteenth century, but it was not until the Mughal period (1585–1758) that the industry achieved its full potential.[73] During the Afghan period (1758–1819), the industry received its first setback as a result of the establishment of the Dagh-Shawl department during the governorship of Haji Dad Khan (1776–83), who imposed a crushing excise tax on shawls.[74] In spite of this tax, however, the Kashmiri shawl industry prospered toward the end of the eighteenth century with the increasing European, particularly French, demand for these prized articles of fashion. With the increase in European demand, shawl looms in the city of Srinagar increased from 12,000 in 1783 to 24,000 in 1813.[75] It was one of Napoleon's former generals, Allard, employed in Ranjit Singh's army in 1822, who established a direct link between Parisian shawl manufacturers and those in Kashmir.[76] Furthermore, by this period the Kashmiri shawl was the universal symbol of aristocracy across the Indo-Persian world. The successor states of the Mughal empire

---

exported to France; the remainder were exported through native (British-Indian) bankers, primarily in Lahore, and sold at London auction sales, the buyers being nearly all French. Bates, *Gazetteer*, 59.

[72] Until 1871, the Jammu and Kashmir government derived revenues of Rs 600,000 per annum from taxation on shawls. See Lawrence, *The Valley of Kashmir*, 440.

[73] Hajji Mukhtar Shah Ashai, *Tract on the Art of Shawl Weaving* (Lahore: Kohinoor Press, 1887), unpublished trans. from the Persian by K.N. Pandita (Srinagar: Central Asian Studies Department, University of Kashmir), 1–2.

[74] Frank Ames, *The Kashmir Shawl and its Indo-French Influence* (England: Antique Collector's Club, 1986), 25–6.

[75] Ashai, *Tract*, 12.

[76] Ames, *The Kashmir Shawl*, 35.

developed special institutions for the classification of shawls, and the Kashmiri shawl even attained the status of a form of honorific currency in the courts of north India.[77]

In order to obtain sufficient quantities of raw material for the shawls, Kashmiri merchants began to travel as far as Yarkand, Khotan and the lands of the great Khirgiz hordes in Central Asia in as early as the late eighteenth century. These merchants established their warehouses in the whole of Chinese Turkistan and monopolized the wool trade of the region.[78] In turn, merchants from British India and France began to come to Srinagar, commissioning shawls for export to particular markets.[79] The presence of French agents in Srinagar—noted by travelers to the city and by the great shawl manufacturer of the Kashmir Valley, Hajji Mukhtar Shah Ashai—had a significant impact on the shawl industry.[80] First, the designs of the shawls underwent a transformation by the mid-nineteenth century with the intervention of French agents who needed designs to suit their own markets; and second, several imitation shawl industries emerged in France to formulate cheaper methods of shawl production.[81] This signaled the beginning of the decline of the Srinagar shawl trade, which has continued in significantly attenuated form into the present.

The importance of the trade to the Dogras is clear from the fact that their system of grain control was, in principle, geared toward the supply of grain to city inhabitants, most of whom were shawl workers. However, as discussed earlier, this system only benefited those who had access to cheap grain, the rest of the population being subject to high prices that it could scarcely afford. Every *karkandar*, or owner of a shawl factory, had a number of *shaal bafs*, or weavers, under him,

---

[77] C.A. Bayly, *Rulers, Townsmen and Bazaars: North Indian Society in the Age of British Expansion, 1770–1870* (1st Indian edition, Delhi: Oxford University Press, 1992), 59–60.

[78] *A Short History of Chinese Turkistan*, anonymous Persian manuscript, translated and annotated by A.M. Matoo (Srinagar: Central Asian Studies Department, University of Kashmir, 1981), ii, and Ashai, *Tract*, 13.

[79] Veronica Murphy, *Kashmir Shawls: Woven Art and Cultural Document* (London: Kyburg Limited, 1988), 6.

[80] Ashai, *Tract*, 20. Also see Baron Charles Hugel, *Travels in Kashmir and the Punjab; Containing a Particular Account of the Government and Character of the Sikhs from the German of Baron Charles Hugel* (London: John Petheram, 1845).

[81] Murphy, *Kashmir Shawls*, 7.

from 30 to 300 depending on the size of his establishment.[82] The karkandars received a certain amount of shali for distribution to their shawl weavers, which they distributed at arbitrary prices, since they kept accounts of the amount delivered to each weaver, which was then deducted from his monthly wages.[83] The government levied an annual tax of Rs 37 on each karkandar for every shaal baf in his employ.[84]

The royal court controlled the shawl trade through the reinstated and much more powerful institution of the Dagh-Shawl, which levied a heavy duty on shawls at various stages of their production and distribution. Additionally, the government imposed duties on the import of pashm—the raw material for manufacture of pashmina shawls—and the costs involved in the production of the fabric itself inflicted unprecedented damage on the industry. From the time of the sale of pashmina by weavers in the bazaar and its purchase for shawl manufacture, to its dyeing, to its having a pattern worked on it, and to its actual completion, taxes increased exponentially. As soon as one line of embroidery on the completed shawl was finished, it was taken to the Dagh-Shawl, where a rough estimate of its value was formed and on which an ad valorem duty of 25 percent was immediately levied. Of this amount, a portion had to be paid down, after which the shawl was stamped and the manufacturer was at liberty to proceed with the work, the value being adjusted and the balance paid at completion.[85]

Needless to say, the class most severely hit by the heavy taxation was that of the shaal bafs, who ended up paying nearly Rs 5 in taxes out of a maximum earning of Rs 7 or 8 per month.[86] There are numerous descriptions of their misery and the squalor of the conditions in which they worked and lived. Baron Charles Hugel, who visited Kashmir in the 1840s, wrote with much horror about shawl manufactories, "one of the most wretched abodes that my imagination could well picture."[87] Each shawl took months to complete, during which time the weavers toiled away at one and a half annas a day. It would seem that the shaal

---

[82] Most shawl factory owners were Kashmiri Muslim Sunni merchants, while the shawl weavers, dyers, and embroiderers were Kashmiri Muslim Shias. Bates, *Gazetteer*, 53.

[83] Thorpe, "Kashmir Misgovernment," 50.

[84] Bates, *Gazetteer*, 54.

[85] Ibid., 55–7.

[86] Ashai, *Tract*, 15.

[87] Hugel, *Travels in Kashmir and the Punjab*, 120.

bafs were condemned to a lifetime of penury because they were not permitted to leave the Valley, relinquish their employment, or change their employer, "even though they may become half-blind or otherwise decapitated [*sic.*] by disease."[88]

Their resistance to these conditions ultimately contributed to the decline of the industry. In 1847 the weavers assembled and demanded that the Maharaja give them permission to emigrate to the Punjab or change working conditions in Srinagar. Gulab Singh conceded that the weaver was to be paid only according to actual work on the loom and he could change his employer if he so chose.[89] However, these promises were not translated into practice and, gradually, the centers of the industry shifted from Srinagar to Amritsar as the weavers migrated to the Punjab in the hope of better working conditions.[90] The ones who remained attempted to petition yet again; this time it was the Governor of Kashmir, Kirpa Ram, who ignored their pleas for a reduction in shali prices and shawl taxes. Ultimately, in April 1865, they rebelled against the Dagh-Shawl department and its Pandit overseer, Pandit Raj Kak Dhar. Robert Thorpe describes this incident in detail: "In bittered despairing mood, the shawl-bafs made a wooden bier, such as the Muslims use to carry their dead to the place of internment. Placing a cloth over the coffin, they carried it to and from the procession, exclaiming; Raj Kak is dead, who will give him a grave?"[91] The darbar mercilessly crushed this rebellion and along with it, in effect, shawl manufacture.

Shawl merchants, on the other hand, were a powerful class in the city of Srinagar and, arguably, in the Valley of Kashmir, well into the 1870s. Not only were they trading in a commodity that brought the darbar thousands of rupees in revenue, they also determined the darbar's relationship with the outside world. Most travelers to the Kashmir Valley in the nineteenth century visited the houses of shawl merchants, not only to purchase shawls but also to get a taste of the

---

[88] Bates, *Gazetteer*, 54.

[89] Ames, *The Kashmir Shawl*, 42.

[90] The emigration of Kashmiri shawl weavers to the Punjab had begun as early as the 1810s, when they fled Kashmir as a result of Afghan policies. Ludhiana, Amritsar and Islamabad had become centers of the imitation shawl industry by the second decade of this century. See Thorpe, "Kashmir Misgovernment", 51, Bates, *Gazetteer*, 53, and Ames, *The Kashmir Shawl*, 40.

[91] Thorpe, "Kashmir Misgovernment," 52–65.

Kashmiri elite mode of living. Lt. Col. Torrens, who visited Srinagar in the early 1860s, called shawl merchants the "merchant princes of Kashmir," the "most comfortable fellows" who owned the best houses in the city.[92] One of the most prominent shawl merchants in nineteenth-century Kashmir was Hajji Mukhtar Shah Ashai (d.1892), celebrated for shawls produced through the loom system, whose house most foreign travelers to the Valley visited. Ashai's relationship with French merchants began in 1811, when they first sent agents to his house to carry out business regarding the purchase and production of shawls. Subsequently, they placed orders with him direct, without the mediation of agents, a relationship that continued for thirty-two years.[93]

The huge profits made by merchants such as Mukhtar Shah on the sale of shawls to European markets is clear from the fact that the commodity sold at a 500 percent profit on its original cost of production in Kashmir. As Mukhtar Shah himself admitted to John Ireland, the American visitor to the Valley in the 1850s, if labor was as cheap in France as Kashmir, they could make shawls as well as he did. In the 1860s, the wholesale dealers in London, for instance, paid Mukhtar Shah £200 for a shawl that would have fetched him only £50 in Kashmir.[94] At the time Ireland visited Mukhtar Shah's manufactory, his workers were at work on a shawl for Empress Eugenie of France, which would have cost him $650 on completion, but could be sold for $4,000 in London or New York.[95] The export of shawls to Europe reached its apogee in the middle years of the nineteenth century, with an increase in the value of shawls exported from £171,709 in 1850–1 to £459, 441 in 1861–2.[96] In London alone, sales rose from £104,000 to £226,000 between 1853 and 1863.[97]

The decline of the shawl trade was imminent, however, as became clear over the next two decades. Even by 1865, exports had fallen to £254,498.[98] The single most significant extraneous event leading to the decline of the export of Kashmiri shawl manufactures was the

[92] Lt. Col. Torrens, *Travels in Ladak, Tartary, and Kashmir* (London: Saunders, Otley and Co., 1862), 261–2.

[93] Ashai, *Tract*, 20.

[94] Ireland, *Wall Street to Cashmere*, 302.

[95] Ibid., 409.

[96] Ames, *The Kashmir Shawl*, 50–1.

[97] Murphy, *Kashmir Shawls*, 7.

[98] Thorpe, "Kashmir Misgovernment," 51.

Franco-Prussian war of 1870, which caused a sharp fall in the demand for authentic Kashmiri shawls in Europe, particularly France. As Mukhtar Shah lamented, "By 1883, the shawl merchants suffered a 50 per cent loss in their business. In recent years, the loss has gone up to 60–70 per cent as its export from Kashmir to France has been completely blocked . . . There are about 800 owners of shawl workshops and 25,000 workmen who are out of business."[99] By the 1890s the state had withdrawn from the industry and abolished the department of the Dagh-Shawl.[100] By this time, with the emergence of factories that produced shawls, cheaper imitations had begun to be produced in Amritsar and even Europe, and the industry had ceased to be profitable for the government. As significantly, with the replacement of the successor state system in India by the colonial administration, the value of shawls as symbols of aristocracy and forms of currency had declined by the late nineteenth century.

The Indian Catalogue of the Colonial and Indian Exhibition, 1886, stated under Shawls, "This manufacture, which formerly brought half a million a year into Kashmir, is now well nigh moribund. Unless means are taken by Government to preserve it, the art of weaving the finest shawl will probably be extinct fifteen to twenty years hence. The warehouses of London and Paris are full of shawls which find no purchasers, and the value in Kashmir has consequently fallen to a third of what it was ten years ago."[101] Ernest Neve, a Christian medical missionary who lived in Kashmir in the first decade of the twentieth century, wrote that the shawl trade, which received its death-blow with the Franco-German war, never really revived.[102] The production of, and trade in, Kashmiri shawls continues into the present, although the nature of the industry has changed dramatically—from one managed by large shawl trading houses to primarily a small-scale handicraft

[99] Ashai, *Tract,* 36.

[100] M. Ganju, *Textile Industries in Kashmir* (Delhi: Premier Publishing Company, 1945), 46.

[101] Quoted in Murphy, *Kashmir Shawls,* 9.

[102] Ernest F. Neve, *Beyond the Pir Panjal: Life among the Mountains and Valleys of Kashmir* (London: T.F. Unwin, 1912), 236. By 1921, there were only twenty-four shawl weaving factories in Srinagar. See Khan Bahadur Chaudhri Khushi Mohammad, *Census of India, 1921, Vol. XXII, Kashmir, Part I Report* (Lahore: Mufid-i-Am Press, 1922,) 178.

industry managed by the Jammu & Kashmir Government Arts Emporium and a few itinerant traders.[103]

However, what is consistently ignored by scholarship on the Kashmiri shawl trade and industry is that the decline of the powerful class of shawl merchants had far-reaching implications for the evolution of the social and political landscape of late-nineteenth and early-twentieth-century Kashmir. Shawl merchants, having lost their principal source of income with the decline of the shawl trade, began to shift to other trades to maintain their standard of living and influence in society. Since a good number of these merchants were also involved in the management of shrines in Srinagar, their first move on facing hardship was to re-establish control of shrines. This led to bitter disputes over the control of religious spaces in the city, beginning in the 1890s, between leading members of the Kashmiri Muslim elite. These internal contestations over sacred space, religious identities, and community leadership intensified in the first two decades of the twentieth century as the Valley's political economy underwent its most significant transformation.

The Impact of Colonial Intervention I:
The Land Settlement, 1885–1914

According to colonial records, land settlement operations in the Kashmir Valley, which began in 1887 and continued through 1893, were pivotal in transforming the Valley's agrarian and urban landscapes at the turn of the twentieth century. While it is certain that these policies had a profound impact on the region, colonial sources greatly exaggerated some of the changes attributed to the settlement. Perhaps a better way of assessing the impact of the land settlement on Kashmir's political economy is to place it in the larger context of other changes occurring in the region at the time, including the decline of the shawl trade and the political and other policies of the Dogra rulers. It is also worth pointing out that some of the changes ostensibly brought about directly by the land settlement had been set in motion before the late nineteenth century, and it is likely that the settlement helped them gather momentum in a dramatically altered political and economic

---

[103] Raina, *Geography of Jammu and Kashmir*, 145–6.

scenario. I argue here that it is important to study the processes set in motion by the decline of the shawl trade, the centralization of the state structure under the State Council and the British Residency, the land settlement, and the emergence of new forms of industry, since these not only determined the nature of the emergent leadership, they also determined the issues that were raised and debated in the public spheres of the Kashmir Valley.

The land settlement was an aspect of the larger British intervention in the political administration of the state beginning in 1885, which led to the establishment of the British Residency and State Council to run the affairs of Jammu and Kashmir in 1889. Although Maharaja Pratap Singh's accession speech in 1885 had declared that he would "adopt such measures only as are calculated to secure to my subjects their greatest good, and the fullest enjoyment of their rights and privileges,"[104] the movement by the British to curtail Dogra authority had been long under way. The British, while conceding the first Dogra Maharaja's request to not have a British resident placed in his court, had employed the services of a local Kashmiri, Mirza Saifuddin, to spy on his administration and report on the general condition of the state. Saifuddin gave a scathing account in twelve volumes, describing in minute detail the misrule of the first Dogra Maharaja. The British viewed the second Maharaja, Ranbir Singh, with a mixture of admiration and distrust, particularly when the Afghan and later the Russian threat on the northwestern border began to occupy them with increasing urgency in the late 1870s. A combination of events, including a discussion in the British and British Indian press of the brutalities carried out by the Maharaja during the famine of 1877, such as the deliberate drowning of a boatload of famine-stricken Kashmiri peasants in the Jhelum, and the Afghan Amir's declaration in 1880 claiming Chitral as part of Afghan territory, made the British close in on the Kashmiri darbar.[105]

[104] "The Maharaja's speech to the Darbar," Sept. 25, 1885, quoted in *The Civil & Military Gazette*, Sept. 30, 1885. See D.C. Sharma, *Documentation on Kashmir: Documentation of English Language Newspapers of India* (Jammu: Jay Kay Book House, 1985), 22.

[105] N.N. Raina, *Kashmir Politics and Imperialist Manoeuvers, 1846–1980* (New Delhi: Patriot Publishers, 1988), 35–7.

In 1884 Lord Ripon came to the conclusion that there was no alternative but to appoint a permanent Resident in Kashmir. The British presented this direct intervention in the affairs of a princely state not merely as a strategic move to protect the British empire in India, but to alleviate the misery of Kashmiris by reforming the administration.[106] Soon after Pratap Singh acceded to the throne in 1885, he was informed that a British Resident would be placed at the Kashmir darbar. In his speech at Maharaja Pratap Singh's *dastarbandi* (coronation) in September 1885, Oliver St. John, the Officer on Special Duty in Kashmir, stated: "The State of Jammu and Kashmir has fallen behind majority of States of India in progress necessary for the welfare of the people."[107] By 1888, Pratap Singh was, de facto, deposed and control of the administration passed into the hands of the British Residency. In March 1889 the Maharaja was made to sign an edict of resignation that relieved him of all part in the administration, which was placed, subject to the control of the Resident, in the hands of a State Council, under the presidency of Dewan Lachhman Das, and a year later Raja Amar Singh. The Viceroy, Lord Dufferin, accepted the edict with these words: "Notwithstanding the ample resources of your state, your treasury was empty; corruption and disorder prevailed in every department and every office; Your Highness was still surrounded by low and unworthy favorites, and the continued misgovernment of your state was becoming, every day, a more serious source of anxiety."[108] Ostensibly, the British had entered Kashmir to cleanse its administration and alleviate the condition of its people.

The State Council almost immediately assumed all powers of governance and the Maharaja was reduced to giving his approval to all measures enacted by the Council. Furthermore, the Council was composed entirely of Indians imported from British India for the purpose, and followed a policy of recruiting Dogras and other Punjabi Hindus to man all branches of the administration. The Government of India was aware of the need to prevent Punjabis from taking over Kashmiri administration,[109] but the extent to which it was in favor of employing

---

[106] Ibid., 36.
[107] State Department Records, 1885/R-2, Jammu State Archives, 5.
[108] Sufi, *Kashir*, 809.
[109] The Secretary of State for India wrote to the Lieutenant Governor of the

Kashmiris in their stead is debatable. The Dogra darbar cited several reasons for the recruitment of outsiders instead of native Kashmiris to the service, including lack of modern education and their incompetence in the recently instituted language of administration, Urdu.[110] Kashmiri Pandits, the class whose "favorite occupation" was state service,[111] were, needless to say, unhappy with this state of affairs, and soon campaigned to regain their position in Kashmir's bureaucracy.[112]

Soon after its establishment, the Residency persuaded the Maharaja to accept a land settlement of the Valley of Kashmir. In 1887, A. Wingate was appointed to carry out this much-needed task. It is here that the significance of British perception of the economic structures of Kashmir becomes apparent. Following from the tradition of the colonial government in British India throughout the nineteenth century, Wingate made a strong argument in favor of granting occupancy rights to the Kashmiri peasantry. According to him, the land revenue system in place in the Valley had left the coffers of the state empty because of the existence of a class of officials between the state and the peasantry. Additionally, it had created an itinerant peasantry with no interest in cultivating the land. Therefore, to replenish revenue, and to convert a discontented and thriftless peasantry into a contented, thriving community, peasants had to be given interest in the land they cultivated. To achieve this, Wingate argued, it was necessary to fix the state demand at a fair sum for a term of years and establish a system of accounts which would confine the powers of the tehsildars to revenue collection.[113]

North-West Province: "If Nisbet (British Resident in Kashmir), asks you for native officials for Kashmir, I hope you will kindly help him get good men. It is very important to start with reorganisation fairly and to avoid a Punjabi ring." See Foreign Department/Secret/726/E, April 1889, Calcutta Records, National Archives of India, 4.

[110] One of the first steps taken by the State Council after its institution in 1889 was to replace Persian with Urdu as the language of administration, the language being imported alongside numerous administrative servants from neighboring British Punjab.

[111] Ram, *Census of India, 1891, Vol. XXVIII, The Kashmir State*, 163.

[112] This campaign was called the "Kashmir for Kashmiris" movement. G.H. Khan, *Freedom Movement in Kashmir* (New Delhi: Light and Life, 1980), 101.

[113] Wingate, *Report*, 34.

More importantly, Wingate made this system contingent on conferring on the cultivators the possession of the land they tilled. In a scathing criticism of the darbar's policies and of middlemen-bureaucrats, he said:

The Darbar claims to be proprietor of the land. The officials seek to persuade the Darbar that this position implies that the cultivators must have no rights; to maintain this theory, when the cultivators have been dispossessed their complaints must be ignored; the rights of which the Darbar has thus deprived the cultivators and which the Darbar supposes it has reserved to itself, are immediately appropriated by the officials . . . The Darbar appears to be under the impression that it can govern much as a zamindar manages a private estate by farming with tenants-at-will. Any such delusion ought to be dissipated by the facts disclosed in this report and the Darbar should be convinced that the only way it can preserve its own rights is by entrusting them under proper restrictions to the cultivators.[114]

Wingate suggested that the settlement rules declare the state as ultimate proprietor, and at the same time confer the right of occupancy on all persons entered as occupants at the time of settlement *jamabandi* (assessment).[115] We must note that Wingate's arguments were designed to bolster the authority of the state through the foundation of a peasantry determined to defend their lands against encroachments, and willing to pay land revenue. It was to be clearly understood that—

the interests of the Darbar and the interests of the cultivators are identical and that the interests of all middle men whatsoever, whether revenue farmers, tehsildars or quasi-proprietors, are inimical to both. The cultivators desire more food and the Darbar, more revenue, and the whole pundit class live by stinting both. The Darbar cannot protect itself without the assistance of the cultivators nor is any land settlement likely to last which does not engage the active sympathies of the agricultural population in support of State policy.[116]

Wingate ended his report with a warning: "It is for your highness to decide whether the Maharaja is to be master in his own territory or not."[117]

[114] Ibid., 61.
[115] Ibid., 34.
[116] Ibid.
[117] Ibid., 43.

In the tradition of Utilitarians and other free-market advocates, Wingate clearly disagreed with the collection of revenue in kind, which allowed for the state to fix prices of grain and act as the sole grain trader in the Valley. According to him, the price of shali had to rise and fall with the outturn of the harvest, because as soon as it got scarce huge profits were made by revenue officials in charge of collection. The mendicancy of the peasantry was a symptom of this artificial system historically in place in the Valley. However, although he proposed in his settlement rules for the Valley that the settlement be made in cash, Wingate allowed the Darbar "upon report by the Settlement Officer to accept whole or part of the assessment in shali under defined conditions . . ."[118]

Walter Lawrence, who took over from Wingate as Settlement Commissioner in 1890, followed the principles introduced by his predecessor in the land settlement of the Valley. According to the "Lawrence Settlement," as it came to be known, permanent hereditary occupancy rights were bestowed on every person who, at the time of assessment or at the time when the distribution of assessments was effected, agreed to pay the assessment fixed on the fields entered in his or her name in the settlement papers. So long as the assessment was paid, the occupant could not be ejected. However, the right to occupancy was not alienable by sale or mortgage.[119] In the tradition of the Utilitarians, Lawrence was ambivalent toward the development of rural capitalism in the subcontinent: he continued to view the state as the provider of social overhead capital and as the redistributor of resources.[120] He argued at length that giving cultivators the right to alienate their land would create a class of middlemen who would procure land for themselves and rich urban individuals.

The settlement only entered cultivated land as in the occupancy of *assamis* (tenants possessing permanent hereditary occupancy rights), while waste and fallow lands were recorded as *Khalisa*, or state land. Out of this waste-land, however, 10 percent was to be left for collective village usage, such as grazing. Furthermore, the revenue assessment was fixed for a period of ten years, to be paid partly in cash and partly

[118] A. Wingate, *Proposed Settlement Rules for Kashmir* (Lahore: W. Ball & Co., 1889), 18.

[119] Lawrence, *The Valley of Kashmir*, 429–30.

[120] See Tomlinson, *Economy of Modern India*, 44–6, for Utilitarian views on rural capitalism and cultivators' rights.

in kind, depending on the produce of the village. The sundry taxes that the state collected from the peasantry on walnut trees, forests and livestock were included in the land revenue, except pony and sheep taxes. In case of a dispute, the case was to be recorded and decided by the settlement officer. In the case of Hindus and Sikhs, no final entry could be made until the orders of the settlement officer were obtained. Chakdars were made into assamis of the several villages in which their estates lay, and were to be subject to regular assessment rates after their terms for the privileged rates ran out.[121]

Lawrence's decision to take revenue partly in kind and partly in cash was a result of the strong opposition of the administration to the idea of a cash settlement for the Kashmir Valley. There were several complex reasons behind the darbar's and the revenue officials' opposition to a settlement in cash. The most obvious was that a cash settlement would hinder revenue officials from making huge amounts of profits from a sale of grain, which they would have collected in kind from the peasantry. The more significant reason for the darbar's opposition was the issue of supply of grain to the city of Srinagar, which could not be achieved unless a significant amount of the revenue was realized in the form of shali from the peasantry. Although the state was losing a significant amount of revenue by accepting a cash and kind settlement,[122] the urban elite was adamant that the government continue to supply cheap grain to the city.[123] This was particularly important with the decline of the shawl trade and the descent of the weaving class into penury. Hajji Mukhtar Shah had appealed to Wingate to exercise caution in introducing a cash settlement because, "The shawl trade is gone and all the artizans [*sic*] are ruined. If the cultivators are all at once allowed to sell at any price they please, the artizan classes will have to buy dear and will be still further ruined."[124] Taking into account this opposition to a cash settlement and the effects of a sudden change to collection in cash in 1891 by the Governor of Kashmir, which brought

---

[121] Lawrence, *The Valley of Kashmir*, 426–37.

[122] In 1871, the value of the revenue taken in kind was Rs 16,93,077 and that in cash was only Rs 9,62,057. However, the state derived revenues of Rs 6,00,000 from taxation on shawls, an amount that was practically wiped out in the next decade with the decline of the shawl trade. Therefore, the state had a strong financial stake in a cash settlement. See Lawrence, *The Valley of Kashmir*, 440.

[123] Ibid., 438–41.

[124] Wingate, *Report*, 26.

about a scarcity of grain in the city, Lawrence gave each village the option to decide the amount to be paid in cash and in kind, with the power of commuting the amount in kind agreed upon by cash payments.[125]

Additionally, Lawrence attempted to reform the system of collection, storage, and sale of state grain. He fixed the state demand in kind for the first year at 360,000 kharwars, an amount considered too low by advocates of revenue in kind. This amount proved to be more than adequate and prices of grain remained low in the city. State demand was reduced to 300,000 kharwars the next year and by the end of the century had been reduced to 175,000 kharwars for ten years. Unfortunately, this almost immediately led to grain shortages in Srinagar, which continued into the next century, culminating in a grain crisis in 1921 (discussed later). Provided with greater market opportunities, petty traders exacerbated grain shortages by grain hoarding and price hikes. Lawrence himself had persuaded private traders at various staging places where grain was received in the city to undertake the supply of rice and other provisions to the city population.[126] This merely led to the collusion of grain traders and revenue officials, many of whom still acted as grain traders, in continuing to control the grain trade in the Valley.

The extent to which the land settlement was ultimately successful in curbing the powers of the class of revenue officials is debatable. Undoubtedly, the land settlement regarded them as mere assamis who were required to pay their share of revenue. However, Lawrence and later settlement officials still depended on revenue officials to carry out the actual settlement, which required an elaborate machinery that the colonial state was not willing to spare for Kashmir; thus precedent, known only to revenue officials, became the basis for settlement policy. More significantly still, revenue officials now became holders of state bureaucratic positions, such as collector and manager of revenue demand, rather than drawing their position from village custom. Since this meant that they could just as easily be dismissed if they did not live up to the expectations of their official positions, these administrators now redoubled their efforts to collect the revenue on which their jobs depended. As a result, in spite of being converted into a

[125] Lawrence, *The Valley of Kashmir*, 440–1.
[126] Ibid., 442–3.

low-level salaried bureaucrat in the employ of the state, the revenue administrator continued to exercise a fair amount of power in his dealings with the village population. Furthermore, since all land was subject to the settlement, the officials concocted ways to prove their proprietary titles on land; many were even successful in entering themselves into revenue records as proprietors of lands to which they had been specially assigned by the Maharaja in the past few decades, thus contributing to the growing class of urban landholders. It is clear, then, that although revenue officials were initially reluctant to assist in the land settlement of the Valley, most were able to maneuver within the new system and find new power niches in the radically changed context.

This is not to suggest that the land settlement did not disrupt Kashmiri rural society. The disruption was perhaps most visible in the situation of various jagirdars, the older generation of landholders, a class that went through transformation throughout the pre-settlement period. Colonial officials in British India regarded jagir lands as most detrimental to the interests of agriculturists, particularly when farmed out to revenue contractors—which according to them led to an internal derangement of village tenures.[127] As has been discussed above, jagirdars in Kashmir had also assigned portions of their lands to revenue farmers.[128] Additionally, the state had lost control over the parceling out of jagir lands, and over the ways in which they were inherited. This had led to the division of jagir lands among the numerous heirs of a certain jagirdar without reference to any rule. According to settlement officials, thus, jagirs had been fragmented into several small holdings run by jagirdars who had no influence or respect. As H.L Rivett, the settlement officer in charge of assessing jagir villages in the Kashmir Valley, commented in his report:

[127] Colonial officials made similar arguments against jagirs and muafis in British India. See Stokes, *Peasant and the Raj*, 72–5.

[128] Although the British presented this as a recent phenomenon that was ruining jagir lands, there are several instances of jagirdars farming their lands out to revenue contractors during the Mughal period. In fact, in 1694, it was reported to the Mughal emperor that some of his *mansabdars*, who had jagirs in Kashmir, were farming them on to local men. Although the Mughal court disapproved of this practice, there was nothing to prevent a jagirdar from sub-assigning part of his jagir to any of his officials or troopers. See Irfan Habib, *The Agrarian System of Mughal India, 1556–1707* (Bombay: Asia Publishing House, 1963), 328–9.

It was perhaps not the original intention of the State that jagir grants should be divided up among a number of heirs, but rather that they should devolve in entirety to one heir, the Government of course retaining the power to regulate the succession to these grants . . . Jagirdars at present exist absolutely devoid of merit or influence . . . This has resulted in the jagirs being frittered away among several heirs, and in many of the grantees now being in such a miserable state of impecuniosity as to render them contemptible in the eyes of the people.[129]

One such example of the fragmentation of jagir lands in the Kashmir Valley is that of Sultan Safdar Ali in Uttar Machipura Tehsil. Sultan Safdar Ali was succeeded by his two sons, Muzaffar Khan and Haibat Khan; the former received three-fifths of the total grant and the latter two-fifths. When these two men died, their shares were divided up between Muzaffar Khan's two sons and Haibut Khan's five sons. The original jagir was fragmented even further after this division.[130]

The assessment of jagir lands in 1896–7, under the supervision of Capt. J.L. Kaye, Settlement Commissioner, set about to repair the flaws that had beset the system of jagirdari.[131] Although the State Council had ordered the extension of settlement operations to jagir holdings in December 1894 and the institution of a cash assessment in such lands, it was not until 1896–7 that the rules governing jagir lands were laid down on paper. Ultimately, this resulted in the curtailment of the powers of jagirdars and the revenue farmers in whose

[129] Rivett, *Report*, 5.

[130] Ibid.

[131] An almost parallel case of jagir settlement in British India can be found in Sind, where Charles Napier undertook to resume as much as possible of the revenue alienated from the government by various means, including demands for one-fourth of the jagirdars' share of the produce. He attached the greatest importance to releasing all wasteland from the grip of jagirdars, with a view to opening up vast areas of virgin land for the enterprising peasant. Napier's main concern was to secure the loyalty of the Baloch chieftans for the British regime by giving them hereditary titles. Similar concerns propelled the jagir settlement in Jammu and Kashmir; however, as noted in the following discussion, the presence of the Dogra state as an intermediary between the jagirdars and the colonial state led to a somewhat different outcome in the state. See Hamida Khuhro, *The Making of Modern Sindh: British Policy and Social Change in the Nineteenth Century* (Karachi: Oxford University Press, 1999), especially chapter two, for an insightful discussion of the jagir settlement in Sind.

hands their estates had fallen. The Commissioner's report quite clearly suggested the active interference of the state in jagir holdings, along with specifying the status of jagirdars and the tenants on these holdings. *Sanads*, or land deeds, were now to be prepared for each jagir, which specified its precise area and value, the term for which and the conditions under which the grant had been made. Jagirdars, it was stated, were no more than mere assignees of state revenue, and the tenants in jagir tracts were as much tenants of the darbar and entitled to protection as any of its other subjects.[132] Therefore, according to Capt. Kaye, it was necessary to grant them occupancy rights:

> To deprive these tenants, to whom the land means existence and whose only means of livelihood is agriculture, of their dearest right—would be the height of injustice. These cultivators are entitled to the same wise and generous treatment accorded by the Darbar to its other tenants and have patiently awaited the settlement in the belief that they will be given rights similar to those granted to the Khalsa assamis (state tenants) . . . Alike in the interests of the jagirdars and of the cultivators, hak assami (occupancy right) must be bestowed in the latter.[133]

Jagirdars, on the other hand, were not given occupancy or proprietary rights to their estates. The report argued that the jagirdar, to whom the revenue derived from certain lands had been assigned by the darbar, could not possibly be a tenant: "The jagirdar stands in place of the Darbar as the collector or assignee of this revenue only . . . Under the grant he has absolutely no connection with the land, only with the revenue derived from it."[134] Just as the darbar could not be its own tenant in *Khalisa* (state owned) villages, according to Kaye, so too jagirdars could not claim occupancy rights that belonged to peasants.

Striking further at the roots of the jagirdars' power over their tenants, Kaye made a strong case for the continuation of a cash settlement at a fixed rate for a term of years in jagir lands, as had been proposed by the State Council Resolution in 1894. According to Kaye, the system of *gala batai* (crop sharing) had helped to give rise to the class of revenue farmers who had ruined villages by effectively taking them over from jagirdars. Although he saw the need for part cash, part kind, assessment for impoverished jagirdars, cash assessments were perfectly

[132] Kaye, *Note*, 14–17.
[133] Ibid., 14–15.
[134] Ibid., 13.

logical in wealthy jagirdars' estates. Attacking such jagirdars by name, Kaye said:

> For men of the wealth of Diwans Amar Nath and Lachman Das, what necessity is there to continue collections in kind? Apart from a consideration of the valuable land they hold in Kashmir, Jammu and the Punjab, they have also their rasums; they cannot be considered poor men who cannot afford to buy their grain, and the collection of revenue in kind is practically always accompanied by unjust exactions and loss to the assamis. Moreover, they do not live in Kashmir and must sell the grain for cash.[135]

Moreover, Kaye argued that jagirdars had no right to collect cesses or make villagers pay for items of expenditure which were purely personal, thus cutting short the formidable list of taxes extracted by jagirdars from their peasants.[136] In the same vein, the report also denied jagirdars any right to the wastelands that they had included with their original grants over the years. The case of Dewan Amar Nath has been noted. Another prominent example is that of the Naqshbandi Khwajas, a prominent Kashmiri Muslim family of Srinagar, who had been granted jagirs by Maharaja Ranjit Singh, continued later by the Dogra maharajas. This family had added Rs 2500 worth of waste land to their original grant over the course of being in possession of the jagir. As a result of the assessment, the Naqshbandis lost 843 acres of land to the state.[137]

In short, the 1896–7 assessment of jagirs brought all jagir lands in line with the land settlement in the rest of the Valley. However, the extent of the impact on jagirs was not quite as far-reaching as colonial records made it out to be; in any case, the impact was not the one intended by colonial authorities. The jagir settlement and the bureaucratization of the Dogra state exacerbated a process that had been in motion since the mid-nineteenth century, namely the changing composition of the jagirdar class itself. The jagirdars who had held land in the Valley for centuries were the ones who lost portions of their territory to the state as a result of the settlement. The Punjabi and Dogra administrators of the Dogra rulers, instead, replaced them as the new

[135] Ibid., 16–17.
[136] Ibid.
[137] General Department Records, 155/22-R/1925, Jammu State Archives.

class of jagirdars who had been assigned jagirs by the state to ensure their loyalty, thereby bolstering its authority and legitimacy.

Maharaja Pratap Singh's statement, asserting the control of the ruling chief in deciding the terms and conditions of jagirs and defending the rights of the jagirdars, illustrates the relationship between jagirdari and state service:

> The jagirdars form the gentry and nobility of the country and have rendered loyal services to the State—they cannot be overlooked on any account. They should be preferred where there are vacancies. They are essential for maintenance of the State's prestige and their rights should continue as before. The title of Maharaja implies that there are Rajas under him and these jagirdars were meant for serving this purpose.[138]

The rest of his response accepted the regulation of jagir lands under the principles of the land settlement of the Kashmir Valley, since he had very little choice in the matter. The significance of state intervention in jagir lands under the residency administration lies in the fact that it threatened the financial and social bases of the Kashmiri landed elite for the first time, replacing this class with a non-Kashmiri, Hindu landholding one. Colonial documents, such as the 1901 census, record that many landed families of note had lost wealth as a result of the better administration, which had led to a loss of their power and influence: "birth alone, nowadays, being no qualification for employment in the civil service of the State."[139] It was this class—notable within it were the Naqshbandis—that would take on the educational and moral reform of the Kashmiri Muslim community with alacrity in the early twentieth century.

The colonial assessment of the land settlement's impact on Kashmir's peasants was similarly overstated. According to these documents, it would appear that within a few years of the settlement there had emerged in Kashmir a stable, revenue-paying peasantry:

[138] Private Records of His Highness, 1898/13, Jammu State Archives. Over the course of his rule, Maharaja Pratap Singh clashed a few times with the British Resident over the question of terms and conditions of jagirs and muafis, his intervention being almost always in favor of jagirdars.

[139] Khan Bahadur Munshi Ghulam Ahmed Khan, *Census of India, 1901, Vol. XXIII, Kashmir, Part I, Report* (Lahore: Civil and Military Gazette Press, 1902), 9.

The agriculturists, who used to wander from one village to another in quest of the fair treatment and security which they never found, are now settled down on their lands and permanently attached to their ancestral villages. The revenue is often paid up before the date on which it falls due . . . Every assami knows his revenue liabilities in cash and kind, and he quickly and successfully resists any attempt to extort more than the amount entered in his revenue-book . . . The annual dread that sufficient food-grain would not be left for the support of himself and his family has ceased, and the agricultural classes of Kashmir are, I believe, at the present time as well off in the matter of food and clothing as any agriculturists in the world.[140]

The 1901 census noted that cultivators were better off than before and enjoyed peace and prosperity as a result of the settlement, and that considerable areas had been converted into flourishing fields over the past decade. Not only was the peasant not at the mercy of revenue officials, he was now in a position to sell his surplus grain to urban grain traders, thus entering the sphere of legitimate and lucrative trade.[141] More and more wastelands were cultivated, "fields fenced, orchards planted, vegetable gardens stocked and mills constructed."[142] Moreover, with increase in wealth peasants were able to make larger purchases.[143] The focus on the peasant's increasing prosperity by colonial administrators was quite obviously an exaggeration. However, the land settlement did lead to the creation of a class of settled peasants, a class that would become an increasingly important focus of the emergent political discourse in the Kashmir Valley at the turn of the twentieth century.

The negative impact of the land settlement on the peasantry and urban poor is, however, worth discussing. The land revenue demand was not significantly reduced under the land settlement, which meant that those in charge of collecting and managing it continued to exercise a fair amount of power over the peasantry. Even if the peasantry had been released from the grip of revenue officials, as colonial officials claimed, payment of revenue in cash meant that it was now connected

---

[140] Lawrence, *The Valley of Kashmir*, 450–1.

[141] Khan, *Census of India, 1901, Vol. xxiii, Kashmir, Part i, Report,* 10.

[142] Old English Records 34/1891, Jammu State Archives.

[143] *The Imperial Gazetteer of India Vol. xv, Karachi to Kotayam* (Calcutta: Superintendent of Government Printing, 1908; repr., New Delhi: Today and Tomorrow's Printers, 1993), 132.

to the larger economic system, and affected by its downturns and up-swings. Moreover, by converting the hereditary right to occupancy into a juridical one sanctioned by the state, the peasant became a tenant of the state, liable to being ejected from his land and losing his occupancy right simply because he was unable to pay the land revenue in full. Additionally, the settlement entrenched chakdars on their illegally procured lands by recognizing their rights to occupancy in such lands, which helped bolster the new Dogra and Punjabi landed class imported into the Valley by the state. As for the artisans, their access to cheap grain was further restricted as the state began to lose control over the grain trade. The Dogra state, moreover, was ill-equipped to administer this partially installed market-driven economic system.

The transformations brought about by the land settlement in the economic system of the Valley were increasingly aided and abetted by the changing nature of internal commerce and the diversification of external trade at the turn of the last century. As we shall see below, internal trade was converted into a money economy in this period, while external trade became commodity-oriented, as opposed to being solely based on luxury goods such as shawls. The resultant urban growth and the rise of new social classes led to the internal reconstitution of communities alongside the redefinition of their external relationships with other communities and the state.

The Impact of the Colonial Intervention II: Trade and Commerce, 1885–1914

As has been pointed out earlier, the Kashmir Valley was by no means either economically or culturally isolated from the outside world prior to the late nineteenth century. A brisk trade in commodities such as salt, cloth, tea, metals and tobacco was carried out on the backs of Kashmiri peasants as they migrated seasonally between the Valley and the plains of the Punjab. Besides this trade, a class of professional muleteers carried out transactions with Punjab bullock drivers. This trade followed three routes: the Banihal Pass that connected the Valley to Jammu, the Old Imperial Road that ran over the Pir Panjal and reached the railway at Gujrat, and the Jhelum Valley Road which ran along the river Jhelum from Baramulla to Kohala in the Punjab.[144] Additionally, the Treaty High Road, which ran from Srinagar to Leh,

[144] Ibid.

connected the Valley and British India with Central Asian trade. This trade commanded a significant proportion of Kashmiri external trade prior to 1890. Nevertheless, trade from Kashmir into British territory in 1805 was valued at only Rs 141,757, and cowries, piece-goods and shawls accounted for 91 percent of this trade.[145] The shawl trade further bound Kashmir and Chinese Central Asia in a strong economic relationship from the late eighteenth century. Shawls of superior quality, leather, grain and a little tobacco were exported from Kashmir to Ladakh, in return for which shawl wool, salt, and tea were imported. Tea came to Kashmir from China by way of Lhasa and was also a state monopoly.[146]

The improvement in communications with British India, evident from the opening of the Jhelum Valley Cart Road to wheeled traffic in 1890, which connected the Valley to the Punjab, led to an almost instantaneous increase in trade with the Punjab. In 1891–2, the value of imports from the Punjab into Kashmir amounted to Rs 6,616,145 and exports to Punjab to Rs 6,405,088, the total value of the trade being greater than all preceding years and exceeding that of 1889-90, the next best year, by Rs 40,734.[147] Furthermore, exports from Kashmir to the Punjab increased from Rs 53.3 lakhs in 1892–3, to Rs 99.6 lakhs in 1902–3 and as much as Rs 192 lakhs in 1904–5.[148] The value of perishable commodities such as fruits and ghee to the export trade increased dramatically with better communications. Consequently, the value of export trade from Kashmir to British Indian provinces exceeded imports, the total value of trade rising from Rs 10,632,488 in 1901 to Rs 19,931,002 in 1911.[149]

Silk, having replaced shawls in the export economy of the Kashmir Valley, became a commodity of increasing value at the turn of the twentieth century. In 1890 the state took over direct control of the industry to establish it on a commercial footing and by 1900 it had become obvious that Kashmir could produce silk on a large scale. As early as 1904, the state was making a profit of £40,240 from the export

[145] Tom Kessinger, "Regional Economy (1757–1857) North India," in Dharma Kumar, ed., *The Cambridge Economic History of India, Volume 2: c. 1757–c. 1970* (Cambridge: Cambridge University Press, 1983), 245.

[146] Bates, *Gazetteer*, 70.

[147] Lawrence, *The Valley of Kashmir*, 386.

[148] *Imperial Gazetteer*, 133.

[149] Ibid., 60.

of raw silk.[150] After 1905 the exports of raw silk from India included large quantities of Kashmiri silk, and by 1919 the bulk of Indian silk being consumed in the European market came from Kashmir.[151] The raw silk produced in Kashmir increased from 115,748 lbs. in 1906–7 to 215,749 lbs. in 1911–12. The silk industry provided employment to a considerable population of the city of Srinagar and surrounding areas.[152] In 1904–5, as many as 5,000 people in the city were employed in silk-producing operations, and in 1906–7, the number of agriculturists employed as rearers of silkworms was 14,427, a number that had increased to 41,552 by 1911–12.[153] Ratan Rawlley, an expert on the silk industry in the early part of the last century, stated that the Kashmiri agriculturist and artisan had adapted well to modern methods of silk production, and helped to increase the annual output of silk in the state.[154] As a result of the importance of silk to the economy of the state, it remained a government monopoly managed by the department of sericulture.[155]

Clearly, the nature and volume of trade from the Kashmir Valley had undergone a major transformation, leading to a period of urban growth. Trade, coupled with the institution of large public works such as the construction of the cart road and the Gilgit road, and a steady increase in tourism to Kashmir, led to an influx of money into the Valley. The 1901 census noted the general prosperity in the Valley as well as an increase in prices to a considerable degree in the decade from 1891 to 1901. According to the census, prices were expected to go

[150] Sir Thomas Wardle, *Kashmir: Its New Silk Industry, With Some Account of its Natural History, Geology, Sport, etc.* (London: Simpkin, Marshall, Hamilton, Kent and Co., 1904), 53.

[151] Ratan C. Rawlley, *The Silk Industry and Trade: A Study in the Economic Organization of the Export Trade of Kashmir and Indian Silks, with Special Reference to their Utilization in the British and French Markets*(England: P.S. King & Son, 1919), 164.

[152] Khan, *Census of India, 1901*, 11.

[153] Ratan Rawlley, *Economics of the Silk Industry: A Study in Industrial Organization* (London: P.S.King & Son, 1919), 41–2.

[154] Ibid., 44.

[155] Ibid., 45. In the early part of the twentieth century, when the silk industry had just begun to gain a foothold in the Valley, Maharaja Pratap Singh and Raja Amar Singh had stated quite clearly to the Resident that they had no intention of handing it over to those who had been trying to lay hold of it as a private enterprise. See Wardle, *Kashmir*, 49.

higher still due to the recognition of values of free trade and the granting of permission by the state for the export of shali.[156] By 1911, a considerable increase in the population of the Kashmir province was noticeable, which registered a 36.4 percent increase from 1891 to 1911.[157] The city of Srinagar had grown steadily from 1891 to 1911, showing an increase of 6.1 percent in the two decades,[158] and a further growth of 11.5 per cent between 1911 and 1921.[159] While there was a general decline of traditional Kashmiri industries, such as metalwork, woodwork and gabba manufacture, new export-oriented industries had emerged in this period. Therefore, even as centers of traditional crafts—such as Islamabad, which did not develop export industries— gradually declined, Srinagar flourished from being the center of new industries such as silk[160] and tourism.[161] Although the nature of the city's importance to the economy of the Valley had undergone a transformation, it continued to be identified with the Kashmir province and very often the entire state of Jammu and Kashmir.

The increasing availability of money, the sedentarization of the peasantry, and increasing trade ushered in a period of social transition in the Valley. Although colonial officials hailed the rise in population as evidence of a rise in prosperity,[162] not everyone was prosperous in this period. There may have been a rise in wages, but it was not nearly as much as the rise in prices of foodgrains warranted. Gone were the days when ten annas could have, at least in principle, bought poor artisans a kharwar (66 seers) of shali. In 1911, one rupee would buy only 13 seers of the same product, a number that had declined from 18 seers in 1901.[163] Furthermore, the old nobility was clearly in

[156] Khan, *Census of India, 1901, Vol. XXIII, Kashmir, Part I, Report*, 12.

[157] Mohammad Matin-uz-Zaman Khan, *Census of India, 1911, Vol. XX, Kashmir, Part I, Report* (Lucknow: Newul Kishore Press, 1912), 64.

[158] Ibid., 45.

[159] Mohammad, *Census of India, 1921, Vol. XXII, Kashmir, Part I, Report*, 26.

[160] As discussed above, the Srinagar silk industry was a major source of employment for the city population, employing 5,000 people in 1911. See Khan, *Census of India, 1911, Vol. XX, Kashmir, Part I, Report*, 55.

[161] Ibid., 31.

[162] According to the census of 1911, "The safety to life and property that is assured by good and efficient government gives to a people a fuller sense of security, and the peaceful conditions of life that result from it are conducive to a growth of population." Ibid., 57.

[163] Ibid., 61.

decline, including shawl merchants and jagirdars, while revenue officials had come to exercise power within the radically changed context
of the semi-colonial Dogra bureaucracy, itself in the process of definition at the turn of the century. At the same time, high-level administrators of the Dogra state had entrenched themselves as the new
landholding elite of the Kashmir Valley. Peasants, while not particularly
prosperous as a result of the settlement, were now a recognizable class
whose interests became the focal point of movements that were to
emerge in Kashmir in the 1910s, 1920s, and 1930s.

What was the impact of these changes on the political economy of
the city?

Transformation and Conflict in Srinagar City, 1880–1930

The changing political economy of the urban space of Srinagar provided the backdrop for intense debates on community and political
identities that were taking place in the Kashmir Valley at the turn of
the twentieth century. A variety of social and economic tensions that
had been brewing under the surface came to the fore in Srinagar,
particularly in the form of sporadic grain shortages, which culminated
in a grain crisis in 1921. These crises, much like the grain shortages in
British north India in the 1830s and 1840s, were not simply crises of
subsistence, since they also reflected the crises of the old order amid the
halting attempts of the new order to establish itself.[164] Colonial intervention in the state of Jammu and Kashmir was more far-reaching than
the land settlement alone. Most importantly, it entailed the bureaucratization and centralization of the state administration. While colonial officials hailed these changes as ushering in a period of peace and
prosperity in the state, it is quite clear that they ushered in neither peace
nor prosperity for everyone.

Perhaps the most important element of the intervention was the
British belief in the efficacy of a grain market free of state control of
any kind, whether by public distribution or the coercion of grain
traders. It is not an accident that the first of the Srinagar grain crises
took place in 1891, soon after the land settlement and the loosening
of state control over the grain market. As has been pointed out earlier,

---

[164] For a discussion of the relationship between grain crises and urban change
in early-nineteenth-century colonial north India, see Bayly, *Rulers, Townsmen and
Bazaars*, chapter 8.

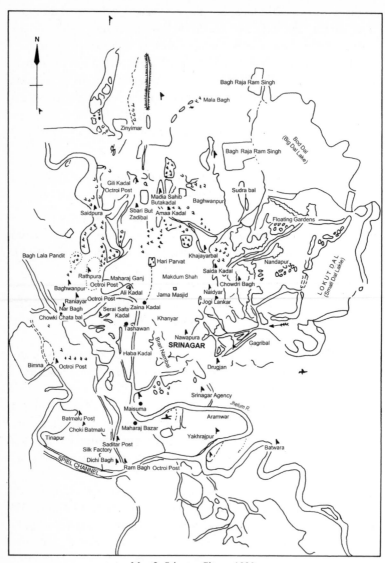

Map 2: Srinagar City, *c.* 1920.
Source: Srinagar State Archives.

the Kashmiri urban population expected the government to ensure a supply of cheap grain to the city, particularly in times of scarcity. As Bayly has noted, government intervention in the grain market was an integral aspect of Indo-Muslim political economy in general. The British, on the other hand, insisted that grain prices should be driven by supply and demand, not state fiat, even in times of severe shortage.[165] This profound disjunction between the Dogra state's belief in the role the state should play in the grain market and that of the colonial administration led to schizophrenic policies that both caused and exacerbated several grain shortages in the city of Srinagar.

That the Dogra administration, local officials, and Kashmiris were against ending the state monopoly on the grain market is clear from the rhetoric on grain dealers that emerged in this period.[166] According to local officials, the retreat of the state from the grain market had led to the rise of grain dealers who brought about grain shortages in the city by hoarding grain and hiking prices in times of scarcity. Jia Lal Kaul Jalali, a Kashmiri Pandit bureaucrat who later became assistant governor of Jammu Province, noted in his book, *The Economics of Food Grains in Kashmir*, that "after the land settlement a class of galladars—grain dealers—came up in Srinagar with whom it became a practice to hoard foodgrains and sell them to the city population at high rates."[167] The Kashmiri poet Azizullah Hakkani, dedicated a poem, "Tamhide Hadisaye Kashmir" (Introduction to the Episode in Kashmir), to describing the grain crisis of 1891, in which he lamented:

> The coffers of the state seem empty,
> It is as though there was no ruler of the land.
> Cheats have become rich by selling grain at the highest possible prices,
> Salt, sugar, firewood, even turnips, are scarce.[168]

---

[165] Ibid.

[166] It is important to note that the system of grain control benefited the state and its officials to a far greater extent than the poorer sections of Kashmiri society, who provided the rationale for its existence.

[167] Jia Lal Kaul Jalali, *The Economics of Food Grains in Kashmir* (Lahore: Mercantile Press, 1931), 55.

[168] Azizullah Hakkani, "Tamhide Hadisaye Kashmir" [Introduction to the Episode in Kashmir], 1892–3, unpublished manuscript in Persian, Acc. # 623, Srinagar State Archives, Kashmir.

6. View of Srinagar city. Chitralekha Zutshi's collection.

The British, on the other hand, regarded high prices in a bad year as desirable, since they created an atmosphere of shortage and stimulated grain dealers to bring grain into a scarcity area.

However, it is likely that British officials resident in Kashmir, much like some of their counterparts in British India earlier in the nineteenth century,[169] allowed for old methods of paternalist intervention in certain circumstances. This is clear from the fact that the Dogra state was allowed to intervene in every single grain crisis that occurred in Kashmir during this period. In 1891 a scarcity of grain, coupled with the spread of cholera—which prevented peasants from coming into the city to sell directly to urban inhabitants—and fires in city granaries, led to conditions approaching famine in the city. Ultimately, at the behest of Lawrence, the state intervened and prompt measures averted a famine.[170] In 1901–2 the city faced grain shortages yet again, when there was a sharp rise in the prices of shali to Rs 3 per kharwar. The Revenue Member's note on this price rise stated that grain traders had artificially created the price hikes by purchasing shali in advance from peasants at favorable rates and hoarding it in the city.[171] Alarmed at the unrest that would ensue, the Maharaja made a plea to the Residency for the reinstitution of state control over the grain trade of the Valley: "The prices have gone up to almost scarcity rates despite the existence of a big untouched store of grains, which the greed of trade has reserved as a mere dead stock and it is for this that the need for the interference of the State government . . . has become imperatively necessary."[172] Subsequently, the state did intervene with a view to limiting the power of the galladar class by requiring them to keep regular accounts of their purchase and sale, which could be examined by the Revenue Department.[173]

The advent of the First World War increased the vulnerability of the Kashmir Valley's economy to the vagaries of the market, leading to the major grain crisis of 1921. This grain crisis derived as much from

[169] Bayly, *Rulers, Townsmen and Bazaars*, 332–3.

[170] Lawrence, *The Valley of Kashmir*, 441–2.

[171] Ghulam Ahmad Khan, "Note on the High Prices of Shali in Srinagar," February 25, 1903 (His Highness's Private Records 1902/5, Jammu State Archives), 10.

[172] His Highness's Private Records 1902/5, Jammu State Archives.

[173] Khan, "Note on High Prices of Shali," 17.

the impact of the World War, as the decision of the Dogra state to intervene in the grain market.[174] Until 1916, the price of shali had remained comparatively low in Srinagar, holding at about Rs 3 per kharwar after the 1901–2 grain shortage.[175] As the effects of the war began to be felt, there was a marked increase in the cost of imported articles, and as the price of local products began to adjust itself to the fall in the purchasing power of the rupee, the price of grain rose steadily.[176] A government note on shali dated May 1918 stated that zamindars (peasants) were selling shali to galladars at Rs 4 per kharwar, and the latter were in turn selling it at double the price.[177] By 1921 the situation had spiraled out of control and the rate of shali had risen to a record high of Rs 18 per kharwar.[178] Moulvi Mohammad Shah Sadaat noted in his diary in 1918 that Kashmiri grain merchants made enormous profits during the course of the Great War.[179] The committee established to investigate the grain crisis also declared unequivocally that abnormal profiteering by grain dealers was responsible for the high prices of shali.[180] Grain dealers were able to get away with such actions, since Kashmir was isolated in the matter of foodgrains and the transport costs involved in making up the deficiency in the Valley through the import of rice from British India or elsewhere were prohibitive.[181]

However, the government itself could not be absolved from its role in this crisis. As a public outcry arose against the high price of shali in Srinagar, the darbar resorted to its time-honored policy and, in 1917–

---

[174] The war had a similar impact on the economy of British India, particularly with regard to grain prices, and prompted the British to relax their extreme free-market principles with reference to the grain market.

[175] *Grain Control in Kashmir*, August 1923, 1. The report of the Board of Grain Control, however, neglects to mention that there was a scarcity of grain in the city in 1906, accompanied by soaring prices of the commodity. See Mufti Mohammad Shah Saadat, *Tarikh-i-Kashmir ki Rozana Diary 1846–1947* [Daily Diary of the History of Kashmir] (Srinagar: Noor Mohammad Ghulam Mohammad, 1997), 633–4.

[176] *Grain Control in Kashmir*, 1.

[177] Political Department 123/1921, Jammu State Archives.

[178] Ibid.

[179] Saadat, *Rozana Diary*, 654–6.

[180] Political Department 123/1921, Jammu State Archives.

[181] *Grain Control in Kashmir*, 13.

18, plunged into a precipitate measure of control. This included the reestablishment of the Mujwaza system, whereby peasants were called upon to deliver shali to government granaries in the city, so that it could be distributed to the city population.[182] Since this measure was imposed on all peasants, including those who possessed no irrigated land and hence did not grow shali, and was carried out without a proper system of accounts, it allowed for wholesale peculation. Peasants were once again at the mercy of state officials, and the galladars, from whom they were forced to purchase grain at double the rate they had sold to the state.[183] Furthermore, the distribution of shali to the city population was badly organized and irregular, and as in previous years the influential were able to have their names included on the distribution list and acquire rice, while the poorer sections of the city simply starved. This measure had a severely adverse impact on the market. As the Report of the Board of Grain Control, established in 1921 to restore the price of shali to the pre-war level, stated:

> The market had been thoroughly upset and a return to normal conditions was not easy to accomplish. State interference had failed. Grain dealers had experienced benefit of heavy profits and would not lightly forgo their advantage. Prices were not expected to fall to the pre-war level: they showed, however, no appreciable tendency to decline and in the late summer months [1921] before the new crop came into the market the rate of grain continued to rise.[184]

The Board of Grain Control undertook to repair the damages rendered to the economic system of the Valley as a result of the high prices of grain and the government's earlier intervention. The first step taken by the board was to bring shali and maize under control and lay down maximum prices for both commodities. The rates prescribed for each locality varied inversely with its distance from Srinagar. Furthermore, the board established a society known as the Srinagar Cooperative Stores in the city, with the object of purchasing and distributing shali and maize to shareholders and others. Shali was to be brought to the city at a rate of Rs 4-1-6 per kharwar and sold at Rs 5-8-0 per kharwar, while the price of maize was eight annas lower. The shareholders of the

---

[182] Ibid., 1–2.
[183] Ibid., 1.
[184] Ibid., 2.

Shali Store, as it came to be called, were to receive a rebate of eight annas per kharwar on shali and maize. The store then issued ration tickets guaranteeing to all city inhabitants above two years of age a monthly ration of eight traks of shali throughout the year. The government also issued orders prohibiting the private import of shali and maize into Srinagar city, as also the export of grain from the Kashmir Valley. Alongside these measures, the board passed anti-Wadh legislation, designed to protect the peasants from the rapacious *wadhdar* (moneylender) by prohibiting the advancement of *wadh* (credit). All wadhdars were to register their claims within a prescribed period, and these were then to be adjudicated by special branches and instalments for repayment were to be fixed in accordance with the financial capacity of the debtors concerned.[185]

The schemes put forward by the board, embodied in the Grain Regulation of 1921, were doomed from the start. As the board had predicted, the grain dealers were unwilling to part with the profits on the sale of grain and did their best to subvert the working of the regulation.[186] The dealers began to offer cultivators higher rates for shali than the maximum legal rates being offered by the State Cooperative Stores. In every village, almost every big landlord, revenue collector, and grain dealer adopted every possible means to prevent the sale of grain to the Shali Store. Invariably, cultivators were not allowed to establish independent relationships with the cooperative stores.[187] Moreover, the commission agents chosen by the board to ensure the transport of grain from the villages to riverside ghats confined their activities to the ghats and availed of every opportunity to loot peasants.[188] Thus, peasants were required once again to part with their grain in kind at rates fixed by the government, and were subject to all manner of oppressions from officials involved in the collection of their

---

[185] Ibid., 2–3.

[186] The presentation of a case for appeal to the Jammu and Kashmir High Court of Judicature in 1922 by a certain grain dealer of Srinagar accused of hoarding grain and refusing to sell it to people reveals the antipathy felt by grain dealers as a class toward the Grain Regulation of 1921. See "Samad Makri versus the State," in *The Punjab Law Reporter, Jammu and Kashmir High Court Rulings, s. 1979–1991 [1922–1934 A.D.]* (Lahore: Punjab Law Reporter Press, 1935), 41.

[187] Political Department 123/1921, Jammu State Archives.

[188] *Grain Control in Kashmir*, 5.

produce. "The Public" presented a petition to the Resident in 1921 blaming jagirdars, galladars and commission agents for causing famine by hoarding grain and preventing its delivery to the city.[189] Jia Lal Kaul Jalali summed up the flaws of the scheme, calling it a state concern that generated finance for the state, rather than a scheme run on cooperative lines to alleviate the distress of the poor, as had been initially intended.[190]

The city population, particularly the poor, continued to starve, since the allotted eight-trak ration was beyond their purchasing power and the store allowed no part-purchase. According to the report of the board, "The result was that the tickets were negotiated. And wealthier people who had good reason to suppose that the Stores would before long exhaust their stocks took advantage of the opportunity to accumulate supplies."[191] More significantly, other lines of division began to appear on the city's body politic. Some Muslims of Srinagar came together to present several petitions to the darbar, claiming to represent the poorest community in the city, which also had the largest population. Ration, they suggested, should be distributed according to a community's proportion of population in the city.[192] Furthermore, they claimed that the Kashmiri Pandit community was conspiring to withhold grain from the Kashmiri Muslim community:

> The Kashmiri Pandits are bent on turning this situation to their advantage to the utter exclusion of their fellow needy brethren, the Kashmiri Muslims. The new scheme for shali distribution can only work if the workers are free of sectarian prejudice. Pandit enumerators exclude the names of Musalmans who deserve rasad [rations], enumerating only their fellow Pandit chakdars, moneylenders and high state officials who don't need it.[193]

The acquisition of grain through the Shali Store had become a playing field for the creation of divisions based on community, a concept that was itself under formulation in this period (as later chapters indicate). As Jia Lal Kaul Jalali had despairingly predicted in his diary in the

[189] Political Department 123/1921, Jammu State Archives.

[190] "Jia Lal Kaul Jalali Private Papers," Srinagar State Archives. The article appeared in *United India and the Indian States*, October 19, 1922.

[191] *Grain Control in Kashmir*, 4.

[192] Political Department 123/1921, Jammu State Archives.

[193] Ibid.

summer of 1918, "Did ye mark among the rights of man, that man was not to die of starvation, while there was bread reaped by him? Hunger whets everything, especially suspicion and indignation."[194] Despite the obvious flaws within the scheme of grain control, the government kept the Shali Store in place into the 1930s with a few modifications, intended to maintain state control on its management.[195]

The grain crises were a symptom of larger changes within the body politic of the Kashmir Valley. One of the foremost in this period was rapid urban growth, which led to a sharp increase in the population of the city as well as a growth of towns dependent on it for the supply of grain. In the decade between 1921 and 1931, the city of Srinagar registered a record 22.5 percent increase in population.[196] There was a significant internal migration of population from rural to urban areas, further swelling numbers in the cities. In 1931, for instance, the average population residing in each town of the Jhelum Valley was 15,510, while the average population for every village was a mere 377.[197]

The most significant factor contributing to urbanization during this decade was the general increase in the state population. In the 1920s, for instance, the Kashmir Province registered a population increase of 65.3 percent.[198] The rise in population meant increased pressure on land since the increase in the area under cultivation was not commensurate with the rise in the number of people dependent on it for food,[199] leading to the movement of people from rural to urban areas in search of employment, various avenues for which had opened up in the cities. The 1931 census listed several reasons for the growth

---

[194] "Jia Lal Kaul Jalali Private Papers," Personal Diary, Srinagar State Archives.

[195] In a State Council Resolution dated September 1922, it was resolved that in future the Shali Stores would work under the Board of Grain Control and would be financed by state capital alone, thus dissolving the managing committee and directorate of the stores. The capital of the private shareholders was to be refunded by the Manager of the stores on application. See General Department 921/C/C4/1922, Jammu State Archives.

[196] Rai Bahadur Pandit Anant Ram and Pandit Hira Nand Raina, *Census of India, 1931, Vol. xxiv, Jammu and Kashmir State, Part i, Report* (Jammu: Ranbir Government Press, 1933), 89.

[197] Ibid., 90.

[198] Ibid., 54.

[199] *Grain Control in Kashmir,* 13.

of towns and rural–urban migration, including the rise of local industries in cities (such as silk manufacture), the growth of marketplaces
into trade centers around villages, and the establishment of an administrative center in a particular district.[200] These factors, coupled with an
increase in wages during the decade, attracted people to towns and
urban centers. Furthermore, internal communications improved
significantly in this period, reflected in the opening of the Banihal Cart
Road, connecting Srinagar with Jammu and other towns of the Punjab
such as Lahore and Amritsar.[201] The improvement of internal and external communications gave a fillip to tourism in the main cities of the
Valley and the consequent migration of traders from rural to urban
areas to hawk their wares.[202]

In keeping with the bureaucratization of the state, the administration
introduced municipal self-government to Srinagar, which exacerbated
the decline of wider institutions of community and urban control that
had bound the city together. At the same time, it injected and insti-
tutionalized conflicts along lines of community, neighborhood, and
class into the political landscape of the city. Maharaja Pratap Singh
announced the Srinagar Municipal Regulation in 1913, whereby the
city's municipal administration was placed in the hands of elected
representatives to "introduce the same system of managing the affairs
of the Municipality in this town, as is in vogue in the towns in British
India."[203] The regulation provided for the election of eight members
representing various communities of the city, with Sunnis getting
three representatives, Shias one, Hindus three, and one representative
being allowed to the Punjabi trading community of the city. In addition, the darbar would nominate sixteen members, eight of whom
were to be officials and the other eight non-officials. The darbar would
also appoint the president of the municipality. Without relinquishing
control over the administration of the municipality, the darbar had

[200] Ram and Raina, *Census of India, 1931, Vol. XXIV, Jammu and Kashmir State,
Part I, Report,* 86.

[201] Ali Mohammad Dar, "Trade and Commerce During Dogra Rule in Kashmir (1846–1947)," (Ph.D. diss., University of Kashmir, 1991), 7–8.

[202] Ram and Raina, *Census of India, 1931, Vol. XXIV, Jammu and Kashmir State,
Part I, Report,* 61.

[203] "Speech of the Maharaja to the Srinagar Municipal Committee, 7th May
1914," in *Jammu and Kashmir State Gazette,* June 1st, 1914.

created a battleground for inter- as well as intra-community contests over political and economic influence in the Kashmir Valley. As early as 1913, when Pandit Anand Koul was appointed the first president of the newly constituted municipality, several petitioners claiming to represent the "Kashmiri Muslim community" sent a telegram to the Maharaja requesting him to choose the vice-president from the Muslim community in the interests of justice.[204]

The ostensible placement of the responsibility of the Srinagar Municipality in the hands of its residents by the darbar at this stage was not accidental. By the second decade of the twentieth century the city had begun to suffer from urban sprawl, congestion and severe sanitation problems. As people congregated in the city and its surrounding areas in search of work, not only did the pressure on foodgrains increase, the competition for jobs intensified as well. The 1931 census noted that castes were not following their hereditary occupations any longer, preferring jobs in labor or government service.[205] Many city inhabitants found employment in the city's silk factory and the grain crises of the preceding years coupled with the poor working conditions in the factory resulted in a strike of factory workers in 1924.[206] The government took swift measures to suppress this uprising, which was portrayed in official records as the Muslim community's attempt at pressuring the darbar to grant them political concessions.[207] Besides labor troubles, urbanization also resulted in a concentration of people of differing religious ideologies in the city, as religious leaders moved to Srinagar from outlying areas in the Valley and the Punjab in search of followers, which, coupled with the competition over jobs and meager resources, intensified conflict.

The internal composition of the city itself had undergone significant transformation at the turn of the century. Centralization of the administration was carried out in tandem with the colonial intervention

---

[204] Private Records of His Highness 1913/12, Jammu State Archives.

[205] Ram and Raina, *Census of India, 1931, Vol. xxiv, Jammu and Kashmir State, Part i, Report*, 102.

[206] Sadaat, *Rozana Diary*, 678.

[207] Khan, *Freedom Movement in Kashmir*, 87. The Dogra state's administrative records suggest that the government could not afford to brook such pressure and had to take effective steps to quell the disturbance. See, for instance, *Administration Report of Jammu and Kashmir State*, 1925–6.

and the consolidation of the Dogra state. One of the more important changes was the reorganization of the judiciary in 1904, which not only made the litigation process more accessible to the population, but also threatened to undercut the traditional occupations of individuals, such as the mirwaiz and mufti, who had provided legal services to the city population. Many of these individuals, who were also associated with the shawl trade and the management of shrines in Srinagar, were already smarting under the decline of the shawl trade and the impact of the land settlement. At the same time, the influence of new social groups—including grain dealers, obvious in the role they played during the grain crises; ascetic traders, such as pirs; urban landholders, most of whom were associated with the new administration; and educated Muslims returning to the city from British India—was on the rise.[208] Later we shall see the tussle for influence between these groups, manifest in the conflicts over sacred spaces and religious identities in Srinagar in this period.

* * *

In short, the land settlement, increased commerce with British India, and the general centralization of the Dogra administrative structure transformed the urban and rural landscapes of the Kashmir Valley. Urbanization brought with the rise of new social classes even as the old elite struggled to exercise power within a radically changed context. The city, where a cross-section of the Valley's population now congregated, became a venue for the competition for scarce resources, along lines of religious community as well as class. The role of the state in exacerbating these tensions can hardly be denied, both at the economic and political levels. As the state began to claim greater responsibility for the welfare of its subjects, it created separate categories based on community for their advancement, thereby giving sanction to a process taking place on the socio-economic level. From the turn of the twentieth century, religious community, defined in variegated ways, became thoroughly imbricated with the expression of political identities in the Kashmir Valley.

[208] Similar processes were taking place in British India in the 1830s and 1840s as a result of the colonial intervention. See Bayly, *Rulers, Townsmen and Bazaars,* Chapters 8 and 9.

CHAPTER 3

Contested Identities in the Kashmir Valley

Do not run from Islam it is the way of God,
O one who is asleep, Awake!, and embrace this bright sun.
I pledge on God who is our creator,
That under the sky Islam is his only religion.
Grateful am I to God who gave us the *Quran*,
That has helped us to blossom from buds to flowers.[1]

The relationship between religious identities, community definitions, and the state underwent significant shifts in content, articulation, and engagement in the Kashmir Valley over the course
of the last two decades of the nineteenth and the first two decades of
the twentieth century. The shifts occurred in tandem with the social,
economic, and political changes set in motion on the Kashmiri landscape in the late nineteenth century. Some of these changes acted
directly on the expression of religious identities, while others provided
the context within which these identities could be used to define
communities in relation to other social groups and the state. Here I
analyse the debates and conflicts generated in Kashmiri public discourse
during this period, which ultimately coalesced around the question of
what it meant to be "Kashmiri Muslim."

In her work on the rise of communalism in north India, Sandria
Freitag argues that since the colonial government viewed Indian society as an aggregate of community interests with particular individuals

[1] Moulvi Mohammad Nooruddin Qari Kashmiri, "Islam ke Mahamid va
Mahasin Me" [The Qualities and Virtues of Islam], 1924 (author's diary from
Private Collection of Moulvi Mohammad Shafi Qari, Srinagar, Kashmir). For a
detailed discussion of Qari's role as an individual Muslim and leader within the
Kashmiri Muslim community, see the third section of this chapter.

representing those communities, integrative rituals that led to the gradual reformulation of collective activities and ultimately the emergence of a politicized religious identity—communalism—as an equivalent and viable alternative to nationalism, were created in public arenas that "had but little reference to the activities of the state."[2] While the Dogra state in Kashmir viewed Kashmiri society not much differently than the colonial state viewed Indian society, the articulation of collective identities in the Kashmir Valley was deeply imbricated with the interventionist activities of this state in public and political arenas. On the one hand, the Dogra state vowed religious neutrality, and on the other it unabashedly identified itself with the Hindu community, its rituals and interests. At the same time, it placed the onus of ritually, politically and socially defining the Muslim community on Muslim leadership, a leadership that could not but function within the ritual and legal framework provided by the state.

This is not to suggest, however, that the Dogra state was the sole reference point for the discourse on communitarian identities among Kashmiri Muslims. Farzana Shaikh's work explores in detail the inadequacy of arguments that focus solely on the consequences of state/colonial policy on Muslim political organization. However, the explanation she suggests instead, that Muslim political action was inspired in large part by "the very real value that Muslims themselves attach to the organization of their politics on grounds of religion and community,"[3] is problematic. While normative constraints certainly played a role in Kashmiri Muslim politics, it does not necessarily follow that within these ideological constraints lay "a quest for political identity as the extension of their religious solidarity . . ."[4] Kashmiri Muslims, as Muslims elsewhere in the subcontinent, framed their identities in relation to their region, class, sect, and a host of other affiliations, and not simply the larger community of Islam. Furthermore, socio-economic changes within the Valley, not all of which were related to state or colonial policies, had as significant a role to play in evolving narratives on religion, community and identities.

[2] Freitag, *Collective Action and Community,* 191–6.

[3] Farzana Shaikh, *Community and Consensus in Islam: Muslim Representation in Colonial India, 1860–1947* (Cambridge: Cambridge University Press, 1989), 126.

[4] Ibid.

On a similar note, while there is no doubt that Kashmiri public discourse at the turn of the twentieth century focused on Islam, it cannot necessarily be interpreted as the rise of "communalism" in the Kashmir Valley.[5] Nor is it axiomatic that Kashmiri Muslim leaders of this period were rank "communalists" interested only in furthering the interests of their own community. Freitag defines communalism as "that ideology of community organized around religion,"[6] that is, a specifically politicized religious identity. Arguably, religious identity was becoming the basis for community formation in Kashmir, or even north India, at the turn of the twentieth century. However, the Kashmiri Muslim case shows that religious identities, variously expressed, had always been a matter of politics and community organization for the Muslims of Kashmir. The expression of Muslim identities in the pre-colonial period, as discussed earlier, was intimately connected to the articulation of belonging to the larger community of Kashmiris and the homeland of Kashmir.

At the turn of the twentieth century, the political exigency of locating and defining an identifiable "Muslim community" on the Kashmiri political landscape led to an intense focus on Islam and its definitions.[7] However, even at this stage, the project was more about asserting cultural difference from the state and the minority firmly entrenched in the power structures of Kashmiri society, than about articulating a politics of communalism or separatism. Moreover, the search for a Muslim community was fraught with conflict and contradictions, and despite the efforts of the leadership to give it concrete shape, a specifically politicized, unified identity did not emerge among Kashmiri Muslims in this period. Class, region, and sect continued to play an important role in mediating the relationship between Islam and community identities in Kashmir. Community interests, even when articulated in response to the perceived advances of the "other"

---

[5] Ayesha Jalal has recognized and questioned the pervasiveness and validity of the term "communalism" in historical scholarship on Muslims in South Asia in several articles and books, most recently *Self and Sovereignty*. Her arguments regarding communalism and its deployment in South Asian historiography will be discussed in detail in chapter six.

[6] Freitag, *Collective Action and Community*, 197.

[7] The focus on religion in articulating community identities was not limited to Kashmiri Muslims in the Valley. Similar processes, outside the bounds of this book, can also be identified among Kashmiri Pandits.

community, could not paper over the intensity of differentiations among Kashmiri Muslims themselves.

Disputes over Sacred Space in Late-Nineteenth-Century Srinagar

Intra-community conflicts around the issue of sacred space and the right to preach in late-nineteenth-century Srinagar provide a key link between the changing politico-economic face of the city and the development of community identities. The conflicts, expressed through petitions and sometimes even physical clashes, were embedded in evolving relationships between urban social groups, illustrating at the same time the halting attempts by Kashmiri Muslims to articulate a shared sense of community through a specific vocabulary that emphasized religion over other affiliations.[8] Competing Kashmiri Muslim elites claiming leadership of the community focused on the same city shrines and their extended systems of religious patronage to assert their influence among Kashmiri Muslims. Here I examine the emergent public discourse in the Valley, which focused intensely on city shrines as symbols of and sites for the evolving ideological and political definitions of Kashmiri Islam, and by extension the Kashmiri Muslim community.[9]

The position of the shrine, variously referred to as a *khanqah* or *ziarat*,[10] in the religious, social, and economic life of the Valley, is legendary. In fact, it forms the basis for assertions of *Kashmiriyat* on the grounds that Kashmiri Islam's close association with shrines has rendered it syncretic. As most students of Indian Islam know well, Kashmir is hardly the only place in the subcontinent where shrines have played a key role in defining religious expression.[11] It is undeniable

---

[8] Srinagar is not the only urban area in South Asia that has a history of conflict and disputes in the nineteenth century. Several cities in South Asia, including Bombay, had "riotous urban contexts" in the mid- to late-nineteenth century. See, for instance, Freitag, *Collective Action and Community*, especially chapter three.

[9] It is important to note that these shrine disputes did not in any way involve or implicate Kashmiri Pandits.

[10] Khanqah connotes a mosque, devotional retreat, or the residence of a saint. A ziarat is a devotional retreat, grave, or tomb of a saint. See Sufi, *Kashir*, vol. I, 125.

[11] Punjab, Bengal, Rajasthan, and Sind are but a few places in the subcontinent where shrines have been an integral part of political, social, and religious life. See,

that shrines were and are a central component of Kashmiri society in general and Kashmiri Islam in particular.[12] What does not necessarily follow is that this renders Kashmiri Islam's practice and ideology unique in the Indian subcontinent. Interestingly enough, shrine disputes in late-nineteenth-century Srinagar were articulated precisely around the issue of whether or not shrine worship was sacrilegious to Islam, an issue that had never before been as contentious among Kashmiri Muslims.[13]

---

for instance, David Gilmartin, "Shrines, Succession and Sources of Moral Authority," in Barbara Daly Metcalf, ed., *Moral Conduct and Authority: The Place of Adab in South Asian Islam* (Berkeley: University of California Press, 1984), 221–40; Christian W. Troll, ed., *Muslim Shrines in India: Their Character, History, and Significance* (Delhi: Oxford University Press, 1992); and Sarah F.D. Ansari, *Sufi Saints and State Power: The Pirs of Sind* (Cambridge: Cambridge University Press, 1992), particularly chapter one.

[12] Pir Hassan Shah Khoiyami, *Tarikh-i-Hassan, Vol. III: Asrar-ul Akhyar* (repr., Srinagar: Ghulam Mohammad Noor Mohammad, 1989), 2. This Persian history of Kashmir was written in the late nineteenth century. In its third volume, which was dedicated to an account of Muslim saints and mystics of Kashmir, the author stated that the soul has a great affinity with the body and on that basis the Sunnis of Kashmir visited the shrines of those loved by Allah and viewed them as a means for a redressal of their problems. Since *Mulk-i-Kashmir* was a place especially blessed by God, he continued, the saints and friends of God born in the Valley had been numerous and their bodies in the tombs still contained their souls, which guided the people in times of need.

[13] In a Persian tract dating from 1834, a pre-eminent Kashmiri Pir, Sheikh Ahmad Traali, defended saint worship as being in keeping with the teachings of the Prophet. Specifically addressed to the non-Kashmiri "Wahhabis," the tract is a lengthy exposition on the necessity and benefits of visiting shrines. It expressly states that Islam does not forbid saint worship, and that visiting shrines is legitimate since the tombs of saints contained their souls, which only became stronger after their death. Based on hadith, Traali argues that the Prophet himself never forbade his followers from going to shrines; there were shrines and mosques of different merit depending on the excellence of the saints who inhabited them, and visiting those of high merit could only bring spiritual benefit to the visitor. According to Traali, far from being un-Islamic, saint-worship is firmly grounded in the principles of the *Quran* and *Hadith*. See Sheikh Ahmad Traali, "Tarikh-u sadad fi tayidi ziaratil kaboor wal istimdad" [The Right way in Support of Visiting Shrines and Seeking Help from Saints], 1834, unpublished manuscript in Persian (Private Collection of Peerzada Mohammad Ashraf, Bemina, Kashmir). See 30n for a definition of the term "Wahhabi."

7. Jama Masjid, Srinagar. Chitralekha Zutshi's collection.

8. Shah-i Hamadaan shrine, Srinagar. Chitralekha Zutshi's collection.

9. Hazratbal mosque, Srinagar. Chitralekha Zutshi's collection.

10. Maqdoom Sahib shrine, Srinagar. Chitralekha Zutshi's collection.

Why then did shrine worship become such a hotly debated issue in late-nineteenth and early-twentieth-century Kashmir? Part of the answer lies in the role played by shrines in the political and economic lives of Kashmiri Muslims. Kashmiri Muslims visited and still visit shrines for health, procreation, longevity, and relief from floods, famine or disease.[14] In addition, shrines provided a venue for Muslims to come together during prayers and preaching, but also more festive occasions, such as periodic fairs at the shrines to celebrate the birth and death anniversaries of the saints entombed therein. As has been pointed out earlier, these fairs, during which pirs and other religious mendicants played a central role, were key sites for rural–urban political and economic exchange. More importantly still, as in other areas of the Indian subcontinent where shrines were repositories of landed wealth and social capital, the patronage of shrines was a clear means of exercising religious and political authority.

The shrines in the Kashmir Valley had revenue-free land grants attached to them that functioned in a manner similar to *waqfs* (endowments) in the rest of the Muslim world. Some of these grants dated from the Sultanate period, when Muslim sultans had endowed waqfs to shrines as a means of asserting their authority in times of political turmoil.[15] One of the earliest recorded and extant waqfs in Kashmir is that of the Khanqah-i-Mualla shrine in Srinagar. The Khanqah-i-Mualla's *waqf-nama*[16] (endowment deed) illuminates the social and political significance of the shrine in the Kashmir Valley, particularly the shrine of Shah-i-Hamdaan. Dating from January 1399, and signed and sealed by Ali Muhammad Hamdaani, the son of the Sayyid Muhammad Hamdaani, the deed is a testament to state support for Islam in Kashmir.[17] Clearly, the Khanqah-i-Mualla's waqf was a

---

[14] Mohammad Ishaq Khan, "The Significance of the Dargah of Hazratbal in the Socio-Religious and Political Life of Kashmiri Muslims," in Troll, ed., *Muslim Shrines in India*, 178.

[15] Parmu, *A History of Muslim Rule in Kashmir*, 71–90.

[16] "English Translation of the Waqf-nama of Khanqah-i-Mualla," in Parmu, *A History of Muslim Rule in Kashmir*, 472–5.

[17] Before the arrival of Sayyid Ali Hamdaani, a Sufi mystic from Hamdaan in Persia, to Kashmir in 1379, Islam had not made much appreciable progress in Kashmir, particularly since the state did not encourage the conversion of its subjects. Sayyid Ali Hamdaani, escaping Timurid persecution in Persia, was granted

symbol of political legitimacy for both Sultan Qutb-ud-Din and Sultan Sikandar Shah, since its creation sustained and then rendered the dynasty, in a way, immortal. In addition, the deed laid down the basis for the management of shrines in the Valley by appointing a *mutawalli* (custodian) to control the affairs of every shrine. This individual had access to revenues of villages attached to the shrine as well as alms received from visitors to the shrine, and had to dispense them according to the terms of the deed. Most significantly, the deed demanded non-interference from the state in the shrine's management, thereby seeking to ensure that the shrine and its dependants would remain untouched by the vagaries of political fortune.

Similar deeds governed other shrines dotting the Kashmiri landscape, although not all were endowed by the ruling dynasty. Given the centrality of the shrine to the social life of the Valley, the attachment of waqfs to shrines was a means of expressing one's social position as well as ensuring continued social prominence. There are several instances of elite members of society sponsoring the foundation of waqfs in the name of khanqahs and shrines in Kashmir.[18] As Gregory C. Kozlowski points out in his work on Muslim endowments in British India, the festivals and celebrations attached to shrines, "whether part of the great, little or familial traditions were occasions for the distribution of food, clothing or money, opportunities for the sponsors to assert their

---

asylum by Qutb-ud-din (1374–89), the reigning Sultan of Kashmir. Hamdaani and his band of disciples took it upon themselves to teach the Sultan the laws of the sharia and convert the population of Kashmir to Islam. Sultan Qutb-ud-Din embraced the principles of Islam into his own life and also that of his rule, the outward trappings of which now became Islamic. In keeping with the influence exercised by Hamdaani in his life and rule, the Sultan laid the foundation for the shrine at Khanqah-i-Mualla, alongside endowing land for the maintenance of its edifice and assembly of men and animals. Qutb-ud-din's son and successor, Sultan Sikandar Shah, who came to power without his sanction and amidst the opposition of his mother, clearly assumed the reins of government through the support of the Sayyids who had escaped from Timurid Persia and considered Sayyid Muhammad Hamdaani, Sayyid Ali Hamdaani's son, as their spiritual head. As a result, Sultan Sikandar Shah endowed several villages for the upkeep of the Khanqah-i-Mualla and it was during his rule that the present edifice of the Khanqah-i-Mualla was constructed and its endowment deed recorded. See Parmu, *A History of Muslim Rule in Kashmir*, 104–18.

[18] Sufi, *Kashir*, vol. II, 388–9.

claim to patron status."[19] Furthermore, the office of the mutawalli, who was chosen from the extended family of the donor, ensured their access to the financial resources of the shrine. Since this individual was answerable to the larger community in which the shrine was located, waqfs usually made some provision for abuses of power by such individuals.

Given the importance of the shrine to Kashmiri Muslim life, it is not surprising that the changing economic context of the Valley led to the manifestation of social and political tussles around shrines and shrine worship. It is also not surprising that those involved in shrine disputes belonged to social groups, such as shawl merchants, landed groups, and the religious elite, who were aware of their loss of financial and social status. Faced with the possibility of social and economic obsolescence in the late nineteenth century, the reassertion of control over shrines—which provided access to wealth and power—became an increasingly expedient move for these groups, inevitably leading to conflict. A discussion of the main characters involved in, and actual manifestation of, one such dispute over the issue of who had the right to preach at particular shrines of Srinagar city, will serve to clarify some of these contentions.

The prominent trading family of the Ashais, under the leadership of Hajji Mukhtar Shah Ashai, a wealthy shawl trader who was particularly affected by the decline of the shawl trade in the 1870s, was one of the main characters in these incidents.[20] Hajji Mukhtar Shah claimed descent from the family of Sayyid Ali Hamdaani and the Ashai family had been involved with the management of his tomb at Khanqah-i-Mualla for several generations.[21] Mukhtar Shah himself had given several donations for the repair and refurbishment of the shrine over the years and was in charge of its rebuilding in the mid-1880s. Other shawl merchants were also involved in the administration of the Khanqah-i-Mualla shrine over the course of the period.[22]

The Naqshbandi and Shaal families, led by Khwaja Hassan Shah Naqshbandi (b. 1854) and Khwaja Sanaullah Shaal (d. 1893–4), also

---

[19] Gregory C. Kozlowski, *Muslim Endowments and Society in British India* (Cambridge: Cambridge University Press, 1985), 4.

[20] See the section on the shawl trade in chapter two.

[21] Sadaat, *Rozana Diary*, 613.

[22] Mohammad Shah Sadaat, *Jannat-ul-Duniya* (Lahore: Mahir Electric Press, 1936), 31.

played a role in this saga. As we have seen, the Naqshbandis were a prominent family of Srinagar who had jagirs worth Rs 2500, the original grant having been made by the Sikh ruler Maharaja Ranjit Singh, a significant portion of which they had lost to the Dogra state under the jagir settlement rules.[23] In addition, they were involved with the administration of several shrines in Srinagar, particularly the shrine of the Muslim saint Khwaja Naqshbandh Sahab, after whom the family took its name. Khwaja Hassan Shah Naqshbandi remained the mutawalli of the shrine, which had a jagir attached to it from Chak times.[24] The Shaals were also owners of lands, orchards and houses spread out over the Valley of Kashmir. Khwaja Sanaullah Shaal was responsible for the repair of the Naqshbandi shrine and the khanqah of Sultan-ul-Arifeen in Srinagar.[25] Kashmiri Muslim landed families like the Naqshbandis and Shaals were gradually becoming a thing of the past as a new non-Kashmiri landed class tied to the Dogra administration rose in their stead. Members of the traditional landed elite, to make matters worse for them, could not seek recourse in government service, since they lacked the educational qualifications required for such an endeavor.

Two other important characters in the incidents include the Mirwaizes (head preachers) of the city of Srinagar: the Mirwaiz Kashmir, who preached at the main mosque of the city, Jama Masjid, and the Mirwaiz Hamdaani, who preached at the shrine of Shah-i-Hamdaan, also known as Khanqah-i-Mualla.[26] The role of preachers and other members of the religious elite of Srinagar had likewise come under considerable strain as a result of the increasing centralization and bureaucratization of the Dogra state. Staking one's claim over the

---

[23] General Department Records, 155/22-R/1925, Jammu State Archives, 15.

[24] Sufi, *Kashir*, vol. II, 349.

[25] Sadaat, *Rozana Diary*, 619.

[26] The two Mirwaizes hailed from the same family that had split in the early nineteenth century as two brothers vied for the position of head preacher at the Jama Masjid. One of the brothers moved his sphere of influence to Khanqah-i-Mualla, while the other stayed on at Jama Masjid as the head preacher of the city. The descendants of the former identified themselves as Mirwaiz Hamdaani and those of the latter retained their position as Mirwaiz Kashmir of Jama Masjid. Based on an interview with Professor Nooruddin Zahid, Badgaam, Kashmir, April 23, 1998.

preaching centers of the city, thus, was critical to the continued exercise of authority by members of this social group. The right to preach at a shrine not only gave the preacher access to the inhabitants of that particular locality who frequented the shrine, and would turn to him for legal and other guidance, but, as significantly, gave him access to the considerable financial resources of the shrine, such as alms, administrative funds, and the trade earnings in its vicinity.

The dispute appears to have begun when the Mirwaiz Kashmir began preaching at shrines in *mohallas* (localities) that were considered the sphere of influence of Mirwaiz Hamdaani. In 1888, Hajji Mukhtar Shah Ashai led a deputation of Sayyids, Pirzadas and traders of the Muslim community to the Maharaja's palace with a petition on behalf of the administration of the Khanqah-i-Mualla asking him to pass a law that would prevent Yahya Shah from preaching at shrines which were, by custom, relegated to the authority of the other Mirwaiz. The Governor of Kashmir, Deewan Badri Nath, informed Mukhtar Shah that the authorities, dedicated to religious neutrality, could not interfere in the internal religious affairs of a community. He further emphasized the importance of maintaining harmony within the community. However, he stated that since it was the responsibility of the government to see to the maintenance of law and order, His Highness had passed an order allowing *wazkhaani* (preaching) in mohallas by one or the other Mirwaiz provided it had the consent of all the resident Muslims of that locality. The order banned the Mirwaiz Kashmir from preaching at shrines in those localities where more than a hundred resident Muslims were against his preaching.[27] In effect, thus, he was legally forbidden from preaching at Khanqah-i-Mualla.

The Mirwaiz Kashmir's supporters, principal among them Shaal and Naqshbandi, reacted immediately by sending their own volley of petitions to the Maharaja with a view to curbing Mukhtar Shah's activities. These petitions claimed that Mukhtar Shah was inciting people against the Mirwaiz Kashmir's preaching so that he could retain his influence at Khanqah-i-Mualla. One petition stated that the Mirwaiz's preaching should not be banned since he was primarily responsible for teaching Kashmiris the revelations of the *Quran* and the words of the Prophet Mohammad, in the absence of which Kashmiri Muslims

[27] Vernacular Records 161/S.1947 [AD 1890], Jammu State Archives.

would be unaware of the meaning of Islam. But some individuals, they continued, who were bent on creating discord, "want Yahya Shah (Mirwaiz) to stop preaching and the people to forget their religion."[28] In the meantime, Yahya Shah continued to preach at shrines from where he had been expressly forbidden by the government, which fined him Rs 200 as punishment.[29] Disputes between followers of the two sides, at times manifest as riots, broke out sporadically in the late nineteenth century.

A consideration of the vocabulary of the dispute suggests that it was more than simply about competition for economic and political control. By framing the dispute in terms of religious ideology, the contenders were attempting to define and appropriate the Kashmiri Muslim collectivity itself. The petitions of the two sides to the government poured vitriol on each other for representing a defiled version of Islam. The Mirwaiz Kashmir was labeled a Wahhabi,[30] referring to one who is against saint worship, while he accused his opponents of being *mushriks*, or sacrilegious saint-worshippers. A petition against Yahya Shah from the *khadims* (administrators) of the Khanqah-i-Mualla shrine stated quite clearly that Yahya Shah went about preaching Wahhabi doctrines under the guise of being Hanafi.[31] They continued,

[28] Ibid., 2.

[29] Ibid., 4.

[30] The term Wahhabi comes from the movement launched by Abdul Wahhab, an eighteenth-century Arab reformer against the worship of saints and visits to shrines. In British India, most Muslims who were regarded as potential threats to colonial rule were labeled Wahhabis, a term that implied fanaticism. In particular, the term was used to describe the movement organized by the followers of Shah Walliullah, Shah Abdul Aziz (1746–1824) and Sayyid Ahmad of Rai Bareilly, who sought to reform Indian Islam. In the Kashmir Valley, the significance of Wahhabism lies in what the term "Wahhabi" implies, namely a person against saint worship, and hence shrines, as well as a potential threat to the state.

[31] Hanafi is the school of Islamic jurisprudence that follows the legalist interpretations of Imam Abu Hanifa (699–766), who was considered a champion of leniency and mercy. Sayyid Abdur Rahman, who is said to have introduced Islam to Kashmir, belonged to the Hanafi order, and Sayyid Ali Hamdaani, although himself a Hanabali, urged the continuance of the Hanafi school of law in Kashmir. Most Kashmiri Sunni Muslims are, therefore, of the Hanafi persuasion. See Sufi, *Kashir*, vol. II, 611–18. Although the schism between "Hanafi" and "Wahhabi" appeared first in the 1880s, membership to the Hanafi school would become the

"The shrines of the city, belonging to our ancestors, are for the prayers and preaching of the Hanafi sect, not for preaching that goes against religion itself."[32] Thus, they pleaded with the government to allow various sects to conduct their prayers and preaching at different times at the six shrines of the city. In yet another petition, the pirs and khadims of Srinagar shrines directly blamed Yahya Shah for attacking their religion through the preaching of Wahhabi doctrines that he had imported from Hindustan. Yahya Shah's followers, in reply, labeled the managers of the shrines, their khadims and followers—*mushriks*—or those who have committed *shirk* by assigning partners to Allah, and thus gone against the most important tenet of Islam—*tawhid*—or the unity of God.

The name-calling by the two sides illuminates several significant details on internal contestations over identity and authority being conducted among Kashmiri Muslims at the time. By calling the administrators of the Khanqah-i-Mualla shrine mushriks, Yahya Shah and his followers were questioning their very authority as religious leaders, since the label implied they were committing sacrilege against Islam. At the same time, they were claiming that authority not only over preaching but also over the definition of Islam—and consequently leadership of the Kashmiri Muslim community—for themselves. Similarly, the other side was attacking the very basis of Yahya Shah's authority by calling him a Wahhabi, a term implying an attitude against saint worship and shrines, which were central to the practice of Islam in Kashmir. Furthermore, the term also implied an anti-Dogra and anti-British attitude, which could, in that period, result in serious consequences for the individuals involved. Maharaja Ranbir Singh had actively repressed any signs of the "Wahhabi" movement in

---

primary form of identification for Kashmiri Sunnis in the first three decades of the twentieth century, when the ideas of the Ahl-i-Hadith influenced the tone of the disputes within the community. See the third section of this chapter, on emergence of the Ahl-i-Hadith.

Besides these theological differences, it is important to note that Kashmiri Muslims were also divided into various castes, such as Shaikhs, Saiyids, Mughals, Pathans, Gujars, Bakarwals, Doms and Watals, not to mention the main sectarian division between Shias and Sunnis. See Lawrence, *The Valley of Kashmir*, chapter XI.

[32] Vernacular Records 161/S.1947, Jammu State Archives, 4.

the Kashmir Valley and Maharaja Pratap Singh was determined to do the same.[33] Aware of the damning nature of such an accusation as well as the danger to their livelihood if Wahhabi ideas did gain a foothold in the Valley, the custodians of shrines saw it in their interest to label Yahya Shah a defiler of the tombs of saints.

As a result, the consequences of the dispute were severe for Mirwaiz Yahya Shah, since the government was more willing to countenance mushriks than Wahhabis. The Governor of Kashmir passed an order in 1888 banning Yahya Shah from preaching at twenty-two shrines in Srinagar and its mofassil.[34] This order conveniently helped the Maharaja present himself as the protector of "Kashmiri" rituals of the people against the onslaught of outside ideas. Yahya Shah, in the meantime, had to face the chastisement of several highly respected pirs of the community for being avaricious and power-hungry. One such individual, Sheikh Ahmad Tarabali, wrote a letter to Yahya Shah requesting him to stop his drive for establishing control over preaching in the city. Tarabali wrote that it was advisable to limit preaching to one's own mohalla and its surrounding areas, so that the possibility of religious schism was reduced. Tarabali's recurrent references to Yahya Shah's greed illustrates the serious nature of the latter's bid to establish control over preaching in areas that had traditionally been outside his sphere of influence. Moreover, Tarabali took this opportunity to present his own view on the raging debate on the nature and practice of Islam in a lengthy exposition on the necessity and benefits of visiting shrines and worshipping saints. He wrote: "Our ancestors who are enshrined in these shrines have dedicated their lives to the maintenance of the *sunnat* [tradition of the Prophet] and *shariat* [Islamic law] and should not be labeled un-Islamic, nor should fingers be raised against them calling them *biddat* [innovations]."[35]

The petitions that went back and forth from the two sides to the government and the government reports on the issue bring forth two general perspectives on the nature of shrine disputes in the late nineteenth century. The pirzadas and administrators of shrines presented

[33] Lawrence, *The Valley of Kashmir*, 285.

[34] Vernacular Records 161/S.1947, Jammu State Archives, 5.

[35] Sheikh Ahmad Tarabali, "Tarabali's Letter to Yahya Shah," unpublished manuscript in Persian (Private Collection of Mufti Mohammad Maqbool, Srinagar, Kashmir).

the disputes as an issue of religious ideology, and demanded that the Maharaja's ruling on the issue take into account the religious sensibilities of the people, which were being threatened by men such as Yahya Shah. However, this side also recognized the role played by what they termed as "money" in the disputes, intimating that the preachers and their supporters were involved in the disputes for financial gain.[36] The police report, on the other hand, dismissed the disputes as being related in any way to religion, instead defining them as domestic wars between two families over social influence: "The real matter is," the report stated, "that Khwaja Sanaullah and Hajji Mukhtar Shah have started a dispute amongst themselves and now the Waizes [preachers] have chosen sides in the dispute . . . The people are illiterate and don't understand the preaching of either of the two Mirwaizes and call each other Wahhabi and Mushrik as a result."[37]

By denying the role of religious ideology in the dispute, the state was clearly stating its position *vis-à-vis* what it termed sectarian conflicts: at best ostensible neutrality and at worst dismissal. And yet the shrine disputes were expressed partly in the context of the evolving nature of the Dogra state itself, which, despite its avowed religious neutrality, drew on symbols of the Hindu faith to assert its legitimacy to rule over its newly acquired territory. In practice, this meant that the Dogra state gave differential patronage to Hindu and Muslim sacred spaces, as Hindu shrines and temples came under the special protection of the state.[38] As the state withdrew from its role in protecting and ensuring the maintenance of Muslim shrines, the onus for this endeavor fell on the Muslim community. The tussles over rights to preaching and the definitions of Islam were, therefore, an integral aspect of the drive to redefine cultural values in the face of perceived threats to the continued existence and maintenance of sacred spaces. This entailed drawing the contours of a Kashmiri community, defined primarily by religious identification, while also locating within it a leadership that was capable of negotiating with the state on its behalf.

[36] Vernacular Records 161/S.1947, Jammu State Archives, 4.

[37] Ibid.

[38] Hindu religious spaces in the state were brought under the administration of a special department, the Dharmarth, established by the Dogra state specifically for this purpose. See Rai, "Question of Religion in Kashmir," especially chapter two. See also the last section of chapter one of this book.

Homeland and Community in Kashmiri Discourse
at the Turn of the Twentieth Century

This is Kalyug,[39]
It is heading towards the end of time.
They are destroying the city,
Breaking down the houses to create little villages.
Nooruddin's prophecy that the good people will fall and the mullahs
    will rise,
Rivers will dry up and drains roar like rivers,
People from London will occupy China and Gilgit,
Are all coming true.[40]

The intensity of the crisis, both spiritual and temporal, facing Kashmiris at the turn of the twentieth century is captured in the Kashmiri masnavi "Akhir Zamaan" (The End of the World). The poem reflects the deep kinship between the spiritual and the temporal, the religious and the regional elements of Kashmiri identities. Ultimately, the poem is a lament for the Kashmiri, not necessarily Muslim, loss of sovereignty under the rule of a long line of non-Kashmiri rulers, of which the Dogras were the most recent. I argue here that expressions of a religious collectivity in Kashmir were inextricably bound up with the definition of a Kashmiri regional identity. In the same vein, although religious affiliations were important, it is apparent that regional aspirations for a prosperous Kashmir, where the just ruled, still colored the discourse of this period to a significant degree.

"Akhir Zamaan," penned in 1904 by a Kashmiri poet, Ali Shah Khoiyami, made a clear distinction between the land of Jammu, from where the ruler hailed, and the land of Kashmir, from where hailed the tillers of the soil. More significantly, by recounting the list of outsiders who had ruled Kashmir for centuries, the verse resonates with a deep sense of alienation and resentment between the rulers and the Kashmiri population, regardless of the religion of the former and the latter. For the poet, state laws that declared the land to be the property of the state and prevented Kashmiris from utilizing the bounty of the land best exemplified the denial of sovereignty to Kashmiris. So he asked:

---

[39] Kalyug can be defined as the modern, contemporary era, considered the most morally degenerate of the four eras in the Hindu temporal cycle.

[40] Ali Shah Khoiyami, "Akhir Zamaan" [The End of the World], unpublished manuscript in Kashmiri (Private Collection of Shafi Shauq, Srinagar, Kashmir), 1.

The poor would eat in abundance from the forests,
Animals, birds, and flowers alike.
Then came the order that for hunting
One needs a license.
How much will they loot,
What will they answer to God?
Our ruler is so greedy that even Mulberry leaves have built him a treasure,
Even then he is not satisfied.
Mulk-i-Kashmir is being plundered from all directions.[41]

The masnavi "Akhir Zamaan" illuminates Kashmiri society in a state of flux, when hitherto powerful classes were losing influence and the powerless were becoming increasingly important, when the state was becoming more interventionist, and when it seemed to Kashmiris that the very laws of nature were threatened. The poet's recognition of the transformation was couched in the acceptance of a Kashmiri identity that transcended religious community and social class:

Muslims and Hindus are both deceptive,
Driven by a desire for property.
Who is rich and who is poor?
Everyone is deceitful.
Hear what Ali Mir Shah says,
Akhir Zamaan is our destiny.[42]

A proliferation in the number of histories of Kashmir written by Kashmiris in the late nineteenth century further demonstrates the interaction between the ostensibly competing visions of religiously informed and regionally based cultural identities. Mostly written in Persian, and some anonymous, these histories attempted to establish a written record of the past of a region with distinct boundaries.[43]

---

[41] Ibid., 5.

[42] Ibid., 6.

[43] Some histories dating from the late nineteenth century are: Hassan Shah Khoiyami, *Tarikh-i-Hassan*; Pandit Ramju Dhar, "Kaifiyat Intezame Mulk-i-Kashmir (1760–1880)" [Description of Administration of Mulk-i-Kashmir], unpublished manuscript in Persian, Acc. # 1913 (Persian and Arabic Manuscript Section, Research and Publications Department, University of Kashmir, Srinagar); Nath Pandit, "Gulshan Dastoor" [Customs of the Garden] unpublished manuscript in Persian, Acc # 2314 (Persian and Arabic Manuscript Section, Research and Publications Department, University of Kashmir, Srinagar); and Mirza Saifuddin, *Khulasatul-Tawarikh*[Summary of History] (repr., Srinagar: Gulshan Publishers, 1984).

Significantly, these histories, whether by Muslim or Pandit writers, began with a description of the geography of the Kashmir Valley, which determined the course of its political and social development and endowed it with a distinct identity. Moreover, the histories subscribed to the same origin myth, with certain variations, that led to the creation of the Kashmir Valley. In this myth, Kashmir emerged as a *mulk* (homeland, country) from underneath a lake. For Pandit authors this happened after Kashyap Rishi drained the lake of its contents, including a demon; and for Muslim authors, after the recession of Noah's flood. Thus, although couched in their own religious traditions, histories of the Valley endowed the land of Kashmir with antiquity and sanctity to all its peoples.

"Kashmir," wrote Pandit Hargopal Khasta in the first Urdu history of Kashmir, "was called heaven by its Hindu and Muslim inhabitants, both of whom had their places of worship and pilgrimage in the Valley itself and some people even said that Moses passed away in the Valley."[44] In Khasta's mind, there was no doubt that Kashmir was unique precisely because it encompassed people of different religious communities who did not have to leave its boundaries to fulfill their religious obligations. Similarly, even though the historians identified the rulers of Kashmir by their religious persuasion, they remained the "rulers of Kashmir" and not "Kashmiri rulers." Whether Mughals, Afghans or Sikhs, not only did these rulers pillage the land and tax its people, but more significantly, they did not belong to the land, nor were they one of its peoples. It is important to note, thus, that the conscious articulation of a Kashmiri regional identity both included and transcended religious, class, and other affiliations.

State, Community, and the Law: Politicization of Kashmiri Muslim Identities in the Early Twentieth Century

Increasingly, the discourse on the region moved backstage as recovery of the self under foreign rule came to be formulated in terms of defining a religious collectivity, articulated in relation to a more interventionist and overtly Hindu Dogra state, and to an extent the British

[44] Pandit Hargopal Khasta, *Tawarikh-i-Guldasta Kashmir* [A History of Kashmir] (Lahore, 1877; repr., Srinagar: City Book Center, 1994), 26. It is interesting to note that this history reflects a sense of regional identity, and at the same

Residency. As we have seen, the tussles for social influence and political power among Kashmiri Muslims were set against the backdrop of the changing political economy of the Kashmir Valley. As the British intervention in Kashmir, ostensibly on behalf of the hapless Kashmiri Muslim masses, gathered momentum, the nature of the Dogra state was also undergoing transformation. Claiming religious neutrality while at the same time defining itself through its identification with the Hindu collectivity, the state nevertheless began to increasingly arbitrate in Muslim intra-community disputes, thereby endowing a distinctly political identity on the Kashmiri Muslim community. The Dogra state emerged as the primary, although not exclusive, point of reference for Kashmiri Muslim communitarian discourses of the early twentieth century.

Mirwaiz Yahya Shah's son, Moulvi Rasool Shah (1854–1909), took over the mantle of Mirwaiz Kashmir after his father's death in 1891. He claimed the leadership of the Kashmiri Muslim community through his efforts on the educational front, presenting education as a means for the unification of Kashmiri Muslims under his definition of Islam.[45] The ideological basis of the divisions among Kashmiri Muslims continued to be salient, as the syllabus of the school founded by Rasool Shah, the Madrasa Anjuman Nusrat-ul-Islam, clearly stood against "innovations" such as saint worship and preached the doctrine of *tawhid*, or the unity of Allah. Even as contests over preaching continued to rise dramatically, the Dogra state began to step in to resolve these disputes while giving recognition to a distinct Kashmiri Muslim community in state policies.

Additionally, Mirwaiz Rasool Shah's attempts at pressurizing the state to return several Muslim places of worship—which had been in use by the government for official purposes—back to the Muslim

---

time sets about drawing the contours of the Kashmiri Pandit community. For instance, Khasta stated that the proximity of temples and mosques in Kashmir was more a matter of convenience than harmony—converts to Hinduism could step into a temple more discreetly this way. He was clearly demanding the recognition of the existence of the Kashmiri Pandit community in the special circumstances of the Kashmir Valley.

[45] Moulvi Mohammad Ibrahim, "Mirwaiz Moulana Rasul Shah," in M.Y. Teng, ed., *Hamara Adab* # 2[Our Literature] (Srinagar: Cultural Academy, 1986), 26–32. See chapter four for a detailed treatment of educational reform movements and their relationship to the state in the Kashmir Valley.

community, further involved the state in the process of the articulation of a unified Kashmiri Muslim identity. These demands, which began in 1900, are a clear indication of an emergent Kashmiri Muslim leadership willing to mediate between the state and community. Mirwaiz Rasool Shah's petitions to the Maharaja began with the demand for the return of the Pathar Masjid, which had been used as a granary for the storage of shali, to the Muslim community at the turn of the century.[46] The petitions continued through to the next decade, becoming more vociferous in the second decade of the twentieth century. Significantly, these demands were couched in the knowledge that the Residency would support the claims of the Muslim community for return of its places of worship, if not to the community then to the archeological department of the state.[47]

The Mirwaiz's demands on behalf of Kashmiri Muslims, however, did not necessarily imply the existence of a unified or coherent Muslim community. In fact, the petitions demanding that the state recognize the existence of a Kashmiri Muslim community appeared simultaneous with the intensification of disputes over preaching and definitions of Islam in Srinagar. Even as the Mirwaiz faced opposition from the administrators of the shrines of Srinagar, he asserted his authority by sending yet another petition to the Maharaja for the return of a mosque or place of worship to the Muslim community, of which he was now self-proclaimed leader and representative. With the return of sacred spaces to the community becoming a possibility, the question of community leadership and spheres of influence in the city became more salient issues.

Coeval with the foundation of the Anjuman-Nusrat-ul-Islam and Mirwaiz Rasool Shah's first petition to return Pathar Masjid to the Muslim community, a dispute broke out between his followers and the *khadims* (administrators) of the shrines of Khanqah-i-Mualla and Makhdoom Sahib. The dispute was framed, significantly, in terms akin to the earlier shrine disputes—the right to preach an unadulterated form of Islam—to which both sides claimed authority. While Mirwaiz

---

[46] Vernacular Records 1957/40, Jammu State Archives.

[47] See Vernacular Records 1957/40, Vernacular Records 1959/41, Political Department 55/E/3/1911, and Political Department 104/B/125/1911, Jammu State Archives. See also chapter three in Rai, "The Question of Religion in Kashmir," for a detailed discussion of archeology as a site for Kashmiri Muslim protest.

Rasool Shah preached that Mohammar Habshi was not a companion of the Prophet, the Khanqahi group asserted that he was one of the Prophet's companions.[48] When Rasool Shah preached at the shrine of Makhdoom Sahib against the wishes of its mutawalli, the latter took a petition to the Maharaja to prevent the Mirwaiz from preaching at his shrine. At the same time, Rasool Shah sent his petition to the Maharaja asking the state to guarantee the Mirwaiz family tradition of preaching at Makhdoom Sahib. When the state did allow him to continue preaching at this shrine, the outcry from the other side became so vociferous that the Maharaja had to rescind his previous order.[49] Once again, while this dispute was framed in theological terms, the issue at stake was the leadership of the community, since the two sides now claimed not only to represent a normative religious ideal but also a religious community.

Apart from the leadership, the social groups involved in these disputes clearly saw their involvement in terms of increasing their social and political influence within the city. It is hardly accidental that the shrine disputes and grain shortages happened simultaneously, since both reflect the rising fortunes of commercial groups, including grain dealers and ascetic traders such as the pirs, both eager to match their economic influence with social recognition through association with Kashmiri Muslim sacred spaces. At the same time, the competition between these groups might have been partly responsible for the ideological vocabulary of the disputes. The Mirwaiz Kashmir, with his stance against shrine worship, attracted the support of grain dealers and other petite bourgeoisie groups in localities such as Chinkral mohalla, Jama Masjid, and Zaina Kadal.[50] The main supporters of Mirwaiz Hamdaani, who preached in favor of shrine worship, were not surprisingly the pirs and mutawallis of shrines, who would be rendered obsolete in the absence of shrine worship. The followers of the two sides supported one and as vociferously opposed the other

---

[48] Sadaat, *Rozana Diary,* 626.

[49] Vernacular Department 1959/65, Jammu State Archives.

[50] This is evident from the large numbers of petty traders that gave monetary support to the Mirwaiz's educational institution, the Madrasa Anjuman Nusrat-ul-Islam. See *Halat wa Rouidad,* Annual Report of the Convocation of the Madrasa Anjuman Nusrat-ul-Islam, 1912 (Srinagar: Salgram Press, 1912), 63–81.

form of Islam, with a view to enhancing their own influence at the expense of other groups.

The state, threatened with a breakdown of law and order, took immediate action to quell the disputes, which erupted into physical clashes in 1910. Instead, it succeeded in drawing the lines of discord even more sharply, since they now had behind them the force of law. The Governor of Kashmir passed an order in July 1910 that laid out the jurisdiction of the two preachers within the city of Srinagar. The order stated that every mosque and shrine in the city should be registered as the preaching place of one or the other Mirwaiz through conferral with the mutawallis, who would decide which Mirwaiz had the hereditary right to preach at their shrine. Furthermore, the order instituted a procedure whereby the mutawalli had to inform authorities of his intention to invite a preacher to preach at his shrine fifteen days in advance of the event. Although the Governor had declared that "these restrictions are not intended to be permanent and will be withdrawn as soon as conditions cool down,"[51] the order only led to increased discord among Kashmiri Muslims. After all, the jurisdiction of the two Mirwaizes was to be legalized by the order of the state and the mutawallis were to be authorities on the issue. Clearly, the time was ripe to confirm one's position within the shrine management through declaration of allegiance to a particular Mirwaiz.

The reconstitution of the urban space of Srinagar, partly responsible for and partly a product of the involvement of social groups and the state in shrine disputes, was a key part of the articulation of a communitarian identity. The Governor's order divided the Muslims of Srinagar based on locality. Whereas earlier it had been possible for both Mirwaizes to preach at a mosque in a particular locality, henceforth the residents of a locality chose which Mirwaiz would preach at their local mosque. For instance, when consulted, the residents of Shahidganj mohalla, in consultation with the mutawalli of the Shahidganj mosque, informed the authorities that although both Mirwaizes had preached at their mosque, in accordance with the order they had chosen the Mirwaiz Kashmir as their sole official preacher.[52] Most Srinagar localities participated in the literal division of the city into spheres of influence based on the location of sacred spaces on its landscape.

[51] Political Department 176/P/91/1910, Jammu State Archives.
[52] Vernacular Records 1968/7, Jammu State Archives.

As a result, the implementation of the order turned out to be more complicated than had been anticipated by the authorities. The decision of a mutawalli to invite a particular Mirwaiz to preach at his shrine frequently met with opposition from some quarter of the mohalla in which the shrine was located. The resultant dispute usually found its way into the court system and the lines of dissension between administrators of the shrine and followers of the Mirwaizes grew increasingly sharper. For instance, in 1911, Siddique Bhatt, the mutawalli of Drogjan mosque, applied to the tehsildar to allow the Mirwaiz Kashmir to preach at the said mosque. Some residents of mohalla Drogjan immediately reported to the tehsildar's office pleading that the Mirwaiz not be allowed to preach there since his preaching created a breach of peace. Both Mirwaizes fired off petitions to the Governor's office demanding that they should be allowed to preach at the mosque because the residents of the mohalla were in their favor.

Upon conducting an inquiry into the matter, the Governor's office discovered that Siddique Bhatt was not, in fact, the real mutawalli of the mosque, but only a minor figure in the administration who had invited Mirwaiz Ahmad Ullah to the mosque to malign the real mutawalli, a certain Abdulla Jan. The Governor's office further discovered that 12 men of the mohalla were in favor of Mirwaiz Ahmad Ullah's preaching and 15 were in favor of the Hamdaani Mirwaiz. The Governor ordered that since the application for Mirwaiz Ahmad Ullah's preaching came from an individual who was not a mutawalli, it could not be allowed. However, if the real mutawalli applied for it, the government could consider such an invitation.[53] Through its decision, the state had not succeeded in resolving the issue; instead it had created discord within the administration of the Drogjan mosque, between the residents of the mohalla Drogjan, and recognized, once again, the dispute between the two Mirwaizes.

Seemingly unaware of its role in exacerbating the dissension, the state carried on its discourse of neutrality while at the same time defining the dispute in sectarian terms. In his speech to the Mirwaizes, mutawallis and *raises* (notables) of Srinagar, the Maharaja reiterated:

> It has always been one of the first principles of my rule that the fullest liberty should be enjoyed by my subjects in religious matters, but the religious toleration on the part of the ruler can be beneficial to his subjects

[53] Vernacular Records 1269/1968, Jammu State Archives.

only if they are able to perform their religious rites and observances in a peaceful and orderly manner . . . Is it not a matter of great regret that religious discord from some time past has produced most unhappy differences between the two sects of the Mohammadans of Kashmir?[54]

Significantly, in the same speech, the Maharaja also declared the appointment of a Muslim governor for the province of Kashmir, "in order that the interests of the Mohammadans of that province may be fully looked after."[55] Then, he warned that if the Muslims of Kashmir were going to waste their energy in discord, no efforts the state made on their behalf would be successful. Clearly, the state was granting political recognition to the specific needs of the Muslims of Kashmir as a community. It was also, however, giving legal sanction to the divisions within the community. Not only were these divisions now "sectarian" and hence irreconcilable, but Kashmiri Muslims had to strictly adhere to the decisions of the state in the resolution of the disputes. The Maharaja passed an order soon after the above speech in which he issued a warning that any individual found in contravention of state orders on the preaching disputes would be "proceeded against according to law and shall moreover be deprived of all favors and privileges enjoyed by him on our behalf."[56]

The legal aspect of state intervention and its impact on the articulation of communitarian identities by Kashmiri Muslims is worth considering in some detail. As the Dogra state's development of a centrally regulated court system proceeded, disputes became increasingly entangled in the legal vocabulary of the state. Muslims turned to state institutions such as law courts for a settlement of their disputes,[57] thus unhinging themselves from community institutions while at the

---

[54] Political Department, 144/P/91/1910, Jammu State Archives.

[55] Ibid.

[56] Ibid.

[57] From the records of this period, which include countless petitions and incidences of legal wrangles, it appears as though the judicial system of the state had been created for the express purpose of settling preaching disputes among Kashmiri Muslims. As Ali Shah Khoiyami had noted in his masnavi: "Those who fight are subjected to criminal trial/The Police swear by their scared books and yet give false evidence/Everyone is determined to create chaos/People now believe in trials." Khoiyami, "Akhir Zamaan," 5.

same time creating a new reference point for community identities: the self-contradictory Dogra legal system. Borrowing heavily from their colonial masters, the Dogras imported the contradictions inherent within the system of colonial law in British India, particularly the Punjab. This was especially evident in the realm of custom, which British administrators by the late nineteenth century had begun to focus on as a source of law.[58]

Drawing on colonial policies in the Punjab, where revenue collectors had been directed to ascertain the customary practices in each village, in 1915 Maharaja Pratap Singh appointed Pandit Sant Ram Dogra, Assistant Settlement Officer, Kashmir, to prepare a consolidated code of tribal custom prevalent in the Kashmir Valley.[59] Dogra toured the Valley exhaustively and compiled his inquiries into the *Code of Tribal Custom in Kashmir*, which for all intents and purposes elevated the custom(s) prevalent in different localities, districts, tribes and villages of the Valley to the level of law.[60] The codification of custom was part of the movement by the state to amend, consolidate, and declare laws to be administered in the state of Jammu and Kashmir, which found fruition in the Sri Pratap Jammu and Kashmir Laws Consolidation Act, 1977B (1920). Based on Dogra's Code, the Sri Pratap Act, while granting primacy to Hindu and Muslim personal law, recognized customary law in cases where it had altered or replaced personal law. Thus, in questions regarding succession, inheritance, family relations, waqfs, caste or religious usages and so on, the rule of decision was to be as follows:

[58] Michael R. Anderson, "Islamic Law and the Colonial Encounter in British-India," in Arnold and Robb, eds., *Institutions and Ideologies*, 176, and Jalal, *Self and Sovereignty*, 145–6.

[59] It is important to note that in part the motivation behind the codification of custom in the Punjab, and probably Kashmir as well, was the need for an assessment of landholding rights, since the agricultural classes followed customary law in matters of inheritance and division of landholdings. See Anderson, "Islamic Law and the Colonial Encounter," 176, and Imtiyaz Hussain, *Muslim Law and Customs (With a Special Reference to the Law as Applied in Jammu and Kashmir)* (Kashmir: Srinagar Law Journal, 1989), 119.

[60] Mohammad Altaf Hussain Ahangar, *Customary Succession Among Muslims (A Critical Appraisal of Judicial Interpretation in Kashmir)* (New Delhi: Uppal Publishing House, 1986), 45.

The Mohammadan law where the parties are Mohammadan and the Hindu law in cases where the parties are Hindus, except in so far as such law has been by this or any other enactment, altered or abolished or has been modified by any custom applicable to the parties concerned which is not contrary to justice, equity or good conscience and has not been by this or any other enactment declared to be void by any competent authority.[61]

Whether this act intended to give primacy to one or other type of law is debatable. However, the result of the consolidation of laws and the concomitant codification of custom in Kashmir was similar to that in the Punjab: Dogra's *Code of Tribal Custom* came to be recognized as the law in state courts, particularly since there was no parallel body of Muslim law that litigants could draw on. This is clear from the observation of the full bench in a high court case that, "In the Valley this book was recognized as laying down the law on the subject incorporated therein and nobody questioned its authority."[62] Until Sant Ram Dogra wrote the *Code of Tribal Custom in Kashmir*, there was no such thing as general custom in the Valley. The people of the Valley were governed by custom not in the shape of a uniform code, which could be universally applicable, but on heterogeneous rules based on local custom, family custom, tribal custom, district custom, and village custom, which at times functioned simultaneously and at others to the exclusion of one or the other.[63] For instance, in the realm of custom, it was possible at the same time to be both the member of an agricultural clan and the resident of a locality; at other times, one could claim an identity based solely on one's locality to the exclusion of one's clan identity.

The codification of custom into law meant that the ambiguities and inconsistencies that had governed the lives of Kashmiris, and their legal decisions in a whole host of disputes, were replaced by what purported to be the exact science of customary law. Since Hindu and Muslim personal law could be negated if a litigant proved the existence of a custom, the laws of religious communities often ceased to have a

---

[61] *Laws of Jammu and Kashmir [Being a collection of the State enactments in force in the Jammu and Kashmir State]*, vol. I (3rd ed. Srinagar: Jammu and Kashmir Government Press, 1972), 223–6; and Syed Tassadque Hussain, *Customary Law and the Indian Constitution* (New Delhi: Rima Publishing House, 1987), 13.

[62] Ahangar, *Customary Succession*, 51.

[63] Ibid., 37.

considerable impact on legal decisions meted out in state courts.[64] As a result, the divisions within the Muslim community came into sharper focus, since customary law cut across religious boundaries, being dictated by tribe, locality, district, and so on. And yet, the *Code* did not entirely obscure the importance of one's religious identity, since almost all customary laws included primary religious identification as one of their salient features, particularly when it came to issues of shrine management.

For instance, the *Code* recorded the customary law as it related to mutawallis of shrines in the case of Sunni Mussalmans of Srinagar as— "If a Mutawalli embezzles the property of the Ziarat, the *Qazi-ul-Waqt* (judge of the time) is authorized to dismiss the Mutawalli. In default of the *Qazi-ul-Waqt* the majority of the respectable Muhammadans can dismiss him."[65] The consequences of this code are self-evident: since an unwritten custom had now been recorded, it could be used in a court of law to bring charges against a particular shrine manager and depose him in favor of a more amenable caretaker. At a time when shrines had become the terrain for battles over influence and power, such a code only served to add fuel to the already blazing fire. The state went a step further and ensured that these battles would in fact be brought forward before law courts, through the passage of a law that enabled "persons interested in religious endowments [to] sue before the Civil Court the trustee, manager, or superintendent of such mosque, temple, or religious endowment, for any misfeasance, breach of trust or neglect of duty, committed by such trustee, manager, or superintendent . . ."[66]

As far as religious law was concerned, while the Sri Pratap Act allowed for its exercise in state courts in certain civil matters, the Dogra state did not make a concomitant attempt to compile Islamic law, as the British had attempted to do in India.[67] The onus for this responsibility was left entirely on the Kashmiri Muslim leadership. For

[64] The codification of custom had a similar impact in the Punjab. See Jalal, *Self and Sovereignty*, 146.

[65] Sant Ram Dogra, *Code of Tribal Custom in Kashmir* (Jammu, 1930), 247.

[66] *Laws of Jammu and Kashmir [Being a collection of the State enactments in force in the Jammu and Kashmir State]*, vol. II (3rd ed. Srinagar: Jammu and Kashmir Government Press, 1972), 526. The law was entitled "The Religious Endowments Act of 1977" (1920).

[67] Anderson and Jalal give detailed analyses of colonial endeavors toward

the leadership, there was but one way out of what must have seemed like a conundrum: focus on the production of a corpus of Muslim personal law that could be used to override custom, as provided for by the Sri Pratap Consolidation Act. However, this raised its own set of issues. First, it took for granted the existence of a unified Kashmiri Muslim community that would be willing to adhere to personal laws over custom—now easily accessible due to its codification—that had governed them for centuries. In a related matter, the impending compilation of Muslim law brought out sectarian divisions among Kashmiri Muslims. After all, if a corpus of Muslim law was to be written practically for the first time, whose law would it be: Sunni or Shia, Hanafi or Ahl-i-Hadithi, to name but a few divisions? These sectarian differences gradually aligned themselves along lines of division already existent in the community.

So while it would appear that religion was the primary identifier for Kashmiris in the late nineteenth century, if placed in the context of political and legal developments it becomes clear that it functioned alongside and in relation to other identifications based on region, class, and sect. Kashmiri Muslims were far from a unified community in the late-nineteenth and early-twentieth centuries, and yet, in a political atmosphere that recognized them solely on the basis of their identification with a coherently defined religious collectivity, the identity and interests of the Kashmiri Muslim "community" became central to the public discourse of this period. However, presenting community interests to the state did not obscure divisions, but instead heightened the simultaneous battles over the meaning of Kashmiri Islam, indeed of belonging to the Kashmiri Muslim community, which were now carried out increasingly over the rich site of Kashmiri, Urdu, and to a lesser extent Persian, poetry.

Poetic Renditions of Kashmiri Muslim Identities

Before the cause of Kashmiri Muslims could be taken before the state, it was imperative to define the community in distinct terms. However, the definitions were as variegated as the opinions about them. It was

---

producing a unified Muslim and Hindu law, the only two categories under which all indigenous legal arrangements were subsumed, and the resultant simplification of both the sharia and the shastras. See Anderson, "Islamic Law and the Colonial Encounter," 172–6; and Jalal, *Self and Sovereignty*, 148–53.

in the dissemination of this discourse, not so much about Muslim interests as about what it meant to be Kashmiri Muslim, that the burgeoning print and publications market played a significant role. Here I explore these debates over definitions of "Kashmiri Muslim" and the "Kashmiri Muslim community" that erupted in the Kashmiri print media during the first three decades of the twentieth century.

The print and publications market in early-twentieth-century Kashmir was still in its infancy, since the Dogra state's laws, such as the Jammu and Kashmir State Newspapers (Incitements to Offenses Act), 1914, gave officials the right to forfeit any newspaper and its press for inciting any form of "violence."[68] As a result, most of these debates were carried out not in newspapers but in informally and privately published pamphlets, usually of poetry, and sometimes polemical tracts. Poetry was a logical choice in a society that was largely unlettered, yet where community activities such as shrine visitations and gatherings at booksellers' shops revolved around recitations of songs and poetry.[69]

"I am writing this book in poetic form to prevent Muslims from being misled, since memorizing poetry is simple and makes the subject matter more interesting,"[70] wrote Sheikh Ahmed Waiz, a Kashmiri pir, in his preface to a tract against "Wahhabis."[71] The bent of the tract

[68] *Laws of Jammu and Kashmir*, vol. I, 207.

[69] Jalal describes the potency of the press and publications market, particularly poetry, in disseminating ideas in the largely unlettered society of the Punjab. See *Self and Sovereignty*, chapter two. Interestingly, many of the treatises and pamphlets of poetry discussed in this section were published in printing presses in the Punjab.

[70] Sheikh Ahmad Waiz, *Rajumul Wahhabiya Najumul al-Shahbiyya* [Throwing Stones at the Wahhabis] (Lahore: Kohinoor Press, 1912), 2.

[71] In most writing from Kashmir, including government documents, the terms Wahhabi and Ahl-i-Hadith were used interchangeably. Historically, however, this is an inaccurate assumption, since the two sects varied significantly on theological issues: while the Wahhabis followed the Hanabali school of Islamic law, the Ahl-i-Hadith specifically did not follow any of the four schools of Islamic jurisprudence, relying instead on the authority of the *Quran* and *Hadith*. The similarity between the two sects rests simply in the fact that both spoke out against saint worship in their drive to "purify" Islam. It is important to note that the organizers of the "Wahhabi" movement in India, Shah Abdul Aziz and Sayyid Ahmed of Rai Bareilly, made a submission to the colonial government after the Wahhabi trials, pleading that they be referred to as Ahl-i-Hadith. See Jalal, *Self and Sovereignty*, 27.

against "Wahhabis" points to the continued importance of the issue of shrine worship to Kashmiri Muslim identities in this period. Although Kashmiri nationalist histories and the votaries of *Kashmiriyat* claim that shrine worship was an accepted and integral part of Kashmiri Islam and consequently that the Kashmiri Muslim community has been an identifiable and immutable entity over centuries, it is clear from this analysis that even a regional community of Muslims in the Indian subcontinent, although purporting to be a unified and cohesive entity, was in fact deeply divided along ideological, social, and economic lines.

The influence of the Ahl-i-Hadith on the conflicts over Kashmiri Muslim identities cannot be overemphasized.[72] As the Kashmir Valley came into closer contact with British India, the sect saw the Valley, where shrine worship was endemic, as a ripe ground for the education of Muslims in the true tenets of their faith. Rabidly against the concept of saints and shrine worship, the Ahl-i-Hadith made tactical alliances with local Kashmiri ulema who had similar ideological leanings, thereby inserting themselves in local disputes over community and identity. It was widely believed that the family of Mirwaiz Kashmir of Jama Masjid had Ahl-i-Hadith connections, since one of their followers, Hassan Shah Batku, had left Srinagar to study with Nazir Husayn in Delhi, and had returned to Kashmir to propagate the sect's beliefs through the Mirwaiz Kashmir. Another Ahl-i-Hadith leader, Anwar Shah Shupiani, hailing from Shupian, a village situated twenty-nine miles from Srinagar, moved the center of his activities to the city in the 1910s. He founded an Ahl-i-Hadith mosque in the Zaldagar mohalla in the city, where he preached against shrine worship.[73] Although the

---

[72] This movement had its roots in the exclusive preoccupation with the traditional corpus of hadith by a group of nineteenth-century ulema in British India, principal among whom were Siddiq Hasan Khan and Nazir Husayn, who regarded it as the principal source of law and the ideal guide to social behavior and individual piety. The creed of this movement, as stated by Siddiq Hasan Khan, is that it does not follow, either in broad canonical principles or in the minutiae of law, any of the four juristic schools of Islam, instead binding itself to the *Quran* and tradition (sunna and hadith) of the Prophet. See Aziz Ahmad, *Islamic Modernism in India and Pakistan 1857–1964* (London: Oxford University Press, 1967), 114–15.

[73] Bashir Ahmed Khan, "Ahl-i-Hadith Movement in Kashmir 1901–1981" (M.Phil. thesis, University of Kashmir, 1984), 48 and 114.

Mirwaiz Kashmir never overtly admitted his support for Shupiani, it was assumed that the two were ideologically of the same bent.[74]

There are several possible reasons for the successive Mirwaizes' support of the movement. First, it gave them an ideological basis drawn from the holy texts of Islam to label their opponents defilers of Islam. In a related issue, the Ahl-i-Hadith, with its focus on the *Quran* and *Hadith*, could in theory provide the necessary means for the compilation of a corpus of Islamic law that was so sorely needed to unite Kashmiri Muslims. Moreover, the Ahl-i-Hadith leaders were prolific writers who believed in the power of the written and spoken word to spread the message of true Islam. The poetic tracts, mostly in Kashmiri, circulating in the city and the Kashmir Valley in general, were geared toward educating the illiterate and forsaken Kashmiri Muslim masses of the *Quran* and doctrines of Islam. Shupiani, for instance, wrote tirelessly throughout his life, composing poetry and prose against the peculiarly Kashmiri Muslim practices associated with shrines, such as *Khatam-i-Sharif* and *Milad-i-Sharif* (anniversary of the Prophet's birthday).[75]

The discourse of this period was peculiar in that it consciously targeted Kashmiri peasants. This class had come into prominence with the incessant efforts of the British Residency to alleviate its position through land settlement operations. While these efforts had not been entirely successful—the peasants continued to toil under the burden of heavy revenue assessments and the threat of ejection from their land for non-payment—the settlement and the rhetoric associated with it elevated the class to a prominent position. It was clear to those who staked a claim to the leadership of Kashmiri Muslims that such an endeavor was impossible without the support, and more significantly, inclusion, of the peasantry into definitions of the Kashmiri Muslim community. This required, however, that the peasants be awakened to their Muslim identity; thus, much of the poetry generated in the 1910s and 1920s was aimed directly at the peasantry. *Greeznama* (Story of

---

[74] Several members of the Mirwaiz family were overt or covert followers of the Ahl-i-Hadith. Since the overt declaration of belonging to the Ahl-i-Hadith would have had severe consequences for the Mirwaiz of Jama Mosque, he remained a closet member of the sect. His brother was a fervent member of the Ahl-i-Hadith in the early twentieth century. Based on an interview with Professor Nooruddin Zahid, Badgaam, Kashmir, April 23, 1998.

[75] Khan, "Ahl-i-Hadith Movement," 126–36.

the Peasant), by Maqbool Shah Kraalwari, a lengthy exposition into the religious fickleness of the Kashmiri Muslim peasant written in the mid-nineteenth century, was published in this period. According to Kraalwari, the cultivator, a deceitful figure determined not to part with his grain, was also a tepid Muslim who knew nothing of true Islam. He wrote:

> They [the peasants] regard the mosque and temple as equal,
> Seeing no difference between muddy puddles and the ocean.
> They know not the sacred, honorable or the respectable,
> They are unaware of the sharia, the millat, or Islam.[76]

Furthermore, in the tradition of Persian love legends that were sung in every corner of the Valley, Islamic legends in Kashmiri, which described the life and exploits of the Prophet and his companions, mostly taken from the *Quran*, captured the Kashmiri publications landscape in the 1910s. In one such poem, *Yak Hikayat* (A Story),[77] for instance, the poet Mahmood Gami related the story of the descent of Angel Gabriel to the Prophet Mohammad in a dream to inform him that his *ummat* (Islamic community) had fallen from the righteous path prescribed to them by the *Quran* and would be burnt on the Day of Judgement. Upon hearing this, Gami narrated, the Prophet left his room and retreated into a cave to ask Allah for forgiveness for his people. His companions followed him into the cave and begged the Prophet's forgiveness, asking him to rise and rejoin the community. Finally Fatimah, flanked by her two sons Hassan and Husain, entered the cave and promised to sacrifice her sons to Allah so that the ummat could be spared the fires of hell. Upon hearing this, Allah sent Gabriel back to the Prophet to accept Fatimah's sacrifice. This story was meant not only to educate people about the message in the *Quran*, but more significantly to impart to them a Muslim identity in belonging to the Islamic brotherhood.

The poetry generated by the movement squarely placed the blame for the irreligious state of affairs in the Kashmir Valley at the doorstep of the pirs and petty ulema associated with shrines spread out across Kashmir. Since a clear bid for leadership required the consolidation of the disparate ulema under one figure, it had to be impressed on them

---

[76] Kraalwari, *Greeznama*, 5.

[77] Mahmood Gami, *Yak Hikayat* [A Story] (Srinagar, 1913).

and their followers that they required the guidance of someone learned in Islam. Several anti-pir poems were published in tandem with poems directed at the peasantry, the most prominent among them being *Pirnama* (Story of the Pir) by Maqbool Shah Kraalwari and *Malnama* (Story of the Mullah) by Khalil Shah. In *Pirnama*, Kraalwari lamented the general decline in the morality of Kashmiri society:

> Something strange has happened to these times,
> Nothing is in its right place, whether ordinary or important.
> People leave the real and stick to the superficial,
> Nobody follows the laws of the shariat.
> All of a sudden religious values have disappeared,
> Whatever is against religion becomes the law of the land.[78]

The poet was outraged by the apparent lack of religiosity amongst natives of the Valley. But that was not all, since this terrible lack of knowledge of Islam was the result of the pirs' influence on the people:

> The pir recites the fatiha and the community says ameen,
> They gather around him.
> And promise to sacrifice their selves and families for him,
> While the pir bestows on them blessings of prosperity.[79]

Not only does this verse blame pirs for creating blind faith among their followers, it questions their ability to be effective leaders and educators of the Kashmiri Muslim community.

Similarly, the author of the *Malnama*, Khalil Shah, seems to take an almost perverse pleasure in condemning Kashmiri mullahs:

> Mullahs are deceitful and treacherous,
> They are far removed from religious doctrines.
> For some money, they will fall from their faith,
> They talk of *tawhid* but are brokers of lust. [80]

The poem describes in detail what Shah perceived as anti-Islamic practices indulged in by pirs and their followers, such as gorging themselves during *Ramzaan*, the Muslim holy month of fasting, and cheating the

[78] Maqbool Shah Kraalwari, *Pirnama* [Story of the Pir] (Srinagar, 1913), 3.
[79] Ibid., 7.
[80] Khalil Shah, *Malnama* [Story of the Mullah] (Srinagar, 1913), 2.

poor and helpless of their hard-earned money. In yet another poem, which appears to have been printed around 1912, entitled *Habblullah* (The Rope of God), the poet struck a more threatening tone and warned Kashmiri Muslims of the punishment awaiting them for committing *shirk* by seeking help from pirs and saints. He wrote:

> Take the way of the *sunnat* and the *shariat*,
> Cut off the strings of *biddat*.
> Those Muslims who seek the help of the pirs and fakirs,
> Are deprived of the word of the *Quran*.
> Read the *Quran* and commit your life to the religion of the Prophet,
> Leave ignorance and accept *tawhid*. [81]

What is interesting about this particular poem is that the poet, despite being a pir himself, believed that Kashmiri Muslims needed to read and embrace the *Quran* and *Hadith* to comprehend the real meaning of Islam.[82]

Most of these poems were framed against Hanafis, who were by this time generally associated with favoring shrine worship and the role of pirs in the religious life of the Valley. In retaliation, Hanafis launched their own invectives. After all, they were as convinced of the purity of the Islam they professed as their detractors were convinced of its anti-Islamic character, since both sides attempted to approximate the same normative ideal. One such Kashmiri tract, entitled *Shamsher-i-Birhana bar Dushmanani* (Naked Sword), by Abu Abdul Hai Pir Ghulam Ahmad Hanafi Kashmiri, declared that the Ahl-i-Hadith were not in reality followers of the hadith, but instead *Ahl-i-Biddat* and *Ahl-i-Hawa*, or the followers of innovations and selfishness respectively. Quoting a hadith to prove his point, Pir Abu Hai wrote that the Prophet had predicted that a cunning man would rise and start a movement in Najd, Arabia, which would go against the principles of Islam. The author claimed that Abdul Wahhab, the founder of the Wahabbi sect, was this individual, who had declared all Muslims apart from himself and his followers, kafirs, or non-believers.[83]

---

[81] Pir Ghulam Ahmed, *Habblullah* [The Rope of God] (Srinagar, 1912).

[82] Based on an interview with author's grandson, Peerzada Mohammad Ashraf, from whose private collection the manuscript was acquired, Bemina, Kashmir, April 18, 1998.

[83] Abu Abdul Hai Pir Ghulam Ahmad Hanafi Kashmiri, *Shamsher-i-Birhana bar Dushmanani* [Naked Sword] (Amritsar, 1906), 1–16.

The same tract included a speech by the individual responsible for its publication, Ghulam Mohiuddin Hundu, entitled *Takrir Dilpazir Dar Islahe Qaum* (Speech for the Good of the Qaum). Although appealing for the unification of the community, the author clearly took one side in the debate. In an eloquent defense of saint worship, the speech declared:

> We should be grateful to the saints, who showed us the path to Islam, otherwise we would have been uttering Ram-Ram in the house of idols. The shrines and khanqahs of Kashmir are avenues for the discussion of the lives of those who devoted their lives to the conversion of non-Muslims to Islam . . . It is not right to criticize these men of God. We cannot even repair our mosques and these men built so many houses of worship where Kashmiris could accept Islam. This is not religion or religiosity. We should first look into our homes and make ourselves Muslim before casting stones at others.[84]

The author used the conversion of Kashmiris to Islam as justification for the pervasiveness of saint worship in the Valley, since it was these saints who introduced Islam to the people. He also implied that if Kashmiris were denied saint worship, they would lose contact with their Islamic antecedents, and ultimately with Islam itself. Additionally, it was necessary to emphasize the Islamic antecedents of the shrines to ward off any insinuation by the other side that these structures, as also the practices associated with them, were in any way "Hindu."

More importantly, however, the speech was addressed to the *qaum*, in this case the Kashmiri Muslim community, and lamented the "sorry state that Muslims are sunk in, beset by extremism and moderation." The author stated that the Kashmiri Muslim community could not hope to be successful, rid itself of its ignorance, and advance, unless it cleansed itself of its sectarianism. While on the one hand Kashmiri Muslims had made their ancestors their ideals, without regard for the *Quran* or *Hadith*, extremist Muslims on the other side "caused one to shiver."[85] The author presented the actions of the ulema of British India as the model for the unification of the Kashmiri Muslim community. If Muslim scholars and ulema in British India could establish anjumans in successive cities with the intent to bridge the gaps between

[84] Ghulam Mohiuddin Hundu, *Takrir Dilpazir Dar Islahe Qaum* [Speech for the Good of the Qaum] (Amritsar, 1906), 17.

[85] Ibid., 16.

the followers of Ahl-i-Hadith and Hanafis, then why could not Kashmiri ulema do the same, the author asked.

This speech represents a subtle shift in Kashmiri public discourse, from a focus on defining Islam to recognizing the need to preserve the unity of the community so that its interests could be presented to the state. By the 1920s, although far removed from reality, the idea that the Kashmiri Muslim community was a unified entity with an identifiable interest had become embedded in discourses on Muslim identity in Kashmir. This was most evident in the gradually evolving Muslim educational demands to the state (discussed in the next chapter). The Mirwaizes and their followers had tangentially included the peasantry in their battles over the true meaning of Islam; however, they had made no effort to politically organize Kashmiri Muslims. Furthermore, their influence remained restricted to urban areas, leaving 78 per cent of the Kashmiri Muslim community, comprising largely of peasants,[86] outside the ambit of their concerns and debates. Although still unable to politically organize the community, the third decade of the twentieth century saw the emergence of a new leadership geared toward the unification of Kashmiri Muslims with an intent to presenting their demands to the state.

Urban Politics and the Emergence of a New Muslim Leadership

Here I trace the emergence of a new Kashmiri leadership on the urban political space of Srinagar in the 1920s, a moment that was, as I discussed earlier, a particularly volatile one in the history of this city. By the 1920s, it had become clear to the emergent Muslim leadership that internal unification was needed if Kashmiri Muslims were to acquire political recognition commensurate with their numbers and have their demands taken seriously by the state. Internal unification, however, was not as easily forthcoming as this leadership had anticipated. Yet the discourse of this period clearly reflected the lofty political agenda of the leadership: to return Kashmiri Muslims to their past glory by educating, elevating, and unifying them into a cohesive community under the banner of Islam. Further, this narrative identified Kashmiri

---

[86] Mohammad, *Census of India, 1921, Vol. XXII, Kashmir, Part I, Report,* 163.

Muslims in oppositional terms to Kashmiri Hindus to a greater extent than earlier narratives of Kashmiri Muslim identity, which had remained focused on debating the meanings of Kashmiri Islam.

The narratives on Kashmiri Muslim identities in the 1920s were set against the backdrop of greater contact with British India, the impact of education, the rising influence of the press and publications market on the common Kashmiri, the rise of Srinagar as the center of competing ideologies, and the general economic discontent of the Valley's inhabitants. As we have seen, the effects of the First World War had begun to make themselves felt in the grain crisis of 1919, which was exacerbated by the state's blundering measures towards its alleviation. General unrest was all-pervasive as prices rose abnormally during this decade, particularly those of foodstuffs, which increased by 150–200 per cent on account of the War.[87] With the integration of the Valley and British India, increasing numbers of Muslims had begun to travel to the Punjab and Islamic centers of higher learning across state borders. The Census of 1921 noted that, "the Kashmiri not only contributes to the growth of population in the state, but he adds considerably to the population of all important towns in the Punjab, which are situated along the State border or the main railway line."[88]

Contact with the Punjab and the limited spread of education had encouraged a concomitant expansion of the publications market, particularly in Srinagar. The circulation figures for newspapers in English and Urdu showed an exponential increase in the decade between 1911 and 1921. While the number of daily or weekly newspapers in circulation in the state in 1911 had not even been recorded, by 1921 their circulation in the state had risen to a staggering 2,000, with the number for English newspapers being as high as 450.[89] Additionally, between 1911 and 1921 the number of books in English, Urdu and even Kashmiri that circulated in the state had increased significantly, their number being 858, 266 and 30 respectively.[90] Most of these books, pamphlets and tracts were published at printing presses in

[87] Ram, *Census of India, 1931, Vol. XXIV, Jammu and Kashmir State, Part I, Report*, 21.
[88] Mohammad, *Census of 1921, Vol. XXII, Kashmir, Part I, Report*, 26.
[89] Ibid., 126.
[90] Ibid.

Lahore and Amritsar, further attesting to the growing relationship between Punjabi and Kashmiri politics. The expansion of the publications market, coupled with the concentration of population in urban centers, particularly Srinagar, facilitated the dispersal of religious and political ideologies among urban inhabitants.

Although restricted to upper-middle-class urban Muslim families, education had a significant role to play in the politics of Kashmiri Muslim identities in this period. Several Muslims passed the level of secondary school and went on to institutions of higher learning in British India. While in British India, these men gained more than just an education. They came into contact with movements among Indian Muslims, such as the one represented by the Aligarh Muslim University, the Khilafat movement, and the ideologies of new sects, most prominent among which were the Ahmadiyyas. Upon returning to Kashmir infused with the fervor of new ideas and armed with academic and professional degrees, these men found the Dogra state unwilling and unable to accommodate their needs. Facing the prospect of unemployment and a seemingly rapidly disintegrating community, they consolidated into a leadership that would lead Kashmir out of Dogra rule.

The leadership had a willing following among the numerous Kashmiri Muslim educated yet unemployed youth. Kashmiri Muslims registered the highest increase in the number of literates between 1921 and 1931 of all communities in the state of Jammu and Kashmir.[91] It is particularly significant that the number of literates in Urdu, the official language of the state, increased by 99.2 per cent in this decade.[92] Unemployment, however, had also begun to make its presence felt, particularly among the educated. That the Census Commissioner of the 1931 census chose to abandon the attempt at enumerating educated unemployment within each community for fear of the consequences is proof enough that this number was high during this decade.[93] Moreover, the largest number of the educated-unemployed possessed academic degrees, such as BA, MA, and MLC. It was these

[91] Ram, *Census of India, 1931, Vol. XXIV, Jammu and Kashmir State, Part I, Report,* 257.

[92] Ibid., 261.

[93] Ibid., 224.

men with hard-earned academic degrees and qualified in the language of administration who, eventually forced to take employment in low-level, low-paying positions in the state educational system, began to question the authority of the state through an organized political movement. Although glaringly prejudiced in its reasoning, the 1931 census recognized the possibility of discontent within this class: "The stylish living that comes so easy to the English literate at school and college when they live on the hard-earned money of their parents is difficult to keep up at a later age when the employment they get does not bring them abundance of money and they have to pool their small earnings in a joint family. Their discontent is thus easily understood."[94]

The emergence of a new Kashmiri Muslim leadership has to be further contextualized within the rise and impact of the Ahmadiyya movement in the Kashmir Valley. The Ahmadiyya movement, founded by Mirza Ghulam Ahmad in Qadian (a small town in the Punjab), began as a rural, small-town middle-class religious resurgence in the late nineteenth century, specifically 1889. The Ahmadiyyas soon found themselves frowned upon by mainstream ulema for the Mirza's self-declaration as the much-awaited *mahdi* (messiah).[95] The movement's relationship to the Kashmir Valley in the late nineteenth century rested on the Mirza's claim that Jesus was brought down alive from the cross and traveled East looking for the lost tribes of Israel, until he settled in Kashmir. The Mirza asserted that Jesus died in Kashmir and lay buried in the Khanyaar quarter of Srinagar.[96]

By the 1920s, however, the Ahmadiyya presence in the Kashmir Valley had begun to assert itself beyond Jesus' tomb in Srinagar. The petitions to the government on behalf of Ahmadiyyas of the Kashmir Valley testify to the growth of the sect during the decade. Moreover, they illuminate the growing involvement of the Punjabi center of the Ahmadiyya movement in Kashmiri Muslim political affairs, despite the movement's assertions to the contrary. For instance, in 1922 the Additional Secretary to the leader of the Ahmadiyya community sent

[94] Ibid., 225.

[95] Spencer Lavan, *The Ahmadiyah Movement: A History and Perspective* (New Delhi: Manohar Book Service, 1977), 11–50.

[96] Paul C. Pappas, *Jesus' Tomb in India: Debate on his Death and Resurrection* (Berkeley: Asian Humanities Press, 1991), 69.

a petition to the Maharaja on behalf of the Ahmadiyyas of the Kashmir Valley, who were "put to much trouble by local officers of the state not being acquainted with our movement."[97] He requested that the government circulate letters to local subordinate officers telling them that the Ahmadiyya community "is a perfectly loyal community, purely religious, and allows no kind of political agitation against ruling government."[98] Notwithstanding such assertions, the Ahmadiyyas formed the core of the emergent leadership that would question the very political existence of the Dogra state.

There were several internal and external reasons for the increasing Ahmadiyya influence on the affairs of Kashmiri Muslims from the third decade of this century. The movement, which had appealed to a "literate and middle class group of followers who found the Mirza's charismatic preaching and prophesying a much-needed element in the stagnating Islam current in the Punjab at the turn of the century,"[99] held a similar appeal for Kashmiri Muslims who came into contact with the movement while at educational institutions in the Punjab. These educated, middle-class Kashmiri Muslims, mostly doctors, lawyers, publishers and teachers, played a significant role in spreading the movement in the Valley,[100] so that by 1931 the number of Muslims identifying themselves as Ahmadiyya in the Kashmir province had risen to 2,955.[101] Furthermore, the Punjabi leaders of the movement saw Kashmir as a ripe ground for spreading their movement. In 1928, a prominent Lahori Ahmadiyya leader,[102] Khawaja Kamal-ud-Din, visited Srinagar with a view to publicly introducing the movement to the Kashmiri Muslim community.[103] This was the beginning of a

[97] Political Department Records 116/Mis-29/1922, Jammu State Archives, 9.

[98] Ibid.

[99] Lavan, *The Ahmadiyah Movement*, 95.

[100] Based on an interview with Professor Nooruddin Zahid, Badgaam, Kashmir, April 29, 1998.

[101] Ram, *Census of India, 1931, Vol. XXIV, Jammu and Kashmir State, Part I, Report*, 308.

[102] In 1914, the Ahmadiyya movement split into Lahori and Qadiani Ahmadiyyas. While the Lahoris were more overtly political, the Qadianis preferred to declare themselves non-political. Their clearly political role in Kashmir, however, points to the contrary. See Lavan, *The Ahmadiyah Movement*, 98.

[103] K.A. Tareen, "The Great Ahmadiyya Mosque at Srinagar (A Brief Historical

protracted Ahmadiyya involvement in Kashmiri Muslim politics, particularly in the 1930s and 1940s.[104]

If one descends from the realm of high politics, however, it becomes clear that the most significant impact of the Ahmadiyya movement, particularly in the 1920s, lay in the rise of a new leadership among Kashmiri Muslims, which, through its association with the movement, redefined Islam as a means to a greater political end for the Kashmiri Muslim community. Individual Kashmiri Muslim Ahmadiyyas played a crucial role in disseminating the ideas of the movement, which ultimately led to debates over the politics of Kashmiri Muslim identities. One such Ahmadiyya, Moulvi Mohammad Abdullah Vakil (1864–1948), from Shupian in the Kashmir Valley, moved to Srinagar as a pleader in the Jammu and Kashmir High Court, after his return from Qadian in the early 1920s.[105] He began a meeting group known as the *Dars-i-Quran* at his residence in Qalamdanpora, Srinagar, where educated Kashmiri Muslims gathered to discuss the verses of the *Quran*. The meeting group soon became a forum for the discussion of general issues, political and religious, facing the Kashmiri Muslim community and developed into the Anjuman Ahmadiyya Ishaat-i-Islam, founded in the 1930s.[106]

Another prominent Ahmadiyya figure from this decade embodying the rise of a new Kashmiri Muslim leadership was Moulvi Mohammad Nooruddin Qari Kashmiri (1894–1934). The son of a mullah of small means, Qari went on for higher education at the Punjab University, where he received the Munshi Alim degree. Since his father had come under the influence of the Ahmadiyya movement in the late nineteenth century, Qari decided to go to Qadian and was officially inducted into the sect after studying under Moulana Nooruddin, the leader of the movement. On his return to the Valley, Qari took up a position as Arabic teacher at the Government High School, Srinagar. Besides teaching, however, Qari wrote prolifically in Kashmiri, translating the

---

Survey)," in *Basharaat-E-Ahmadiyya, A Biannual International News Magazine of Ahmadiyya Anjuman Ishaat Islam, Lahore*, December 1996: 19–23.

[104] See chapters five and six.

[105] Tareen, "The Great Ahmadiyya Mosque," 19.

[106] Ibid., and based on an interview with Professor Zahid, Badgaam, Kashmir, April 29, 1998.

Quran and several Islamic juristic works into the language.[107] More importantly, however, he composed numerous poems which, though not of high literary quality, were read and recited by Kashmiris throughout the Valley. They relay a sense of the transformation of the Kashmiri Muslim leadership and the position of Islam within its agenda. Additionally, Qari gave an impetus to the indigenous publishing industry in Srinagar by printing his own works and, in the late 1920s, financially supporting the founding of the biggest publisher and bookseller in the Kashmir province, Ghulam Mohammad Noor Mohammad, who printed and sold his works, along with most other political, social, and religious tracts written during this period.[108]

Despite his short life, Qari had a tremendous impact on Kashmiri Muslims and their vision of Islam's role in their community. His simple and clear translations made Islam and its core texts more accessible to Kashmiris. In the work entitled *Hayat-ul-Nabi* (The Life of the Prophet), for instance, Qari discussed in detail the life history of the Prophet and included controversial issues from his life that were a part of the hadith. Significantly, he focused on issues that had relevance in the Kashmiri context, such as polygamy and the Shia–Sunni conflict over the will of the Prophet, designed to bring about consensus within the community.[109] In another major work entitled *Kashur Masal Kitab* (Book of Juristic Verdicts in Kashmiri),[110] Qari translated major juristic verdicts from the Hanafi school into Kashmiri so that Kashmiris could resolve religious issues in the community without referring to the *waizes* (preachers), who were, in Qari's view, responsible for the stagnation and disintegration of the Kashmiri Muslim community.

The verdicts discussed in this book were a response to the conflicts over legal issues among Kashmiri Muslims and sought to unite the community by compiling a corpus of Islamic law to replace the customs recently codified by the state. The first of its kind in the Kashmiri language, the book was divided into three sections: Beliefs; Worship

---

[107] Based on an interview with Qari's grandson, Moulana Mohammad Shafi Qari, Lal Bazaar, Srinagar, Kashmir, November 26, 1997.

[108] Based on an interview with Professor Zahid, Badgaam, Kashmir, May 5, 1998.

[109] Moulvi Mohammad Nooruddin Qari, *Hayat-ul-Nabi* [The Life of the Prophet] (Srinagar: Privately Printed, 1921).

[110] Qari, *Kashur Masal Kitab* [Book of Juristic Verdicts in Kashmiri], 2nd edn (Lahore: Rafiq-i-Am Press, 1929).

and Rituals; and Verdicts relating to issues in business, trade, agriculture, and so on. The popularity of the work can be gathered from the fact that four editions were published in the last century—1923, 1929, 1986 and 1993—in years that, significantly, coincide with great political upheaval in the Valley. Prominent Kashmiri Muslims of Srinagar hailed the book as a significant contribution to Islam in Kashmir, since it "rendered minute religious discourses comprehensible to all."[111] Qari aimed yet another book, *Kashur Haar Baghe*,[112] a translation of an Arabic text on the division of property according to the Hanafi school of jurisprudence, directly at Kashmiri Muslim agriculturists in an attempt to rid them of their dependence on customary law in questions of inheritance. Clearly, Qari had taken over the agenda of the religious leadership: to unite the community under the laws of Islam so that the divisive force of customary law could be relegated to the background.

In spite of the significance of his books, it was Qari's poetry that served as a vehicle for the transmission of his potent vision of Islam for the Kashmiri Muslim community. For Qari, Islam was not simply a vision of past glory and power, but rather a means for the attainment of material wealth, and ultimately, political sovereignty. Thus, although goading the Muslims to embrace Islam in its purity by rejecting the guidance of the waizes, Qari also expected Muslims to take control of their destinies, and unite with the aim of seizing political power. In one of his poems, he wrote:

> Look at the others, how united they are,
> Internal divisions do not rent them asunder.
> We have so many internal wars,
> That all our wealth is wasted on them.
> Muslims, awake to the reality!
> Awake and be united.
> Do not believe the blasphemous fatwas any longer,
> Attain victory on the creators of dissension and conflict. [113]

This particular verse, from the poem *Dard-i-Dil wa Haqiqat-i-Haal* (The Aching Heart and the Reality of the Situation), clearly aimed at

---

[111] Moulvi Mohammad Abdullah Vakil, "Review," in Qari, *Kashur Masal Kitab*, 35.

[112] Qari, *Kashur Haar Baghe* (Lahore: Karimi Press, 1926).

[113] Qari, *Dard-i-Dil wa Haqiqat-i-Haal*[The Aching Heart and the Reality of the Situation] (Srinagar: Privately Printed, 1922), 2.

effacing the divisions that had appeared among Kashmiri Muslims in the past few decades. Moreover, significantly, the verse conveys a sense of the existence of separate communities with distinct identities by pointing to the fact that while other communities stood united, the Muslim community was squandering its wealth and energy on frivolous conflicts.

Although not overtly articulated, the message was clear: other communities would continue to hold power unless the Muslim community shook off the leadership of preachers responsible for the disarray within its ranks. The acquisition of education was, in Qari's view, central to this project of unification, since it would not only enlighten Muslims, but also provide them with the tools to attain wealth on the road to political power.[114] Qari recognized that if Muslims were to take advantage of state educational and service quotas, directed towards a community now recognizable only in terms of its individual members' religious identification, they had to unite under the banner of Islam. Islam, the only unifying factor for Kashmiri Muslims otherwise divided along lines of locality, social status, class, and sect, could not be allowed to become a force of dissension. Religious unity, in his view, necessarily preceded the articulation of a political identity. Although Qari does reflect a sea change in the Kashmiri Muslim leadership's agenda, what makes his writings especially compelling is that they represent an individual Kashmiri Muslim's relationship to his religion and community. While anchored to the community, Qari clearly aimed to reconfigure its contours through his individual faith in the philosophy of the Ahmadiyyas.

It was for this reason, among others, that the religious leadership represented by the Mirwaiz of Jama Masjid did not appreciate Qari's ideas and were quick to label him a kafir who was misleading Muslims for his own ends. To this Qari responded:

> When kafirs have not yet become Muslim,
> Then how could a Muslim have become a kafir?
> All those who recite the Kalima,
> Are brothers like the *ansaars* of Medina.[115]

---

[114] See chapter four for a detailed discussion of Qari's role as an educator.

[115] The companions of the Prophet who migrated with him to Medina to escape persecution in Mecca.

Progress in harmony and brotherhood,
And fire itself will be turned into a garden of flowers.[116]

Qari's translation of the last section of the *Quran*, published in 1925,[117] generated particular consternation among religious leaders, and a decade later Mirwaiz Moulvi Yusuf Shah published his translation of the same section of the *Quran* with a critique of Qari's work. In the preface to this work, the Mirwaiz wrote:

> My grandfather [Mirwaiz Yahya Shah] was the first to translate the last chapter of the Holy *Quran* into Kashmiri because he wanted Kashmiri Muslims to learn about the book. There was no need for another translation of the chapter. Unfortunately, a member of the Ahmadiyya community published his own translation of the last chapter, using it as a vehicle for the propagation of his own beliefs. He changed the *Quran* to suit his own faith so that he could convert people to the Ahmadiyya sect.[118]

From the above it is clear that Ahmadiyyas represented a threat to the authority of the Mirwaiz, which he was not willing to countenance. Since the Mirwaiz of Jama Masjid was opposed to Ahmadiyyas, his traditional rivals, the Mirwaiz Hamdaani and his followers, fell on the side of the Ahmadiyyas.[119] The addition of a new character to antagonisms that had their origins in the 1880s exacerbated tensions, determining the contours of political factionalism among Kashmiri Muslims for the next two decades.

Apart from the impact it had on the leadership of the community, the Ahmadiyya influence on Kashmiri Muslims was apparent in more subtle ways during the 1920s. No discussion of this decade in the Indian subcontinent is complete without an examination of the Khilafat movement and its impact on the politics of the districts and states involved. Significantly, despite the preponderantly Muslim population in Kashmir, the Khilafat slogan did not seem to arouse the passions it did in other parts of British India and the native states. In 1919, the Resident in Kashmir wrote to the Political Secretary to the Government

[116] Qari, *Dard-i-Dil,* 2.

[117] Qari, *Kashur Tafsir* (Lahore: Rafiq-i-Am Press, 1925).

[118] Moulvi Mohammad Yusuf Shah, *Kashur Tafsir* (Amritsar: Sana-i-Barki Press, 1935), 2.

[119] Based on an interview with Shafi Qari, Srinagar, Kashmir, November 26, 1997.

of India that "The Muhammadan population of Kashmir appears as yet to evince but little interest in the welfare of Turkey and the consequences which must result from her entry into the war and her subsequent defeat. There is at present no cause for apprehension as far as the Kashmiri Moslems are concerned."[120] The indigenous religious leadership perceived the Khilafat issue as a further threat to their already embattled position in the Valley and actively opposed its proponents in Srinagar.[121] Furthermore, since the leadership that was beginning to take its place in the 1920s had Ahmadiyya leanings, it followed the lead of the Ahmadiyya movement in Punjab with its staunch loyalty to the British government during the Khilafat agitation.

This is not to suggest, however, that the Khilafat and non-cooperation movements raging in British India failed to have an impact on the Kashmiri political landscape. Government records make several references to the formation of a Khilafat Committee, Srinagar, in 1920 under the auspices of the Khilafat Committee, Lahore. However, that the government was not unduly concerned by the activities of this organization suggests that Kashmiri Muslims were not overly enthusiastic about the Khilafat cause. Moreover, the meetings that were held in the various localities of Srinagar in 1920 in an attempt to disseminate the ideas of Hindu–Muslim unity and fraternization among the Kashmiri population were not organized under the auspices of the Khilafat cause. Instead, they were largely organized by Kashmiri Pandits who had recently returned from British India and believed that Kashmiris should unite to counteract the effects of skyrocketing food prices through a social reformation of their communities. The Muslims who did join these meetings lamented the apathy of the general population to their cause and exhorted Kashmiri Muslims to join hands with Pandits and sacrifice meat-eating and wasteful expenditure, and observe economy in relation to their daily expenses. While the speakers at these meetings did not voice opposition to the Maharaja or the British government, they did publicly propose the importance of Kashmiri "national" unification to further social causes.[122]

[120] "Lt. Col. Bannerman to Political Secretary to Government of India in the Foreign and Political Department," Foreign and Political Department R/1/19/667/1921, India Office Library and Records, London (microfilm), 4.

[121] The Mirwaiz of Jama Masjid announced to his congregation that the Khilafat agitation held no meaning for the Muslims of Kashmir. See Khan, *Freedom Movement in Kashmir*, 84.

[122] Political Department 209/45-C/1920, Jammu State Archives.

Much like in the rest of British India, by the mid-1920s the political atmosphere of Kashmir was characterized by the articulation of antagonistic communitarian identities. This development was strengthened by the efforts of the state toward endowing the two communities with separate political identities in the previous decades. The granting of full powers to Maharaja Pratap Singh in 1923 and his declaration of an impending representative assembly[123] further emphasized the importance of formulating well-defined community identities. In the same year, the appointment of a committee by the state to present the definition of State Subject meant that Kashmiris would be given a fair opportunity to enter state service.[124] Raja Hari Singh, Senior and Foreign Member of Council, notified all officers of the state that "in future no non-state subject shall be appointed to any position in the Jammu and Kashmir State, without the express approval of His Highness in Council . . ."[125] The solidification of separate political identities in this period was by no means limited to Kashmir, since constitutional changes in British India, such as the Morley–Minto and Monatgu–Chelmsford reforms, had produced similar results in British Indian politics.

* * *

The early twentieth century had set the stage for the emergence of a public discourse on identities that utilized religion as a political tool while attempting to transcend its "communal" component. By the 1920s, as the influence of the religious leadership receded from the political arena, there emerged an educated, professional leadership that demanded more than simply rights to preach at shrines and educational opportunities for the Muslim community. This new leadership, with a firm basis of support in the Kashmiri Muslims settled in the Punjab, the financial backing of the influential Ahmadiyya community, the belief in the mobilizational power of Islam as the means to material and political sovereignty, and Srinagar as the center of operations, was able to consolidate the Kashmiri Muslim community more effectively than ever before. Although included in the political agenda of the new

[123] General Department 103/1923, Jammu State Archives.
[124] General Department 14/1923, Jammu State Archives.
[125] General Department 213/1923, Jammu State Archives.

leadership, the community was not necessarily united, however. The political and economic changes of the 1930s, combined with the agenda of the new leadership, brought forth stark cleavages that had divided the Muslim community in the previous decades—now these were translated and appropriated into political factions. Most significantly, the leadership of the 1930s and 1940s articulated a vision of Kashmiri nationhood, not only in the context of the shifting communitarian identities in the Valley, but also the discourse of Indian nationalism in British India.

CHAPTER 4

Education, Class, Language, and Identity

I n this chapter, I approach the relationship between narratives on
Kashmiri Muslim identities, definitions of class, issues of language, and the Dogra state's political agenda at the turn of the twentieth century from the perspective of the discourse on education in the
Kashmir Valley. The focus on improving the educational status of
Kashmiri Muslims provided the religious leadership with a concrete
agenda to consolidate its position with the community. At the same
time, its engagement with the Dogra state on this issue infused an economic and political component into the ostensibly religious narrative
on identities that characterized the political culture of this period. By
the third decade of the twentieth century, the leaders and then the
beneficiaries of educational reform movements in the Kashmir Valley
battled for political supremacy and the right to define religious, regional, and national identities.

Most scholarship on the British Indian educational system focuses
either on the system as a hegemonic device created by the colonial state
to control its Indian subjects,[1] or on educational institutions as the key
to the development of Indian nationalism and "political consciousness."[2] In the Kashmir case, there is no evidence to suggest that the

---

[1] See Gauri Viswanathan, *Masks of Conquest: Literary Study and British Rule in
India* (New York: Columbia University Press, 1989), and to a lesser extent, Nita
Kumar, *Lessons from Schools: The History of Education in Banaras* (New Delhi:
Sage Publications, 2000), for a detailed discussion of this perspective.

[2] There are numerous works on this issue, including Krishna Kumar, *Political
Agenda of Education: A Study of Colonialist and Nationalist Ideas* (New Delhi: Sage,
1991); Suresh Chandra Ghosh, *Indian Nationalism: A Case Study for the First
University Reform by the British Raj* (New Delhi: Vikas Publishing House, 1985);

Dogra state, while borrowing heavily from colonial rhetoric and ideology on education, was at all invested in educating its Kashmiri subjects with a view to either producing a class to help run its administration,
or inculcating in Kashmiris the notions of citizenship and national
identity. However, since the educational system was drawn, willy
nilly, into the ongoing centralization of the state machinery prompted
by British intervention, and since the colonials also insisted on mass
education, the Dogra state could not but delineate an educational
agenda.

The state's fumbling attempts to articulate its policies for the education of its Kashmiri subjects, and the ambivalent nature of the
content of this enterprise, determined to some extent the Kashmiri
Muslim leadership's educational program. But, more importantly, the
Muslim leadership's rhetoric on education, language, class, and government employment, in turn, had an impact on the educational and
other policies of the Dogra state toward its Muslim subjects. Thus, it
would be erroneous to view the Dogra state's education system simply
as a means of hegemonic control over the Kashmiri population. Instead, the system and the discourse generated by it were key aspects of
a rapidly changing social, economic and political context that involved
the reconstitution of the state as well as Muslim community identities
in a dialectical process.

Aparna Basu, *The Growth of Education and Political Development in India, 1898–
1920* (Delhi: Oxford University Press, 1974); and for Kashmir, Hari Om, *Muslims of Jammu and Kashmir: A Study in the Spread of Education and Consciousness,
1857–1925* (New Delhi: Archives Publishers, 1986). A select few works have
related education to questions of occupation, class, language, religious identity
and social status, producing a more complex picture of the ground realities of
education in colonial India. For instance, although Nita Kumar's work does make
a general argument for the hegemonic and homogenizing nature of the colonial
educational enterprise, it also very effectively relates education to issues of class,
gender, occupation and technologies of social production. For other works, see
Narayani Gupta, *Delhi Between Two Empires, 1803-1931: Society, Government,
and Urban Growth* (Delhi: Oxford University Press, 1981), chapter 4; Ayesha
Jalal, *Self and Sovereignty*, chapter 3; and for postcolonial India, Suzanne Hoeber
Rudolph and Lloyd I. Rudolph, eds., *Education and Politics in India: Studies in
Organization, Society, and Policy* (Cambridge: Harvard University Press, 1972).

Education and the Dogra State, 1846–1889

Akin to pre-colonial systems of education in India and pre-national educational systems in Europe, indigenous Kashmiri education in the early nineteenth century was firmly rooted in the diverse traditions of communities, localities, castes and religious traditions. Nita Kumar describes education in eighteenth-century Banaras as a system where "we see the instance par excellence of heterogeneity, with patronage of a variety of institutions and systems of teaching; of political coexistence and tolerance between them; and of a discursive assumption of the legitimacy of multifarious learning practices."[3] In Kashmir, pandits and moulvis imparted education to local Hindu and Muslim boys in pathshalas and madrasas. These institutions, inextricably bound to temples and mosques, respectively, were run through community support and imparted basic religious and mathematical education to students.[4]

Other educational institutions in the Valley included indigenous schools in the houses of pandits who taught Persian to both Hindu and Muslim boys in return for a fee of two to four annas a month, depending on what parents could afford. The education imparted in such institutions followed the traditional system of Persian education whereby students were taught the alphabet, easy stories, and then Persian classics such as the *Bostan* and *Gulistan*, without necessarily mastering their content. The ordinary student would finish his course with the *Hurkaram* and *Sikandarnama*, and those with a desire to go further would memorize *Sakinama*, *Shirin Khusroo* and other such legendary works. Letter writing, calligraphy and a little arithmetic were also taught in these schools.[5] Education was intermeshed with the structures and functions of caste groups, religious sects, and localities.

The early Dogra rulers, placed at the head of the newly established

---

[3] Kumar, *Lessons from Schools,* 14.

[4] C.E. Tyndale Biscoe, *Kashmir in Sunlight and Shade: A Description of the Beauties of the Country, the Life, Habits, and Humor of its Inhabitants and an Account of the Gradual but Steady Rebuilding of a Once Down-trodden people* (London: Seeley, Service & Co. Limited, 1922), 253.

[5] Charles Girdlestone, *Memorandum on Cashmere and Adjacent Territories* (Calcutta: Foreign Department Press, 1874).

state of Jammu and Kashmir, did not intervene in the indigenous educational system. Gulab Singh, the first Dogra Maharaja, was too busy consolidating his dominions to pay much attention to the educational status of his subjects. His successor, Maharaja Ranbir Singh, was the first to take an active interest in education. The system of education that prevailed under his rule continued to be dictated by indigenous functional concerns, although Ranbir Singh encouraged religious education through a study of classical languages—Persian, Arabic and Sanskrit. However, in keeping with the religious tenor of his rule, Ranbir Singh's ultimate aim was to spread classical Hindu learning among his Dogra subjects. Thus, the shrine he consecrated to the worship of Rama, known as the Raghunath Temple, became a center of classical Sanskrit learning where several hundred Brahmin pupils were trained in various branches of Sanskrit scholarship. The Raghunath Temple institution also housed a translation department where moulvis helped translate Arabic and Persian works on philosophy and history into Sanskrit and a staff of pandits translated the whole range of the Dharamashastras into Hindi and Dogri.[6] According to Sir Aurel Stein, this was done in "order to facilitate the exchange of ideas which the Maharaja in a spirit of true enlightenment desired to promote between the representatives of Hindu and Mohammedan scholarship in his dominions."[7] Additionally, the Ain-i-Dharmarth provided for the maintenance of six hundred students in various temples of the state.[8] Education, as envisaged by Ranbir Singh, was to be the sole preserve of the ruling class and religious elite.

In principle, however, Ranbir Singh believed in providing education for all classes of his subjects and made feeble attempts at founding a few state-supported institutions. The darbar opened two schools in Srinagar, one for teaching Sanskrit to Kashmiri Pandits and the other for teaching Arabic to Kashmiri Muslims.[9] By 1872, there were five state-supported institutions in Srinagar—Madrasa Nava Kadal, Madrasa Maharaj Gunj, Madrasa Rainawari, Madrasa Basant Bagh and Madrasa

[6] Sufi, *Kashir*, vol. II, 790–1.

[7] Aurel Stein, *Catalogue of the Sanskrit Manuscripts in the Raghu Natha Temple Library of His Highness, the Maharaja of Jammu and Kashmir* (London: Luzac, 1900; repr., Bombay: Nirnaya-Sagara Press, 1983), vi.

[8] Sufi, *Kashir*, vol. II, 791.

[9] Om, *Muslims of Jammu and Kashmir*, 21.

Aishakol, with students numbering 192, 68, 71, 54 and 51 respectively.[10] The number of educational institutions in the entire state in 1872–3 remained at 44.[11] Apart from meager government funding to educational institutions,[12] there was no concerted effort on the part of the state to promote education among the mass of the population, which, far removed from the scholarly activities of the Dogra court, continued its involvement in community- and caste-based educational institutions. In fact, the government was opposed to the school established by the Christian Missionary Society in Srinagar in 1880, which had only five pupils.[13] It is obvious that in this period the state did not consider education either its responsibility or a priority.

Education, the Dogra State, and Kashmiri Muslims, 1889–1915

The education system of the state of Jammu and Kashmir underwent a dramatic shift with the deposition of Maharaja Pratap Singh from the throne in 1889 and the establishment of the British Residency and State Council to direct the affairs of the princely state. Education became a central component of the state's drive toward centralization and bureaucratization along the lines of British India. Along with bringing the education system under its purview, however, the state found itself responsible for the education of its subjects, most of whom were Muslim. I suggest here that since the Dogra state was ill-equipped and unwilling to take on this responsibility, its educational policies in this period were fraught with ambivalence toward mass education in general and Muslim education in particular. At the same time, the response of the Kashmiri Muslim leadership to the Dogra state's halting attempts at articulating its philosophy of education is useful in

[10] Sayyid Mohammad Farooq Bukhari, *Kashmir me Arbi Sher wa Adab ki Tarikh* [The History of Arabic Poetry and Literature in Kashmir] (Srinagar: Jammu and Kashmir Academy of Art, Culture and Languages, 1993), 56.

[11] *Gulab Bhawan Research Series*, vol. I (Jammu, 1979), 5.

[12] The administration report of 1873 mentions the existence of state schools only in the city of Srinagar, where state expenditure on education amounted to Rs 36,372. See *Administration Report of Jammu and Kashmir State, 1873*, 114.

[13] *Proceedings of the Christian Missionary Society in Africa and Asia for the year 1884–85* (London, 1885), 122.

gauging the ways in which the contours of the emergent public discourse on Kashmiri Muslim identities was shaped within the political framework provided by the state.

The Dogra state's policies in the field of education in the late nineteenth century can only be understood in terms of the British colonial project of education. Education had become central to the project of colonialism in British India by the early nineteenth century. If the empire that had already been won by the urban bourgeoisie had to be preserved for profit, then the dominant groups in Indian society had to be included in the colonial enterprise. This involved the creation of a civil society among the natives and their inculcation into the ethos, rules and symbols of the new order, which could only be achieved through education. Education thus had a significant role to play in the transformation of a commercial institution into a colonial state.[14] As C.A. Bayly has pointed out, the English East India Company had attempted to do this through a mixture of military domination and political suasion. The changes in the educational system introduced in the early nineteenth century were part of this process. For instance, Persian was abolished in official correspondence in 1835 and the government's weight was thrown behind English-medium education.[15]

At the same time, the idea of different types of education for different classes came to define the British educational system in India. As propounded by J.S. Mill and Macaulay, the elite would gain Western education through the English language and the rest of the population would be consigned to studying their own languages, while receiving Western ideas from the elite through "downward filtration."[16] Entrusted as it was in the hands of Indians of status and wealth, education was also supposed to be the chief agency for accomplishing the great moral agenda of colonialism: the eventual conversion of natives to Christianity, since Englishmen governing India were deeply concerned with the development of character.[17] Ironically, Western education became, in time, a symbol of secularism for many among the Indian elite.[18] And, this elite, which not only became a strong arm of

[14] Kumar, *Political Agenda of Education*, 24–6.

[15] Bayly, *Indian Society and the Making of the British Empire*, 122.

[16] Viswanathan, *Masks of Conquest*, 149.

[17] Kumar, *Political Agenda of Education*, 34, and Rudolph and Rudolph, eds., *Education and Politics*, 16.

[18] Kumar, *Political Agenda of Education*, 39.

the colonial government, but also its most stringent critic by the late nineteenth century, was to become one of the important products of the colonial educational system in India.

Lord Curzon's viceroyalty marked a turning point in the government's education policy, coming as it did after the openly anti-British atmosphere of 1897,[19] which British officials perceived as being a direct result of English education. Curzon presented education as more than an intellectual demand in India, being socially and politically important for the natives. According to him, in India "education was required not primarily as the instrument of culture or the source of learning, but as the key to employment, the condition of all national advance and prosperity and the sole stepping stone for every class of the community to higher things."[20] However, privately he admitted that "our system of higher education in India is a failure; it has sacrificed the formation of character upon the altar of cram; and the Indian University turns out only a discontented horde of office-seekers, whom we have educated for places which are not in existence for them to fill."[21] To address these flaws, he reiterated the policy of government intervention in education and pushed for the central control of a planned education system. Despite his idealistic rhetoric, thus, his policies aimed to protect educational institutions, particularly universities, from the "baleful influences of the ambitious and politically interested Indians."[22] The colonial state seemed unable to reconcile its educational, language, and employment policies in the various provinces of British India.

[19] This atmosphere was clearly visible in Poona, where Bal Gangadhar Tilak and other leaders had launched a bitter attack on the government's anti-plague policies. This ultimately resulted in the murder of Col. Rand, the Collector and Plague Commissioner of Poona, on June 22, 1897. The assassins were subsequently tried and executed. Tilak was accused of sedition and sentenced to eighteen months' imprisonment.

[20] Quoted in Basu, *Growth of Education*, 6.

[21] Quoted in Ghosh, *Indian Nationalism*, 25. The view that the colonial educational system in India had proven to be inadequate and unsatisfactory was widely held in early-twentieth-century England, particularly among educators. This perspective is expounded on at length in Leonard Alston, *Education and Citizenship in India* (London: Longmans, Green, and Co., 1910). Alston was director of non-collegiate studies in economics and history, Cambridge University, and had served as temporary professor at Elphinstone College, Bombay.

[22] Rudolph and Rudolph, eds., *Education and Politics*, 17.

Once the British had de facto taken over the administration of Jammu and Kashmir, the state government could no longer follow a policy of non-intervention in matters of education. The crucial difference, however, was that in Kashmir the main reason behind the education of native subjects in British India—the creation of a class among the elite that could help with the task of administering the vast country—did not exist; and, having learnt from the experience of their colonial masters, the Dogras did not intend abetting the emergence of such a class either. In the late nineteenth century, when this class was already well entrenched in British India, the Jammu and Kashmir state simply imported these individuals to run its growing bureaucracy. As P.N. Bazaz so scathingly put it: "Armies of outsiders trailed behind the officers from the plains with no more interest than to draw as much as they could, and then to depart leaving behind their kindred as successors to continue the drain; and thus was established a hierarchy in the services with the result that profits and wealth passed into the hands of the outsiders."[23]

The replacement of Persian with Urdu in 1889 as the court language and subsequently as the language of administration, further justified the import of Punjabis into the state administration. That the government did not intend creating a class of people to administer the state is clear from the State Council's opinion that mere literary education without a technical component "only serves to create a class of discontented candidates for clerical duties whose aspirations the State cannot afford to meet."[24] As late as 1909, the Resident in Kashmir, Sir Francis Younghusband, was to admit to the Secretary to the Government of India in the Foreign Department that there was a distinct tendency among these officials of the state to "secure Kashmir not for the Kashmiris, still less for the British, but for the Punjabis and other Indians."[25] This would have far-reaching consequences for the cause of Kashmiri as the medium of instruction in schools as well as the language of state administration.

[23] Bazaz, *The History of the Struggle for Freedom in Kashmir*, 135.
[24] *Administration Report of Jammu and Kashmir State, 1893–94*, 46.
[25] Sir Francis Younghusband, "Confidential Note on Kashmir Affairs for 1907–8," Foreign Department R/1/19/358, July 1908, India Office Library, London (microfilm).

As a result of the import of Punjabis into the state administration, there was a lack of urgency in the state's efforts at promoting education among local Kashmiris. Claiming a stringency of funds, the State Council did not carry out educational reforms in the first few years of its rule, though it did recognize the need for formalizing and centralizing the system of education in the state.[26] As early as 1889, Pt. Bhimshember Nath, Inspector Schools, recommended to the State Council that maktabs and pathshalas be brought under the purview of the department of education.[27] By the beginning of the twentieth century, the state had already introduced important reforms that would begin the process of state regulation of the educational system. Rules regarding the duties of inspecting officers were framed and introduced, the question of constituting Jammu as a center for high school examinations was successfully settled, and a uniform standard of tuition and admission fees was adopted for all secondary schools in the state.[28]

There were a few weak attempts by the state at expanding educational institutions in this period. The administration reports of 1890–1 noted the lack of proper school buildings and methods of teaching in the mofassil and the need for opening more primary schools. A few primary schools were established by the state in this period, with the number rising from 8 to 31 during 1891–2.[29] There was a corresponding increase in the number of students in town and village schools from 836 in 1889–90 to 4,214 in 1892–3.[30] The Council also took steps to encourage private enterprise to promote education. Bhag Ram, the Home and Judicial member-in-charge of the state education department, went to the extent of appealing to the private purses of the

[26] The growth and centralization of bureaucracies was one of the most widespread processes in most princely states subsequent to British intervention in their political structures. Furthermore, just as the Dogra state's bureaucracy was composed of Hindus imported from the Punjab—since the Dogra rulers continued to draw their legitimacy from this region—bureaucracies in most princely states were manned by people loyal to the Maharajas. See Jeffrey, *People, Princes and Paramount Power*, 18–20.

[27] "Information on Education in Kashmir," Vernacular Records 194/1957, Jammu State Archives.

[28] *Triennial Administration Report of Jammu and Kashmir State, 1901–4*, 556.

[29] *Administration Report of Jammu and Kashmir State, 1890–1*, 99.

[30] *Administration Report of Jammu and Kashmir State, 1892–3*, 72.

Maharaja, the Resident, the rajas, members of the council and other notables to "prove very liberal in putting our hands in our pockets for subscribing to education." He intended to use this money "in providing poor, deserving students with scholarships, fees, and so forth."[31] Even so, private institutions were growing at a much faster rate than public educational institutions in this period. For instance, while the number of public institutions for males and females between 1901–4 increased by 24, the number of private institutions increased by 75 in the same period.[32]

By the early twentieth century, however, the state began to present itself as the promoter of education among all its subjects. Translated into actual government policy, this meant the rapid creation and consolidation of a state educational bureaucracy. School curricula in the state were reorganized along the lines of the Punjab University syllabus and affiliated to the university. As a result, the Kashmiri language was relegated to the background in all educational and administrative matters, even by the Kashmiri Muslim leadership. Maharaja Pratap Singh endowed an arts college in Jammu to commemorate the visit of the Prince of Wales in 1905. The state set up a Normal School in Srinagar in 1906, increased the number of scholarships to the middle and high departments of schools, and opened girls' schools in several parts of the state. The darbar also instituted a number of college scholarships for Kashmiris to study in Lahore. Dr Annie Besant started a Hindu College in Srinagar in 1905, which was taken over by the government in 1911 and renamed Sri Pratap College. The darbar even began to recognize the need to encourage education among Muslims of the Valley and sanctioned scholarships for Muslim boys studying in Srinagar High School, while also appointing an Arabic teacher for the school.[33] The *1910–11 Note on Education* proudly proclaimed the existence of 2 colleges, 5 high schools, 24 middle schools, 172 primary schools, 8 girls' schools and 1 teachers' training school in the state.[34] By the second decade of the century education had become one of the most telling symptoms of the growing centralization of the Jammu and

[31] Ibid.

[32] *Triennial Administration Report of Jammu and Kashmir State, 1901–4,* 563.

[33] "Note on the State of Education in Jammu and Kashmir State," Education Department 7/17EM/1906–11, Jammu State Archives.

[34] Ibid.

Kashmir state bureaucracy, and of a greater economic and political integration of the state with British India.

By 1907 it had become clear that the state was lagging behind in developing schemes to impart education to the vast majority of its subjects, since it considered education to be the preserve of the elite. The British Resident, Sir Francis Younghusband, had impressed on the foreign minister the need for improving the educational department of the state with a view to extending education.[35] Furthermore, he asked the future educational conference to suggest the best type of education to be given to various classes.[36] As a result, the review of educational policy in 1907 emphasized the need to provide education to the whole cross-section of the population. And, in a statement that best exemplified the liberal British view of different types of education for different classes in society, the Maharaja proclaimed that mass education could be accomplished only if—

> Instruction is as obviously useful and helpful as food, clothing and fresh air, and the aim should be to make everyone fit for some definite calling in life, to give each the opportunity of developing himself to the fullest, to make the agricultural class better agriculturists, the merchant class good businessmen, the artisans useful handicraftsman, the fighting class brave soldiers, the ruling class efficient governors and the intellectual class thinkers and writers. The ancient should retain the glory of the ancient civilization with all the old manliness, courtliness, charity and respect for parents and for authority and add to it the thoroughness, energy and scientific, practical and public spirit of the present day.[37]

The Dogra state seemed to have imported the British Indian administrative structure for its educational system along with its ideological content.

The state's acceptance of the idea that education should be restricted to the upper tier in society is reflected in the education minister's negative response to the Maharaja's directive that he draw up a scheme for free and compulsory primary education in the state. The education minister rejected the idea of primary education on the grounds that such a measure would be seen as tyrannical by the majority of the

[35] Political Department 101/P-102/1907, Jammu State Archives.

[36] Old English Records 279/1907, Jammu State Archives.

[37] "Note by Daya Kishen Kaul," Private Secretary to Maharaja, dated August 26, 1907, Private Records of His Highness 279/1907, Jammu State Archives.

Kashmiri population, which was not aware of the duties of citizenship. The minister stated that if the wage-earning children of uneducated parents were forced into schools, the parents would consider it "zoolum" (tyranny) and in the absence of public-spirited men to explain the benefits of such a measure to the public, it should not be undertaken by the state.[38] According to the state, then, it was not the responsibility of the government to educate the Kashmiri population or inculcate in them the duties of citizenship, but for community leaders to encourage education among members of their respective communities. In the matter of state educational policy in this period, it is clear that the Dogra state did not conceive of Kashmiris as citizens and did not intend to make them citizens of the state through education.[39]

In response to the idea of compulsory primary education, the Inspector of Schools suggested that Meghs and Dooms, low-caste Kashmiri Muslims, should not for the present be required to send their boys to school.[40] The Headmaster of the Hindu High School, Srinagar, articulated the state's concerns on mass education in more concrete terms. Expressing dislike for the fact of upper-class Hindu and Muslim boys studying alongside those of lower classes, he suggested that schools be classified according to the classes of subjects living in Srinagar:

> The Hindus and the high-class Mussulmans will not like to see their children learn a profession while surrounded by the other Mussulman children, at least for some time till these come up to the standard of Hindu children or the children of high class Mussalmans . . . It is not at all desirable that the children of the Hanjis [boatmen] and sweepers and the like should be allowed to mix with other children.[41]

[38] Old English Records 101/P-102/1907, Jammu State Archives.

[39] That the Kashmiris were not "citizens" of the Dogra state is obvious from the denial of civil, political and social rights to them by the state. T.H. Marshall's influential work argues that "the right to education is a genuine social right of citizenship . . . Fundamentally it should be regarded, not as the right of the child to go to school, but as the right of the adult citizen to have been educated." See T.H. Marshall, *Class, Citizenship and Social Development, Essays by T.H. Marshall* (Connecticut: Greenwood Press, 1973), 81–2.

[40] "Scheme for Imparting Education to the Masses in Kashmir," Political Department 101/P-102/1907, Jammu State Archives.

[41] Ibid. In 1891, the percentage of Hanjis to the Muslim population was approximately 4.47 per cent, most of whom lived in and around Srinagar. See Lawrence, *Valley of Kashmir*, 313.

The issue at hand, clearly, was one of class rather than religious affiliation, since the elite of both communities was expected to and did gain an education. Tellingly, at this stage, the state discourse on education rarely focused on the backwardness of Kashmiri Muslims in education. In the following years, however, the state was forced to recognize the fact that there was a congruence between class and religious affiliation, since most agriculturists were uneducated Kashmiri Muslims while most administrators were educated Punjabi Hindus, and to a lesser extent Kashmiri Pandits.

The state did not intend to keep the lower classes uneducated, however. It was interested in imparting to them a different type of education. Punjabi officials who ran the state saw no need for educated Kashmiris threatening their hold on the meticulously controlled bureaucracy. They did, however, feel the need for economic returns on their educational reform policies. This was possible only if technical education was imparted to the agriculturists and artisans with a view to making them more efficient in their respective occupations. In discussing the subject of technical education in 1893–4, the State Council had expressed the opinion that, "in the best interests of the country and the people," steps should be taken to "encourage technical education, because mere primary or high literary education unattended by technical instruction was to the agriculturist a curse rather than a blessing . . . It literally incapacitates him to follow his occupation."[42] By 1908, Amar Nath, the Foreign and Education Minister, gave a more ringing endorsement to technical education for the same reasons: "Unless," he said, "the spread of technical education and study is given its proper place in the scheme of education in the state, the department will omit out of its programme of reform one of the most important items for converting the subjects of the state into useful citizens and thriving businessmen."[43] Since citizenship was a hollow concept for the Dogra state—with its sole focus on the duties of the subjects toward the state but devoid of a guarantee of political and social rights to them—the Kashmiri lower classes had to remain satisfied with technical and vocational training, which was not formalized until the establishment of the Amar Singh Technical School, Srinagar, in 1914.[44]

[42] *Administration Report of Jammu and Kashmir State, 1893–94*, 46.
[43] Old English Records 147/W/202/1908, Jammu State Archives.
[44] Om, *Muslims of Jammu and Kashmir*, 64.

The state's focus on class in defining the role of education in Kashmiri society meant that the majority of the Kashmiri Muslim population remained uneducated in this period. Even at the beginning of 1910, there were only 15 educated Muslim males as compared to 453 Hindu males per thousand of population in the Jhelum Valley.[45] By the census of 1921, this number had jumped to a mere 19 for Muslims, while going up to 508 for Hindus.[46] Even among the few Muslim literates in the Valley, the largest number was of the Babazadas, or the mullahs and pirs, the traditionally educated caste among the Muslims of Kashmir who were associated with shrines and mosques across Kashmir.[47] This caste remained disgruntled because the new system of education was unable to absorb the increasing numbers of the unemployed within its ranks, resulting from a fall in the numbers of makhtabs in this period.[48] The second most educated caste among Kashmiri Muslims was the Sheikhs, i.e. the converts from Hinduism at the time of the advent of Islam.[49] The Muslim agricultural castes had no representative among the educated in the Census of 1911. Kashmiri Pandits were the most educated social group in the Valley, and the state as a whole. The Census of 1911 explained away the lack of literacy among the Muslims of Kashmir by stating that education did not hold any value for the Kashmiri Muslim agricultural classes, who formed the majority of this community and who "would rather retain their children for cattle-grazing, crop-watching and other agricultural pursuits than send them to school."[50] A folk saying among the Muslim agricultural castes was used to sum up their attitude toward education: "Education brings ruin. It is by ploughing that a good living can be ensured."[51]

Nevertheless, the number crunching by census operations in Kashmir served to bring into the limelight the "backwardness" of Kashmiri

[45] Khan, *Census of India, 1911, Vol. xx, Kashmir, Part I, Report,* 169.

[46] Mohammad, *Census of India, 1921, Vol. xxii, Kashmir, Part I, Report,* 121.

[47] Khan, *Census of India, 1911, Vol. xx, Kashmir, Part I, Report,* 163.

[48] The Census of 1911, while lamenting the marginal diffusion of education in the state, stated that one of the ways in which the state could introduce primary education of a truly popular type would be by employing the services of village mullahs and pirs. See ibid., 167.

[49] Ibid., 170.

[50] Ibid., 167

[51] Quoted in Om, *Muslims of Jammu and Kashmir,* 82.

Muslims in the field of education, among other areas, this being a re-
curring theme in colonial discourse on Muslims of British India since
the 1871 publication of W.W. Hunter's *The Indian Musalmans*.[52]
Walter R. Lawrence, settlement commissioner, performed a similar
role in the Kashmiri context through his book, *The Valley of Kashmir*,
first published in 1895, in which he expounded at length on the dismal
condition of Kashmiri Muslims and their exploitation by Kashmiri
Pandits.[53] In the context of early-twentieth-century Kashmir, where
social change threatened to dislodge the Muslim elite, the emergence
of this idea on the political landscape provided them with a sound
pretext for regaining their foothold in the community as well as the
political arena. Furthermore, the emergent Kashmiri Muslim leadership,
precisely from the classes that were losing out in the new political structure due to their lack of English education, recognized the need for
promoting the educational interests of the Muslim community as a
whole. It was clear to them that the indigenous system of education
was no longer enough if Muslims were to be integrated into the state
system of education, and ultimately state government.

The time was certainly ripe for the moral and educational reform
of Kashmiri Muslims, particularly given the increasing interest exhibited
by Punjabi Muslim organizations in their social condition. As I said
earlier, Mirwaiz Rasool Shah claimed leadership of the Kashmiri
Muslim community through his activities on the educational front,
founding the first reform association for Kashmiri Muslims, with an
affiliated school. Founded in 1889 with the financial assistance of emi-
nent Punjabi Muslims, the Anjuman Nusrat-ul-Islam—literally meaning the Society for the Victory of Islam—sought to unite the Kashmiri
Muslim community around the concept of tawhid, or the unity of
Allah. The Anjuman opened its doors to all Muslim sects, to cleanse
the Kashmiri Muslim community of its "un-Islamic" aspects. A madrasa was soon attached to the Anjuman with a view to improving the
lot of the Kashmiri Muslim population through pure Islamic education.

[52] W.W. Hunter, *The Indian Musalmans* (first published 1871, repr., Delhi:
Indological Book House, 1969).

[53] Apart from exposition, Lawrence also cited statistics to prove his points: In
the year 1891–2, out of a total population of 757,433 Muslims, only 233 were
being educated in state institutions, while out of a total population of 52,576
Hindus, 1,327 were receiving state instruction. See Lawrence, *The Valley of
Kashmir*, 228–9.

The aim of the school until the early years of the twentieth century was to provide its students with a traditional Islamic education in order to create a class of religious leaders who would guide the community on the path of pure Islam. The traditional syllabus of the school, with an emphasis on Arabic and Persian to facilitate memorization of the *Quran*, bears testimony to this goal.[54] Within a few years of the foundation of the Madrasa Anjuman Nusrat-ul-Islam similar moves were made by heads of various shrines to establish schools. For instance, the *sajjadanashin* (spiritual head) of the Khanqah-i-Mualla Shrine, Pir Yusuf Shah Khanqahi, helped found a school in the courtyard of the shrine, which was also dedicated to furthering religious education among Kashmiri Muslims.[55]

The political and economic needs of the time, however, dictated that these institutions alter their nature and project. Although the Madrasa Anjuman Nusrat-ul-Islam was turning out mullahs with an ability to recite the *Quran* in good numbers, none of them was literate in Urdu, the language of administration. State schools needed teachers who could teach a variety of subjects in Urdu, while the mullahs were trained in Arabic and Persian.[56] As a result, Moulvi Rasool Shah reorganized the madrasa along the lines of Anjuman-i-Himayat-i-Islam, Lahore, and a new building was constructed for it in 1901. Munshi Mahboob Alam, editor of *Paisa Akhbar*, Lahore, and Hakim Mohammad Ali Lahori raised Rs 400 for the school, and finally the Maharaja of Baroda came forward with Rs 2000 for the repayment of the building loan. A few years later, in 1905, the madrasa, now renamed the Islamia School, became a recipient of state grant-in-aid and was converted to a high school in 1912. The school provided a course of study that included a firm grounding in Islamic theology along with a study of secular subjects. The Mirwaiz Hamdaani, not to be outdone, also transformed the syllabus of the Khanqah-i-Mualla school to include both English and religious education.[57]

The Muslim leadership's vision for the Kashmiri Muslim community in this period is reminiscent of the European Enlightenment ideal of

[54] *Halat wa Rouidad*, Annual Report of the Convocation of the Madrasa Anjuman Nusrat-ul-Islam (Lahore: Hindustan Steam Press, 1913), 2.

[55] Sadaat, *Jannat-ul-Duniya*, 34, and Sadaat, *Rozana Diary*, 618.

[56] General Department 1609/E-17/1923, Jammu State Archives.

[57] Sadaat, *Jannat-ul-Duniya*, 55.

progress through the moral uplift of society. This vision re-created the dichotomy characteristic of colonial as well as Indian nationalist discourse: a morally superior teacher and a society whose character was in need of reform. The task of reforming society entailed not only making Kashmiri Muslims aware of their inadequacies, but also awakening them to the benefits of modern education, which was an inextricable component of a truly Islamic unified society. The aims and objectives of the Madrasa Anjuman Nusrat-ul-Islam shed light on the twin agenda of the Muslim leadership of this period: "to ensure religious and worldly education for Muslim children who are backward in education" and "to create an aptitude for reforms, social awakening and mutual unity amongst the Muslim community."[58]

The Mirwaiz leadership subscribed to the vision of the Islamic period in Kashmiri history as the ideal, when illiteracy was allegedly unknown. It was during this period that the Muslim community, united under an Islamic authority, attained the zenith of civilization and made Kashmir the envy of the world. Most speeches delivered at annual convocations of the school hearkened back to this Islamic period in Kashmiri history when it was a center of learning and scholarship.[59] In his speech to the annual convocation, the general secretary of the Anjuman lamented the march of time that had transformed Kashmir from a land dedicated to patronizing Persian and Indian masters of art and letters to a poor country with an illiterate population of Muslims. Both natural and political calamities, in his view, had played their part in plunging this paradise on earth into the darkness of illiteracy.[60] The leadership had made the period of Islamic rule in Kashmir synonymous with a high level of education among Kashmiri Muslims and subsequent periods with illiteracy and ignorance. Needless to point out that, even in the Islamic period, education had been the preserve of the elite, regardless of religious affiliation.

Thus, for members of the Anjuman, the ignorance besetting Kashmiri Muslims was a symptom of the larger malaise of Islam's decline in Kashmir, caused by the loss of temporal authority. However, much like the Muslims of British India in the late nineteenth century, the

[58] *Halat wa Rouidad*, 1913, 1.

[59] *Halat wa Rouidad*, 1912–15.

[60] *Halat wa Rouidad*, Annual Report of the Convocation of the Madrasa Anjuman Nusrat-ul-Islam (Srinagar: Salagram Press, 1912), 2.

reattainment of this temporal authority was not the main focus of the leadership's vision. Instead, their goal was an internal regeneration of the Kashmiri Muslim community, so that Muslims might recover their Islamic identity through education. In his speech to the annual convocation in 1912, Mohammad Ayub, a student at the Islamia High School, described Islam as a sick child in need of its mother's sympathy and care. He continued by giving the example of Sir Sayyid Ahmed Khan, who had laid the foundation of Aligarh College for the advancement of the Muslim community.[61] At the same convocation, Moulvi Salamuddin Nahwi hailed the Mirwaiz as the savior of the Kashmiri Muslim qaum and the Anjuman as the victory of Islam.[62] In a convocation speech, Pir Abdullah Shah Kamri, mutawalli of Ziarat Sayyid Qamar Sahab, exhorted Muslims to be faithful to their religion, which, according to him could only be achieved through gaining education.[63] A poem presented at this function by Moulvi Ghulam Hassan Vakil captures the Kashmiri Muslim elite's appeal to the community to rise out of its stupor:

> Until when will I be worried about this qaum?
> Until when will I cry and complain like women?
> Until when will I mourn the condition of my qaum?
> Until when will I hang my head like a dying flower?
>
> I present to you the courage and determination of Sir Sayyid,
> I will also sacrifice myself for the qaum like him.
> If our qaum is steeped in the sea of ignorance,
> Then only he is a man who saves people from drowning during the
>   storm.[64]

The recurrent references to Sayyid Ahmad Khan in the discourse of this movement are significant because they point to the self-perception

---

[61] Ibid., 40–1.

[62] Ibid., 29. It is essential to note that in the discourse of the Muslim leadership in this period, "nation" and "community" were synonymous under the term *qaum*. In some instances in the use of the term, reference was clearly being made to a religio-political community, at other times to a regional collectivity, and in yet others to both. At no time, however, was this term used to refer to a territorially defined nation-state.

[63] Ibid., 25.

[64] Ibid., 31.

of the Muslim leadership as modernizers. Although its leadership was composed entirely of the religious elite, this movement developed a discourse which attempted to provide for the regeneration of the Muslim community alongside its advancement in Western education. Unlike British India, where the Deobandi and Farangi Mahali ulema were launching bitter critiques of Sayyid Ahmad Khan, the Kashmiri religious elite had appropriated his methods as a model for the educational and ultimately economic advancement of the Kashmiri Muslim community. Another appeal to the Kashmiri masses asked: "who will save your qaum from this deteriorating condition? Neither a king, nor a ruler, nor a preacher or any administrator; only self-help can make a nation exemplary. God helps those who help themselves."[65] Khwaja Mohammad Maqbool Pandit went so far as to give the example of Japan and Germany as nations that had risen from their helpless condition to claim their God-given position in the world.[66] What was explicit in these remonstrations by the Muslim elite was that it was not the king or the preacher or the administrator, but rather the educated, who would raise the moral fiber of society. However, for the educated at the forefront of this movement, the furtherance of true Islamic tenets remained essential to the "progress" of the community.

In the face of an overtly interventionist Hindu state, educational institutions became a means of defending Islam, and through them the collectivity itself. This project is amply illustrated in an incident that was meticulously recorded by a poet at the turn of the century. Witty and humorous, the Kashmiri poem entitled, significantly, *Aijaze Quran* (Miracle of the *Quran*), describes an incident in 1891 in which a Kashmiri Pandit bureaucrat in the Dogra administration stormed into a madrasa near his house in Nava Kadal, Srinagar, and insulted the moulvi and the *Quran*. According to the poet, Pandit Hargopal Khasta demanded that the moulvi stop the loud recitation of the *Quran*; when the moulvi refused to comply, Khasta threw the holy book on the ground. Furious at this insult, some Muslims of Srinagar organized a deputation to the Maharaja, which began at the Khanqah-i-Mualla shrine and grew in size as it passed through the five major

[65] *Halat wa Rouidad,* Annual report of the Convocation of the Madrasa Anjuman Nusrat-ul-Islam, (Srinagar: Privately Printed, 1900), 10.

[66] *Halat wa Rouidad,* Annual Report of the Convocation of the Madrasa Anjuman Nusrat-ul-Islam, (Srinagar: Privately Printed, 1915), 15.

shrines of the city. The Maharaja promptly rejected their petition to expel Khasta from the state, asking them to appeal through the court system instead. The custodians of the Hazratbal and Naqshbandi shrines then petitioned the Resident, on whose personal intervention Khasta was banished from Jammu and Kashmir in 1891.[67]

More significant than the veracity of the details of this incident is the fact that it was recorded at the turn of the twentieth century and clearly asserts the authority of the Muslim leadership on the community's educational institutions against threats from the state. Furthermore, the poem frames the incident in religious terms. It does not describe a random insult to a random individual, but instead an insult to the Kashmiri Muslim collectivity through the insult of its most sacred book. It is also significant that the incident ends in success for Kashmiri Muslims and their representatives, who are able to challenge the legitimacy of the Dogra state by appealing to the higher authority of the British colonial state. The defense of the religious collectivity through the protection of its educational institutions was an integral aspect of the articulation of identities by Kashmiri Muslims in relation to both the Dogra state and the British Residency.

Since this identity was inextricably linked to the Muslim leadership's vision of progress for the individual Muslim, henceforth the Muslim community's moral and economic well being would be measured in terms of the success or failure of its educational career. As Munshi Ghulam Mohammad Khadim declared at the second annual convocation of the Madrasa Anjuman Nusrat-ul-Islam: "No *qaum* can progress and no *qaum* can claim to be civilized until it has reached the zenith of its educational career."[68] Progress now not only meant the community's adherence to a particular version of Islam, but also its acquisition of modern education. The latter was becoming increasingly important as its benefits became apparent. Thus the general secretary

---

[67] M.Y. Teng, "Kashiri Adbuk Godnyuk Sahafati Dastavez" [The First Journalistic Tract of Kashmiri Literature], in Teng, *Talaash: Tahkiki te Tabkidi Majmoonan Hinz Sombran* [Quest: A Collection of Essays on Research and Critical Studies] (Delhi: J.K. Offset Prints, 1988), 36–54. The poem was probably recorded around 1899–1900. This type of incident was common in other parts of the subcontinent as well, and the response of the colonial state in such instances was similar to that of the Dogra state in Kashmir.

[68] *Halat wa Rouidad*, 1900, 6.

of the Anjuman lamented in 1913 that the Kashmiri masses were not interested in education due to their abject poverty, but now that the educated from state and other schools had attained high posts in the administration, and traders had benefited from these educational centers, Muslims had to come to their senses.[69]

In spite of its efforts, however, the Anjuman Nusrat-ul-Islam and its educational reform movement remained a Srinagar-based institution supported by a wide cross-section of the population of the city. The fact that its influence did not penetrate beyond the Srinagar conurbation is clear from the list of over 600 contributors to the organization, only 20 (3 percent) of which were individuals from other parts of the Kashmir Valley, mainly Islamabad, Bandipora and Sopore, the rest being from Srinagar. One of the more obvious reasons for the institution's limited sphere of activity was its links to the ruling dynasty, bureaucracy, and Muslim organizations of the Punjab.[70] The language in which its convocation sessions were conducted was Persian or Urdu, neither of which was spoken or understood by the vast majority of Kashmiri Muslims, the former being the language of the Kashmiri literary and religious elite, the latter the language of administration.[71] Although poetic and other tracts in Kashmiri—these included common people in their debate on identities—had captured the publications market by this time, they were not considered worthy of inclusion in educational institutions. By promoting Urdu at the expense of Kashmiri, these institutions were creating a gap between education and the public sphere, defined largely by publications in Kashmiri, which is perhaps the reason why the educational reform movements had such a minimal impact on the Muslim masses.

Furthermore, the appeals made at these functions were directed more toward the elite in the hope of donations, than toward the masses. Donors to the society included the Maharaja, his private secretary, the head mufti of Srinagar, petty and big traders of the city, and powerful Kashmiri Muslims from the Punjab.[72] Additionally, Punjabi officials of state did their utmost to sabotage the Anjuman's efforts to

[69] *Halat wa Rouidad,* 1913, 3.

[70] *Halat wa Rouidad,* 1912, 63–81.

[71] The table of principal languages in the Census of 1901 did not even include Urdu as a language worthy of consideration.

[72] *Halat wa Rouidad,* 1912, 63.

spread its influence outside the city because, the Anjuman claimed, they were fearful for their monopoly on government jobs. The convocations of the madrasa charged the Punjabis with spreading misinformation among agriculturists, such as the fact that the Anjuman was anti-Islamic, and if they sent their children to the Anjuman's schools the government would have to increase land revenue.[73]

For obvious reasons, the educational status of Kashmiri Muslims remained at a low level throughout this period, especially when compared to that of Kashmiri Pandits. After all, the expectation of modern educational achievement from cultivators, a novel idea in itself, would not by itself ensure its success, particularly since the medium of instruction was alien. On the other hand, Kashmiri Pandits, the Hindu minority in the Valley and mainly an administrative class, found it imperative to gain an Urdu/English education to retain their foothold even on the lower rungs of administration. They had recognized early on that the state was not interested in promoting education among Kashmiris because it did not desire to appoint them to government positions. This led to the "Kashmir for Kashmiris movement" for securing the rights of Kashmiris against outsiders, on the basis of the fact that Kashmiri Pandits were as educated and qualified as Punjabis, who formed the bulk of the administration.[74] This ultimately led to the formation of a committee for the definition of the term "state subject" in 1910 in order to limit government employment to such persons as fitted the category.[75] Although the definition, finally submitted by the State Council in 1912, placed Kashmiris who had been in the state for generations on the same footing as outsiders who had acquired a *rayatnama* (special order) from the Maharaja,[76] it did

---

[73] *Halat wa Rouidad,* 1912–15.

[74] Khan, *Freedom Movement in Kashmir,* 101. The "Kashmir for Kashmiris" movement was not unique to the princely state of Jammu and Kashmir. Similar movements for securing the rights of state subjects characterized the political landscapes of several princely states at the turn of the twentieth century, including Mysore, Travancore, Hyderabad, and Kolhapur. See Jeffrey, *People, Princes and Paramount Power,* 22.

[75] "Terms of Reference for the Committee appointed to define the term 'State Subject' 1923" (Srinagar: K.M. Press, 1923), General Department 14/1923, Jammu State Archives.

[76] The 1912 definition of "State Subject" was the following: (1) All bonafide subjects of His Highness the Maharaja Sahib Bahadur. (2) All persons who have

imbricate the legal definition of Kashmiri subjecthood with education and, consequently, employment in government service.

One can detect a gradual transformation in the agenda of the Kashmiri Muslim leadership by the beginning of the 1910s. The advent of the British on the Kashmiri political scene and the simultaneous state regulation of the education system had given the Kashmiri Muslim leadership the opportunity to press its social and political demands on the state. Since the Dogra state was modeling its education system on British lines, it also followed that those who went through the system would be advantageously placed for state employment. Moreover, the Kashmiri Muslim leadership could always point to colonial educational policies toward Indian Muslims, some of which were designed to provide incentives for Muslim educational progress.[77] Education thus came to mean more than just an advancement of Kashmiri Muslim civilization, since it now also held the additional rewards of employment in government service—the traditional preserve of Kashmiri Pandits. This, combined with the decline in the traditional system of Muslim education,[78] enhanced the Kashmiri Muslim leadership's stake in being recognized by, and included in, the state system of education.

Supported by Muslim organizations of British India, particularly the Punjab, the Kashmiri Muslim leadership began demanding that the state play a more active role in redressing the discrepancy between the educational status of the two communities of the Valley. Kashmiri Muslim expatriates in the Punjab had retained emotional and familial ties to their soil and felt compelled to raise the banner of freedom for Kashmir and their brethren in the Valley, thus launching bitter

---

tendered a duly executed rayatnama and have acquired immovable property in the state. (3) All persons who have resided within the State territories for not less than 20 years and are subject to the laws and regulations promulgated from time to time by His Highness the Maharaja. (4) The descendants of the persons mentioned in the foregoing clauses. See ibid.

[77] The Resolution of 1885 adopted by the colonial state was emphatic in its directive that a special section of the annual education reports should be devoted to the Muslim community so that the government could be kept informed about its progress in education. See Peter Hardy, *The Muslims of British India* (Cambridge: Cambridge University Press, 1972), 122.

[78] The 1915–16 Note on Education stated that twenty-four makhtabs run by moulvis had to be closed during that year. See Education Department 321/E-11/ 1914, Jammu State Archives.

critiques of the Dogra administration.[79] In its 1913 address to the
Maharaja, the Kashmiri Muslim Conference—one of the main Kashmiri Muslim expatriate organizations in the Punjab—made a strong
case for improving the status of Muslim education in the state by employing Muslim teachers in state schools, as well as providing religious
education in these institutions. If, the Conference claimed, enough
educated Muslims did not exist in the state, then Muslims should be
imported from British India to teach in state schools. The Conference
kept up its pressure on the darbar to requisition the services of competent Mohammadans, preferably Kashmiri Muslims from the Punjab,
for educational services within the state.[80] It is essential to point out
that Kashmiri Muslim expatriates in the Punjab faced discrimination
in terms of recruitment to the army, educational institutions, and
other areas. Therefore, petitioning the Dogra state for the recruitment
of Kashmiri Muslims from the Punjab into educational institutions
clearly had an economic motivation.

The Dogra state's initial response to these moves was one of dismissal. The Maharaja made a supercilious reply to the Conference,
particularly toward the idea that more Muslims would be attracted to
schools if their teachers were Muslims: "Once upon a time, the fame
of Kashmir as a literate country was well-established and then the
Pandits were usually, if not exclusively, the teachers of Persian to
Mohammadans." He continued, "In matters of imparting and receiving
education, all questions of creed and nationality should be set aside."
In the same reply, the Maharaja also declared that orders had been issued by the education department for the employment of moulvis in
all primary schools which had more than ten Muslim boys on their
rolls.[81]

Throughout this period, the state followed schizophrenic policies
towards the creation of a distinct category for Muslims within the
state's educational system. While the 1908 State Educational Conference had dismissed Khan Sahib Peerzada Mohammad Hussain's
proposal regarding the advancement of Muslim education in the state
as of a "purely sectarian nature and hence not proprietary to be taken

---

[79] For a more detailed discussion of the politics of Kashmiri Muslim expatriate
community in the Punjab, see Jalal, *Self and Sovereignty*, 352–60.

[80] Political Department 217/P-96/1913, Jammu State Archives, 1.

[81] Ibid., 2–3.

up,"[82] in 1914 the state appointed a Mohammadan Assistant Inspector of Schools whose "chief duty was confined to the improvement and propagation of education among this backward community."[83] The education department had also provided seventy primary schools with Arabic teachers for making education popular and raising the number of Muslim scholars in public schools.[84] By doing so, in its view the state was bridging the gap between secular education as provided by state schools and religious education as provided by madrasas, so that Muslims, seen as being inherently more religious, would be attracted to these schools.

The government seemed oblivious to its own role in reifying the religious community through its educational policies. In 1911, the Maharaja had proclaimed the introduction of religious education in all schools and colleges. All students were to be provided with instruction in their own religion by moulvis, pandits or priests based on their sacred texts, in "separate rooms."[85] This not only led to the co-optation of religious faith by the Dogra state, but also to the appropriation of its definition by the religious leadership of the communities. Although under the same roof, students were reminded each day of their separateness from other students, based on the teacher's monolithic version of their religion. While the Dogra state declared its neutrality in matters of religion, it unabashedly promoted distinct religious identities among its subjects through state schools.

Since the colonial state was the Dogra state's main inspiration, the ambiguities and inconsistencies in British education and language policies could also be noted in Kashmir. These are most comparable with the Punjab, where the script, the medium of instruction in government schools, and the language of administration were far removed from the regional vernacular.[86] A similar situation prevailed in Kashmir, a fact never raised or addressed by the state or the Muslim leadership. Instead, the state focused on the issue of languages most suited for religious instruction. Hence, the Inspector of Schools, Srinagar, stated

[82] Political Department 101/P-102/1907, Jammu State Archives.

[83] *Administration Report of the Education Department, Jammu and Kashmir State, 1914–15*, 7.

[84] Ibid.

[85] Education Department 59R.R./1911, Jammu State Archives.

[86] See Jalal, *Self and Sovereignty*, chapter three.

in 1912 that if the policy of moral and religious education in schools was to be successfully implemented, then provision had to be made for the teaching of Hindi to Hindu boys, in the same way that Urdu was taught to Muslim boys. This led to the abolition of Sanskrit and Persian in primary departments of schools in 1911 so as to enable boys "to receive a better grounding in their own vernacular tongue i.e. Urdu or Hindi before they take up a study of a classical language like Persian or Sanskrit in the Secondary schools."[87] The Dogra state had made Urdu synonymous with Muslim education and Hindi with the education of Hindus, developing parallel systems of "vernacular" education, such as in the North Western Provinces, ignoring the glaring fact that neither Kashmiri Hindus nor Kashmiri Muslims spoke anything other than their regional vernacular, Kashmiri, in either their homes or places of business.[88] This might explain the absence of a language controversy generated as a result of this blatantly sectarian policy.[89] It is also important that the complete unwillingness to implement the mother tongue as the medium of instruction was in large part responsible for high illiteracy rates among Kashmiri Muslims.

What is most peculiar, perhaps, is the complete silence among the Muslim leadership on the subject of Kashmiri as the language of instruction in schools. This silence is an interesting comment on the class basis of the educational reform movements in Kashmir. Since education in the Kashmiri language would have benefited the lower classes the most, but not appreciably served the interests of the elite (since their main motivation in acquiring an education was to be conversant in the language of the administration, Urdu), the Muslim leadership was unwilling to raise the banner of Kashmiri as the medium of instruction. Kashmiri thus became a victim of the interests of

[87] *Administration Report of the Education Department, Jammu and Kashmir State, 1911–12*, 4.

[88] This is the case in contemporary Kashmir as well, where Kashmiris interact with each other in their regional vernacular at home, on the streets, in shops, in administrative offices, in places of business, and so on, while the language of administration is Urdu and English, with the former being more prominent at lower levels.

[89] Since Kashmiri was not to be the language of instruction or administration, the question of the script it would be written in did not arise. The Valley did witness a communitarian debate on script in the early 1940s, but that had very little to do with Kashmiri. For a detailed discussion of this controversy, see chapter six.

the early-twentieth-century Kashmiri Muslim elite, which, while purporting to represent a wide cross-section of the Muslim community, clearly framed its demands to serve the interests of its upper-tier.[90] In effect, then, the narrative on Kashmiri Muslim identities elided over linguistic assertions for Kashmiri.

The sole area of education where the state and leadership were willing to concede the necessity of Kashmiri as the language of instruction was in the education of girls, and even in this case it was never implemented. The state and representatives of the community seemed more concerned with the religious education of females rather than the efficacy of the education being imparted to them. Until 1920 the management of government girls' schools was left largely to advisory committees, private managing bodies composed of leading members of religious communities, and the schools themselves were connected to particular communities.[91] The state recognized that communities would perceive interference in women's education as an attack on their religious sensibilities. The "religious prejudice of the people of Kashmir and their prejudice against education, especially that of females,"[92] were cited as reasons for the placing of the education of their girls in the hands of advisory committees. However, these committees remained under the charge of the education department and conducted supervision over the general work of schools in accordance with the rules sanctioned by the Education Minister for that purpose.[93] This gave state sanction to overtly religious policies recommended by the advisory committees, such as closing Muslim girls' schools on Fridays instead of Sundays for the reason that "women are supposed to be more religious and their education will suffer if Fridays, a day of Muslim sabbath, is not a holiday in girls schools."[94]

The growing nexus of state and community educational institutions was visible not simply in the area of women's education. Following

[90] It is interesting to note that in the Punjab, the call to introduce Punjabi as the medium of instruction in educational institutions was met with opposition from the Muslim elite, who saw in it a conspiracy to keep Muslims uneducated in the language of administration, Urdu, and a move to divide Muslims and Hindus. See Jalal, *Self and Sovereignty*, 133–8.

[91] Education Department 100/R.R./1915, Jammu State Archives.

[92] Ibid.

[93] Education Department 134/R.R./1920, Jammu State Archives.

[94] Education Department 100/R.R./1915, Jammu State Archives.

from colonial policies, the public funding of private institutions through the system of grants-in-aid had become the norm in Kashmir.[95] By 1915 the darbar had brought all religious educational institutions of the Valley—none of which could survive without the annual state grants-in-aid that increased steadily through the years—under its direct control. Educational officers made regular reports on the status of these schools, "the staff and standards" of which were not "as could be desired." But since the aim of these institutions was "spreading education amongst a backward community,"[96] the darbar continued to sanction the grants year after year.[97] In 1911 the state took over two aided religious schools, the Hindu High School and the Fateh Kadal Hindu Middle School, to "place them on an improved basis." In 1918 the education department directly intervened in the affairs of the Islamia High School, where the state-loaned headmaster had accused the president of the Anjuman Nusrat-ul-Islam, Mirwaiz Ahmadullah, of embezzling school funds. After a volley of letters to the Education Minister from the Mirwaiz demanding a dismissal of the headmaster, a managing committee was established at the behest of the state to run the school. The chairman of this committee was to be versed in religious sciences and modern education and the secretary in educational methods in vogue. The members consisted of a mix of the traditional religious elite of Srinagar and government officials.[98]

Clearly, the indigenous school of previous decades had been successfully transformed into an arm of the state and the traditional

[95] The public funding of private institutions was the educational norm in nineteenth-century England. In 1854, the directors of the East India Company wrote: "The most effectual method of providing for the wants of India . . . will be to combine with the agency of the government the aid which may be derived from the exertions and liberality of the educated and wealthy natives of India . . . We have, therefore, resolved to adopt in India a system of grants-in-aid which have been carried out in this country [England] with very great success." Quoted in Rudolph and Rudolph, eds., *Education and Politics*, 15.

[96] Political Department 76/P-11/1914, Jammu State Archives.

[97] In 1914–15, the darbar was giving grants-in-aid to 14 such institutions in the entire state, including 25 makhtabs and pathshalas as compared to 11 institutions in 1911–12. See *Administration Report of the Education Department 1911–1912*, 4 and *Administration Report of the Education Department, 1914–15*, 9.

[98] Political Department 260/24-C/1918, Jammu State Archives. The committee members included Hassan Shah Naqshbandi; Moulvi Sharifuddin, Head Mufti, Srinagar; Moulvi Atiqullah, Secretary Anjuman Nusrat-ul-Islam; Ali Sahab,

teacher into its paid servant. The informal system of indigenous education that had prevailed in Kashmir only four decades earlier was systematically converted into a state-sponsored system, far more centralized and homogeneous in nature. Education, thus uprooted from the community and attached to the state, was unable to live up to the expectations created by the state's own ambivalent rhetoric on the education of the masses as well as its conflicted language and religious policies. In the coming decades, the backwardness of Muslims in the field of education, and the insistence on state recognition of Muslims as a separate category in the field, became central components of the Kashmiri Muslim leadership's political rhetoric.

Education, Kashmiri Muslim Demands, and the Dogra State, 1916–1930

The Dogra state could no longer ignore the growing intersections between religious affiliation, education, language and employment, which by 1930 had become firmly entrenched in the political structure of Jammu and Kashmir. Here I argue that the state's educational policies in this period were geared toward creating a separate political category for Muslims and defining it in social and cultural terms borrowed from the discourse of the Kashmiri Muslim leadership, thus vitiating its own rhetoric on religious neutrality. The Kashmiri Muslim leadership, in its turn, attempted to appropriate this category to further the economic and political interests of the Muslim community.

The Second Educational Conference of Jammu and Kashmir in 1915 did not dismiss the suggestion of its Muslim members that a subcommittee consisting of the Muslim religious elite of the city of Srinagar should be set up to draw up and submit a scheme for Muslim education.[99] At the same time, the President of the Conference also proclaimed the need for Sanskrit, Arabic and Hindi teachers in all Middle and High Schools, "these languages being critical for religious

---

President Committee Khanqah-i-Mualla; Khwaja Ghulam Mohammad Sahab, employee Silk Factory; Khwaja Ghulam Hassan Shaal; Khwaja Ghulam Mohiuddin Trambu; Khwaja Ghulam Mohiuddin Kausa; Moulvi Ahad Shah, Headmaster State School, Rainawari; Asadullah Shah; General Farman Ali Khan; and Ghulam Mohammad Ashai.

[99] This committee included the two Mirwaizes and Khwaja Hassan Shah Naqshbandi and ultimately did not submit a scheme for Muslim education. See Political Department 199/P104/1915, Jammu State Archives, 2.

instruction." It was also at the same meeting that the Minister of Education, Dewan Bishen Das, recommended a more direct involvement of the Government of India in the educational affairs of the state.[100] This ultimately led to the appointment of Mr Sharp, Educational Commissioner of the Government of India, who was loaned to the Kashmir Darbar for a period of two months, to submit a report on the condition of education in Kashmir. The Sharp Committee Report, quoted widely by Kashmiri Muslim organizations inside and outside the state, contributed significantly toward crystallizing the idea of Kashmiri Muslim backwardness in education.

The Sharp Committee Report went beyond the state in delving into the reasons for the low educational status among Kashmiri Muslims. Maintaining the colonial focus on class, the report pointed out that poverty and the agricultural class basis of Kashmiri Muslims was the reason for the lack of literacy among them. The committee felt that the Muslim community in the state was so overwhelmingly poor that Muslims could not send their children to schools. Therefore, liberal grants and scholarships should be kept aside for Muslim students and institutions, at primary, secondary and college levels. Furthermore, the report recommended the institutionalization of technical education in the state, pointing out that the provision of practical education ought to be one of the state's most urgent priorities. Since the overwhelming majority of Muslims in the state belonged to the agricultural community, the modern curriculum of state schools held no value for them. Hence, Sharp recommended the foundation of mechanical, agricultural, horticultural, carpentry and cattle-breeding schools.[101] While the government had been discussing technical education as early as 1893–4, they did not see it as a means of attracting the state's agricultural classes to education so much as making them better at their own occupation. With the Sharp Committee Report, the concept of the organization of education according to the needs and abilities of various classes became entrenched in the state. At the same time, by focusing on the education of the agricultural class, the report highlighted the importance of Muslim cultivators to Kashmiri political discourse.

Sharp's report did not merely stop at that, however: it did much to valorize the category of religious community in the state organization

[100] Ibid.

[101] "Sharp Committee Report," in Ghulam Rasool, *Education in Jammu and Kashmir: Issues and Documents* (Jammu: Jay Kay Book House, 1986), 151–6.

of education. For instance, the report recommended the appointment of a Muslim teacher to Sri Pratap College, Srinagar, and the State High School, Srinagar, and the appointment of Muslim headmasters to some middle schools of the city. Recognizing that in 1916 enough Kashmiri Muslims did not exist who could be employed in these posts, Sharp observed that, "Numerous outsiders of the Hindu faith have been appointed to offices, and however laudable the desire of the Darbar to employ only subjects of the state, there seems a good case, in view of His Highness's Muslim subjects, for relaxing the rule in case of Mohammedan teachers until there is a supply of Mohammedan graduates in the State itself."[102] Inadvertently, or perhaps not so much, the report had spoken in favor of Punjabi Muslim organizations, thus promoting the possibility of importing Muslims into the state and encouraging further appeals and petitions from such entities.

By the end of the second decade of the twentieth century and the beginning of the third, the demands of the external and indigenous organizations on behalf of Kashmiri Muslims were becoming increasingly embroiled with larger political issues, both in Kashmir and the Punjab. In its resolutions, the All India Kashmiri Muslim Conference held at Rawalpindi in 1918 demanded yet again that efficient Muslims should be imported into state service from the neighboring British territory. And, in view of the fact that 95 per cent of the population of the state was Muslim, the Director of Public Education or at least the Personal Assistant to the Education Minister should be Muslim. More significantly, the Conference expressed its "strong and emphatic disapproval" of the introduction of Hindi in state schools, because "the measure will tend to create a split among Hindus and Mohammedans of the state."[103] The Education Minister's reply to the above charge was indignant. He said that Hindi was not the official language of the state and nowhere in British India was its teaching prohibited. "The State," he continued, "cannot do differently, as to do otherwise would be to depart from its position of religious neutrality . . . If Hindi can be regarded as the cause of split between two classes, I do not see why should Urdu and Persian be not put in the same heading."[104]

Interestingly, the state's discourse on the educational status of

[102] Ibid., 153.
[103] Political Department 229/P-102/1918, Jammu State Archives.
[104] Ibid.

Kashmiri Muslims was derived to a great extent from the Muslim leadership's heightening laments on the backwardness of Muslims in this field. This was a convenient means through which the state could outline its achievements in promoting Muslim education, without taking any responsibility for the community's backwardness, since they were given to "apathy and ignorance." The Education Minister complained: "Mohammadans of lesser qualifications are accepted in the Normal School, but still they would not come." He continued that the government had opened a training school for mullahs in Sopore, but only three out of seven mullahs attended the institution.[105] Instead of recognizing this as possibly a form of resistance by the traditional teachers of Kashmir to the state control of education, the minister saw it as another example of Muslim ignorance, a product of their poverty and lower-class mentality.

Even as the discourses of the Muslim leadership and the state converged on the issue of the slow progress of education among Muslims, the two increasingly diverged on the means to redress this situation. The state claimed that it was doing its best to promote education among Muslims while the Muslim leadership held the state responsible for the small numbers of educated Muslims and even smaller numbers of Muslims employed in government service. In the 1920s the demands of the Muslim leadership gradually moved away from the provision of education by the state to the benefits offered by education in government service. After all, the Maharaja himself was declaring that "in the race of life, nothing tells more effectively than higher qualifications . . . it is merit and merit alone which is the key for advancement in life these days."[106] As in all areas of governance, however, the Maharaja placed the responsibility for advancing educational merit among Muslims at the doorstep of their leadership.

In 1922 the President of the Anjuman Nusrat-ul-Islam, Mirwaiz Ahmadullah, presented a representation to the State Council for consideration. In this representation, he clearly accepted the flaws of the Kashmiri Muslim community—such as their apathetic attitude toward English education—as the reason for their illiteracy. However, just as clearly, he pointed to the duty of the government in alleviating this apathy by promising educated Muslims employment in government

---

[105] Ibid.
[106] General Department 103/1923, Jammu State Archives.

service. The remedies that followed in this representation make it clear that, by the early 1920s, the demands of the Kashmiri Muslim elite had gone beyond the provision of educational opportunities for Kashmiri Muslims. The platform of education had become a means for their leadership to force the state to acknowledge the distinct demands of the Kashmiri Muslim community, which derived from its particular economic and political situation in the state.

Following from the recommendations of Sharp, the Mirwaiz went on to list the absence of Muslim teachers in state schools, the absence of schools imparting practical education in many villages, and the meagerness of scholarships to Muslim students as reasons for their low educational status. Albeit respectfully, he demanded that the state recruit Muslims who had taken a lead in education to responsible positions. Since the number of young Muslim men educated in English was then limited, he stated: "such of them as are well-read in Urdu and Persian may be appointed in departments such as Settlement, Revenue, Police, Customs, Municipalities and Sericulture and where Muslims with necessary qualifications for these and other departments are not available, requisition may be made from the Anjuman." The Mirwaiz also demanded that all primary schools have a staff of Muslim teachers, and state high schools have Muslim headmasters and inspecting staff. His other demands included provision for a special Muslim adviser attached to the Education Minister and extraordinary help for Muslim students and institutions such as the Islamia School.[107]

The last three demands of this representation, however, are most significant, since they reflect the changing political climate of the Valley. The Mirwaiz demanded that the Council abolish the begar system, return the mosques that were still under state control to the Muslim community, and, considering the numerical strength of the Muslim population, allot them seats in the representative assembly that might be brought into existence in the future.[108] Added on to the representation in the hopes that the Council would consider them, these demands were an attempt by the religious leadership to recover its rapidly declining role as representative of Kashmiri Muslims.

The government, not willing to recognize the importance of these particular demands, ignored them as "not concerning the education

[107] General Department 1609/E-17/1923, Jammu State Archives, 1–3.
[108] Ibid., 3–4.

department." Instead, the State Council focused on what it saw as the purpose of the Mirwaiz's representation: education. In his reply to the Mirwaiz, the Home Member placed the entire burden of the backwardness of the Muslim community in education and state employment squarely on the community itself. In rhetoric reminiscent of provincial governments in colonial India, he stated that the real cause of Muslim backwardness was their apathy and incapacity to take advantage of the facilities of education placed before them by the government. According to him, mullahs were primarily responsible for fostering this attitude among Muslims.[109] He claimed that whenever there was a vacancy in a high school or middle school, a Muslim graduate or undergraduate seldom came forward and the position went to a Hindu. As far as the employment of Muslims in state service was concerned, the member stated that posts could not be reserved for Muslims, "because if this is done, members of other communities will also make a similar representation. Besides, if the suggestion of the President is accepted, it would mean that a large number of posts should not be filled as long as qualified and efficient Muslims are not available."[110] This, of course, was not possible in the interests of the efficient administration of the state.

It was clear that the darbar was willing to concede the distinctness of the Kashmiri Muslim identity only in so far as it could be used to explain the community's backwardness. In the Home Member's response to the Mirwaiz's representation, the Kashmiri Muslim community was presented as a community handicapped by its religion, which had much in common with its "brethren community" in British India. The response went into a detailed discussion of this "besetting sin of their community all over India." In Delhi province, the Home Member stated, the Muslim community could not plead poverty and neglect by the government as reasons for their backwardness in education. And yet, in this center of Muslim culture and civilization, the Muslim community was doing very poorly in the field of education.[111] "The fact is," he concluded, "any culture that is foreign to their mode

[109] Ibid., 5.

[110] Ibid.

[111] It is not necessary to point out the utter fallacy of this statement. For a discussion of the educational politics of the Muslims of Delhi, see Gupta, *Delhi Between Two Empires*, particularly chapter four.

of living and thinking or any education that is not based on the tradition of the *Quran,* has been regarded with disfavor by their religious heads and so far been kept under a ban."[112]

In keeping with the view of the Muslim community as "handicapped," at a speech delivered in 1923 at the prize distribution ceremony of Sri Pratap College, Srinagar, the Maharaja emphasized the benefits of education and the responsibility of the Kashmiri Muslim leadership in instilling the awareness of the need for education in the community. He declared that his government's educational policies and standards, modeled after the British government, provided equally for all communities of the state: "I have been all along impressing upon my Mohammedan subjects the supreme necessity of education and if they are lagging behind, they are themselves to blame." He then appealed to the "Mohammadan gentlemen of light and learning" to impress upon the community the need for education.[113] Clearly, the state still did not recognize that the need to provide incentives for education to its subjects was its responsibility.

And as far as the leadership was concerned, it was not able to match its rhetoric on mass education with concrete demands in this field, as is clear from its lack of support for the regional vernacular. Instead, the "Mohammadan gentleman of light and learning" took their demands to the Viceroy of India, since they considered the colonial state a champion of Muslim rights. In a memorial to the Viceroy on his visit to the state in 1924, the leadership made a last-ditch effort to act as representatives of a united Kashmiri Muslim community, at the same time openly challenging the authority of the Dogra state.[114] The memorial appealed to the British sense of justice and democracy by describing Kashmir as "one of the remotest outposts of the British Empire."

Although education remained central to their demands, the backwardness of Muslims in this field was not seen as the community's fault, but instead as a charge that was leveled against the community

[112] General Department 1609/E-17/1923, Jammu State Archives, 5.

[113] General Department 103/1923, Jammu State Archives.

[114] The darbar perceived this as a particularly insidious blow to its authority, since the British had only recently granted full powers to Maharaja Pratap Singh in 1922.

by the state with the express purpose of excluding its members from government service. While the religious leadership used similar arguments to chastise Kashmiri Muslims, they resented its use by the state. The memorial was constructed around the issue of the exclusion of Muslims by the state from government posts on the basis of their lack of educational qualifications: "The cultivators, mostly Muhammadan, build up the wealth of the state and support a vast army of state officials. Thus, the Muslims demand a proper share in the administration of the state for consuming and enjoying a fair portion of the wealth they produce and to safeguard the interests of the community."[115] Additionally, the leadership emphasized Kashmiri Pandits as the "other" community, which, in contradistinction to their own, had access to not only scholarships and grants for education, but also government service.

Needless to say, the State Council took swift action against the authors of the memorial who had clearly subverted the legitimacy of the Dogra state in Kashmir. The select committee appointed by the State Council to consider the grievances presented in the memorial refuted them in detail, attributing their seditious nature to the work of "agitators from British India." Certain local Muslims had visited British India, according to the committee report, and returned to disseminate the idea that the Viceroy was visiting Kashmir to replace the Hindu dynasty with Muhammadan rule. Saaduddin Shaal, held primarily responsible for the memorial, was expelled from the state, to be allowed back in only through the orders of the Maharaja-in-Council. Hassan Shah Naqshbandi, another primary offender, was divested of his jagir.[116] The remaining signatories to the memorial were reprimanded and warned.[117]

This was a severe blow to the turn-of-the-century Muslim leadership. Even at the height of their power, Muslim educational institutions such as the Madrasa Anjuman Nusrat-ul-Islam and the Khanqah-i-

[115] Political Department E-13/1931, Jammu State Archives.

[116] It is interesting to note that these two memorialists were descendants of the families who had been involved in shrine disputes of the late nineteenth century, the Shaals and Naqshbandis. Even in the 1920s, this rapidly declining elite was struggling to maintain its social status and foothold in Kashmiri politics.

[117] Political Department E-13/1931, Jammu State Archives.

Mualla School had limited spheres of influence, as did their leaders, who remained embroiled in disputes over rights to preaching their definitions of Islam during the course of this period. By the middle of the 1920s, another class of leaders had begun to emerge in Kashmir. These individuals had been the first to take advantage of the combined efforts of the Muslim leadership and the state at encouraging Muslim education and received higher education in British India.[118] As discussed earlier (chapter three), Moulvi Muhammad Nooruddin Qari Kashmiri straddled the two types of leadership and best exemplifies the transition in Kashmiri Muslim politics in the 1920s. Qari also represents the dual role of the mullah class as part of the state system of education, and a class that would ultimately question the ability of the Dogra Maharaja to address the political demands of the Kashmiri Muslim community.

Qari was a resident of Srinagar who studied in Punjab University and went on to become a follower of Moulana Nooruddin, the head of the Ahmaddiya community in Qadian. Returning to Srinagar in the wake of the Sharp Committee Report, he was employed as an Arabic teacher in the State High School, Srinagar.[119] In the 1920s and early 1930s, Qari became one of the most vociferous opponents of the religious leadership of the Kashmiri Muslim community. He accused the waizes, or preachers, of keeping the true message of Islam from the people, thus submerging Kashmiri Muslims in ignorance. Significantly, he recognized the value of the Kashmiri language in alleviating the benightedness of Kashmiri Muslims and wrote prolifically in the vernacular. It was his verses, however, which became the most popular among the people of Srinagar and the mofassil.[120] Strung together in

---

[118] See the last section in chapter three for a detailed discussion of the emergence of this new leadership. The impact of the new, more belligerent leadership could also be felt in Jammu, where some Muslims founded the Youngmen's Muslim Association in the late 1920s, under the leadership of Hamid-Ullah, advocate, Allahrakha Sagar, Choudhury Ghulam Abbas, Hakim Sahib, and Mr Quraishi. The main aims of this association were to spread education among Muslims and to defend Islam against attacks by men professing other religions. See Khan, *Freedom Movement in Kashmir*, 76.

[119] Interview with Moulana Mohammad Shafi Qari, Srinagar, Kashmir, November 26, 1997.

[120] Ibid.

simple Kashmiri, these verses appeared on the back covers of his longer books and chose to focus on the importance of education for Kashmiri Muslims. One such poem, *Teleem Par, Taleem Par* (Gain Education, Gain Education) began with the hadith that proclaimed the duty of all Muslims to gain education, then asked them to awaken as the caravan of progress had left them behind:

> You are sunk in disrespect,
> Fallen, hunched up.
> Look at your own condition now,
> You are being cursed by passersby.
>
> Knowledge is the biggest wealth,
> It does not fear fire or thieves.
> The one who gained knowledge well,
> Wealth will follow him.
>
> One who remains uneducated,
> Dies an ignorant death each day.
> He lives like cattle,
> Read and become human again.[121]

To Qari, education was ultimately a means for the attainment of the unity of the community, which had been lost under the leadership of the waizes.

The numerous references to wealth in his poetry illustrate a significant distinction between the goal of education as envisaged by the two types of leadership. Unlike the earlier leadership, Qari's ultimate project was not merely the moral, but also the economic and political alleviation of Kashmiri Muslims. What further distinguished him from the earlier leadership was that he wrote all his works in Kashmiri. The use of Kashmiri is particularly significant not only because it was the language of the people, but also because it was a language consistently ignored by the Dogra state in its educational policies and the Muslim leadership in its demands. By writing in Kashmiri, thus, Qari was emphasizing the regional identity of the Muslim community that had been so far suppressed by the Dogra state. In another of his popular poems, *Dard-i-Dil wa Haqiqat-i-Haal* (The Pain of the Heart and the Reality of the Situation), he wrote:

---

[121] Nooruddin Qari, *Teleem Par, Teleem Par* [Gain Education, Gain Education] (Srinagar: Self-Published), 1.

The Muslim is without a doubt helpless,
Worried, tired and unemployed.
No doubt there are many preachers,
But their religion is money, not advice.
Other communities do not have preachers,
But look how smart they are.
They have knowledge, wealth, power and prestige,
Which is why they are the leaders and rulers.
But in us there is no wealth of knowledge,
Ignorance has reduced us to ashes.[122]

In 1925, when Maharaja Hari Singh succeeded to the throne of Jammu and Kashmir, a new Muslim leadership had already defined its agenda. Although he presented himself as an enlightened ruler whose "dearest wish" was educating the subjects of even the remotest corners of his state, his reign ushered in the end of Dogra rule of Jammu and Kashmir. Educated at Mayo College, Ajmer, Hari Singh was hailed by Kashmiri Muslim organizations as a "highly enlightened ruler under whose wise and sympathetic guidance . . . the people of this great state are sure to advance in various spheres of human activity."[123] This praise was quickly followed by a long list of demands by the All India Kashmiri Muslim Conference, which would set the tone for the rest of Hari Singh's rule, despite his attempts at furthering the cause of education.

Hari Singh took the initiative of opening several new schools in the mofassil, such as the Hari Singh High School in Baramulla, and raising the standards of several others, such as the Hanfia Middle School in Anantnag, which became a high school in 1926. The education department even began to take steps to provide Muslim teachers in schools situated in localities with a preponderantly Muslim population.[124] He also took into account the recurrent demand of the All India Kashmiri Muslim Conference and introduced free compulsory primary education in all municipal areas of the state in 1930.[125] However, his rule was fraught with increasing animosity between

---

[122] Qari, *Dard-i-Dil wa Haqiqat-i-Haal,* 2.

[123] "Address by All India Muslim Kashmiri Conference, Lahore," General Department 145/150-G/1925, Jammu State Archives.

[124] Education Department 222-U/1926, Jammu State Archives.

[125] Mohammad Ishaq Khan, *History of Srinagar 1846-1947: A Study in Socio-Cultural Change* (Srinagar: Aamir Publications, 1978), 161.

communities, whose definitions by this time had been appropriated by a new educated leadership as unified, immutable entities that could relate to each other only in oppositional terms.

The decade in which the discourse on education would become secondary to the discourse on Kashmiri Muslim and Kashmiri Pandit political representation was already under way. The Anjuman Nusrat-ul-Islam petitioned the government at the institution of the Examination Board in the education department, which did not admit third-division graduates, undergraduates and matrics. This board, the Anjuman contended, would further restrict the already small number of Muslims in the department and had given rise to feelings among Muslims that the only reason the department had instituted these rules was because a majority of Muslims would not fit this description.[126] By the time the state announced the formation of the Civil Service Recruitment Board in August 1930, not only had the new Kashmiri Muslim educated leadership taken over, but, more importantly, their demands had gone far beyond education into the realm of service recruitment.

The state could no longer use its old strategy of pointing to the small numbers of educated Muslims to explain away their lack of representation in government service, since the Muslims petitioning them were products of the state educational system. The Reading Room Party's[127] petition to the Cabinet after the Civil Service Recruitment Board rules were passed by the state in 1930 began with the point that the paucity of Kashmiri Muslims in government service had so far been explained away through their low educational qualifications. The representation pointed out that although such a claim could to a certain extent apply to services requiring degree qualifications, it could hardly apply to low-level posts and non-gazetted appointments, from which Muslims had been excluded by the Hindu heads of department, who cared little for Muslims. Additionally, the petition stated that there were plenty of educated Muslims in the state now, waiting for employment. The main accusation against the government remained that there were no

---

[126] General Department 1190/Misc 35/1930, Jammu State Archives.

[127] Sheikh Mohammad Abdullah established the Reading Room Party, the forerunner to the All Jammu and Kashmir Muslim Conference, in 1930, primarily as a venue to discuss social and political problems facing the Kashmiri Muslim community. For details, see next chapter.

incentives for Muslims to gain education, since the possession of degree qualifications was a matter of no advantage to them.[128]

Even as the religious leadership succeeded in elevating educational reform to the status of political agenda, its rhetoric on Muslim backwardness in education was readily appropriated by the state. As a result, while the state recognized Kashmiri Muslims as a separate category in the 1920s, particularly in the realm of education, it continued to eschew its responsibility for providing incentives to Muslims to get educated, instead placing this burden squarely on the community leadership. After all, according to the Dogra state, Muslims were condemned to remaining backward in education due to their religious proclivities. The emergent leadership of the 1930s, however, soon forced a change in this attitude.

* * *

The discourse on education, conducted between Muslim educational reform movements, private educational institutions, and the state system of education, provides an important perspective on the changing relationship between the Muslim community leadership, itself in the process of transformation, and the Dogra state at the turn of the twentieth century. The institutionalization of education into a branch of the state, and the concomitant link between education and government employment, had led to the realization of the Dogra state's worst fear, articulated as early as 1893. A class of educated Kashmiris, who not only spoke for themselves but also their uneducated brethren, were clamoring for employment in government service. The state could no longer camouflage its inaction in the rhetoric of class or religion. The new leadership was willing (at least at the level of discourse) to cut across lines of class and sect to organize Kashmiri Muslims under an anti-government banner. Education, in the coming decades, was to become deeply imbricated with a more belligerent discourse on political, economic and social rights for Kashmiris, not merely as subjects, but as rightful citizens of the state. The locus of historical initiative had shifted to a new Muslim leadership.

---

[128] General Department 1190/Misc 35/1930, Jammu State Archives.

CHAPTER 5

The Politics of Identity

Religious Community, Region, and Nation in Kashmiri Discourse

I n the 1930s, the rhetoric of belonging to a religious collectivity became inseparable from the discourse on rights and freedoms that formed the core of the emergent Kashmiri Muslim movement. As I have shown, this was not a novel phenomenon on the political landscape of the Valley. Since the late nineteenth century, Kashmiri Muslim leaders had been attempting to internally reform and define the boundaries of their community while also demanding that the state recognize them as a separate entity. This was particularly because the Dogra state defined itself and its right to rule solely based on its religious affiliation, and, much like its colonial counterpart in British India, categorized its subjects singularly on the basis of their religious affiliations.

However, what was different about the new Muslim leadership that took over in the wake of the 1931 incidents was that it more concretely linked religious affiliation with political demands by claiming rights for Kashmiri Muslims based on the ideal of a just Islamic society. Furthermore, since this leadership ultimately sought to replace the autocratic rule of the Dogras with Kashmiri self-rule, the articulation of a "national" ideology was imperative to its project. The leadership soon discovered, however, that the creation of a "nation" on the bedrock of religious identifications without taking into account religious/cultural difference was a parlous enterprise, particularly in a political structure built to guarantee the rights of a particular community. Here I chart the emergence and articulation of a Kashmiri nationalist discourse as it attempted to negotiate religious affiliations, regional identities, a Hindu state, and political organizations of British India, with the ultimate aim of granting citizenship rights to all Kashmiris as citizens, not subjects of the state.

1931: Events, Meanings, and Outcomes

The concept of *Kashmiriyat* and the events of 1931 both have pride of place in Kashmiri historical narratives. While the former is used to extol the uniqueness of Kashmiri identity and nationalism, both of which have shunned religious animosity, the latter becomes a dramatic example of the rise of political consciousness in the Kashmir Valley. The apparent contradiction between the two seems lost on authors of the Kashmiri nationalist narrative. The religious syncretism that *Kashmiriyat* so proudly claims as its inheritance was nowhere in evidence during the events of 1931, nor in the discourse generated in their aftermath. In fact, 1931 inaugurated the emergence of the much-dreaded term "communalism" in the political discourse of hitherto "non-communal" Kashmir.

Reams of paper have been devoted to the incidents that took place in the princely state of Jammu and Kashmir from April to July 1931, most accounts geared toward illustrating the groundswell of public opinion against the atrocities of Maharaja Hari Singh's regime. As P.N.K. Bamzai put it, for instance: "It is from that date that the people took upon themselves the task of securing for themselves the right of democratic self-rule."[1] The fact that 1931 was the beginning of anti-Dogra political activity in Kashmir is highly overstated. Despite the fact that the public arena was severely proscribed in the state prior to 1932, the Kashmiri Muslim leadership had crafted and laid claim to a public space in which they debated and defined their political agenda as well as the contours of their community identity. What cannot be doubted, of course, is that 1931 explicitly changed the course of Kashmiri politics, steering it toward the anti-colonial politics of British India.

The incidents of 1931 began in Jammu Central Jail with the alleged insult of the *Quran* by a Hindu constable. Although the charges against the Hindu constable were dismissed, this was soon followed by

---

[1] P.N.K. Bamzai, *Culture and Political History of Kashmir, Vol. 3, Modern Kashmir* (New Delhi: MD Publications, 1994), 732.

the discovery of a few pages of the *Quran* in a Srinagar drain. A follow-up incident occurred in June, when Abdul Qadeer, a Punjabi who had come to Kashmir in the service of a European visitor and was later alleged to be an Ahmadiyya, delivered a seditious speech during a meeting of Kashmiri Muslims at the Shah-i-Hamdaan shrine. The police promptly arrested him and the date of his trial at Srinagar Central Jail was set for July 13, 1931. The final explosion that has forever stamped this date on the annals of Kashmiri history took place when a restive crowd and the police clashed outside the Central Jail, followed by general rioting during which Muslim men destroyed the shops and homes of Pandit landholders, moneylenders, and petty officials in the city.[2]

Although the scribes of Kashmiri nationalist histories would have us believe otherwise, the 1931 incidents cannot be studied in isolation. They were intimately connected to the larger socio-political context of the late 1920s and early 1930s in the Kashmir Valley. As already pointed out, by the late 1920s, a new Kashmiri leadership had begun vigorously demanding the active intervention of the Dogra state in redressing the political and economic grievances of Kashmiri Muslims. This was evident in their representation to the government on behalf of Kashmiri Muslims on the constitution of the Civil Service Recruitment Board in 1930. According to the representation headed by Sheikh Mohammad Abdullah, the government had instituted the board at this particular juncture to create hurdles for Kashmiri Muslim young men who were qualified and willing to join the services.[3] Despite the government's refusal to change the recruitment rules, the belligerence of the new leadership was evident from this representation.

Additionally, the economic situation of the Valley was in steady decline from the late 1920s. By the early 1930s, the worldwide economic depression had begun to have an impact on a wide cross-section of Kashmiri society. The slump in trade beginning in 1930 and fall in the price of agricultural produce led to increased rural–urban migration. However, the urban factories that had provided jobs to the immigrants

---

[2] Bamzai, *Culture and Political History of Kashmir*, Vol. 3, 731 and Barjor Dalal, *Report of the Srinagar Riot Enquiry Committee S. 1988 (1931)* (Srinagar: Pratap Government Press, 1931), 19–21.

[3] P.N. Bazaz, *Inside Kashmir* (Srinagar: Kashmir Publishing Co., 1941; repr., Azad Kashmir: Verinag Publishers, 1987), 100–1.

in the 1920s were now in a state of collapse.[4] Newspaper editorials from this period lamented the rise in unemployment, the decline of factories such as the silk factory, and the acquisition by moneylenders and *mahajans* of those lands that had been made over to the peasants as part of the conferral of proprietary rights by the government.[5]

Although the government had passed a Land Alienation Act in 1926 to control the transfer of land by sale or mortgage, which disallowed the transfer of the newly acquired rights to any but a member of the agricultural classes and prohibited an alienation of more than 25 percent of any holding for a period of ten years, the peasants exercised this right in full for the liquidation of debt. These sales increased the fragmentation of holdings and transferred much of the land to members of agricultural classes who were not cultivators. This in turn resulted in the reduction of the state's aggregate food supply and difficulties of feeding a rapidly increasing population. Additionally, it led to soaring land prices, which the richer classes in the Valley, usually non-agriculturists, were willing and able to pay.[6]

Finally, the 1931 events in Jammu and Kashmir have to be viewed in the all-India political context of the period. Although Kashmir was far removed from the Purna Swaraj resolution adopted by the Indian National Congress in 1929 and the Civil Disobedience campaigns of the early 1930s, the people of Kashmir, particularly their leadership, were greatly affected by the heated political atmosphere in India.[7] The full-scale impact of British Indian politics on the politics of the Kashmir Valley is evident when one analyses the interpretations of 1931 by the Maharaja's administration, the "impartial" British inquiry committee heads investigating the incidents for the British, and the emergent

[4] Political Department D-6/1934, Jammu State Archives and *Trade Report of the Jammu and Kashmir State (1935–38)* (Jammu: Ranbir Government Press, 1940), 1–3.

[5] "The Empty Promises of the Government," *Sadaqat,* Srinagar, January 26, 1934.

[6] Capt. R.G. Wreford, *Census of India, 1941, Vol. XXII, Jammu and Kashmir* (Jammu: Ranbir Government Press, 1943), 14–15. The state passed a follow-up Land Alienation Act in 1938, which allowed for the alienation of land only "where the alienor is not a member of the agricultural class, or where the alienor and alienee are members of an agricultural class." See *Laws of Jammu and Kashmir,* vol. III (3rd ed. Srinagar: Jammu and Kashmir Government Press, 1972), 581.

[7] Wreford, *Census of India, 1941, Vol. XXII, Jammu and Kashmir,* 103–4.

Kashmiri Muslim leadership—which saw 1931 as a great political opportunity. By far the most significant impact of the events of 1931 was the entry of the term communal into the Kashmiri political arena. From 1931 onwards, Kashmiri politics and politicians, not unlike their Indian counterparts, would come to be judged on the communal–national gauge.[8]

Even before the events of July 13, the British were busy predicting agitation on "communal lines" in the cities of Jammu and Srinagar. The reports of the British Resident from the first half of June 1931 were rife with ominous references to the restless Muslims of Jammu and Srinagar who were attempting to secure a larger share of posts in the Kashmir government, for which they would necessarily resort to communal disturbances.[9] Maharaja Hari Singh, taking his cue from the Resident, issued a message to his "beloved people," expressing his regret at the "communal strife" that had been observed in certain sections of the cities of Jammu and Srinagar. The message promised to consider the legitimate requests of the people, provided "the leaders of the various communities take immediate action to put a stop to all political activities tending to prevent the re-establishment of friendly relations between them."[10] The British, as also the Maharaja, would necessarily view any action on the part of Kashmiri Muslims to secure political and economic rights as "communal" in nature, implying that it was directed specifically against another religious community, and more significantly against the Dogra state.

[8] The communal/national dichotomy had been in use in British Indian provinces since the early twentieth century. In Bengal, for instance, the gradual distancing of leading Muslim associations headed by Abdul Latif and Syed Amir Ali from the Indian National Congress in the 1890s prepared the ground for the use of these dichotomous terms by "nationalist" politicians. However, their use became more widespread and loaded during the time of the Swadeshi movement (1905–8). By the end of the first decade of the twentieth century, Bengali Muslims had begun to discuss defensive interpretations of communalism in the format of "good" versus "bad" communalism. For a detailed discussion see Semanti Ghosh, "Nationalism and the Problem of Difference: Bengal, 1905–1947" (Ph.D. dissertation, Tufts University, 2000).

[9] "Report of the Resident in Kashmir," June 19, 1931, Foreign and Political Department, R/1/29/689/1931, India Office Library, London, 5 (microfilm).

[10] "His Highness's Message to My Beloved People," ibid., 2.

July 13, 1931 confirmed their worst fears. The peaceful and placid Kashmir Valley, where religious communities had lived in complete harmony since time immemorial, as the discourse on *Kashmiriyat* claimed, had ultimately fallen into the communal trap. The Barjor Dalal Committee, appointed by the Maharaja to inquire into the causes of the disturbances of 1931, presented them not as a movement against the Maharaja's person or his reign, but as a Muslim movement against the Hindus of the Valley, many of whom held positions of power within the government. According to the committee report, even extremist Muslims had full faith in the Maharaja and the laws he had enacted for the betterment of his subjects. But they complained that "a section of the Hindus had overpowering representation in the government and that section oppressed the Mohammadans."[11] In the same vein, the report made incessant references to the communal riots of 1931, the means of re-establishing communal peace, and the future prevention of communal tension in the state. Even when it did admit that the incidents of 1931 might represent the genuine political and economic grievances of the Kashmiri Muslim population, the admission was couched in the knowledge that Muslim leaders used these grievances to incite their followers into communal disharmony:

> The grievance [paucity of state Muslims in state service] does exist . . . the grievance becomes more acute when the Mohammadans themselves find that they have no ability to satisfy their natural desire for a voice in the Government of the State . . . this dissatisfaction is a perpetual source of embitterment of the Mohammadan intellegentia [*sic*] and an incentive to them to excite the masses by illusive [*sic*] religious grievances in order to force the Government to accept their claim for a much larger share in the State service than they enjoy at present.[12]

According to the report, then, the large proportion of Kashmiri Muslim masses had been duped by their leadership into blurring the boundaries between their religious and economic grievances, thereby communalizing the 1931 movement.

How else were the British to reconcile the uniqueness of the Kashmiri identity and its ethos of tolerance with this sudden outbreak of

[11] Dalal, *Report of the Srinagar Riot Enquiry*, 45.
[12] Ibid., 35.

a "communal epidemic?" Another explanation, expounded on at length by the British since it also conveniently obscured the culpability of the Dogra state in engendering Muslim protests, laid the blame at the doorstep of Punjabi Muslim communal organizations and newspapers that had taken it upon themselves to incite Kashmiris. G.E.C. Wakefield, the minister-in-charge of the police, political and foreign departments at the time of the disturbances, noted that the leading exponents of the Punjabi Muslim communalist press—the *Inqilab*, the *Siasat* and the *Muslim Outlook*—questioned the Kashmir government at every step, its every action "anathemised as a deep-laid design on the part of the state authorities to frustrate the legitimate progress of Mohammedans and to undermine their rights and privileges."[13] According to him, had it not been for the influence of the All India Kashmiri Muslim Conference, Lahore, and other communal organizations and newspapers, the Muslims of the state would not have raised the cry of "Islam in danger" during the incidents of April and June 1931. The Dalal Report stated that the dogmas of the All India Kashmiri Muslim Conference were adopted wholesale by the Youngmen's Muslim Association of Jammu and Srinagar and the Kashmir government's hesitation in nipping their agitation in the bud led to the later developments.[14] That the Maharaja also perceived his hitherto calm subjects to have been corrupted by Punjabi Muslims is clear from his proclamation after the events of 1931: "His Highness expects his subjects, who are peaceful by nature to shake off the evil influence, to shun violence and crime and to behave, as they have done in the past, as law-abiding citizens."[15]

It suited the British and the Maharaja to explain away the 1931 disturbances as communal and the outcome of persistent agitation from outside the state. However, the voices of Kashmiris had become too loud to ignore. A Jammu Muslim organization, the Youngmen's Muslim Association, actively presented the community's case to the Maharaja in the months following the events of 1931. The inroads the

[13] G.E.C. Wakefield, "Note by Mr. G.E.C. Wakefield on the Causes of Unrest Amongst the Mohammedans of the Jammu and Kashmir State," Political Department E485/13/1931, Jammu State Archives, 15.

[14] Dalal, *Report of the Srinagar Riot Enquiry*, 23.

[15] General Department 16/Pr-1/1931, Jammu State Archives.

term "communal" had made into Kashmiri politics is clear from a representation, made by a deputation of Muslim representatives of Jammu and Kashmir to the Maharaja, devoted almost entirely to proving that Kashmiri Muslims were not communal. However, the representation did not stop at simply articulating their secular nature and their loyalty to the person of the ruler; it went on to declare that Hindus of the state were, in fact, the communal ones. The representation was mainly concerned with accusing Kashmiri Pandits and Hindu organizations of the Punjab for spreading nefarious propaganda against Kashmiri Muslims that labeled them communal: "True to their traditions, these Pandits reduced the Muslims to utter helplessness from whom petitions were not even received, by hiding their property to pretend that they were looted by Muslims."[16]

Whether it was Kashmiri Hindus or Kashmiri Muslims who were communal is moot, since the term has been misrepresented and misapplied in South Asian historiography.[17] What is more significant is that the Kashmiri Muslim demarche was correct in pointing out that 1931 should not be dismissed as an outburst driven by religious passion, since it was the outcome of years of oppression. Furthermore, it emphasized the fact that simply because the demands of Kashmiri Muslims were couched in religious terms did not mean that they could be branded communal. According to the representation:

[16] "Representation made by the Deputation of Muslim Representatives to His Highness," August 15, 1931, Political Department 87/P/1931, Jammu State Archives, 3.

[17] Ayesha Jalal argues that scholars and politicians alike have used the term communalism as a pejorative Other of nationalism to connote the exclusionary project of Muslim politics in South Asia, thereby conflating the Muslim religiously informed cultural identity with the politics of cultural nationalism. According to her, exploding communalism may perhaps be the only means of "genuinely rethinking and renegotiating the perennial problem of difference and identity in South Asia as a whole." See Ayesha Jalal, "Exploding Communalism: The Politics of Muslim Identity in South Asia," in Bose and Jalal, eds., *Nationalism, Democracy and Development*, 76–103. However, the term "communalism" was a very real label for those who applied it to their opponents and those who were at its receiving end. Therefore, while deconstructing the term is a valid and necessary enterprise, the term itself cannot be simply wished away in a discussion of Kashmiri politics of this period.

The causes of the present troubles and the tale of oppression to which the Muslim subjects have been and are being subjected have a long history behind them and it would be no place to mention them here. Suffice it to say that the non-Muslim community was actuated by definite purpose to interfere with the religious affairs of the Muslim subjects and the ball was set rolling by the officers of the government, for example the prohibition of Khutba-i-Id-ul-Zuha, the insult to the holy Quran, the dismantling of mosques, the stoppage of azan, were heart-rending events of a nature which grievously wounded the religious feelings and prestige of the peaceful Muslim subjects and they were so impressed by the shortsightedness of the authorities that they considered Islam to be in danger.[18]

The Muslim representatives were clearly underscoring the liability of the government in creating a public space with religious contours, which slotted and gave differential patronage to individuals based on their membership of particular religious communities. This also demonstrates the importance of the term "communal" in the Kashmiri political context and the need felt by the new leadership to separate themselves from it. Although it was not until the end of the decade that the leaders adopted the term "national" as a counterpoise to it, the process of defining political parties and persons through their adherence to a "communal" or "national" agenda was under way in Kashmir.

Until the early 1930s, the only public activism permitted by the Dogra state was under the auspices of societies for socio-religious reform, which were allowed to function on the condition that they eschew all forms of political activity, a condition that most ignored. These societies, such as the Dogra Sabha, Arya Samaj, Hindu Sahayak Sabha, Sanatan Dharma Yuvak Sabha, and Anjuman Nusrat-ul-Islam, to name a few, campaigned for the reform of their individual communities and caste groups.[19] The division of the public sphere along lines of community in the early twentieth century ensured that the politics of the 1930s was also played out in terms of communitarian interests, and in a vocabulary imported from British India. The significant difference, of course, was that while the earlier organizations had

[18] "Representation made by the Deputation of Muslim Representatives to His Highness," August 15, 1931, Political Department 87/P/1931, Jammu State Archives, 5.

[19] For further elaboration on this point, see Rai, "Question of Religion in Kashmir," chapter five.

represented fairly narrow class or caste interests within communities, the organizations that emerged in the early 1930s claimed to unite and represent a cross-section of their particular communities.

On the heels of the above representation, representatives of the Jammu and Kashmir Muslims presented a memorial to the Maharaja on October 19, 1931, for the specific purpose of presenting Kashmiri Muslim demands to the administration. The representatives attempted to set themselves apart from the external influences of communal Punjabi Muslims, stating that their suggestions "did not owe their origin to any artificial agitation," but instead the hardships that Muslims had been laboring under for centuries had forced them to conclude that "without the reforms and improvements contained in this humble memorial the lives of the Muslim subjects of Your Highness will continue to be extremely miserable."[20] Although the memorial recommended the setting up of an independent inquiry commission to investigate the events of July 1931 and the actions of officials during the disturbances, along with the release of political offenders, these measures related to the events were not the motivation behind the memorial.

The new leadership was determined to gain full political mileage out of 1931 by drawing the administration's attention to the origins of the disturbances. The economic and political disabilities suffered by the people, in turn, could only be addressed through widespread reformation of the structures of the state. As the memorial warned, albeit respectfully, "subjects can enjoy real peace only when they have been conceded the right to an effective share in the legislation of the State and of criticising the administration."[21] To this end, the memorial gave a detailed description of the proposed constitution for the state of Jammu and Kashmir, which included a guarantee of the fundamental rights of religion, speech, press, platform, assembly and equality of treatment of all state subjects, and the formation of executive and legislative bodies to carry out the will of the people. Significantly, the

[20] "Memorial of the Jammu and Kashmir Muslims presented to His Highness Raj Rajeshwar Maharajadhiraj Shri Maharaja Sir Hari Singh Ji Bahadur Inder Mahinder, Sipar-i-Saltanat-Inglishia, G.C.I.E., K.C.V.O., A.D.C., Maharaja of Jammu and Kashmir," Srinagar, October 19, 1931, Political Department 83/1931, Jammu State Archives, 2.

[21] Ibid., 5.

memorial demanded that the rules for election to the legislature should be framed so that the "elected representatives of the different religions are returned in proportion to the number of their respective adherents." The same principle of communal proportion was to be observed in recruitment to all grades of services, based on the minimum qualification. Hence, if a requisite number of Muslims of high education was not available, the government had to recruit from less qualified Muslims in preference to better-qualified non-Muslims.[22]

Notwithstanding their claims to the contrary, the Kashmiri Muslim leadership's truculence was partly a result of the support they enjoyed from Punjabi Muslim organizations. Significant among them was the All India Kashmir Committee, which had been vocal in Kashmiri Muslim affairs since the beginning of the century. Other organizations supporting the Kashmiri cause were the Anjuman-i-Himayat-i-Islam, Lahore, and the Anjuman-i-Kashmiri Musalman, both of which were patronized by Muhammad Iqbal. By the time 1931 rolled around, all manner of Punjabi political groups had appropriated Kashmir for their own purposes, with Hindu and Muslim newspapers crying Muslim and Hindu conspiracy respectively while discussing the events of 1931.[23]

What further complicated the situation by October 1931 for both the British and the Dogra government was that the Ahrar party, watching Kashmir slipping through their fingers into the hands of the Kashmir Committee, decided to send *jathas* (bands of volunteers) into state territory through the Jammu province. They claimed that the Kashmir Committee was run by Ahmadiyyas for the propagation of their sacrilegious sect in Kashmir. Mirpur and Jammu districts were soon engulfed in rioting; here Muslim crowds made the Hindu moneylending class a target of looting and arson. Ultimately, one company of British troops had to be dispatched to Mirpur and two others to Jammu to contain the bedlam. An alarmed Government of India issued an ordinance on November 7, 1931, prohibiting the sending of jathas into the state.[24] Although the Ahrar agitation in Kashmir soon dwindled from lack of support and factionalism, it

[22] Ibid., 8–10.

[23] Jalal, *Self and Sovereignty*, 351–6.

[24] "Report of the Resident in Kashmir," November 3, 1931, Foreign and Political Department, R/1/29/689/1931, India Office Library, London, 1 (microfilm).

certainly jolted the Dogras and the colonial government, since the Ahrars refused to give up their stance as saviors of Kashmir.[25]

The British did not want the already far too restive Punjab to be drawn into a rapidly deteriorating situation in Kashmir. An expeditious end to the Kashmir crisis suited the British the most, a fact that was not lost on the Kashmiri Muslim leadership.[26] Although the Kashmir government announced the appointment of B.J. Glancy to head an independent commission to consider Muslim and non-Muslim demands, the new leadership was in a position to put continued pressure on the darbar to meet their demands even before Glancy arrived on the scene. As the Resident wrote in his fortnightly report from Kashmir, "The Jammu leaders showed a disinclination, unless further immediate concessions were announced, to comply with the Darbar's request that they should get in touch with the Ahrar party with a view to stopping a further incursion of jathas from the Punjab."[27] Jammu Muslims had lost sympathy with the Ahrars and Kashmiri Muslims had the support of the Ahmadiyyas, but the leaders of both communities continued to use the Ahrars as a threat to force the darbar into concessions. The strategy evidently worked since the darbar rescinded the special taxes on Bakarwals (goat herders) to placate Jammu Muslims and restored the Pathar Masjid to the Kashmiri Muslim community before Glancy's arrival.[28] Fifty thousand Muslims gathered at the opening ceremony of the mosque, where they passed a resolution declaring the mosque "the centre and symbol of unity among all Muslim sects in Kashmir." Additionally, the meeting demanded that the government immediately grant adequate funds for the repair of the mosque.[29]

The purpose behind the darbar's actions and the newly belligerent

[25] For a discussion of the Punjabi context for the Ahrar intervention in Kashmir, see Jalal, *Self and Sovereignty*, 356–63.

[26] In his letter dated October 9, 1931 to the Maharaja, the Resident conveyed the Government of India's message regarding the disturbances involving Ahrars and Ahmadiyyas: "It seems of vital importance to the Government of India that Your Highness's government should satisfy public opinion immediately and it is prepared to have an enquiry made by an absolutely impartial officer into the alleged grievances with a view to the redress of those established to be reasonable." See Political Department 422/1931, Jammu State Archives.

[27] "Report of the Resident in Kashmir," November 3, 1931, Foreign and Political Department, R/1/29/689/1931, India Office Library, London, 4 (microfilm).

[28] Ibid.

[29] Political Department 83/1931, Jammu State Archives.

stand of the Muslim leadership was evident to the minority communities in the state, particularly Kashmiri Pandits. Faced finally with the prospect of being reduced to a numerically insignificant minority in the political and economic structures of the state, some Kashmiri Pandits retaliated with alarm. Disgusted at the Hindu Maharaja for not protecting their life and property during the riots of 1931, they petitioned the Viceroy and Governor General of India, presenting their community as "enlightened, educated, law-abiding," which was under siege from the local Muslim community that was "barbarous and ignorant." Since they had "drunk deep at the fountain of English learning and culture more than any other community in the state," some Kashmiri Pandits asked the Viceroy to protect their life and property.[30] They recognized that the only means through which they could get special attention from the British was if they declared themselves to be a beleaguered minority. To establish this status, they had to separate themselves from Kashmiri Muslims, which they did by stating that their community was the first to gain education and serve actively in the service of the state, thus deserving better treatment than they had received from the government.

Kashmiri Pandits had received a rude shock, not so much through the events of 1931, as through the darbar's previous and subsequent "pro-Muslim" actions, since they had believed that their pro-regime stance and their fact of being Hindu would keep their position within the state administration intact. The statements of the Kashmiri Pandit Sudhar Sabha and Sanatan Dharma Youngmen's Association after the 1931 events were devoted to describing the darbar's pro-Muslim policies, such as special scholarships, special education officers, financial aid for the reconstruction of their mosques and so on, which had encouraged the Muslims to carry their demands to the logical conclusion. "In every department of public life," charged one statement, "the Muslim is the spoiled child and the Hindu the step-child of the government."[31] And this in spite of "the historical importance of the

[30] "Petition from certain Kashmiri Pandits of Srinagar to the Viceroy and Governor General of India," September 26, 1932, Office of the District Magistrate, Kashmir, 340/1931–2, Srinagar State Archives.

[31] "Statement of Kashmiri Pandit Sudhar Sabha, Srinagar to Prime Minister, His Highness's Government," August 8, 1931, Political Department 96/89/1931, Jammu State Archives, 4.

Kashmiri Pandits which entitle them to special protection."[32] The representations did not stop there, however, and presented the Kashmiri Pandits not only as a historically enlightened community, but also a historically persecuted one. During 600 years of Muslim rule, claimed this pamphlet, "the majority of them [Kashmiri Pandits] were converted to Islam at the point of the sword, and large numbers had to leave hearth and home . . . The inherent love of learning did, however, assert itself; and he adapted himself to altered conditions of life and mastered the Muslim culture and literature."[33] The Muslims, with the sole object of obliterating the community, carried this historical tradition forward into 1931 with the loot, murder and rape of Kashmiri Pandits. The statements included meticulous lists of Kashmiri Pandits materially and physically injured during the disturbances.

Needless to say, this proved the "non-communal" nature of Kashmiri Pandits, while Kashmiri Muslims threatened to ruin the fabric of the society through their "communal" actions. Recent events had proven beyond doubt, claimed the representation, that "we cannot look on things through communal glasses while Mussalmans have presented their claims on communal grounds."[34] Despite claiming to be non-communal, however, some Kashmiri Pandits joined other Hindus in demanding special protection from the ruler based on their common religious affiliation. Reminding the Maharaja of his Hindu antecedents, which made him duty-bound to protect his Hindu subjects, these Kashmiri Hindus warned the Maharaja that they were the "solid backbone" of his rule in Kashmir and he could not afford to alienate them. However, the "vacillating surrendering policy of Your Highnesses government has set the Hindus a-thinking if the State authorities have really ceased to function in the matter of protecting the person and property of Your Highness's loyal subjects. Hindus' confidence in Your Highness's government has suffered a rude shock."[35]

[32] "Representation of Sanatan Dharma Youngmen's Association, Srinagar for Submission to Enquiry Commission to Investigate the Disturbances," Political Department 96/89/1931, Jammu State Archives, 2.

[33] Sanatan Dharma Youngmen's Association, Srinagar, *Kashmir Hindus and the Recent Disturbances* (Lahore: Bharat Printing Works, 1931), 1.

[34] "Representation of Sanatan Dharma Association," Political Department 96/89/1931, Jammu State Archives, 2.

[35] "Memorial on Behalf of Hindus of Different Shades of Opinion of Jammu

Despite the communitarian rhetoric in the aftermath of the 1931 crisis, which flourished the bogey of the "other" religious community in order to paper over its own fractured reality, the tensions were far from motivated by religion. There is no doubt that the leaders of both communities claimed to represent issues specific to their own community while labeling the other side communal. And that the avowedly "Muslim" and "Hindu" elements from British India jumped in the fray to support their respective Kashmiri brethren. However, the tussle between Kashmiri Muslims and Kashmiri Pandits in and after 1931 was more about political and economic representation than religious antagonism. Kashmiri Muslims, tired of being excluded from education, the government, and the lower rungs of the administration, rallied around the cry of "Islam in Danger" raised by youth recently returned from British India with professional degrees. Significantly, the looting following the Central Jail incident was concentrated in the Vecharnag locality of Srinagar, home to Kashmiri Pandit petty administrators and moneylenders. A certain Pandit moneylender, Kailash But, told the Dalal Commission that "among the rioters many who [*sic*] were my debtors took special care to see that my documents and other papers were completely destroyed."[36] The rioting on July 13, 1931 was not that of a frenzied mob looking to kill in the name of religion, but one intended to redress the immediate economic grievances of Kashmiri Muslims.

Kashmiri Pandits, a minuscule minority in the Valley who had been gradually losing their traditional foothold in the administration with the establishment of the British Residency and the import of Punjabi Hindus as state administrators, saw the new bellicosity of Muslims as the final nail in their coffin. If the government accepted Muslim demands, as it seemed inclined to do, then Kashmiri Pandits would be

---

and Kashmir State presented to His Highness," October 29, 1931, Political Department 96/89/1931, Jammu State Archives, 5.

[36] Political Department 399/S-96/1931, Jammu State Archives. This kind of activity on the part of the indebted, particularly among the peasantry, has been well documented by Sugata Bose in the case of Bengal. According to Bose, 1930 was the turning point in the attitudes of the Bengali peasantry, mostly Muslim, when they began to attack the houses of Hindu moneylenders with a view to destroying the debt bonds held by them. See Sugata Bose, *Agrarian Bengal: Economy, Social Structure and Politics, 1919–1947* (Cambridge: Cambridge University Press, 1986), 190–1.

deprived of their traditional means of employment. Since Muslims numerically far exceeded Pandits, it would not be long before they manned all government departments. Rumors that the government was giving into Muslim demands for communal representation abounded during the time. This is clear from the increased number of telegrams, letters and memorials from Pandit organizations addressed to the Prime Minister of Kashmir or the Maharaja himself, expressing reservations and resentment on the moves to sacrifice Pandit interests to satisfy Muslim demands.

A particular letter went so far as to ask the Prime Minister to confirm the rumor whether "His Highness has issued a circular reserving 50 percent of all appointments for Muslims, the other 50 percent being for the other communities," and warning that "I should be able to tell my constituents that the rumor is false, otherwise we can come to a clash with forces of law and order."[37] In their memorial to the Maharaja, Kashmiri Pandit representatives categorically stated that "we are opposed to giving statutory recognition to the vicious principle of communal representation." Further expressing fears on their economic position the memorial stated:

> It was proved by our spokesmen before the Riots Enquiry Committee that about a thousand of our educated men: Matriculates, Undergraduates, B.A.'s, B.Sc's, M.A's, M.Sc's, I.F.S's and LL.B's are without service . . . In recent years about a hundred Kashmiri Pandit educated men have settled outside the State . . . The Government has in the past on numerous occasions passed over the claims of our qualified men and given preference to men of indifferent worth of other communities . . . The glaring truth is that Kashmiri Pandits are being excluded from service because they are Kashmiri Pandits.[38]

The state in general and the Maharaja in particular were caught between the overwhelming upsurge of Kashmiri Muslim public opinion and the rancor of Kashmiri Pandits at being the objects of sacrifice to placate Muslim demands. Walking the tightrope, the Maharaja attempted to assure Kashmiri Pandits that their best interests would be

[37] "P.N Bazaz's letter to Prime Minister," February 12, 1932, Political Department 308/P-S/119/1931, Jammu State Archives.

[38] "Memorial of Demands presented by the Kashmiri Pandits to His Highness, the Maharaja of Jammu and Kashmir," October 24, 1931, Ex-Governor's Records 401/1931, Srinagar State Archives, 3.

kept in mind, although "you will be the first to recognize that with the steady growth of education in other communities the position of advantage which your community has enjoyed in the past in regard to State service, cannot continue."[39] Apart from the two communities, the pressure from the British to resolve the crisis was increasing daily as the Ahrar *jathabandi* continued in the Jammu province. The Government of India was sufficiently concerned that the Viceroy wrote in his telegram to the Secretary of State for India, "So long as active jathabandi continues, there is cause for considerable anxiety . . . The danger will remain that justly or unjustly Kashmir will be made a pretext for Muslim organization when this seems likely to serve the community's [Punjabi Muslims'] purpose."[40] British troops had already entered the state and the Resident was pressing the Maharaja to accept a deputation of outside Muslims to conduct an inquiry into the happenings of 1931. A ruler who had declared in his accession speech that "my religion is justice" was faced with the prospect of keeping his word. The foremost issue that the Maharaja ordered the Glancy Commission to investigate was the "complaints . . . in regard to any conditions or circumstances which might tend in any way to obstruct free practice of any religion followed by any community in my State."[41] He did not, however, accept the Government of India's view on allowing a deputation of outside Muslims to conduct an inquiry in the state, so as to prevent demands of a similar nature by Hindus.[42]

The Maharaja's attempts at keeping Kashmir isolated from the outside world had already failed. Kashmiri Muslim politics continued to be played out as much inside as outside the state. The leadership of the 1930s made full use of the financial and moral support of organizations sympathetic to their cause in British India. Further attesting to the imbrication of politics in British India and Kashmir, the 1931

[39] "Maharaja's Reply to Representation from Kashmiri Pandits," October 29, 1931, Ex-Governor's Records 401/1931, Srinagar State Archives, 4.

[40] "Telegram from His Excellency the Viceroy (Home Department) to H.M.'s Secretary of State for India," December 19, 1931, Foreign and Political Department, R/1/29/823, India Office Library, London, 15 (microfilm).

[41] "Gist of Orders issued by the Maharaja," Crown Representative Papers of India, Foreign and Political Department, R/1/29/823, India Office Library, London, 3 (microfilm).

[42] Ibid.

incident and its aftermath brought with it the language of inclusionary Indian nationalism into the Valley. "Communal" became the pejorative term with which to slander one's political opponents. Although not in widespread use yet, the term "national" would soon appear as the foil of communalism. The emergence of Sheikh Mohammad Abdullah on the Kashmiri political landscape and the foundation of the All Jammu and Kashmir Muslim Conference illuminate the intricacies of these processes.

1932–1933: The Rise of Sheikh Mohammad Abdullah and the Muslim Conference

Sheikh Mohammad Abdullah (1905–82), a master political strategist who dominated Kashmiri politics for five decades, was born into a poor Kashmiri Muslim family from Sorah, a suburb of Srinagar. A beneficiary of the educational reform movements among Kashmiri Muslims in the early part of the century, Abdullah went on to obtain a Master's degree in chemistry from Aligarh Muslim University. Returning to the Valley in early 1930 along with other Kashmiri Muslims such as Mirza Afzal Beg and G.M. Sadiq, Abdullah found employment as a schoolmaster at the State High School, having failed to acquire an administrative job. Along with Beg, Sadiq, and the Ahmadiyya leader Mohammad Abdullah Vakil, he organized an association known as the Reading Room Party at Fateh Kadal, Srinagar, with the view to discussing the problems facing the Muslim community.[43] On the eve of the 1931 crisis, Abdullah was one among many obscure young people filled with discontent over the state of affairs in Kashmir. So how did he manage to rise above the fray, claim the mantle of sole representative of Kashmiri Muslims, and acquire the position of Prime Minister of Jammu and Kashmir in late 1947?

Abdullah succeeded in the chaotic political atmosphere of the 1930s because he was astute enough to predict the course of politics, foresee political challenges, and was sufficiently lacking in scruple to take advantage of them. He most effectively wove the Islamic concepts of a just society and individual rights into his organization's agenda,

---

[43] Alastair Lamb, *Kashmir: A Disputed Legacy, 1846–1990* (Karachi: Oxford University Press, 1993), 90–2.

which appealed to Kashmiri Muslims precisely because social and political rights had been denied them based on their religion, a religion that emphasized justice and social equality. Recognizing the value of allying in early 1930 with the older religious leadership, which had a strong base of support, Abdullah set about making inroads into the favor of the Mirwaiz Kashmir. Recently succeeded to the position after his uncle's death in early 1931, a young Yusuf Shah was suitably impressed by Abdullah's religious devoutness, and extended the Jamia Masjid as the organizational center for Abdullah's political activities.[44] At the same time, Abdullah continued to get financial assistance from the All India Kashmir Committee and other pro-Ahmadiyya organizations, arch-rivals of the Mirwaiz family. He understood that the religious prestige of the Mirwaiz family would be necessary if Islamic concepts were to be used to unite the Kashmiri Muslim community. On the other hand, the Ahmadiyyas in the Valley, with their contacts in the Punjab, would prove valuable for the financial and structural support they could extend to the movement.

Abdullah was able to assume the mantle of sole representative of the Kashmiri Muslims soon after the events of 1931 precisely because he had the moral support of the Mirwaiz Kashmir and the structural support of the All India Kashmir Committee. By rallying the Muslims around the cry of "Islam in Danger" and presenting the community as a unified entity, Abdullah ascended to the status of the "strongest local champion of Muslim demands," who had a "following greater than any other local leader."[45] In an interview with the *Civil and Military Gazette* in July 1932, Abdullah posed as a conduit between the masses and the government: "I am fully in favor of giving them a chance of overhauling the administration and redressing our genuine grievances. I shall, as far as possible, try to co-operate with the administration and help it in reconstructing the State. This, however, depends on . . . the future policy of the administration itself."[46]

Carrying forward his political advantage, Abdullah set about giving

[44] Sadaat, *Rozana Diary*, 694–5.

[45] "Telegram from the Resident in Kashmir," November 11, 1931, Crown Representative Papers of India, Foreign and Political Department R/1/29/823, India Office Library, London, 7 (microfilm).

[46] "Welcome Change in Affairs in Kashmir: S.M. Abdullah's View," *Civil and Military Gazette*, Lahore, July 9, 1932, Political Department 83/1931, Jammu State Archives.

his following and their demands an organizational shape. With the support of the Reading Room Party organizers, Sadiq and Beg, and the Mirwaiz Kashmir and Mirwaiz Hamdaani, Abdullah inaugurated the All Jammu and Kashmir Muslim Conference in 1932. In his presidential address at its first session on October 15, 1932, he called on Kashmiri Muslims to unite, gain education, and be prepared to serve notice to the government as well as to participate in assembly elections as soon as they were called. At the same time, he recalled the past glory of Kashmiris, which was lost when they became the slaves of non-Kashmiri rulers. Emphasizing that the Kashmiri Muslim movement was non-communal, he went on to accuse the administration of holding communal views, which had led them to insult the *Quran* and injure the religious feelings of Kashmiri Muslims.[47] At this stage, the Muslim Conference was a Kashmiri Muslim organization, whose main objective was to unite Kashmiri Muslims under one political umbrella through an appeal to their sense of belonging to an Islamic community. Abdullah recognized the political dangers of claiming to represent a community wracked by internal discord. And, from the outset, he was unable to reconcile the communitarian card he played with the national one. As the decade progressed, the internal contradictions in Abdullah's politics became glaringly obvious.

Mirwaiz Kashmir Yusuf Shah was the first to raise the banner of revolt against Abdullah's ambivalent politics. Recognizing that Abdullah was far from a sycophant who would follow in his footsteps, the Mirwaiz broke away from the Muslim Conference in 1933 and formed his own political organization, the Azad Muslim Party Conference. The alleged reason for this breakup was that the Ahmadiyyas controlled the Muslim Conference with a view to proselytizing their faith among Kashmiri Muslims. Labeling Abdullah and his supporters "the Pathar Masjid leaders," the mutawalli of Hazratbal mosque, during the inaugural session of the Azad Party Conference, stated that the fundamental principle of these men was the preservation and spread of Qadianyat in the Kashmir Valley, since they were puppets in the hands of the Qadianis.[48] As discussed in earlier chapters, the activities of the

[47] "Presidential Address by Sheikh Mohammad Abdullah at First Session of All Jammu and Kashmir Muslim Conference," October 15–17, 1932, Srinagar, in Mirza Shafiq Hussain, ed., *The Political Struggle of Kashmiri Muslims, 1931–1939: Selected Documents* (Srinagar: Gulshan Publishers, 1991), 219–29.

[48] "Reception Address by Khwaja Abdul Rahim Bhande at First Session of

Ahmadiyyas in the Valley had been threatening to the religious leadership since the 1920s. Their obvious success on this front could not but have rankled the Mirwaiz Kashmir, who devoted much energy in formulating elaborate theological arguments to prove the Ahmadiyya movement heretical.

It was no accident then that in his presidential address on the founding of the Azad Party the Mirwaiz drew attention to the role played by his family in the Kashmiri Muslims' struggle for their rights, labeling the Anjuman Nusrat-ul-Islam as the first stage in "our collective thinking." His activities in 1931, when the Muslim holy book was insulted, was, according to him, the logical continuation of this role. However, as soon as he realized that the Ahmadiyyas controlled this movement and would not let the Ahrars help the Kashmiri people, he struck out on his own, realizing that "to stay out of politics would be a crime against Islam."[49] Undoubtedly, the fact that his family's traditional rival, the Mirwaiz Hamdaani of Shah-i-Hamdaan shrine, supported Abdullah, also played a role in the Mirwaiz's decision to separate himself from the movement. Moreover, Abdullah's political orientation was becoming increasingly anti-government, despite his repeated claims of loyalty to the Maharaja, and the Mirwaiz Kashmir had no intention of alienating the government and jeopardizing the traditional financial patronage enjoyed by his family. Significantly, also, the trader class who financed the Mirwaiz family's philanthropy and formed its primary basis of support, was in favor of remaining aloof from Sheikh Abdullah and the Muslim Conference, a movement that was increasingly putting forth the demands of the peasantry and laboring classes.[50]

In a letter to the Maharaja asking for a reconsideration of the order banning religious sermons, the Mirwaiz expressed his sincere loyalty to the government. He claimed that he had dissociated himself from

---

Jammu and Kashmir Azad Party Conference," December 3, 1933, Srinagar, in Hussain, ed., *The Political Struggle*, 249.

[49] "Presidential Address by Mirwaiz Mohammad Yusuf at First Session of Jammu and Kashmir Azad Party Conference," December 3, 1933, Srinagar, in Hussain, ed., *The Political Struggle*, 265.

[50] Political Department 188/PS-7/1934, Jammu State Archives.

the 1931 movement so that he could preach religious sermons exhorting people to remain peaceful. Additionally, he stated that when he realized that Sheikh Abdullah and his party wanted to launch an agitation against the government, and "thereby plunge the country in the depths of destruction," he opposed their mission. He asked them to stop the agitation immediately and dispense with "Mirzaies [Ahmadiyyas] and such revolutionary men." In return, however, he got brickbats from the Sheikh and his followers, who prevented him from preaching in several localities of the city. Along with the hatred of these people on account of his loyalism, his livelihood was now being threatened by the order of government banning religious sermons, while "to allow Sheikh Mohammad Abdullah to deliver speeches on all topics is beyond justice."[51]

He then used the opportunity to request the Maharaja to remove the restrictions that had been placed on the Mirwaiz Kashmir's preaching through legal enactments in previous years, and, as significantly, to reserve the Pathar Masjid solely for offering prayers. The Mirwaiz was attempting not only to maintain his family's position within royal circles, but also to wrest political control from Abdullah by regaining the right to preach at city shrines. That he requested to have the Governor of Kashmir's order of 1910 rescinded—which had laid down the preaching jurisdictions of the two Mirwaizes—illustrates that he was obviously keen on re-establishing his waning authority in the city. And, by appealing to restrict the Pathar Masjid for prayers, he was striking at the roots of Abdullah's popularity in the Kashmir Valley. Not only had the divisions of the early twentieth century reappeared on the Valley's political landscape in the 1930s, but the symbols that had informed the political culture of the 1910s and 1920s reappeared now in the public sphere of the Valley.

Although Sheikh Abdullah claimed to be a national leader far removed from the concerns and methods of the earlier leadership he so quickly seemed to have replaced, his political rhetoric and tactics in the early years had much in common with those of the religious leadership. He continued to use Islam as the primary focus of community organization, since the parameters within which the public and political

---

[51] General Department 132/P-18 1932, Jammu State Archives.

could function in the state were defined by religion. In a highly symbolic move, Abdullah organized a meeting of Kashmiri Muslims at the Shah-i-Hamdaan shrine soon after the events of 1931, which was attended by the Mirwaiz Kashmir, the first member of the Mirwaiz Kashmir family to visit the shrine of his traditional adversary.[52] Additionally, Abdullah reclaimed the most potent symbol of the Kashmiri Muslim community's struggle to be recognized as a social and political entity with certain rights by the state, the Pathar Masjid, as his political platform. The return of the mosque to the community by the Maharaja, was, after all, the first political victory of the 1931 agitation. In a letter to the Prime Minister, Abdullah noted that, at the opening ceremony of the mosque, "the vast gathering of Kashmir Muslims which is representative of all Muslim sects resolves that, as this Mosque symbolises perfect unity among the various Muslim sects, no waaz or speech would be allowed in it which may be likely to break the unity and injure the feelings of any sect."[53]

Supporters of the Muslim Conference apotheosized Sheikh Abdullah as their savior, a prophet sent by God to intervene on their behalf. The poetry composed in the early 1930s presented the movement as the Kashmiri Muslim struggle to regain their rights in the face of intense persecution. A Kashmiri masnavi published in 1932 entitled *Noah's Ark, or the True Voice*, hailed the voice of truth and justice that had descended on Kashmir through Abdullah. The poem likened the 1931 incidents to the martyrdom of Hassan and Hussain at Karbala:

Look at the light of faith, the greatness of Allah
Who are the real Muslims?
Only they became famous who died for their rights,
And embraced the way of the royal jails.
Those faithfuls were shot in the chests
And sacrificed their lives, look at the greatness of Allah.[54]

[52] Sadaat, *Rozana Diary*, 699.

[53] "Letter from Sheikh Abdullah to the Prime Minister, Jammu and Kashmir State," November 30, 1931, Political Department, 83/1931, Jammu State Archives.

[54] Babu Fakirullah Khan Sahab, *Safinaye Nooh, almaroof Sach Aawaaz* [Noah's Ark, or the True Voice] (Amritsar: Ahmadiyya Press, 1932), Political Department 384/Pol 10/1932, Jammu State Archives.

Other pamphlets declared that the exalted Abdullah arrived on the scene to "lift the burden of oppression off the shoulders of Muslims."[55] Although he was terrorized by the government and incarcerated, he continued to work for Muslims and said: "I am a Muslim, devoted to my community . . . If the ruler puts me to death, another Muslim will succeed me and will never turn back; we are several thousand in number. But even then I shall feel that my coreligionists are being oppressed."[56] Another part of the same pamphlet entitled, "Well done, Lion of Kashmir," stated that Abdullah "bore the standard of the faith." He "came boldly into the field. He suffered jail three times for our sakes, and denied himself the necessaries of life, saying that his brethren in Islam were being persecuted."[57]

The incidents of 1931 were central to the erection of this persona around the figure of Sheikh Mohammad Abdullah. According to his followers, the Sheikh, who had by now been elevated to the status of *Sher-i-Kashmir* (Lion of Kashmir), had stepped forward in 1931 to receive the cauldron of oil that was prepared by the oppressors for his community, since "he depended on God alone for support."[58] For many Kashmiri Muslims, Sheikh Abdullah was not so much a figure who represented the Kashmiri regional identity but a figure who personified the ideal Muslim. This is significant, especially since a discussion of *Kashmiriyat,* the celebrated symbol of Kashmiri identity, was entirely absent in the political discourse of this tumultuous period. In the early 1930s, this discourse drew unequivocal lines of division between religious communities.

For Kashmiri Muslims, Kashmiri Pandits were far from their brethren in their fight against injustice; in fact, they were arrayed on the side of their enemies. Abdullah could explain this enmity to the British Indian press as a clash of interests between Pandits and Muslims for jobs. For his followers, however, the enmity was definable in religious

---

[55] *Mousiki Kashmiri ka Nava Hissa* [The Ninth Part of Kashmiri Music] (Lahore: Inqilab Steam Press, 1932), 4, Political Department 383/Pol 10/1932, Jammu State Archives.

[56] Ibid., 5.

[57] *Mousiki Kashmiri ka Dassva Hissa* [The Tenth Part of Kashmiri Music] (Lahore: Inqilab Steam Press, 1933), 2, Political Department 383/Pol 10/1932, Jammu State Archives.

[58] Ibid., 6.

terms, as Abdullah himself took pains to point out to them on numerous occasions. The Pandits had become the "Satan's brood," who
"knows nothing of the truth,"[59] while the Muslims "the slaves of
Hazrat Mohammad Sahib," who gave proof of "the same steadfast-
ness"[60] as their ancestors during the time of adversity and persecution.
Similarly, many Pandits recognized that they were the targets of Muslim hostility because they were Hindus, since "Muslims identify all
Hindus with the Raj, and sometimes they call the present Raj as Bhatta
[Pandit] Raj."[61]

The leaders of the Muslim Conference unabashedly used religion
as a marker of identity for the community that had been excluded from
the political and economic framework of the state based precisely on
this very identifier. That some Kashmiri Pandits did work within the
framework of the Muslim Conference for the goal of responsible government illustrates that the movement was not exclusivist in nature.
However, by the beginning of the next decade the Muslim/National
Conference leadership would exclude most voices of dissent from
Kashmir's political arena based on the national/communal dichotomy.

The similarity between the public discourse in the first two decades
of the century and the early 1930s is further evident within expressions
of dissension among Kashmiri Muslims. The followers of the Mirwaiz
Kashmir and Sheikh Abdullah expressed their disagreements in terms
reminiscent of the division between the Ahl-i-Hadis and Hanafis at the
turn of the century. The Mirwaiz Kashmir, whose ancestors had been
at the forefront of the movement to discredit petty ulema for misleading
Kashmiri Muslims, himself became the object of criticism for the same
reason. Labeled the *bakras* (goats) by the *shers* (lions, or, Abdullah's
followers), the Mirwaiz and his followers were the object of much
ridicule in the 1930s. In a poem entitled "Che-Bakra" (Of Goats), an
anonymous pro-Abdullah writer presented the duplicity of preachers
such as the Mirwaiz:

> Sometimes he comes as the messiah into our sacred places,
> And other times he gets angry, this is the two-facedness of the Bakra.
> Sometimes he preaches the message of love and brotherhood,

[59] *Ninth Part of Kashmiri Music,* 3.

[60] "The Place of Resurrection—Kashmir," *Sadaqat,* Srinagar, July 14, 1933,
Political Department 223/ PP 2/ 1933, Jammu State Archives.

[61] Jia Lal Kaul Jalali, "Notes on 1931," Personal Diary, Srinagar State Archives.

And other times he encourages disputes, this is the way of the Bakra.
Sometimes he merges with the Qadianis,
And other times he becomes an Ahrari, this is the religiosity of the Bakra.[62]

Not only did the writings accuse the Mirwaiz of being dishonest and deceitful, but also of leading the Kashmiri Muslim community down an erroneous path. For the last forty years, alleged an article, Muslims had been under the influence of *wazkhani* (preaching) by religious preachers, which was "senseless and frustrating." When the profession of preaching became a hereditary occupation, the article continued, the preachers established their monopoly on different mosques and formed their parties and followers, as "Poor Muslims became their instruments in this newly politicized game, and the common land where Muslims were to hold prayers became the private property of the preachers on which they fought their battles." The article then appealed to Muslims to recognize the reality of the preachers and stop following them, since "the community was crying at them and shedding tears of blood."[63] Clearly, the Mirwaiz had been clubbed in the same category with other preachers, regardless of differences of opinion, and had to suffer its consequences.

Apart from abstract accusations of falsehood, the pro-Abdullah group charged the Mirwaiz and other preachers on two concrete points. First, through their incessant disputes with each other, the preachers had prevented Kashmiri Muslims from uniting as a community. "Sheikh Abdullah," on the other hand, "knew well that if there was anything that ruined the Kashmiri Muslims it was their sectarian differences and disunion."[64] And second, the Mirwaiz's loyalty to the government was seen as a betrayal of the community. Most political tracts and poems against the Mirwaiz drew attention to the fact that he had turned his back on Sheikh Abdullah and the Muslim community, which made him a traitor: "May God curse such traitors/ This treachery, this belligerence, this is the standard of the Bakra."[65] Another warned the Mirwaiz that all his machinations,

[62] Anonymous, "Che-Bakra" [Of Goats], 1932, unpublished manuscript in Kashmiri (Private Collection of Peerzada Mohammad Ashraf, Srinagar, Kashmir).

[63] Mohammad Rashiduddin, "Taziyanae Ibrat," *Sadaqat*, Srinagar, May 18, 1933.

[64] "Golden Tulip of Kashmir," *Sadaqat* (Shaheed Number), July 14, 1933, Political Department 223/PP 2/1933, Jammu State Archives, 6.

[65] Anonymous, "Che Bakra."

including the formation of the Azad Party, would not re-establish his lost prestige, since "It [Sheikh Abdullah's personality] has become enshrined in the hearts of the people whence the Mirwaiz cannot oust it. His country-men know what sacrifice the Sheikh has made for their sake."[66]

Notwithstanding the general similarities in the rhetoric of the early twentieth-century leadership and the leadership of the 1930s, that there were some significant differences between the two can hardly be denied. As I said earlier, the religious leadership had failed, even at the level of discourse, to unite Kashmiri Muslims under a single political agenda. Their main aim had been to reform Kashmiri Muslim society, which they saw as being tainted by un-Islamic influences, while at the same time demanding that the state recognize Kashmiri Muslims as a distinct entity. The policies of state in the early twentieth century that endowed Kashmiri Muslims with a distinct political identity based on religion had also succeeded in legally sanctioning the dissensions within the community. Furthermore, the religious leadership had drawn its influence mainly from Srinagar and its mufassil, and had been unsuccessful in founding an organization that attained state-wide, even Valley-wide, popularity. Since its base remained urban, the vast majority of the Kashmiri Muslim population, the agriculturists, fell outside its sphere of influence. Most significantly, the religious leadership had sought to work with the state, not against it, to achieve its modest demands for the betterment of the status of Kashmiri Muslims.

Sheikh Mohammad Abdullah and his political organization, as we have seen, was based on the concept of a unified Kashmiri Muslim community, defined by the Islamic ideal of social and political rights for all its members. In a departure from the earlier leadership, Abdullah's rhetoric focused on Islamic concepts known to most Kashmiri Muslims, rather than judging them based on their practices. It is important to point out, however, that even in the 1930s the Kashmiri Muslim community was severely divided, in spite of the movement's discourse that transcended sectarian and class differences in presenting the common demands of Kashmiri Muslims to the state. Second, despite its claims to the contrary, the movement was anti-government, and sought to, if not overthrow the government outright, then at least

[66] "Conspiracy Against Sheikh Mohammad Abdullah," *Inqilab*, Srinagar, July 12, 1933, Political Department 225/PP 3/1933, Jammu State Archives.

to bring about qualitative structural changes within it. Abdullah formulated his political platform through the Glancy Commission, in which he was the representative of Muslims from all districts, localities, and provinces of the Kashmir Valley. Although his organization would remain unrepresentative of both Muslims and Hindus of the Jammu province, a flaw that would cause a rift in the early 1940s, Abdullah claimed to be the sole representative of Muslims of the entire state of Jammu and Kashmir, regardless of their class, sectarian or geographic location.

The demands to the Glancy Commission, its activities, recommendations and the state people's reactions to them shed valuable light on the evolution of Kashmiri politics in the 1930s. The commission, appointed under the orders of the Maharaja in November 1931, primarily to address the religious concerns of the population, became instead a forum for the ventilation of their political and economic grievances. Religious grievances, it became clear, could not be divorced from their social and political contexts. The commission comprised four non-official members, a Hindu and Muslim from Jammu province and a Hindu and Muslim from Kashmir province, presided over by the British officer, B.J. Glancy, who had been lent to the Jammu and Kashmir state by the Government of India. Even before the commission began its deliberations, the Jammu Hindus withdrew their member as protest against its proposed inquiry into the Hindu Law of Inheritance.[67] From the outset, the commission became a site for the expression of dissensions among various community representatives involved in its proceedings.

The communities' foremost demands related to the return of their places of worship, either from state occupation or that of another community. The difference between these demands and those of earlier years regarding the same issue was that not only were the present demands more vociferous and included tracts of land between sacred spaces, but more significantly they were now lodged on a political forum against other communities' claim to the same land. For Muslims, as for Hindus, these claims could no longer be divorced from the larger question of basic rights for the denizens of the state. In a

[67] B.J. Glancy, *Report of the Commission appointed under the order of His Highness, the Maharaja Bahadur dated 12th November, 1931 to Enquire into Grievances and Complaints* (Jammu: Ranbir Govt. Press, 1933), 1.

statement to the commission, the Head Teacher of the Madrasa Deeniye Arbia, Srinagar, linked the religious rights of Muslims to their economic condition, "The condition of Kashmiri Muslims in this Garden of Solomon [Kashmir] is indescribable. Neither do they have any means of economic survival, nor have they been provided with religious freedom."[68] Religious freedom, the statement argued, was essential for human beings, "without which their life was rendered meaningless and there was no difference between them and beasts."[69] Another statement accused the government of denying them rights that were guaranteed to Muslims by the shariat. Denial of proprietary rights on land, occupation of shrines and mosques, the inflated revenue rates, the child marriage prohibition act, and the denial of property rights to a Hindu converting to Islam, the statement claimed, went against the shariat.[70] The law of the land, according to this petition, was specifically designed against Muslims, and forced them, in a sense, to go against the dictates of their religion.

Just as the memorials presented the state occupation of sacred spaces as an injury to the religious sensibilities of Kashmiri Muslims, so too they described the backward educational status of the community as an affront to their religion, which could only be remedied through adequate community representation in the administration. It was clearly no longer sufficient to describe Muslims as backward to explain their low educational status and the concomitant small share in government service held by the community. "I have never heard," wrote Abdullah to the Glancy Commission, "of any truly useful steps having been taken by the Government, to strike at the root causes, that play a prominent part, in alienating the Musalman from Educational Institutions."[71] After all, he argued, the teaching staff of all the Government Schools was Hindu and did not inspire much confidence in Muslim boys, who dropped out of primary schools in large numbers as a result. In spite of these hardships, he continued, the Muslims who

[68] Political Department 23/22/PL/1932, Jammu State Archives.
[69] Ibid.
[70] Ibid.
[71] Sheikh Abdullah, "Some Instances of Muslims receiving Discriminative Treatment," January 13, 1932, Political Department 23/22/PL/1932, Jammu State Archives.

do succeed in passing the higher examinations are not given their share in state services: "The successful Muslim student rots and vegetates on a meagre salary while the misbehaved pandit, returns home a qualified hand, thanks to his Hindu patrons. If under these circumstances the muslims [*sic*] remains in the same rut into which he was forced by the (unfortunate?) fact of his being muslim, is he to blame?"[72] Abdullah went a step further than the religious leadership in placing the onus of responsibility not simply on the state, but specifically a state run by Hindus which patronized only its co-religionists.

An issue submitted to the Glancy Commission that drew heated debate between the Pandit and Muslim communities was the question of the forfeiture of inheritance in the case of those who renounced the Hindu religion. Most Muslim petitions raised this issue as an impingement on their religious freedom, since in practice it meant that a Hindu wishing to convert to Islam forfeited his legal right to inheritance. Although the Glancy Commission concluded that the Muslims of Jammu and Kashmir had no legitimate grievance "in the fact that the State law relating to the consequences of apostasy is based upon the religious laws of Hinduism and Islam,"[73] Muslim representatives viewed this law as a specific affront to the religious rights of those professing Islam.

Hindu and Muslim organizations outside the state loudly defended the claims of their respective communities. The Ahmadiyyas, unsurprisingly, came out in support of the Muslim grievance, stating that "the question is not whether the Hindu *Shastras* shall or shall not be enforced in the Kashmir State. It is quite a different question: Will the *Shastras* be enforced against anyone who has renounced the Hindu religion and become a Christian or a Muslim?"[74] The Kashmiri Pandit reply was that any modification in the Hindu law of inheritance with regard to apostasy, which was similar to the Muslim law regarding the same subject, "is not only an interference with the free exercise of religion of the Hindus but is a flagrant attack upon their religious laws

[72] Ibid.

[73] Glancy, *Report*, 7.

[74] Muhammad Ali, "Hindu Inheritance in Kashmir," *Civil and Military Gazette*, Lahore, January 8, 1932. Muhammad Ali was the President of the Ahmadiyya Anjuman, Lahore.

which have governed the society for ages past."[75] The claims and counter-claims on this issue are significant in illuminating the extent to which the politics of this period was governed by the discourse on religious rights and freedoms. Significantly, even when the grievances concerned were political and economic, they were defined in terms of their impact on the religious sensibilities of the communities involved.

Further, the recommendations of the Glancy Commission judged these grievances based on their religious validity. The sacred buildings or grounds demanded by the Muslim community were to be made over to them immediately. Those that were contested by the two communities were left up to a settlement by the authorities and the "good sense of the communities."[76] Glancy had no intention of exacerbating tensions; he simply wanted to placate Muslims with a view to re-establishing order within the state. Recognizing the importance of educational demands for the Kashmiri Muslim community, the commission's report devoted a whole chapter to their redressal. According to the report, the state had not fulfilled Sharp's recommendations regarding the expansion of primary education or the increase in the appointment of mullahs in primary schools. Accordingly, it recommended that the number of mullahs employed by educational authorities should be increased as rapidly as possible and their transfers should be kept to a minimum as transfers have the effect of driving them out of service.[77]

Additionally, since the proportion of Muslim teachers and staff compared to non-Muslims was regrettably too small to carry out Sharp's recommendations, a list of distinctly Muslim towns and villages would have to be prepared by the state so that educational authorities could concentrate on these towns during their training sessions.[78] The most important aspect of the chapter on education, however, was Glancy's recommendation of the appointment of a special Muhammadan Inspector for Education. According to Glancy, the post of the Assistant Inspector of Muhammadan Education already in existence

[75] Anand Koul, "Hindu Law of Inheritance," *Civil and Military Gazette*, Lahore, February 18, 1932.

[76] Glancy, *Report*, 4.

[77] Ibid., 10.

[78] Ibid., 15.

was not enough because he was treated as just another Assistant Inspector in one particular division. The post of Muhammdan Inspector should not be subordinate to any provincial inspector and the incumbent's duty should be to "attend generally to the progress of Muhammadan education in all grades and to see that the policy laid down by the state authorities is duly carried out."[79]

Further responding to Kashmiri Muslim demands, Glancy recommended the conferral of proprietary rights on agriculturists since the "advantages to be expected therefrom are sufficient to outweigh any objections that can be raised, provided that suitable steps are taken to prevent the concession from abuse." To quell the discontent of the people of Jammu province, the report recommended the suspension of grazing taxes in certain tehsils such as Bhimber, Jammu, Samba, Akhnur, Kathua, Jasmergarh and Mirpur, where pasturage land was reportedly meager, until inquiries into the justification for a permanent remission were carried out.[80] The other recommendations were general yet significant—for instance, the conferral of limited freedom of press, publication and political organization; urging the government to address economic issues such as unemployment through the promotion of industries in the state; and not setting the minimum qualifications for appointment to a government post unnecessarily high so as "to prevent the due interests of any community from being neglected."[81]

Many Muslims of the state did not consider Glancy's recommendations revolutionary enough, although the representatives did put their signatures on the report, since, as one noted, "I would be serving the interests of my community by signing it better than by not doing so." The same individual, Chaudhuri Ghulam Abbas, the Muslim representative from Jammu, wrote a long note of dissent to the report, which argued that Glancy had not addressed all the grievances raised by Muslims in their memorial to the Maharaja. He proposed drastic measures to ensure fair representation for Muslims in civil services and the administration of the state, such as the retirement of all non-Muslims who had attained the age of fifty or been in the service twenty-five years, and the discharge of all non-Muslim temporary incumbents

[79] Ibid., 16.
[80] Ibid., 28–9.
[81] Ibid., 24–5.

so that the vacancies created thereby could be filled by qualified Muslims. Additionally, he "strongly protested" the recommendation to invest the power of making appointments in government departments with the heads of the departments, as had traditionally been the case. Instead, Abbas suggested the formation of a Public Services Commission to safeguard the interests of the Muslim community with regard to proper representation in services, against the prejudicial treatment by department heads.[82]

Prem Nath Bazaz, the Kashmiri Pandit representative from Kashmir, voiced a strong note of dissent on the report's recommendation to "make-over" the Idgah ground to the Kashmiri Muslim community, since "it has not been proved that the Muslims had at any time any better title over the Idgah than they possess at present." According to Bazaz, the Idgah had never been an exclusively Muslim resort and the "making over" of the ground to the community was unacceptable:

> The rights of way, pasturage, recreation and other rights possessed by the citizens of Srinagar are in the nature of rights over a village common. The Muslims' rights over the Idgah are neither less nor more than the right that the Hindu inhabitants of a village may have over the village common . . . No individual or class of individuals can claim any exclusive right over the ground.

Most significantly, the note argued for the right of all communities and classes of Srinagar to dispute "any settlement proposed with regard to the land, irrespective of what the position of the Government in the matter may be."[83] The Glancy Commission did not provide a solution to intra-community disputes, or the contentions between communities and the government; instead, it ushered in an era of legal battles over land.

Apart from the single point of dissent, Bazaz accepted the general proposals of the Glancy Commission as they related to Kashmiri Muslims, thereby incurring the wrath of the Sanatan Dharma Youngmen's Association. A deputation from this organization waited on the Prime Minister in May 1932, requesting that the recommendations of the commission could not be given practical shape so far as they concerned

[82] Ibid., vi–vii.
[83] Ibid., iv–v.

Kashmiri Pandits. The deputation claimed that since Kashmiri Pandits traditionally trained themselves for state service to the exclusion of all other occupations, the Glancy recommendations would entail a loss of their main means of livelihood. It then urged the Prime Minister to consider alternative means of livelihood for them, such as grants of state lands for agricultural purposes when proprietary rights were conferred in Kashmir, and special scholarships to technical schools to facilitate their entry into industrial and other professions.[84]

The government gave its imprimatur to most of the report's recommendations almost immediately after its publication. However, as pointed out above, the government's orders placated neither Muslims nor Pandits. In fact, the report would become a much-used stick with which to beat the darbar into conceding communitarian demands for the next few years. Additionally, the Valley had been seething with discontent throughout 1932 from the deteriorating economic climate. The authorities at Sopore, Muzaffarabad, Poonch, Kotli, Mirpur, Baramulla, and Uri sent frantic telegrams to the government in Srinagar regarding the degenerating law and order situation in these tehsils, where crowds had been clashing with authorities.[85] Finally in September 1932, at the arrest of Sheikh Abdullah and the apprehension of the arrest of other Muslim leaders, some Muslims of Srinagar congregated at Abdullah's house and shouted slogans for the overthrow of the Maharaja's government and the establishment of a Muslim government. The Maharaja promptly handed the city over to the military authorities. Hundreds of telegrams from panic-stricken Pandits poured into the office of the District Magistrate, Kashmir, asking the government to protect their lives and property from hostile Muslims.[86] Although the authorities viewed these disturbances as being directed against the Hindu community, most Muslims felt as beleaguered by the disturbances as Pandits did. As an anonymous Muslim noted: "The recent disturbances, though attempts were made to give them a communal coloring, were purely political, being neither more nor less

[84] "Representation of Sanatan Dharma Youngmen's Association to Prime Minister," May 2, 1932, Crown Representative Papers of India, Foreign and Political Department R/1/29/886, India Office Library, London, 21 (microfilm).

[85] Political Department 71/32/1931–2, Jammu State Archives.

[86] Office of the District Magistrate of Kashmir, 340/1931–2, Srinagar State Archives.

than an open organized rebellion against the Hindu ruler of the state."[87]

The Kashmir Valley stood at the threshold of a major political transformation. Not only had Muslims made their discontent known to the government, it was also clear that despite the administration's moves to redress the situation, there would be no turning back. By 1933, the government could no longer dismiss the movement in the Valley as communal, since its anti-administration rhetoric had become increasingly trenchant. Sheikh Mohammad Abdullah, who had risen to the forefront of the movement in a few months on a specifically communitarian platform, was willing to press his advantage in the direction of the political reformation of state structures, aided by a substantially expanded public sphere as well as press and publications market.[88] Abdullah's steady progression in the direction of the Congress leadership and the discourse of Indian nationalism further attested to a sea change in the political atmosphere of the Kashmir Valley. The realignment of its political rhetoric along lines of the majoritarian nationalism of the Indian National Congress became the Kashmiri Muslim leadership's main objective through the rest of the decade.

1934–1939: A Community, Regional, or National Ideology?

"The government sat satisfied by applying the Glancy chloroform bottle to the nose of the public," noted an editorial in the *Sadaqat* in early 1934, "and thought that the clamourers had become senseless."[89] Clearly, the "clamourers" had no intention of remaining silent. From late 1933, the Kashmiri Muslim leadership began the gradual articulation of the agenda and discourse of the movement in clearly national terms, one that addressed the issues of the Kashmiri nation as a whole. Socialist ideals, which had the potential to unite people of

[87] "Note on the Recent Political Disturbances in Jammu and Kashmir," Political Department 469/1932, Jammu State Archives.

[88] In keeping with Glancy's recommendations, the state repealed the Press and Publications Act of 1971 (AD 1914–15) and passed the Press and Publications Act of 1932, the provisions of which were similar to the press act operative in British India. See *Laws of Jammu and Kashmir*, vol. II, 737–61.

[89] "The Empty Promises of the Government have Ruined Us," *Sadaqat*, January 26, 1934, Political Department 223/PP2/1933, Jammu State Archives.

different religious affiliations under a single political and economic program, became the basis of this movement. More significantly still, the concept of *Kashmiriyat*, with its emphasis on a united, syncretic Kashmiri cultural identity, although not overtly articulated, came to inform the political discourse of this period. Here I trace the move within Kashmiri political discourse from the community to the nation as the basis of organization, a move that ushered in an era of nationalist politics in the Valley that would culminate in the accession of the state of Jammu and Kashmir to India.

As noted earlier, the Kashmir Valley did not escape the impact of the world economic depression. By 1933, the already indigent situation of Kashmiris had further degenerated. The movement of members of the agricultural and laboring classes toward state service was inevitable in these rapidly deteriorating economic conditions. The Muslim Conference leadership had already recognized the importance of this economic change, which is clear from their emphasis on the paucity of Muslims in state services before and during the Glancy Commission's deliberations. This certainly helped garner the support of a cross-section of the population for the movement. From 1934 onward, moreover, the Muslim Conference's program became even more specific to the alleviation of the economic hardships facing the people. "We have achieved a lot," declared Mirwaiz Hamdaani at the reception address of the annual session of the Muslim Conference in 1935, "but we still need to address the issues of unemployment and poverty among the people."[90] In the same session, the Conference passed a resolution condemning the Land Alienation Regulation for not incorporating within it "full safeguards against the defeat of the very object of the enactment."[91] Additionally, the Conference laid out specific demands of the laboring classes during this session.

The articulation of a socialist economic program that could address these issues required the conception of Kashmir as a unified entity with horizontal class divisions as opposed to vertical sectarian/communitarian ones. This shift was clearly discernible in Sheikh Abdullah's rhetoric. In his presidential address at the annual session of the Muslim

[90] "Reception address by Mirwaiz Ghulam Nabi Hamdaani at fourth annual session of the All Jammu and Kashmir Muslim Conference," Srinagar, October 25, 1935, in Hussain, ed., *The Political Struggle*, 371.

[91] Ibid.

Conference in December 1933, he exhorted all Kashmiris to come forward and support the movement:

> The loss of rights is a loss to all, whether he is a Muslim or a non-Muslim. The Muslim Conference has fought for the right of the people and there is no discrimination between a Hindu or a Muslim. I appeal to the non-Muslims that they should stand shoulder to shoulder with us so as to take part in the emancipation of the people, freedom of the nation from the degradation, poverty and slavery . . . there is no reason why Hindus should not join their Muslim brothers on this national front.[92]

This was the first occasion in a public speech when Abdullah claimed to represent not only the Muslim community, but also Kashmiri Pandits.

A split in the ranks of the Kashmiri Pandit leadership abetted Abdullah's move in the direction of formulating a national agenda for the movement. P.N. Bazaz (1905–84), the Hindu representative from the Kashmir Valley on the Glancy Commission, made it clear that he recognized the Kashmiri Muslim movement to attain economic and political rights. A devout socialist by this time who later became a follower of M.N. Roy, Bazaz fervently believed in the separation of religion and politics. Although as leader of the Sanatan Dharma Youngmen's Association in 1931 he had expressed his bitter resentment at the Muslim leadership and its demands on behalf of the Pandit community, by 1933 Bazaz was writing in the Muslim Conference's official newspaper, the *Sadaqat,* in support of the martyrdom of those Muslims "who left their fathers, wives, children and every comfort of this world and sacrificed themselves on the altar of their country."[93]

Bazaz realized that Kashmiri Pandits had no choice but to follow the lead of the majority community of the Valley. In a letter to Mahatma Gandhi explaining the direction of Kashmiri politics, he clearly expressed his belief in nationalism: "It is nationalism that will save our country and our community because neither the Hindus or the Muslims can wipe out the one or the other from the country." Furthermore, he argued that since most Kashmiri Pandits lived among

---

[92] F.M. Hassnain, *Freedom Struggle in Kashmir* (New Delhi: Rima Publishing House, 1988), 79–80.

[93] P.N. Bazaz, "Wreaths of Devotion Offered at the Graves of the Martyrs," *Sadaqat,* Srinagar, July 14, 1933, Political Department 223/PP-2/1933, Jammu State Archives.

Muslims, communalism would endanger their lives; "It is only nationalism that will save such families."[94] In a joint enterprise, Abdullah and Bazaz began the weekly newspaper, *Hamdard*,[95] which later became one of the most trenchant critics of Abdullah's nationalist politics.

By 1933, Abdullah's intention to separate the Conference from the increasingly acrimonious politics of Punjabi Muslims was becoming apparent. Its official mouthpiece, *Hamdard*, roundly condemned all Punjabi Muslim "communal" organizations for having misled the Kashmiri movement since its inception in 1931. Its editorials argued that Kashmiris should stay out of Punjabi politics and address their indigenous political problems themselves.[96] On a more personal level, Abdullah wanted to steer clear of the Ahrar–Ahmadiyya controversy in the Punjab, which was gathering force since the announcement of Ramsay Macdonald's Communal Award in 1932. By 1933, the Ahrars had pressurized the Ahmadiyya khalifa Mirza Bashiruddin to resign as head of the Kashmir Committee and replaced him with Muhammad Iqbal.[97]

Although Abdullah decried this move, it was clear that he did not want to be identified as an Ahmadiyya or an Ahmadiyya sympathizer. Several avowed Kashmiri Ahmadiyya founding members of the Muslim Conference, such as Moulvi Abdullah Vakil, left the organization as a result.[98] Abdullah's apparent break with the Ahmadiyyas was motivated by a host of factors. According to his autobiography, the alignment of the Muslim Conference with the Ahmadiyyas had already

[94] "Letter from P.N. Bazaz to Gandhi," May 8, 1934, (Private Collection of Bhushan Bazaz, New Delhi).

[95] Sheikh Mohammad Abdullah, *Flames of the Chinar: An Autobiography*(New Delhi: Viking, 1993), 46–7; and P.N. Bazaz, *The History of Struggle for Freedom in Kashmir*, 167.

[96] "How did the Communal Mentality become Widespread in Kashmir?" *Hamdard*, Srinagar, February 1, 1936.

[97] The Communal Award of 1932 restricted the franchise to propertied classes; if the Ahrars were to continue their influence among the dispossessed Punjabi classes, they had to accelerate their campaign against the Arya Samajists and the Ahmadiyyas. For this and a discussion of the reasons behind Iqbal's sudden withdrawal of support from the Ahmadiyyas in favor of the Ahrars, see Jalal, *Self and Sovereignty*, 363–70.

[98] "Report of the Resident in Kashmir," September 1935, Foreign and Political Department, R/1/29/1303, India Office Library, London, 22 (microfilm).

caused enough internecine strife among Kashmiri Muslims.[99] A more probable reason was that the Ahrars were carrying out a verbal war against the Ahmadiyyas for being heretics and British loyalists, two charges both Abdullah and his organization could ill afford to be associated with. As significantly, the Indian National Congress unofficially supported the Ahrars in the Punjab; since the Conference was moving steadily in the direction of a pro-Congress politics, they could not be seen publicly supporting the Ahrars' arch-rivals, the Ahmadiyyas.

In the meantime, the Maharaja had accepted the proposals of the Franchise Committee that recommended an elected legislature for the state and announced the foundation of a state assembly in 1934, which was to be known as the Praja Sabha, or the subjects' assembly. The Praja Sabha was to have 75 members, 33 to be elected and 42 to be nominated. The elected members were to be chosen based on the system of separate electorates for communities, with 21 Muslims, 10 Hindus, and 2 Sikhs, through a limited franchise. Candidates for membership to the assembly had to be at least 25 years of age and literate in either the Persian or Devnagari script. The administration and government of the state remained under the control of a council of ministers presided over by the Prime Minister. The assembly was to have no more than the power of interpellation, passing resolutions and discussing the budget. Furthermore, the Maharaja retained the ultimate political power in that the executive was responsible to him and not to the assembly.[100] Sheikh Abdullah recognized that the Praja Sabha was a powerless body. However, he decided that by contesting the elections and winning seats, the Muslim Conference could demonstrate its popularity in the state and use the Sabha as a forum to propagate its ideology of nationalism.[101] In the 1934 elections to the Praja Sabha, the Muslim Conference won all the 21 Muslim seats of the assembly, a fact that might not have been possible had Abdullah not verbally dissociated the Conference from the Ahmadiyyas.

In tandem with distancing himself from Punjabi Muslim politics, Abdullah's move in the direction of Indian National Congress politics continued through the 1930s. At the passage of the Government of India Act of 1935, the Muslim Conference declared that in case

---

[99] Abdullah, *Flames of the Chinar*, 33.

[100] Wreford, *Census of India, 1941, Vol. XXII, Jammu and Kashmir*, 5.

[101] Abdullah, *Flames of the Chinar*, 45.

Jammu and Kashmir decided to join the federation of India, it would be represented by its people as opposed to the Maharaja.[102] Priding itself on being above communalism, *Hamdard* articulated the incipient national ideology of the mid-1930s in its weekly issues. Kashmir attained the status of a mother nation and its inhabitants became the children of Kashyap Rishi. The newspaper contended that the formation of a responsible government in the state rested on the coming together of Hindus and Muslims under one flag since they were the two sons of the mother nation.[103] The impact of the nationalist rhetoric of British India was evident in these articles, as was the growing mistrust of individuals and organizations expressing a joint affiliation for both religious community and national identity.

Jawaharlal Nehru's ideas on nationalism and the future of princely states in independent India appeared often in *Hamdard*, and its editorials rejected the involvement of religion in the articulation of political identities. Furthermore, they recognized the possibility of Kashmir as a part of independent India in the future. As Nehru's "Advice to the Youth of Kashmir" stated:

> Kashmir's destiny is intertwined with that of Hindustan because if Hindustan gains independence then Kashmir will definitely ask for its share . . . The fate of the 8 crore people of the princely states cannot be separated from that of the people of British India. In fact, both peoples are riding in the same boat. If Kashmiris would only recognize that their education, economy and culture was in the hands of an irresponsible government, then nothing could stop them from attaining their rights.[104]

Abdullah and Bazaz extended an invitation to Nehru to visit Kashmir in 1936 in an effort to boost their attempts at establishing a joint Hindu–Muslim national front in politics. Although Nehru declined, Abdullah had the opportunity to meet him in the NWFP the following year, a meeting that so impressed Abdullah that he declared at a press conference in Amritsar: "Our next programme will be to follow the

[102] Ibid., 47.

[103] P.N. Bazaz, "A Clarification of Certain Misunderstandings," *Hamdard*, Srinagar, April 11, 1936, and "The Responsibility of Muslims, Hindus and Sikhs," *Hamdard*, Srinagar, May 9, 1936.

[104] "Pandit Jawaharlal Nehru's Advice to the Youth of Kashmir," *Hamdard*, Srinagar, June 27, 1936.

principles of the Congress Party, and, after returning to Kashmir, I will strive to set up an organization which supports national ideology."[105] True to his word, Abdullah remained pro-Congress in ideology and politics for the remainder of his political career in pre-1947 Kashmir. An important consideration in Abdullah's decision to orient himself with the Congress was quite possibly the Congress's increasingly leftist leanings on social and political issues, which were similar to the socialist ideals being propounded by the Muslim Conference for Kashmir at this time.

The rhetoric of the Muslim Conference during these years resembled the discourse on Kashmiri regional belonging from the pre-colonial period. However, there were some qualitative differences between the two. The rhetoric of the 1930s had moved from the conception of Kashmir as mulk, which can be conceived as land, place, or homeland, to watan, a more territorial conception of the nation. Kashmir was no longer simply a beautiful land that had sunk into oppression, it was a nation with boundaries congruent with the princely state of Jammu and Kashmir that had to be rescued from exploiters through nationalism. This is not to suggest that the territorial boundaries of the Kashmiri nation were fixed in this period: simply that the Muslim Conference presented a more concrete and in some instances territorial conception of the Kashmiri nation. Furthermore, a sense of desperation and anger at the incessant persecution suffered by Kashmiris pervaded this discourse. Several authors quoted Ghalib's famous verse to draw attention to the fraudulence of the appellation of paradise on earth for Kashmir, which was in reality steeped in poverty and decline: "I know the reality of paradise/ But it is a good thought to entertain the heart."[106] In the words of a Kashmiri poet, "They think that decadence comes cheap here/ I say that there is an abundance of sorrow here."[107]

In a gendered rendition of the nation, *Hamdard* published a poem that eulogized Kashmir as a beautiful woman whose external beauty had faded, revealing her hollow insides. Had she acquired any internal beauty endowed by knowledge and education, argued the poet, she would not have been lying on the roadside at the mercy of passersby:

[105] Abdullah, *Flames of the Chinar*, 45–6.

[106] Seemab Akbarabadi, "Paradise on Earth," *Hamdard*, Srinagar, July 31, 1938.

[107] Ghulam Rasool Nazki, "The Story of Kashmir," *Hamdard*, Srinagar, July 31, 1938.

Such beauty and this oppression?
Oh Kashmir I feel sorry for you.
The blood that runs in your veins is cold,
Your face is blooming but your heart is wilting.
But oh beautiful and unfortunate one,
External beauty is not the standard of beauty.
Knowledge forms a part of beauty,
A beauty that never fades.
In a nation that is knowledgeable,
You will never find the indebted and beggars.[108]

Needless to say, this poem simultaneously described the ideal Kashmiri woman, who had the internal strength to fortify the nation against external assault. Another poem exhorted the people of the nation to lay the foundation of nation-building, where brotherhood would prevail and sectarian/communitarian differences would be dispensed with: "Here will be our mosques and here too our temples/ The world will resound with the cries of united nationalism."[109]

The Muslim Conference's discourse on a united Kashmiri nationalism encapsulated the premise of Indian nationalist thought, as described by Dipesh Chakrabarty: "that 'individual right' and abstract 'equality' were universals that could find home anywhere in the world, that one could be both an 'Indian' and a 'citizen' at the same time."[110] While the project of converting the individual Indian into a citizen was fraught with contradictions, in the case of Kashmir the attainment of citizenship rights for individual Kashmiris was even more complicated (as the rest of this book will reveal). In 1936, the elected members of the Praja Sabha staged a joint walkout from the assembly in protest against its unrepresentative nature and called for responsible government.[111] At the fifth session of the Muslim Conference, held at Poonch in May 1937, Abdullah declared in his presidential speech that they had "demanded responsible assembly and independent administration from the beginning of the freedom struggle." And since "last year, the

[108] Ahsan Daanish, "The Indebted Beauty—In Memory of Kashmir," *Hamdard,* Srinagar, February 20, 1938.

[109] Nand Lal 'Talib,' "Message of Nationalism to the People of the Nation," *Hamdard,* Srinagar, July 31, 1938.

[110] Dipesh Chakrabarty, "Postcoloniality and the Artifice of History: Who Speaks for 'Indian' Pasts?" *Representations* 37: Winter 1992, 8.

[111] Abdullah, *Flames of the Chinar,* 46.

demand for a better constitution has not remained the demand of the Muslim majority population of the state," but Hindus and Sikhs had also joined in the struggle.[112] Abdullah further defined the demand for responsible government at the Conference's annual session the following year as the "participation of all those people, who have been forced in various ways by the present system of government to lead the miserable lives as slaves . . . they are not Muslims alone nor the Hindus and Sikhs alone . . . but all those who live in this state."[113]

The Conference issued a manifesto in 1938, the National Demand, with a view to "acquaint our countrymen" with their objective: the acquisition of elementary and basic rights of citizenship through a progressive form of government that would be responsible to the people.[114] Although Kashmiri nationalist discourse bandied about the idea of citizenship, the process whereby Kashmiris were to be transformed from the subjects of the Dogra state and the larger British empire into a citizenry with equal rights was never elucidated. After all, which nation-state was going to give Kashmiris equal rights—a Kashmiri state, an Indian state, or the British paramount power? Furthermore, the leadership could not reconcile the idea of common citizenship with the irksome problem of majority and minority communities so entrenched in the state, especially since the political structures of the "nation-state" that Kashmiris were to be citizens of had not been specified.

Most importantly, a nationalist movement that promised equal citizenship required the participation of minority communities, not their hostility, as seemed to be the case in Kashmir. As a result, the Muslim leadership made attempts to persuade Kashmiri Pandits to join their struggle. They painted the Muslim role in the 1931 incidents, which Kashmiri Pandits viewed with rancor, in nationalistic colors. According to them, the 1931 agitation had not been organized against any particular community; rather, it was a spontaneous movement that had been generated as a result of the social and political

[112] "Sheikh Mohammad Abdullah's Presidential Address at the Fifth Annual Session of the Muslim Conference," Poonch, 13–15 May, 1937, in Hussain, ed., *Political Struggle*, 449–50 and Political Department 237/D-11/1937, Jammu State Archives.

[113] Hassnain, *Freedom Struggle in Kashmir*, 87.

[114] "The National Demand," *Hamdard*, Srinagar, May 7, 1939 and Bazaz, *The Struggle for Freedom in Kashmir*, 168–9.

conditions prevailing in the Valley at the time. The increase in population led to a rise in unemployment among youth, resulting in the 1931 outburst in which they demanded political and social reforms. Unfortunately, since the Muslim Conference was founded in these tense conditions, Kashmiri Pandits had viewed it with suspicion and continued to do so.[115] An article in the special "Responsible Government Number" of the *Hamdard* claimed that the Muslim Conference's demand for responsible government should not be suspected as being an attempt to replace Dogra Raj with Muslim Raj in Kashmir, since only this demand could cure the maladies faced by the people of the state.[116] Nationalism, which would bring with it responsible government and eventually equal citizenship, had now become the panacea for the Kashmiri people.

Led by Abdullah, the working committee of the Muslim Conference decided to formally recognize the transition of their organization into a national body in an attempt to ensure the continued support of the Indian National Congress for their movement.[117] At a special session, the working committee of the Muslim Conference recommended that the appellation of the organization should be changed to the National Conference, "that all such people who desire to participate in this political struggle, may easily become members of the Conference irrespective of caste, creed or religion."[118] On June 11, 1939, the Muslim Conference became the All Jammu and Kashmir National Conference, the bearer of the majoritarian nationalist ideology for the people of the state. Undoubtedly, the leadership intended to present the Conference as an organization of the downtrodden classes. Its flag, for instance, was red in color with a white plough in the center, representing socialist revolution for the Kashmiri peasantry.[119]

More significantly, the formation of the National Conference ushered in an era of anti-British politics in the Kashmir Valley. No

[115] "Responsible Government is our Birthright," *Hamdard*, Srinagar, July 31, 1938.

[116] D.P. Dhar, "Responsible Government and Kashmiri Pandits," *Hamdard*, Srinagar, July 31, 1938.

[117] Abdullah, *Flames of the Chinar*, 49.

[118] "Ghulam Mohammad Sadiq's Address at the Special Session of the Muslim Conference," Srinagar, June 10–11, 1939, in Hussain, ed., *Political Struggle*, 477.

[119] Hassnain, *Freedom Struggle in Kashmir*, 103. Interestingly, red was the color of the Ahrar Party as well, which too claimed to represent the poor and the downtrodden, including the oppressed Kashmiri Muslims.

longer was the Kashmir movement simply against the government of the Maharaja; it had also assumed the status of an anti-imperialist movement in favor of the larger independence of Hindustan. During the inaugural session of the National Conference in 1939, Abdullah drew attention to the 1935 act, condemning the scheme as considering "the people living in the States as animals and . . . is being put into force against their wishes, simply to bind them into slavery."[120] Furthermore, the session resolved that the Conference appreciated and accepted the intentions underlying the Indian National Congress's stance against the policy of the British government toward the political aspirations of the Indian people. In his turn, Nehru, as President of the All India States People's Conference in 1939, adopted the National Conference's demand for responsible government as a demand for the people of all princely states.[121]

The trend within the Muslim Conference leadership to present a nationalist ideology in the mid-1930s did not imply, however, that religion as a marker of identity was relegated to the background. In fact, local leaders continually invoked the religiously informed political identity of Kashmiri Muslims in their political statements and policies. The redressal of Kashmiri Muslim demands still formed the core of the Muslim Conference's agenda, even though the organization verbally assured the minorities that their rights would be guaranteed in any future political structure. Undoubtedly, the expression of a national ideology for most of the leadership did not imply an alienation from their religious affiliation, which formed, after all, the basis of their political support. Local Muslim Conference leaders framed issues in terms of communitarian differences, for instance, the oft-repeated charge that people of other religions were trying to rob Muslims and Muslims stood to gain nothing from their "undue friendship with the Hindus."[122] The 1937 incident in which the Kashmiri Pandit newspaper, *Martand*, allegedly insulted the Prophet Mohammad, precipitated an outcry from Muslim organizations in the Valley. The Muslim Conference condemned the article, but spoke out against the demonstrations, since their rival, the Mirwaiz Kashmir, had organized them:

[120] Ibid., 102.

[121] "The States People's Conference and Kashmiris," *Hamdard*, Srinagar, February 23, 1939.

[122] Meeting of the Muslim Conference at Tajpore, February 1, 1934, Political Department 188/PS-7/1934, Jammu State Archives.

The sole object of the conference is to attain as high a political status for the people of the state as their brethren will achieve in British India. The conference will not allow any aggression on the political rights of the Muslims and therefore though we may brook no wanton attacks on our religion we shall not under its garb permit others to kick up a row. On the other hand we believe we can master courage to warn the Muslims when someone deliberately attempts to mislead them.[123]

Abdullah himself continually struggled to reconcile his religious identity with his national ideology, a struggle that would intensify in the 1940s, particularly after Chaudhuri Ghulam Abbas broke away from the National Conference to revive the Muslim Conference. Abdullah frequently emphasized that, as a nationalist, he was not necessarily anti-Muslim. He pointed out that all Muslims could not possibly have the same political orientation because they had other allegiances; even the *ummat* did not present a united political viewpoint. According to him, what was important in Islam was *deen* (worldview), not *mazhab* (organized religion) and deen taught one to be human and compassionate. Hence, Islam could not be used to create communitarian differences; instead, it could help transcend them to work for the welfare of all communities.[124] Abdullah was drawing attention to the fact that nationalism did not have to be devoid of religious sensibility. For these statements, however, Kashmiri Pandit organizations continually accused him of being a communalist, since he was ultimately a Muslim who favored separate electorates and supported Muslim candidates in local elections.[125] Significantly, however, Abdullah too was quick to label as communalists those of his political opponents who emphasized their religiously informed cultural identity.

The movement of Abdullah's political rhetoric from community to nation did not go uncontested. The Sanatan Dharma Yuvak Sabha, a Kashmiri Pandit organization, was the most trenchant critic of the Muslim Conference during this period. According to the Yuvak Sabha, the Muslim Conference, notwithstanding its claims to the contrary, did not represent Kashmiri Pandit interests. And although the Sabha recognized the necessity of Kashmiri Pandits adapting to the

[123] Political Department E-110/1937, Jammu State Archives.

[124] *Hamdard,* Srinagar, July 9, 1939.

[125] *Martand,* Srinagar, May 19 and 20, 1937, Political Department 237/D-11/1937, Jammu State Archives.

new circumstances, it expected the government to ensure the community's survival.[126] The rhetoric of the Yuvak Sabha indicates the extent to which the concepts of majority and minority communities had penetrated the political thought of the Kashmir Valley: "Denied the privileges of the majority on account of the smallness of our numbers, we are at the same time denied the protection due to a minority and doubly due to a minority community with our history, services and educational attainments."[127] The suspicion toward the Muslim Conference was so great that the followers of the Yuvak Sabha believed that the success of this organization would mean an annihilation of non-Muslims from Kashmir and the fulfilment of the pan-Islamic scheme that included Kashmir within its ambit.[128]

Importantly, though, not all Kashmiri Pandits subscribed to the Yuvak Sabha's extreme views. Jia Lal Kaul Jalali, a Kashmiri Pandit bureaucrat who held independent political views on the events of the decade, represents the complexity of Kashmiri Pandit attitudes towards the Muslim Conference. Jalali was not a member of the Yuvak Sabha, although he could identify with the roots of their discomfiture at the prevailing political conditions in the Valley. According to him, Muslim leaders were alienating Kashmiri Pandits through their demands, which he did not consider nationalist by any definition:

> What do the Muslims agitate for? Just that they wanted the Maharaja to go, and "murdabad" was their "national" war cry. But when it became impossible to change Hindu Raj to Muslim Raj, they rallied with a wash over to profess allegiance, loyalty, faith and affection for the Maharaja, clamoring for the dismissal of non-Muslims, particularly the Kashmiri Pandits. And for this turnover . . . the government of Maharaja Hari Singh must concede . . . In the course of the year the employment problem will have been solved by returning Kashmiri Pandits from government service en bloc to make room for the non-Pandit . . .[129]

Although Jalali criticized the methods of the Muslim Conference, he did not wholly disagree with their ultimate objective. He stated that

[126] "Memorial to His Highness on Behalf of Kashmiri Pandits," Political Department D-6/1934, Jammu State Archives.

[127] Ibid.

[128] "P.N. Bazaz's Letter to Mahatma Gandhi," May 8, 1934 (Private Collection of Bhushan Bazaz).

[129] "J.L.Kaul Jalali's letter to Lala Sahib," August 30, 1936, Private Collection of Jia Lal Kaul Jalali, Srinagar State Archives.

Kashmiri Pandits also craved for "nothing more or less than a resolute, progressive, efficient government," which would ensure "its protection and the recognition of its special rights."[130] Furthermore, Jalali recognized that Pandits were dependent on Muslims in Kashmir. However, their confidence in the Muslims had suffered a blow with the events of 1931–2 and it was the responsibility of Muslim leaders to restore this confidence among Pandits.[131]

Jalali, as most Kashmiri Pandits and members of other minority communities, held ambivalent feelings toward the Kashmiri Muslim movement since they not only felt excluded from it, but also frequently found themselves labeled the enemy. While supporting the Muslim Conference throughout the 1930s, P.N. Bazaz continually reminded its leaders to make special efforts to assure the minority communities of adequate representation in any future political structure.[132] Sardar Budh Singh, a Sikh who worked tirelessly for the cause of the Muslim Conference, nevertheless felt within his rights to remind the organization of its responsibility to demand joint electorates in municipal elections to boost its "national representative character." Failing to do so would deprive the organization of its right to demand either responsible government or appeal to Hindus to join its movement.[133] By the 1940s, however, several minority individuals at the forefront of the "nationalist" movement separated themselves from it, accusing the leadership of following a brand of majority nationalism that did not address the demands of minorities.

Despite these critiques, the Muslim, and later National Conference presented Kashmiri nationalism as an uncomplicated, all-encompassing entity. But it was becoming clear that the discourse on common citizenship had not been successful in eliding over the more entrenched idea of rights on the basis of religious enumeration. As the majority and minority community dilemma threatened to bring down the foundations of Kashmiri "nationalism," Sheikh Abdullah turned increasingly to concepts such as *Kashmiriyat* to provide sustenance to the rapidly crumbling national edifice. *Kashmiriyat* did not emerge

[130] Jalali, "Note from Sept. 1936," Personal Diary, Srinagar State Archives.
[131] Ibid.
[132] P.N. Bazaz, "The Biggest Complaint of Minorities against the Muslim Conference," *Hamdard*, Srinagar, May 1, 1937.
[133] Sardar Budh Singh, "It is a Dream to Search for Nectar in a Communal Mirage," *Hamdard*, Srinagar, August 29, 1936.

ex-nihilo from the soil of Kashmir; it was a product of the collusion of Kashmiri and Indian majoritarian nationalisms, both of which needed to obscure the inherent contradictions in their logic and rhetoric.

* * *

Even as regional identity came to be elevated to a nationalist creed in the public discourse of the late 1930s, religious identities were relegated to the realm of confused nationalists or outright communalists. Undoubtedly, religion remained the primary marker of identity for most Kashmiris even in this period; however, in the atmosphere of majority nationalism, those who openly professed a primary identification with their religious community were viewed with suspicion. In keeping with the political atmosphere in which even the appearance of a term signifying religious identities was suspicious, the All Jammu and Kashmir Muslim Conference became the All Jammu and Kashmir National Conference in 1939. Kashmir now stood at the threshold of its final and complete inclusion into the politics of British India. As the Kashmiri national organization assumed the majoritarian character of its counterpart in British India, the voices of the Kashmiris who rejected its political project were lost in the resultant political din. It remains for us to excavate these voices, which attempted, until the very moment of partition, to steer Kashmir away from its turbulent future.

CHAPTER 6

Kashmiri Visions of Nationalism and Regionalism

The 1940s are the most intensely written about decade in the history of Kashmir. Even those authors who discuss the region's contemporary politics feel compelled to mention the 1940s, particularly their second half.[1] Not only did the contentious event of Kashmir's accession to India take place in this period, it was at this time that Kashmir consciously entered the Indian nationalist imagination, serving as a metaphor for the ideals of secularism and democracy in the newly independent Indian nation-state. Not surprisingly, the writing on this subject has remained embroiled in the question of whether Kashmir belongs to India or Pakistan, ignoring in the process the crucial events taking place in the informal arenas of Kashmiri politics. Here I shed different light on the decade by exploring the debates and discussions on Kashmiri identity and sovereignty being carried out in such arenas, including hitherto ignored newspapers, pamphlets, and books.

If Sheikh Abdullah had succeeded in introducing the idea of a Kashmiri nation into the political discourse of the Valley, he certainly failed in the 1940s to translate this into concrete politics. Harboring vague ideas about the possible autonomy of the state at the lapse of British

---

[1] There are more than 400 works that wholly or in part examine the 1940s. Some examples are: Hassnain, *Freedom Struggle in Kashmir*; Sardar Mohammad Ibrahim, *The Kashmir Saga*, 2nd edn (Mirpur: Verinag Publishers, 1990); Devendra Swarup and Sushil Aggarwal, eds., *The Roots of the Kashmir Problem: The Continuing Battle between Secularism and Communal Separatism* (Delhi: Manthan Prakashan, 1992); Verinder Grover, ed., *The Story of Kashmir, Yesterday and Today*, 3 vols (Delhi: Deep and Deep Publications, 1995); Hari Jaisingh, *Kashmir: A Tale of Shame* (Delhi: UBS Publishers, 1996); and Prem Shankar Jha, *Kashmir 1947: Rival Versions of History* (Delhi: Oxford University Press, 1996).

paramountcy while also maintaining an ingratiating attitude toward the Congress at the expense of Kashmiri public opinion, Abdullah, to an extent, bears responsibility for the emergence of the state as a divided entity in 1947. At the same time as the National Conference's discourse conflated region and nation, it struck an even more uneasy alliance between nationalism and religious identities, performing in Kashmir a role similar to that of Congress in the all-India context. The popularity of the organization dwindled as it moved away from its emphasis on forging a just society based on Islamic ideals familiar to the population, and began to focus instead on the undefined ideas of nationalism and secularism that specifically disparaged religious affiliation.

Historians of nationalism and religious identities in South Asia, most notably Ayesha Jalal, have pointed out the necessity of re-examining the majoritarian ideology of the Indian National Congress in light of the varied and creative critiques of Indian nationalism articulated by nationalists outside its fold. Far from being "an inclusionary, accommodative, consensual, and popular anti-colonial struggle," Jalal argues, Indian nationalism represented by the Indian National Congress excluded those seeking to accommodate religious differences within the broad framework of Indian nationalism. The resultant creation of the binary opposition between secular nationalism and religious communalism denigrated the affinities to religion as, if not always bigoted, then somehow "less worthy than identifications with the 'nation'."[2]

Much like its counterpart in British India, the National Conference ignored and resisted alternative visions of Kashmiri nationalism and consensual schemes for the future of Kashmir that sought to accommodate religious identities and intra-regional interests.[3] However, the disjunction between the pan-Indian majoritarianism with its "national" and "Hindu" orientation, and the pan-Kashmiri one with its "regional"

[2] See Ayesha Jalal, "Nation, Reason and Religion: Punjab's Role in the Partition of India," *Economic and Political Weekly*, August 8, 1998: 2183. Jalal has also argued this point in "Exploding Communalism: The Politics of Muslim Identity in South Asia," and *Self and Sovereignty*.

[3] Most scholarly works on the Kashmir problem begin their analyses with the All Jammu and Kashmir National Conference, which is accepted uncritically as the most popular political organization in Kashmir in the 1940s in general, and 1947 in particular. Furthermore, the National Conference is seen as pro-Congress

and "Muslim" orientation, already apparent in the 1930s, became increasingly clear in the postcolonial era. Inheriting the mantle of the Dogras with the collusion of the Indian state, the National Conference regime, in the post-independence period, found itself in the almost impossible bind of drawing a bridge between the region and the center while at the same time ensuring Kashmiris' citizenship rights. The politics of nationalism and the discourse on citizenship demanded that the individual be subsumed within a larger entity. In a situation where the relationship between the regional entity, Kashmir, and the singularly defined national entity, India—and their respective religious orientations—had itself not been resolved, there could be no guarantee that Kashmiris would take their rightful place as citizens of either the state of Jammu and Kashmir or the Indian nation-state.

Revivalism vs. Nationalism? Kashmir in the Early 1940s

In an analysis of the beginning of the decade, it is essential to debunk the view that the re-creation of the All Jammu and Kashmir Muslim Conference in 1940–1 was a triumph for the forces of Muslim revivalism in Kashmir, which would ultimately lead to the province's de facto partition between India and Pakistan. This perspective is an integral aspect of the myth that the National Conference represented the majority of Kashmiris, a myth that was perpetuated by the organization itself in the face of increasing opposition from various sectors of the population of the state of Jammu and Kashmir in the 1940s. Furthermore, according to this view, the Muslim Conference stood for the ideals of the Muslim League, which was in favor of the creation of a separate state of Pakistan and the ultimate accession of Kashmir to this Muslim state, while the National Conference supported the Indian National Congress and stood for united nationalism. I believe that this is an exceedingly simplistic reading of a very complicated and, more significantly, evolving relationship between these four organizations through the 1940s.

---

and pro-India, while its main rival, the Muslim Conference, is regarded as pro-Muslim League and pro-Pakistan. See, for instance, Raju G.C. Thomas, ed., *Perspectives on Kashmir: The Roots of Conflict in South Asia* (Boulder: Westview Press, 1992)—in which most of the articles perpetuate these views.

In the wake of the transformation of the Muslim Conference into the National Conference in 1939, Chaudhuri Ghulam Abbas declared: "We are neither Gandhavi, nor Congressi, or Ahrari, or Muslim Leaguers. We are simply Kashmiri and consider our followers Kashmiris who have to be given their rightful place as citizens."[4] This was an interesting comment from a man who was neither Kashmiri, nor spoke the language of the people he claimed to represent. Abbas hailed from Jammu and soon recognized this reality, as also the increasing indications that, despite the National Conference's claims to represent all Kashmiris, the organization primarily served the interests of the Muslims of the Kashmir Valley.[5] The disjunction between the organization's discourse on Kashmiri nationalism, its ideal of citizenship, and the realities of political divisions within the state was already becoming apparent.

Abbas's moves toward reviving the Muslim Conference have to be seen in the light of regional rather than religious tensions between the disparate people of the state of Jammu and Kashmir. If Muslims of the Kashmir Valley were divided along lines of sect and class, then geography and language created an even greater gulf between Muslims of the Valley and Muslims of the Jammu region. Jammu is, for all intents and purposes, an extension of the plains of the Punjab, and the Jammu Muslims spoke Dogri, a dialect akin to Punjabi, which was also the language of the Dogra dynasty. Their co-religionists in the Valley spoke Kashmiri, and had developed, as demonstrated earlier, a vocal political culture in oral media predominantly in that very language.

Ghulam Abbas and Allahrakha Sagar, both of whom, as members, had endorsed the Muslim Conference's resolution that transformed it into the National Conference, revived the Muslim Conference in 1940–1. There were several reasons behind this move, including the fact that the National Conference did not represent Jammu Muslims very effectively, and the increasingly pro-Congress orientation of the organization made many of its members uncomfortable. Ghulam Abbas attempted to extract an assurance from Sheikh Abdullah that the National Conference would remain aloof from external politics.

[4] *Hamdard*, Srinagar, May 27, 1939.
[5] Several National Conference members from Jammu had already absented themselves from its second annual session at Baramulla in September 1940. See *Hamdard*, Srinagar, November 9, 1940.

Upon receiving an unsatisfactory reply, he resigned from the organization. In a speech to his followers in Mirpur, Abbas said Muslims "should rise and hoist the flag of the Muslim Conference in the name of the Prophet of Arabia. According to the *Quran*, the whole world belonged to the Muslims and if they joined the Congress, they would lose sight of their object."[6] The re-formation of the Muslim Conference would, moreover, enable Jammu's leaders to shake off the Kashmir Valley's hegemony in determining the course of political developments in their region.

The reason their movement drew so much ire from the National Conference and its supporters was clear enough, since it directly challenged Sheikh Abdullah's position as the sole representative of the state of Jammu and Kashmir. To add insult to injury, the Sheikh's traditional rival, Mirwaiz Kashmir Yusuf Shah, who had been biding his time since their split in the early 1930s, extended a willing hand of support to Ghulam Abbas, becoming the representative of the Muslim Conference in Srinagar. The National Conference did not take to this new challenge to its authority with dignity. It descended to hooliganism against supporters of the Muslim Conference. However, it was the propaganda of the National Conference against its rival that has had the most lasting impact on the reputation of the Muslim Conference. Newspapers that supported the National Conference—which, incidentally, are the only newspapers that have survived in the government archives of the state—labeled Yusuf Shah a communalist who was desecrating the idea of the jihad by carrying it out against nationalist supporters of the National Conference.[7] "It is stated clearly in the *Quran*," claimed one article, "that the Jews and Christians fell because they accorded their religious heads with unlimited powers. Islamic leaders have not been spared when they have committed crimes against the people, therefore, the removal of the Mirwaiz as a leader of the Kashmiri Muslims will not be a move against Islam in the Kashmir Valley."[8]

[6] Political Department E164/1941, Jammu State Archives, 9.

[7] These newspapers included *Khidmat* and *Khalid-i-Kashmir*, both published out of Srinagar.

[8] "The Mirwaiz's Latest Attempt at Killing the Nation," *Khalid-i-Kashmir*, Srinagar, October 26, 1942.

The National Conference assumed that the Muslim League supported the Muslim Conference, and their criticism of the Mirwaiz was accompanied by a critique of the Muslim League's ability to represent the needs of Kashmiri Muslims. "The Muslim League should accept the fact that the National Conference is the sole representative of the Muslims, Hindus and Sikhs of Kashmir," declared an editorial in the pro-National Conference newspaper, *Khalid-i-Kashmir*.[9] Despite the claims of propagandists of the National Conference, the relationship between the All India Muslim League and Muslim Conference was far from one of unconditional support. In fact, as late as 1936, on his pleasure visit to the Kashmir Valley, the leader of the Muslim League, Mohammad Ali Jinnah, had made no political overtures to the Muslim Conference. In his speech to the Conference, Jinnah stated quite clearly that he did not claim to understand the position of the Muslims of the state of Jammu and Kashmir. However, he emphasized the duty of the representatives of the majority community to assure the minorities of the state, the Hindus, that they would have an equal share in the justice and representation in the state.[10]

In the next decade, the League's ambivalent attitude toward Muslim inhabitants of princely states continued. In 1937, it created a new entity, the All-India States Muslim League under the supervision of Nawab Bahadur Yar Jung, to supervise the affairs of the residents of princely India, thereby excluding them from membership in the League.[11] The Pakistan scheme, as conceived by the Muslim League in 1940, it was obvious, did not include the princely states, not even Muslim-majority Kashmir.[12] It is important to note here, however,

[9] *Khalid*, Srinagar, November 18, 1942.

[10] "Address by M.A. Jinnah," June 3, 1936, in Hussain, ed., *The Political Struggle of Kashmiri Muslims*, 402–3.

[11] Ian Copland, "The Abdullah Factor: Kashmiri Muslims and the Crisis of 1947," in D.A. Low, ed., *The Political Inheritance of Pakistan* (New York: St. Martin's Press, 1991), 222.

[12] Although the Muslim-majority provinces of Punjab and Bengal formed the cornerstones of the League's demand for Pakistan, it is clear that the League faced tough opposition from regional parties in both these provinces in 1940–1. As a result, most of its energies in this period were geared toward increasing its support base against the Unionist Party in the Punjab and the Krishak Praja Party in Bengal. See Ian Talbot, "The Unionist Party and Punjabi Politics, 1937–1947," and Sugata Bose, "A Doubtful Inheritance: The Partition of Bengal in 1947," in Low, ed., *The Political Inheritance of Pakistan*, 86–105 and 130–43. See also

that while the Muslim League may have been focusing its energies on British India, other Muslim organizations and sects in British Indian provinces, particularly in 1930s Punjab, always included Kashmir in their schemes aimed at reconciling sovereignty and legitimacy. The schemes put forth by the Punjabi Premier Sikandar Hayat Khan, and the All India Kashmir Committee under the Ahmadiyyas and later Muhammad Iqbal, are cases in point.[13]

This did not, however, prevent the Muslim Conference from declaring the Muslim League as its political mentor. Chaudhuri Ghulam Abbas stated unambiguously that "the Kashmir Muslim Conference is a part and parcel of the All-India Muslim League."[14] And the Muslim League did make statements that supported the Muslim Conference as a representative of the Muslims of the state, much to the chagrin of the National Conference.[15] This should not be taken to mean that the Muslim League had designs to include Kashmir in its future plans for Pakistan, since the Pakistan idea itself remained fluid until the very eve of partition. Furthermore, at least in the early 1940s, the League regarded Kashmiris as being unfit to participate in its movement. Khurshid Ahmed, who was sent by Jinnah to Kashmir in 1943, wrote about Kashmiri Muslims and their religious leadership, ironically enough, in terms not dissimilar to the way in which they were being described by the National Conference:

> The Muslims of Kashmir do not appear to have had the advantage of a true Muslim religious leadership. No important religious leader has ever made Kashmir . . . his home or even an ordinary centre of activities. Islam, in Kashmir, throughout remained at the mercy of a crop of counterfeit spiritual leaders in the person of the ignorant Mullahs who appear to have legalised for them everything that drives coach and four through Islam and the code of life it has laid down. Cowardice, treachery, lies, cheating, and other abominable things are now the most common features of the Muslims of the country.[16]

Rajit K. Mazumder, *The Indian Army and the Making of Punjab* (New Delhi: Permanent Black, 2003).

[13] For a detailed discussion of these schemes, see Jalal, *Self and Sovereignty*, especially 342–70 and 388–422.

[14] *Khalid*, Srinagar, January 12, 1943.

[15] *Khalid*, Srinagar, November 18, 1942.

[16] Quoted in Copland, "The Abdullah Factor," 223.

While Jinnah abandoned his plans to immediately visit the state in the wake of this report, he did visit the Valley the following year.

In the meantime, the relationship between the National Conference and the Indian National Congress was becoming increasingly less ambiguous. At Sheikh Abdullah's invitation, Jawaharlal Nehru, accompanied by Khan Abdul Gaffar Khan, visited the Valley in 1940 amidst displays of public enthusiasm by National Conference supporters.[17] The organization received lavish funds from Hindus, particularly Punjabi Hindu traders, to organize reception parties for Congress leaders.[18] Nehru expressed his unequivocal support for the National Conference as the sole national organization in the state and attempted to recruit Kashmiris into the anti-colonial struggle being conducted by the Congress. While the matter of acquiring responsible government in the states was an important one, he stated that it paled in comparison to the larger anti-imperial struggle the Indians were engaged in against the British. More significantly, Nehru asked Kashmiri Pandits to abandon thoughts of minority questions and advocated joint electorates for the two communities, labeling separate electorates as the work of communalists. In turn, Sheikh Mohammad Abdullah hailed the Congress for including the programs of the states in its agenda, which aimed at establishing constitutional rule by the princes with the willing co-operation of the inhabitants of princely states. Furthermore, he stated that the idea of vivisecting India was "fantastic, absurd, unworkable, and anti-national."[19]

Both Nehru and Abdullah mutually served the interests of their organizations during this visit, while ignoring the larger questions surrounding Kashmir's status in an independent India. The two organizations consistently elided over the different, and sometimes mutually exclusive, demands of their constituents. Nehru's visit to the state backfired for the National Conference, since it presented incontestable proof to Kashmiris—both Hindus and Muslims—that the organization was a puppet of the Congress and would follow its lead in glorifying the anti-imperial struggle at the expense of the decade-long struggle for responsible government in Kashmir. A police intelligence report from

[17] Abdullah, *Flames of the Chinar*, 50–1.

[18] Bazaz, *The Struggle for Freedom in Kashmir*, 181.

[19] Political Department E 206/1940, Jammu State Archives.

1940 noted that "Sheikh Mohammad Abdullah is losing favor amongst the Muslims because of his nationalistic activities, which the majority feel to be detrimental to their interests."[20] A prominent Kashmiri Muslim leader, M.A. Sabir, the son of the Kashmiri Ahmadiyya Mohammad Abdullah Vakil, who had split with Sheikh Abdullah in 1934, organized a meeting in which he advised people not to co-operate with the National Conference during Nehru's visit to the Valley. "The Congress," he added, "aimed at the annihilation of Islam and India and Nehru had come to Kashmir to make Kashmiri Muslims the slaves of this organization."[21]

Additionally, two prominent Kashmiri Pandit leaders, Kashyap Bandhu and Jia Lal Kilam, resigned from the National Conference in the wake of Nehru's visit. National Conference newspapers immediately labeled them communal and closet supporters of the Muslim Conference. Interestingly enough, however, other articles pointed out that the Kashmiri Pandit members had resigned because they were unable to accept Sheikh Abdullah's personal commitment to Islam and his political commitment to the Kashmiri Muslim cause. In an attempt to rescue Sheikh Abdullah's image, one particular article alleged that Kashyap Bandhu had asked Sheikh Abdullah why he should be considered a nationalist if he called himself a Muslim first and a Muslim last. To this Abdullah replied that the *Quran* instructed him to declare that he was a Muslim first and Muslim last. On being asked again by Kashyap Bandhu whether he would abandon nationalism if the *Quran* instructed him to do so, Abdullah replied that he would renounce any such nationalism that the *Quran* did not expressly support.[22]

As we saw earlier, Abdullah had been attempting to reconcile his overtly "nationalist" stance with his religious affiliation since the late 1930s. This schism in the National Conference's ideology had serious consequences for the organization's project in Kashmir. The need to appear responsive to the demands of the Muslim community became more insistent after the revival of the Muslim Conference and its growing popularity, even among the Muslims of the Valley. In time-honored tradition, Abdullah moved in the direction of establishing

[20] Ibid.
[21] Ibid.
[22] *Khalid,* Srinagar, August 9, 1940.

control over Muslim shrines in an attempt to make his nationalist agenda more responsive to Kashmiri demands for a recognition of their religious—and by extension, their social, economic and political—rights. The National Conference founded the All Jammu and Kashmir Auqaf Trust in 1940 for the development, maintenance, and control of religious places, including the Hazratbal shrine (the repository of the holy relic of the Prophet Mohammad) and the religious sites that the state had returned to the Muslim community in the 1930s. Abdullah was named its founder president.[23] While the trust busied itself in decorating the inner chamber of the Hazratbal shrine and the Idgah, in another symbolic move Abdullah set up the National Conference's press on the lands of the Pathar Masjid, from where its weekly newspapers were published.[24]

Despite the establishment of the Auqaf Trust and Abdullah's fiery speeches against Hindu politics and religion during the course of 1940, it is evident that by 1943 Sheikh Abdullah and his organization were rapidly losing their popular mandate in Kashmir. The Devnagari–Persian script controversy, which broke out in the state in the wake of the government order on the medium of instruction in schools, further illuminates the challenge presented by the Muslim Conference to the National Conference, particularly in the Valley. Against the recommendations of the Educational Reorganization Committee, in September 1940 the government ordered that: "The language should be a common one, viz., simple Urdu. But for reading and writing, both the Devnagari script and the Persian script should have equal recognition. The textbooks to be used in imparting instructions in the various subjects should be same but printed in both scripts." Additionally, teachers were expected to have a knowledge of both scripts and, if they did not, to "learn it to the satisfaction of a prescribed authority within a period of one year."[25]

The National Conference's stance on the medium of instruction issue was double-edged, and again illuminated the inability of its leadership to reconcile the "religious" and "regional" aspects of its ideology.[26] While Abdullah made public speeches exhorting his

---

[23] *Trust Deed* (Srinagar: All Jammu Kashmir Muslim Auqaf Trust, 1973), 1–3.

[24] *Trust Deed* and Abdullah, *Flames of the Chinar*, 53–4.

[25] Political Department 29/10/1940, Jammu State Archives.

[26] It is important to note that the government order was not much different

followers to fight until the government's order was rescinded since it was a move to foist Hindu culture on Muslims,[27] pro-National Conference newspapers regarded the order as an attempt by the government to divide Hindus and Muslims within the national movement. According to one article, the only means through which a people could assert a common nationality was through a common script. By imposing two scripts, the Dogra government had sown the seeds of communal discord within Kashmir's body politic with the ultimate aim of stunting the national movement. Furthermore, the author alleged that the Hindustanis diverted their energies on meaningless controversies such as script and language while ignoring the demands of their national movement. The Kashmiris, however, should not be inclined to follow their lead, since "neither was Urdu the language of the Muslims, nor was Hindi the language of the Hindus."[28]

The author was, of course, correct in pointing out that neither Kashmiri Hindus nor Muslims spoke Hindi or Urdu; they all spoke Kashmiri. However, instead of advocating Kashmiri as the language most suited to be the medium of instruction in schools and the language of the Civil Service examinations, pro-National Conference newspapers asserted that Urdu possessed what was required for it to be the common language of Kashmiri nationality since it adapted to changing circumstances while preserving its essential qualities.[29] The eight National Conference Praja Sabha members followed Abdullah's lead and made fiery speeches against the Pandit community for instigating the government to pass the dual script order and resigned their seats.[30] The National Conference thus gave the debate on scripts a communitarian color, thereby obscuring the class biases of the Kashmiri

---

from the resolution adopted by the working committee of the National Conference in reference to the Kashmir Civil Service Examinations in 1939. Resenting the exclusion of the recognized court language of the state, Hindustani, from the list of both compulsory and optional subjects prescribed for the Kashmir Civil Service examinations, the resolution "strongly urges its inclusion as one of the compulsory subjects, facility to be given to the candidates to use either Persian or Devnagari script as they like." See *Khalid*, Srinagar, January 12, 1940.

[27] Political Department E224/B196/1941 and Political Department E216/B182/1941, Jammu State Archives.

[28] *Khalid*, Srinagar, December 14, 1940.

[29] *Khalid*, Srinagar, October 10, 1941.

[30] Bazaz, *The Struggle for Freedom in Kashmir*, 186–8.

"national" movement, which had once again ignored, along with Kashmiri, the interests of the lower tier of society. Given the National Conference's narrative on united nationalism, it is surprising that the organization did not adopt Kashmiri as the symbol of Kashmiri national identity.[31]

The Mirwaiz, as a representative of the Muslim Conference, registered a more complex response to the government orders on dual scripts in state schools. In a long petition to the Maharaja, the Mirwaiz alleged that the introduction of Devnagari was not only an attack on common nationality but also an attack on Islam in Kashmir. The imposition of Devnagari on the people of Kashmir was an attempt by the government to spread Hindi in the name of simple Hindustani. For the Mirwaiz, those who had introduced this measure were contemptuous of Urdu because it was associated with the Muslim community, because its vocabulary was derivative of Arabic, and because it was written in the Persian script. Such animosity toward the language of the majority community of the state could only be interpreted, stated the Mirwaiz, as "enmity towards Islam." For him the introduction of Devnagari into the state school system was just another means through which the Dogra state was attempting to "Hinduize" Kashmir. Not only had the government steadily reduced the study of Arabic in schools over the years, it had also begun to allot Hindu titles to places, buildings and associations, for instance, the conversion of the name of the town of Islamabad to Anantnag. [32]

Interestingly, the Mirwaiz interpreted the government orders as not simply an attempt to acculturate Kashmiri Muslims, but also to "create a lingual split between the Muslims of the Kashmir and that of the Punjab," a policy that could only stem from the Mahasabhaite, Gandhian and Nehruvian mentality which aimed to "crush the national spirit of the Muslims." He noted that:

[31] Although the organization's meetings were conducted in Kashmiri, at least in the Valley, its newspapers and other publications were solely in Urdu, with occasional articles and poetry in Kashmiri. Perhaps this was because Kashmiri had the potential to divide as much as unite the movement—since its adoption would raise the acrimonious issue of the script in which the language should be written. Whatever the reason, this had created a split between the Valley's oral culture, conducted largely in Kashmiri, and print political culture, further attesting to the growing gulf between the National Conference and the Kashmiri people.

[32] Political Department E224/B196/1941, Jammu State Archives, 9–13.

The persons responsible for enforcing the Wardha system of education here must keep in view that even those who have sold themselves to the Congress through the Congress "mass contact" have opposed this scheme along with us . . . because being away from the influence of Wardha, Islam has taken the upper hand over Gandhi and the Congress though it was their claim of being Congressites that, in the first instance, emboldened the Prime Minister to adopt this anti-Islamic policy.[33]

The Mirwaiz clearly opposed Gandhi's proposal to merge Hindi and Urdu into a common language of the masses called Hindustani— which the Mahatma claimed could be written in either script[34]—as just another attempt by the Congress to annihilate the "social, cultural, religious, and national qualities of the Muslims." That the Government of India had been successful in introducing Hindi in the Devanagari script to an equal position with Urdu in the Persian script as an official language of the Central Provinces in 1900 was proof enough for the Mirwaiz that the Congress was responsible for the order. What was more significant to the Mirwaiz, however, was that the Hindi movement had been defeated in the Punjab, where Urdu retained its official status. The fact that, while the Punjab had remained untouched by Congress machinations, Kashmiris were being forced to accept another script could mean nothing other than a Congress attempt to divide Punjabis and Kashmiris. Such policies could only, warned the Mirwaiz, push Kashmiri Muslims into the arms of those who propagated the anti-Congress Pakistan scheme.[35]

More importantly, the Mirwaiz pointed to the incongruity of the introduction of Devnagari in Kashmir given the fact that even non-Muslims in the state had conducted the business of administration in Persian and then Urdu, and "there was never any movement in the state in favor of the Hindi language or Devnagari script, no request was made for its introduction until the arrival of the present Prime Minister . . . and no community claimed it as its own language."[36] Furthermore, he argued that if the language of the people did have to be introduced, the government should have introduced Kashmiri in

[33] Ibid., 11.

[34] For a detailed discussion of Gandhi's ideas on language, see Paul R. Brass, *Language, Religion and Politics in North India* (London: Cambridge University Press, 1974), 135.

[35] Political Department E224/B196/1941, Jammu State Archives, 4.

[36] Ibid., 9.

schools since that was the native tongue of the Kashmiris. As he put it quite plainly, "Our common dialect is Kashmiri and common language Persian. Arabic is the religious language of the Muslim subjects."[37]

The Mirwaiz seemed to be more in tune with the interests of the Muslim masses, most of whom were illiterate precisely because their leaders had never raised the banner of the vernacular tongue as the medium of instruction. Furthermore, as the Mirwaiz rightly noted, the government order would push the Muslim masses even further back in education just as they had started making progress in the field and "thus leave the non-Muslims the unrivalled monopoly of Government Service, and similar other things." The Kashmiri Muslim student was already under a heavy burden, and this order would mean he had to acquire four languages: "In addition to English, Persian according to custom, Urdu and Devanagari according to law, and Arabic according to religion."[38]

Some Kashmiri Pandits, who had been smarting under concessions made by the state in favor of Kashmiri Muslims, saw an opportunity to regain lost ground through this controversy. A few established a Hindi Parishad and the Hindu League to propagate the reading of Hindi in Srinagar.[39] Hindu organizations in Jammu and Mirpur, such as the Rajput Amar Khashtriya Sabha and the Hindu Rajya Sabha, in the meantime hailed the orders and organized Hindi Pracharini Sabhas to agitate for the replacement of Urdu with Hindi as the court language of the state. They argued that if the court language of Hyderabad—whose ruler was a Muslim while his subjects mostly Hindus—could be Urdu, then the language of Jammu and Kashmir—whose ruler was Hindu while his subjects were mostly Muslims—should be Hindi.[40]

While there may have been some truth to the allegations that the introduction of dual scripts was the government's attempt at dividing

[37] Ibid., 13.
[38] Ibid., 7–8.
[39] Political Department E206/1940, Jammu State Archives.
[40] Political Department E164/1941, Jammu State Archives. Movements for the introduction of Hindi in state schools and the administration were of very recent origin in Jammu and Kashmir. While most northern provinces of British India were embroiled in Hindi movements in the 1880s, the Jammu and Kashmir State Council declared Urdu as the court language in 1889.

the national movement, the more probable reason was that it wanted to pacify Hindu opinion, which had become increasingly rancorous over the past decade against the state's so-called pro-Muslim policies. In spite of vehement Muslim opposition to the dual-scripts move, thus, the state did not rescind the order. In 1943 the government passed orders approving the vocabulary for the common medium of instruction in elementary schools, namely simple Urdu (Hindustani), stating that the spirit behind this move was "that the vocabulary . . . should, while conforming to the description of 'Simple Urdu,' consist of words which, as far as possible, are common to both Urdu and Hindi and which are easily understandable in the language of common parlance."[41] And, the report of the Ganga Nath Commission, appointed by the Maharaja in 1944 for the evolution of an organic scheme for the administration of the state, by which time the script controversy had all but died down, stated that "These orders [dual-script medium of instruction], if implemented, will encourage the adoption of instruction in Urdu or Hindustani by facilitating the learning of that language in a script more akin to the script at present being used by communities or which has been used in its ancient structure of its spoken language."[42]

The script controversy illuminated the political affiliations of the two main organizations in the state. By 1943, the popular perception of the National Conference as a stooge of the Indian National Congress had become more widespread. During a meeting of the National Conference in Jammu devoted to the establishment of the organization's branch in the city, Sheikh Abdullah was asked the purpose of forming such a branch when a branch of the Indian National Congress already existed there. Although Abdullah reacted to the question with indignation, and a branch of the National Conference was established in Jammu,[43] the incident indicates the extent to which the National Conference had lost favor among Muslims, since they regarded Abdullah as a leader who was more interested in nationalistic activities along the lines of those conducted by the Congress, than in safeguarding their interests.

The Muslim Conference and other political parties of the Valley

---

[41] *Jammu and Kashmir Government Gazette,* March 4, 1943, 53.

[42] *Shri Ganga Nath Commission Report on Administration of Jammu and Kashmir State,* November 1944, Jammu, 433.

[43] Political Department E206/1940, Jammu State Archives.

registered a tepid reaction to the National Conference's declaration of total support for the Quit India movement begun by the Congress in India in 1942.[44] While the movement electrified many parts of India, Kashmir remained relatively quiescent during the course of the agitation. Unable to tolerate the growing popularity of the Muslim Conference, which stood in the way of the National Conference's aims, pro-National Conference newspapers slandered the organization and its founders as tools of imperialists. Instead of spreading the message of unity among various communities of the state, according to the articles in these newspapers, the Muslim Conference had spread the cry of "Islam in danger" for its own political purposes, making it impossible for Kashmiris to stand united against Nazism, Fascism, and imperialism.[45] In the 1943 session of the National Conference held at Mirpur, Abdullah further aligned himself with the goals of the Indian National Congress by declaring that "As Muslims, we must believe that India is our home. We have been born of this earth and we will go to the same earth. India is our motherland and it will remain our motherland. It is our duty to free our motherland and our homes from the slavery of the foreigners."[46] Through this declaration, Abdullah not only replaced Kashmir with India as the homeland of the Kashmiris, but also privileged Indian national identity at the expense of Kashmiri regional identity, when there was no easy correlation between the two.

At the same time as its discourse was becoming increasingly alienating, the National Conference's alliances with Gopalaswami Ayyengar, the unpopular Prime Minister of the state, convinced many Kashmiris that Sheikh Abdullah was willing to go to any lengths to gain political power. Instead of holding by-elections to fill the seats that had been vacated by the National Conference members in the wake of the script controversy, the Prime Minister proposed that since the National Conference was the "acknowledged popular" party, the candidates suggested by the Conference could be nominated by the special orders of the Maharaja to fill the vacant seats in the legislature. The working committee of the National Conference agreed readily. This move could not but have incited protests from the other political parties, particularly the Muslim Conference, which would probably have won at least a few seats given the changing political scenario, had elections

---

[44] *Khalid*, Srinagar, September 1 and 6, 1942.

[45] *Khalid*, November 2, 1942.

[46] Quoted in Hassnain, *Freedom Struggle in Kashmir*, 115–16.

been held.[47] By 1943 the National Conference had betrayed Kashmiris by not only subordinating their movement to the Congress, but, more importantly, its collaboration with the Dogra state threatened to jeopardize the very raison d'être of the movement.

The association of the National Conference with the government, furthermore, did not simply have an impact on the realm of high politics. The effects of the acute economic crisis during the war, which led to soaring inflation and famine in parts of British India, also affected the economic situation in Kashmir. The winter of 1942–3 registered a shortage of fuel in the Valley, and there were shortages of grain both there and in Jammu province. The government set up fuel and grain committees to supply fuel and grain to inhabitants of the provinces who were hardest hit. The Prime Minister appointed a National Conference member, Bakhshi Ghulam Mohammad, as the Muslim member of these committees. This resulted in a hue and cry from several sections of the population which alleged that the committees had refused them grain and fuel because of their affiliation with the Muslim Conference. The press reported that corruption was rampant at the depots and a big portion of the fuel went to the black market, the profits of which were shared by committee officials.[48]

The results of National Conference policies and tactics were apparent in the political atmosphere of the Valley by 1943–4, as the informal arenas of politics resounded with voices of dissent against the organization. Significantly, some Kashmiri leaders rejected the political agendas of both the National and the Muslim Conference as unrepresentative of Kashmiri interests. These critics questioned ideas of "secular" and "communal" nationalism, while attempting to creatively redefine the terms and reconfigure the concept of nationalism.

The Critique of "Nationalism" and "Communalism" in Kashmiri Political Discourse

Here I examine the voices of dissent launched against the National Conference in the atmosphere of uncertainty surrounding the inhabi-

[47] *Rahnuma*, Srinagar, November 10, 1942.

[48] Editorials and articles in the *Khalid, Khidmat, Rahnuma*, and *Hamdard*, December 1942–May 1943. Other regional parties, such as the Unionist Party in Punjab, also faced a decline in their popularity and authority as a result of wartime dislocations and the colonial state's intrusive rules and regulations around the same time.

tants of the princely state of Jammu and Kashmir in the mid-1940s. Neither the National Conference nor its most formidable rival, the Muslim Conference, seemed to possess the answer to the peculiar situation the Kashmiris found themselves in by the middle of the decade. While the Indian National Congress and the Muslim League stood in a position to bargain with the British for the future of their particular constituents, the future of the princely states had become murkier than ever during the course of the Second World War. Furthermore, the two main political parties in the state seemed bent on following the lead of and getting directives from the two main political parties of British India, neither of which was particularly interested in the political or other predicaments of the inhabitants of princely states. The Government of India, in the meantime, while willing to carry out their treaty obligations with the princely states in the future, did not seem in a particularly strong position to do so.

It is necessary to examine the changes taking place at the level of political reforms in British India to contextualize the political predicaments facing the princely states and their inhabitants in this period. Although the Montagu–Chelmsford reforms of 1919 had allowed for the creation of a Chamber of Princes as a special assembly for the rulers of the states, through which their collective opinion could be sought by the Viceroy and their will expressed to him,[49] the British first gave serious thought to questions regarding paramountcy and the status of princely states in the future constitutional makeup of India in the Government of India Act of 1935. Since the concept of Dominion Status for India had become a definite possibility from the end of the First World War, the British could no longer ignore the problem of princely states. In an attempt to incorporate princely states into the future political structures of India, as much as to perpetuate British rule, the Government of India Act provided for the creation of a Council of State and a Federal Assembly, in which the representatives of princely states would act as a counterpoise to the elected representatives of the Indian provinces. The princely states that voluntarily agreed to participate in the dispensations of the act "were to be granted well over a third of the seats in the Council of State (up to 104 as opposed to 156 for British India) and exactly a third of the representation

---

[49] *Report of the Indian States Committee 1928–1929* (London: His Majesty's Stationary Office, 1929).

in the Federal Assembly (with 125 seats as opposed to 250 from British India)." States were allotted seats based on their populations; hence Hyderabad received five seats, while Jammu and Kashmir was allocated three.[50]

The act specified separate conditions for provincial autonomy and the creation of an all-India federation. While the provinces were to become autonomous after the first general elections, federal autonomy was dependent on the voluntary accession of half the princely states to the Indian Union. Needless to say, there was no reason to believe at the time that the princes would be willing to do so, given the scale of internal autonomy exercised by them in their states and the infancy of political movements against their rule in the middle of the 1930s. Recognizing this fact, the National Conference had voiced its critique of the act in 1935. In any case, the 1935 act created more problems than it settled in relation to the future of princely states. Most importantly, by creating the concept of the Instrument of Accession, the act put forth the possibility of a state deciding not to join the proposed federation. The pertinent question this raised, of course, was what status such a state would have within the British Commonwealth. Moreover, what would happen if paramountcy, as the special relationship between the Crown and the princely states had come to be defined, lapsed in future in the case of those states that had refused to sign the Instrument of Accession?[51]

The status of the princely states became a matter of greater concern to British and Indian leaders during the course of the Second World War. Not only were the British beleaguered both militarily and economically by 1943, the rulers of the states, in direct contrast to the Indian leadership, had rallied to the British cause quite unanimously during the war. The *Jammu and Kashmir Government Gazette* regularly printed proclamations of loyalty to the British government and solidarity with their war against Fascism throughout the war years. The British may have been grateful for these admissions of support by princes, but given the extent of the economic damage suffered by Britain during the war it was conceivable that they would not be able to

---

[50] Alastair Lamb, *Incomplete Partition: The Genesis of the Kashmir Dispute 1947–48* (Hertingfordbury: Roxford Books, 1997), 11.

[51] For a detailed discussion of these questions, see Lamb, *Incomplete Partition*, 10–13.

fulfil their role as the paramount power for the states at the end of the war. In spite of this, the Cripps Mission, sent by Churchill to India in 1942 to come to terms with nationalist leaders, made a set of assurances to the princely states. As far as those states which decided to accede to an Indian union were concerned, "the Crown will cease to exercise paramountcy over them." For those who chose not to accede to an Indian union, Cripps stated that "His majesty's government will make the necessary provision to implement their treaty obligations . . . Non-acceding States need have no fear that their treaties, so far as these are concerned with their relations with the Crown, will be revised without their consent."[52] Despite these assurances, British policy toward princely states would change dramatically in 1946. (Its impact on Jammu and Kashmir will be discussed later in this chapter.)

Suffice it to say that in the mid-1940s, in the eyes of the inhabitants of the princely state of Jammu and Kashmir, the princely hold on their state seemed to be intact. More importantly, the movement against the Dogra dynasty that had been initiated a decade back had outlived its usefulness. With the possibility of British withdrawal from the subcontinent, Indian nationalist leaders of various hues had begun to meddle in Kashmiri affairs without recognizing the peculiar situation of the people of the state. Moreover, Kashmiri political organizations seemed bent on preventing the state from following an independent political course. It was in this context, when the political future of Jammu and Kashmir seemed uncertain, that some Kashmiris attempted to articulate alternative visions of Kashmiri nationalism.

The Kashmiri leader who protested most vociferously against the direction of Kashmiri politics in the mid-1940s, and continued to do so until his death in 1984, was Prem Nath Bazaz. Bazaz was born in 1905, the same year as Sheikh Mohammad Abdullah, into a Kashmiri Pandit family of Srinagar. Like Abdullah, he was educated in state institutions being opened up through the government's increasing interest in mass education, and acquired a Bachelor's degree at the local Sri Pratap Singh College in Srinagar. He went on for further studies to Punjab University and, after graduating, found employment as a clerk in the Chief Engineer's office at the Public Works Department in Srinagar. However, throughout the 1920s, he also began to establish

[52] Quoted in Lamb, *Incomplete Partition,* 13.

strong connections with newspapers in British India, particularly Lahore, and began a second career as a journalist, writing articles for the *Akhbaar-i-Am,* Lahore. In the early stages of his involvement in politics, Bazaz was pro-Gandhi and pro-Congress and attended the annual Congress Session at Lahore in 1930. He also participated actively in the States People's Conference. After his return from these meetings, he resigned from government service, having decided to devote his life to politics.[53]

Bazaz began his political career as the president of the Sanatan Dharma Yuvak Sabha, which was at the forefront of representing Kashmiri Pandit interests to the Dogra state in the wake of the incidents of 1931. As president, Bazaz toured the Kashmir Valley to unify and awaken Kashmiri Pandits to impending changes in the political structures of the state. By 1933 Bazaz had recognized that Kashmiri Pandits had no choice but to join hands with the Muslim Conference, which had recently been established to further the demands of Kashmiri Muslims: in his words, he "found his way into the politics of the masses."[54] This heralded the beginning of Bazaz's association with Sheikh Abdullah that lasted close to a decade. As editor of *Hamdard,* Bazaz spearheaded the movement to transform the Muslim Conference into the National Conference. In spite of his involvement with the Muslim Conference, however, Bazaz felt increasingly alienated from the organization and its leaders. The pages of *Hamdard* continually warned the Conference to divorce itself from the politics of British India, which, it was evident in the late 1930s and early 1940s, the organization was unwilling to do. In the wake of the script controversy, during which Abdullah made anti-Hindu speeches, Bazaz resigned from the working committee of the National Conference in November 1940, and a few months later, from the Conference itself.[55]

Bazaz's break with the National Conference is significant since it reflects the disillusionment felt by several Kashmiri Pandit leaders with the organization's agenda and its claim to speak on behalf of all Kashmiris. Bazaz's discomfort with the Conference, however, stemmed

[53] Prem Nath Bazaz, "Chronology of Prem Nath Bazaz's Life and Works" (Private Collection of Bhushan Bazaz, New Delhi), 1.

[54] "Letter from Prem Nath Bazaz to Jawaharlal Nehru," July 15, 1936 (Private Collection of Bhushan Bazaz, New Delhi).

[55] Bazaz, "Chronology," 5.

from far more than the fact that the organization did not represent the interests of Pandits. The close alignment of the Conference with the politics of the Congress was particularly distasteful to Bazaz. Bazaz had been moving away from Gandhian and eventually Congress politics throughout the 1930s. He had been taken aback by Gandhi's dismissive reply to his letter asking for advice on the path Kashmiri Pandits should follow in the political movement in Kashmir: "Seeing that Kashmir is predominantly Mussalman it is bound one day to become a Mussalman State. A Hindu prince can therefore only rule by non ruling i.e., by allowing the Mussalmans to do as they like and by abdicating when they are manifestly going wrong."[56]

Further, Jawaharlal Nehru's replies to Bazaz's queries about the peculiar problems facing Kashmir were just as dismissive. In a 1936 letter to Bazaz, Nehru categorically stated that Kashmir was part of the larger issue of Indian independence, hence the intricacies of the Kashmir situation were immaterial: "It is clear that the ultimate fate of Kashmir, as of the other Indian States, is bound up with that of India as a whole. So that the larger struggle for Indian independence governs the situation and the more or less local struggle in Kashmir must be viewed in the light of the Indian struggle." Moreover, Nehru condemned pan-Islamism and Pakistan as "the veriest nonsense."[57] It was evident to Bazaz that Congress leaders would readily sacrifice the interests of Kashmiris at the altar of Indian independence.

In 1943 Bazaz launched a strident critique of the Indian "nationalism" of Gandhi, the Indian National Congress, and the Kashmiri "nationalism" of their puppet organization, the National Conference, in a pamphlet entitled *Gandhism, Jinnahism and Socialism*. By this time, Bazaz had become a fervent follower of M. N. Roy and had been instrumental in founding the Kashmir Socialist Party in 1942, as well as supporting the Kisan Mazdoor Conference as alternatives to the political hegemony of the National Conference. Comprising a collection of articles by Bazaz, this pamphlet was an extraordinarily perceptive critique of the hegemonizing and homogenizing agendas of the Congress and the National Conference. In an article titled "Politics and Religion," Bazaz condemned Gandhian politics for dragging religion

[56] "Gandhi's Letter to Prem Nath Bazaz," May 15, 1934 (Private Collection of Bhushan Bazaz, New Delhi).

[57] "Nehru's Letter to Prem Nath Bazaz," July 7, 1936 (Private Collection of Bhushan Bazaz, New Delhi).

into the political arena. Admitting that he was once a follower of Gandhi, Bazaz stated that he soon realized that Gandhi was neither a nationalist nor a revolutionary. While Gandhi had undoubtedly awakened the Indian people, the tactics he used for the purpose had introduced a canker into the Indian body politic. To Bazaz, religion was a matter of faith that lay in the realm of an individual's personal affairs and did not belong in the political arena.[58]

In another article Bazaz stated that the politics of the Congress was the politics of revivalism and reaction. The Congress, according to him, was a party run by Hindu capitalists, whose agenda was certainly not to ensure social and economic rights to all classes of the Indian population, but to keep wealth and political power in their own hands. Their bigoted policies, masquerading as nationalism, had produced what Bazaz called the "Bogey of Pakistan." In an article of the same title, he argued that the biggest threat to the Congress was Jinnah and Pakistan, but Gandhi himself was responsible for the creation of Jinnah. Jinnah's politics, even though he was not a particularly devout Muslim, appealed to the Muslim masses because he provided an alternative to the Congress, which to them represented Hindu nationalism. And just as Gandhi was a creation of Hindu capitalists, Jinnah was a creation of Muslim capitalists. Jinnahism, in his view, could not be eradicated without the eradication of Gandhism. The difference between Hindus and Muslims, stated Bazaz, lay not so much in their religion as the political objectives of their leaders. While the Hindu political party "wanted to throw the British out and take over the rule of India without sharing it with anyone, the Muslim leaders wanted to unify their religious community with a view to being able to gain some participation in government."[59]

According to Bazaz, only the fact that Congress leaders were unwilling to share power in an independent India could explain their fear of Pakistan, since Pakistan was no more than the acceptance of the Muslim right to rule in Muslim-majority provinces:

> Pakistan is even today functioning in the Muslim-majority provinces such as Punjab, Sind, NWFP, and Bengal, where Muslim Prime Ministers are running their governments. This too is Pakistan. The only difference that may happen now is that if any of these provinces wishes, it can separate

[58] Prem Nath Bazaz, *Gandhism, Jinnahism, Socialism* (Srinagar: Nishat Electric Press, 1944), 5–6, 16, and 58.

[59] Ibid., 31–51.

itself from the central government. If this will bring independence to India, then those Hindus who think of themselves as the sole representatives of Indian independence, why can't they accept the idea of Pakistan?[60]

The Congress media was responsible, as Bazaz noted, of creating a fear of Pakistan among Hindu masses. It was absurd to think that the establishment of Pakistan would lead to a genocide of Hindus and the imposition of the sharia. In another characteristically perspicacious comment, Bazaz stated that, contrary to the claims of the Congress Hindu leadership, India had never been united from Kashmir to Kanyakumari, either culturally or politically. In fact, nationalism itself was a new concept for India and needed new means of interpretation. He warned Hindus that they could hope to rule India only with the active and willing participation of Muslims. The Hindu–Muslim question, for that reason, had to be settled before independence, not put off, as the Congress stated, until after independence.[61]

For Bazaz the problems India faced were economic, not communal. But unlike Nehru he accepted that the communal problem existed and had to be overcome if India was to progress toward economic liberation for its masses. The masses of both communities were poor and backward, while their leaders were too busy serving their own political interests to pay attention to them. "What kind of independence are we fighting for?," he asked. "It is well enough to say that we will throw the British out of India, but who will replace them? If the socio-economic status quo of the pre-independence period continues in the independent India, then what difference would independence have made to the common people?" According to Bazaz, leaders like Nehru and Gandhi bandied about the idea of independence without addressing the economic issues facing the people, because they had no answers. "Of what use," he asked again, "is the independence of the capitalists?"[62] Clearly, Bazaz viewed socialism as the answer to India and Kashmir's problems and presented it as an alternative to Gandhism, Jinnahism and Fascism. The Kashmir Socialist Party, in line with the Radical Democrats in India, declared the Second World War a class struggle in which the forces of socialism were fighting against the forces of Fascism—yet

[60] Ibid., 78.
[61] Ibid., 76–7.
[62] Ibid., 113–17.

another reason, according to Bazaz, why the demands for independence should have been shelved until socialism had won the war.[63]

It is evident that for Bazaz the Indian National Congress was neither nationalist nor representative of the interests of the Indian population. Unfortunately for Kashmir and Kashmiris, the National Conference played a similar role in the state. "The National Conference does not represent national interests or democracy simply because its title is National or it appears to be popular," argued Bazaz. "Hitler may have been popular but he was never democratic, while Lenin was not a popular man when he led the revolution of 1917 and furthered the cause of Russian democracy." Both the Congress and the National Conference, according to Bazaz, were mainly in favor of political reforms to suit their own political interests while paying no attention to social and economic uplift of the people. The National Conference, furthermore, had abandoned its revolutionary program to co-operate with the government, ostensibly because of the war situation, but in reality to gain political power. "It is clear beyond doubt," stated Bazaz, "that the Conference has ceased to be a revolutionary nationalist body which had come into existence to express the inner urge of the suppressed and tyrannized masses."[64]

Bazaz was not the first in the state to express his discomfort with the National Conference. From a radically different perspective, but for similar reasons, the Hindu newspapers of Jammu had hailed the recreation of the Muslim Conference, since they felt that the term "national" in the title of the National Conference was just a means to mask the majoritarian ideologies of the organization. *Sudarshan* and *Amar* of Jammu stated that an overtly communal organization such as the Muslim Conference was much more acceptable and far less dangerous for Hindu interests than the National Conference, where communalists had disguised themselves as nationalists. An article claimed that the sole aim of the National Conference was the replacement of Hindu Raj with Muslim Raj, and while the Muslim Conference was also against Hindu Raj, since it was a communal organization it would be more willing to garner the endorsement of the minorities for its programs. The National Conference, however, simply by virtue of

[63] Ibid., 118.
[64] Ibid., 44–7.

the fact that it proclaimed itself to be national, sought no such sanction. The article further questioned the dangers of the nationalism of the National Conference by pointing out that when it put forth its demands the government regarded these as representative of all the inhabitants of the state, when they clearly were not. On the other hand, the government dismissed the demands of the Muslim Conference as communal.[65]

Several prominent Kashmiri Muslims, too, disputed the National Conference's claim to be the sole representative of Kashmiris, mostly on the grounds that it had betrayed their trust by aligning not only with the Dogra government but also with the Indian National Congress. However, they were equally opposed to the Muslim Conference's pro-Muslim League ideology. In an article in *Hamdard*, Pir Abdul Ahad Shah eloquently defended Kashmir's right to self-determination. He stated that neither the Congress nor the Muslim League could intervene in the affairs of the native states. If, he argued, Pakistan indeed stood for the self-determination of Muslims, then why couldn't Kashmiris have the right to self-determination? Furthermore, he said that Kashmiris would not simply accept the Muslim League's attitude whereby it ignored the interests of the people of the native states unless they joined Pakistan. The Kashmiris' right to self-determination could not, in his view, be ignored in Hindustan's movement toward independence.[66]

Hamdard represented the strongest voice of dissent against the invasion of "nationalism" and "communalism" into the body politic of the Kashmir Valley. Most significantly, it defended the right of Kashmiris to decide their own fate in the impending political transformations in the Indian subcontinent. An article by a Kashmiri Pandit activist rejected the Indian National Congress as the answer to the problems of the states, since the organization would bring independence to the rajas and maharajas of the states, while their subjects continued to toil under autocratic rule.[67] It is evident that by the mid-1940s Kashmiris had become increasingly suspicious of the stance of the Congress and the Muslim League toward native states, a well-founded suspicion given future events in the state. Other editorials implored

---

[65] *Amar*, Jammu, October 25, 1940.

[66] *Hamdard*, Srinagar, November 27 and December 8, 1943.

[67] *Hamdard*, Srinagar, August 15, 1943.

Sheikh Abdullah to abandon his alignment with the Indian National Congress and choose the socialist path to address the issues facing Kashmiris. They pointed out that the economic and political reforms that the National Conference had stood for, when it was still the Muslim Conference, seemed to have been lost in the race to gain political power and the favor of Congress leaders. "Where is the revolutionary," asked one *Hamdard* editorial, "who had appeared as the Prophet to lead the Kashmiris out of their oppressive conditions?"[68] The newspaper and its editor still held on to the hope that Abdullah might change his ways and prove to be the leader he had set out to be during the 1931 movement.

Sheikh Abdullah responded to *Hamdard's* charges by calling it a newspaper of the Kashmiri Pandits, a community whose "standard of success is to acquire clerical posts in offices. My community had also begun to run after government posts, but I convinced them that there were greater goals to be achieved." He went on to say that the people who criticized the Indian National Congress and the National Conference for mixing religion with politics had no experience of politics: "They sit in their government offices, and have made criticism their profession. In the field of practice, their critiques hold no water and cannot be applied." Religion, according to Abdullah, who assiduously labeled all his opponents "communalists," could not be separated from politics.[69]

Abdullah's contention that *Hamdard* represented Kashmiri Pandit politics was grossly misplaced. In fact, the newspaper was as critical of the "reactionary politics" of Kashmiri Pandit organizations as it was of the politics of the National Conference. The lampooning of the Kashmiri Pandit as a conservative figure filled the pages of *Hamdard* in the 1940s. In a satirical poem on the primary organization of the Kashmiri Pandits of the Valley, the Sanatan Dharam Yuvak Sabha, the Kashmiri poet Pitambar Nath Dhar Fani wrote:

Neither do you have a constitution,
nor do you have any responsibilities.
You are an enemy of principles,
and bereft of any objectives.

[68] *Hamdard*, Srinagar, November 16, 1943.
[69] *Hamdard*, Srinagar, July 22, 1943.

You keep claiming with every breath,
to be the spokesperson of the Pandits.
In reality you are simply,
a disciple of the capitalists.[70]

As early as the mid-1930s, Prem Nath Bazaz had declared to Kashmiri Pandits that their future lay in joining hands with the majority community of the state; reaction would only threaten their future in Kashmir. Simply because Bazaz and his newspaper critiqued the majoritarianism of the National Conference does not mean that they represented "communal" or anti-national interests.

The nationalism of the National Conference had come under fire from a variety of fronts by the mid-1940s. Several Kashmiri leaders launched powerful critiques of the vacuity of the organization's nationalism, which was devoid of a revolutionary agenda and had reduced Kashmiris to pawns in the great anti-colonial game being played out in British India. Perhaps Kashmiris would have decided to stay politically connected to India had they been given an opportunity to make their own decision. However, as early as the mid-1940s, they were already voicing their protest against the high-handedness of the organization that was forcing them into a political future over which they had no say.

The National Conference under Siege: Naya Kashmir and Kashmiris, 1944–1946

Despite appearances which suggested, particularly to the British, that the National Conference had the largest following of all the political parties in the Valley, several significant voices of dissent to the organization's ideologies and policies had arisen by the early 1940s. The fact that it was allied with the organization that the British considered the biggest threat to their rule in India, the Indian National Congress, may have been the reason the British viewed the National Conference as the most significant organization in the Valley.[71] It was evident to Kashmiris that despite the Conference's increasingly trenchant narrative

---

[70] "Address to Yuvak Sabha," *Hamdard*, Srinagar, August 14, 1943.

[71] The British Resident in Kashmir, Colonel Barton, noted in a report in 1943: "In the urban areas of the State, particularly in large cities such as Srinagar . . . [the

on nationalism and citizenship, a decade of political agitation under its rubric had brought the people of the Valley no closer to economic or political rights. Here I discuss the effectiveness of moves made by the National Conference to regain its popularity in the Valley in the mid-1940s.

The war had proven especially devastating for the National Conference. Not only was the Conference unable to redress the shortages of food and fuel that beset the population, but more importantly the Muslim Conference made significant strides through its association with the Muslim League toward the end of the war. Jinnah finally decided to make a political visit to the Valley in 1944.[72] An editorial in *Hamdard* noted that Sheikh Abdullah was so unnerved by Jinnah's impending visit that he sent his faithful lieutenants to make overtures to the leader in an attempt to portray himself as a champion of the Muslim League's cause. While pro-National Conference newspapers had quite categorically opposed Jinnah and called him a fanatic a few years earlier, Abdullah made speeches in late 1943 claiming that Jinnah's demand for Pakistan was justified. According to *Hamdard*, unhappy with Kashmiri Muslims thronging to Muslim Conference functions, Abdullah had taken the politically expedient step of announcing his support for the Muslim League and its leader.[73] The National Conference even attempted to hold a welcome reception for Jinnah on his arrival in Srinagar, although such a reception had already been organized under the auspices of the Muslim Conference.[74]

Abdullah's overtures notwithstanding, Jinnah's visit to the Valley in May–June 1944 proved harmful to the interests of the National Conference. In a speech to the Muslim Conference and the Muslim Students' Union, Jinnah declared that for 99 percent of the Muslims of Kashmir the only representative organization was the Muslim

---

National Conference] undoubtedly commands greater support among the Muslim population than does the Muslim Conference . . . There is little doubt that majority of the politically-minded Muslims belong to this party." Quoted in Copland, "The Abdullah Factor," 229.

[72] This was also the beginning of the Muslim League's ascendancy in Punjab and Bengal, as it capitalized on the wartime blunders of its regional party opponents.

[73] *Hamdard*, Srinagar, November 16, 1943.

[74] District Magistrate Office Records 49/2000/1944, Srinagar State Archives.

Conference. He further stated that although it was not his responsibility to put pressure on the National Conference, it was his duty to warn his Muslim brothers about the danger of associating with certain organizations in British India.[75] In another meeting, Jinnah exhorted the people to unite as Muslims under the flag of the Muslim Conference. Recognizing that Jinnah was clearly in favor of the Muslim Conference, the National Conference organized its own meetings during his visit, in which speakers declared that the Hindus and Muslims of Kashmir would not tolerate external intervention in state politics. The police reported that National Conference workers shouted abusive slogans during Jinnah's speeches on other occasions, which led to rioting between the followers of the two organizations.[76]

Hamdard noted that Jinnah's visit was detrimental to the National Conference. The overtures made by Sheikh Abdullah to Jinnah had not only been politically opportunistic, they had turned out to be politically suicidal, since Jinnah came to Kashmir and unequivocally supported the Muslim Conference. If, the editorial noted, Abdullah wanted to gain the support of the League, he would either have to give up his nationalism or end his political career.[77] To make matters worse for Abdullah, after his visit Jinnah began to take a closer personal interest in the affairs of princely states and wrote advisory letters to Ghulam Abbas as well as letters to the Viceroy attacking the oppressive administration of the Dogra government. This may have led to the replacement of the Prime Minister of the state, the pro-Hindu Kailash Haksar, with the more moderate B.N. Rao at the intervention of the Government of India.[78]

It is also clear that the growing popularity of the Muslim League among Indian Muslims during the war, and the increasing viability of the Pakistan demand, was not lost on Kashmiri Muslims. After all, in the correspondence between Rajagopalachari and Jinnah, which had been published in the Kashmiri press, the former had conceded the creation of Pakistan comprising the provinces and parts of provinces where the majority was Muslim.[79] The closer association of the Mus-

[75] *Hamdard*, Srinagar, June 22, 1944.

[76] District Magistrate Office Records 49/2000/1944, Srinagar State Archives.

[77] *Hamdard*, Srinagar, July 30, 1944.

[78] Copland, "The Abdullah Factor," 231.

[79] *Hamdard*, Srinagar, December 10, 1944

lim Conference and the Muslim League had led to the transformation of the Muslim Conference from an organization that had registered dissent against the National Conference to an organization that presented a viable alternative to it. As Ghulam Abbas noted in 1946: "We have stolen a long march on our opponents since the Quaid-i-Azam's visit."[80]

The National Conference had to take drastic steps to recover its ebbing influence among Kashmiris. To this end the organization's members of the Royal Commission, appointed by the Maharaja for the evolution of an organic scheme for the administration of the state, resigned from the commission. They submitted, instead, a comprehensive plan to the Dogra state for economic, social, political and cultural reconstruction. The National Conference adopted this plan, which came to be known as Naya Kashmir, or the New Kashmir Manifesto, at its September 1944 session in Srinagar as the objective of their nationalist party.[81] In his foreword to the manifesto, Abdullah attempted to reclaim his status and the status of his organization as the leader of the Kashmiri masses, both of which were willing to incur sacrifices for their uplift:

> Progress is a continuous struggle—a tempestuous struggle . . . The National Conference has been fighting the battle since the inception of the freedom movement. The struggle has continued but it should have a definite future programme . . . This struggle of ours is the struggle of the workers against those stone-hearted exploiters who as a class of discriminators have lost the sense of humanism . . . In our New Kashmir we shall build again the men and women of our state who have been dwarfed for centuries of servitude, and create a people worthy of our glorious motherland.[82]

The manifesto was a move to give concrete expression to the ideas of citizenship that the Muslim Conference had bandied about since its proclamation of the "National Demand for Responsible Government" in 1939. Naya Kashmir was divided into two parts—the Constitution of the State and the National Economic Plan. The proposed constitution

---

[80] Quoted in Copland, "The Abdullah Factor," 231.

[81] "Naya Kashmir," Unpublished Manuscript (Private Collection of Fidah Mohammad Hassnain, Srinagar, Kashmir).

[82] Ibid., i.

of the state would grant a single citizenship to all inhabitants of Jammu, Kashmir, Ladakh, and the Frontier Regions, including the Poonch and Chenani *ilaqas* (regions). Furthermore, the plan guaranteed equality of rights to all citizens, irrespective of their nationality, religion, race or birth. The administration of *Naya Kashmir* was to be run by a national assembly, elected by the citizens of the state by electoral districts, on the basis of one deputy per 40,000 population, for a period of five years.

The manifesto further envisaged the establishment of councils for national education, cultural uplift, women's rights, communications, and health to ensure the restructuring of all areas of the state. Most significantly, the plan advocated the socialization of all instruments of production and the reorganization of property relationships. It declared that the land belonged to the tiller and the landlord had no right over the land or the peasant. Since the state was agricultural country, the tiller would have the right to own a piece of land that at the time of enforcement of the new law may still be the property of the landlord. Additionally, the tiller would gain freedom from all his debts and the rights to protection against natural calamities as well as access to all the necessities of life.[83]

The extent to which the National Conference regime would adhere to this manifesto in Jammu and Kashmir after Indian independence will be examined later. Suffice it to say here that the New Kashmir Plan was a tall order even on paper, never mind in practice. Most importantly, not only did it give the Maharaja a solemn promise that he would continue to exercise the right of general control over the administration of the state, it did not delineate the status of Kashmir within the future political structure of independent India. The plan seemed to assume that the state of Jammu and Kashmir would be autonomous regardless of the political entities that replaced British rule. Sheikh Abdullah's speech during the National Conference session which adopted the manifesto as its future program did not address, or was at best ambiguous, on this issue. "The All Jammu and Kashmir National Conference," he declared, "has always championed the cause of Hindu–Muslim unity . . . Our duty, along with that of our countrymen, was to support the move for unity."[84]

[83] Ibid., 10.
[84] "Sheikh Abdullah's Speech at 1944 Session of National Conference,"

He went on to say that the independence of India was the essential prerequisite for the independence of state peoples: "So long as the India outside the States' borders continues to be the area for deadlock and depression, thaw will not release the ice-bound politics of the Indian States."[85] Aligning the National Conference with the Indian national movement still further without spelling out whether Kashmiris would be the citizens of an Indian or Kashmiri state, or some version of both, he stated, "The All Jammu and Kashmir National Conference has cherished the unity of the Indian people as its fondest hope and has considered supporting it to be the prime duty imposed by patriotism and love of freedom."[86] To reiterate a point made earlier, although Kashmiris were to be citizens with full citizenship rights, the contours of the state that would grant them these rights and its relationship with the Dogra state, the paramount power, and the future Indian dominion, was still quite unclear.

The attempt by the National Conference to boost its flagging popularity among Kashmiris through the adoption of the revolutionary Naya Kashmir manifesto was only partially successful. Bazaz dismissed it as an "interesting though thoughtlessly drafted document, envisaging the establishment of a communist State yet, opportunistically enough, it guaranteed the perpetuation of the alien Dogra rule in Kashmir."[87] Mirwaiz Yusuf Shah, predictably, labeled Naya Kashmir anti-Islamic,[88] while Kashmiri Pandits represented by the Yuvak Sabha also voiced their concerns against the plan, which threatened to dislodge their position within the administration of the state.[89] According to them, Naya Kashmir ignored the interests of the minorities by attempting to further the rule of the majority.[90] The National Conference, also predictably, responded by labeling both the followers of the Mirwaiz and the Yuvak Sabha reactionaries who were determined to dislodge the Kashmiri people from the path to freedom under the guise of religion.

Unpublished Manuscript (Private Collection of Fidah Hassnain, Srinagar, Kashmir), 2.

[85] Ibid., 3.

[86] Ibid.

[87] P.N. Bazaz, *The Struggle for Freedom in Kashmir*, 220.

[88] *Khalid*, Srinagar, April 30, 1945.

[89] *Khalid*, Srinagar, December 28, 1945.

[90] *Khalid*, Srinagar, June 12, 1945.

P.N. Bazaz was lampooned almost daily in pro-National Conference newspapers as a venal individual who could be bribed for his political loyalties.

However, it was not just the so-called reactionaries who opposed Naya Kashmir. Lala Bansi Lal Suri, a prominent Gandhian member of the National Conference, resigned from the party in the wake of the introduction of the plan. According to him, the National Conference, the Muslim Conference and the Hindu Rajya Sabha were all provincial parties. While the National Conference had no influence in the Jammu province, the Muslim Conference and Hindu Rajya Sabha had no following among the people of the Kashmir Valley. In his resignation speech he stated that he could not continue to be a member of the National Conference because he had been unsuccessful in his attempts to popularize the organization in Jammu, where the people were naturally against the party since they viewed it as a pro-Kashmir organization. Furthermore, the Jammu Hindus perceived the National Conference as a Muslim organization that was against Hindu civilization, culture and rights. He went on to say that the Naya Kashmir plan was not acceptable to everyone in the state, but instead of popularizing it the National Conference was simply interested in tarnishing the reputation of its critics. "Naya Kashmir has some merits," he admitted, "but it has many more shortcomings from the national point of view." According to him, the plan did not take into account the principle of proportionate representation according to population, and by granting Urdu the sole status as the official language it had further proved its anti-national character.[91] The adoption of Urdu as the national language of the state by the manifesto had, in fact, drawn the ire of certain sections of the state's Hindus. The Second Annual Hindi Conference of Jammu and Kashmir declared Sheikh Abdullah and his party "communal" for ignoring Hindi in its future language plans for the state.[92]

Despite these criticisms, Naya Kashmir did propel the Dogra regime into announcing plans for dyarchy on October 2, 1945. According to this plan, two ministerial posts would be given to a Hindu and a Muslim who commanded the confidence of the state legislature. This

[91] *Hamdard*, Srinagar, May 9, 1945.
[92] *Hamdard*, Srinagar, May 7, 1945.

legislature comprised 75 members, of which the Maharaja nominated 35. Of the 40 elected members, furthermore, jagirdars, landlords and government pensioners chose 7, and Hindu and Sikh constituencies elected 11. The National Conference members of the legislature were all Muslim; the other Muslim members belonged to the Muslim Conference or were independents. While the Muslim Conference boycotted this offer, the National Conference sent its nominees to become ministers in the proposed plan of dyarchy. The state was only too happy to induct a member of the National Conference, Mirza Afzal Beg, into its cabinet as Minister for Public Works.[93] This move further alienated Kashmiris from the National Conference, which, it was clear to them, was being rewarded for its compliance with the Dogra state. As Bazaz noted in one of the many editorials he wrote to expose the "conspiracy that lay hidden behind the move to dynamite the citadel of revolution in the state,"—"there was not a ghost of a chance for a member of either the National Conference or the Muslim Conference to be chosen as Minister unless he has the fullest backing of the government."[94]

Discontent with the National Conference reached fever pitch during the following months of 1945. The Muslim Conference, on the other hand, became a martyr, since it had separated itself from the government by refusing the offer of dyarchy. Shortages became more prevalent toward the end of the war, even as prices and taxes were increasing. Kashmiri Muslim peasants, the poorest section of the state population, were especially hard hit by the economic situation, and turned away from the National Conference to redress their problems. The peasants of Anantnag tehsil, which was Mirza Afzal Beg's tehsil— where it was widely believed that, since becoming minister, he had handed over control of the local Cooperative Bank and Cooperative Stores to his family—organized an association to defend their interests. This organization, which came into being in July 1945 as the All Jammu and Kashmir Kisan (Peasant) Conference, elected a young peasant as its president. Soon after, kisan committees emerged in most large villages of the Kashmir Valley and National Conference workers

[93] The Hindu to be appointed as minister under this plan was Ganga Ram, the ultra-loyalist Dogra politician, who was named Home Minister by the Maharaja. See Bazaz, *The Struggle for Freedom in Kashmir*, 222.

[94] *Hamdard*, Srinagar, October 10, 1945.

began to regard them as opponents. The Conference high command made it clear to the committees that it resented the growth of the peasant movement outside its confines.[95]

Sheikh Abdullah recognized his party's loss of support, particularly at the grassroots, and the disillusionment within its ranks. In an attempt to salvage the party's reputation, Abdullah yet again resorted to external support and invited top leaders of the Congress and the States People's Conference to the National Conference's Sopore session in 1945. It is important to note that each time the National Conference was faced with a political challenge, it resorted to emotional and physical violence against its opponents, or sought the support of organizations external to Kashmir. It did not bode well for the future of Kashmir that the party considered as the representative of all Kashmiris was unwilling to accommodate political and ideological differences from within and without its ranks. Rather than redressing the issues that Kashmiris had voiced, the visits of Nehru and other Congress leaders only served to reiterate the fact that the National Conference was determined to bring the political movement in Kashmir even closer to India. In a speech in honor of Moulana Abul Kalam Azad, Abdullah declared that "our future and our fate is connected with the freedom struggle of India."[96]

Undoubtedly, the high command of the Congress, particularly Nehru, believed, or wanted to believe, that the National Conference and its leader represented the majority of Kashmiris. In statements that proved harbingers for the future, Nehru exhorted Kashmiris, particularly Kashmiri Pandits, to follow the lead of the National Conference if they wanted to remain in Kashmir. In a speech to the National Conference, Nehru stated that Kashmir was fortunate to have a leader like Sheikh Abdullah. He went on to say that those non-Muslims who claimed that the National Conference represented Muslim interests because there were more Muslims in the organization were simply making excuses for their reactionary ideas. After all, the state was majority-Muslim, and it followed that the National Conference would have more Muslim than Hindu members. He advised those who leveled these charges that "if they wanted to live in Kashmir, they

---

[95] In an incident in Anantnag, some members of the National Conference who attempted to impress this on the peasants were handled roughly and had to leave the district. Bazaz, *The Struggle for Freedom in Kashmir*, 224–9.

[96] Quoted in Hassnain, *Freedom Struggle in Kashmir*, 130.

should join the National Conference, or bid goodbye to their country."[97] In another speech to the Yuvak Sabha, Nehru said he was irritated by Kashmiri Pandit slogans, and that the community was deceiving itself by thinking that they could put up a strong opposition to the National Conference.[98]

Significantly, Nehru's speeches assumed not only that the independence of Kashmir was integrally connected to the independence of India, but also that, once Kashmiris had overthrown Dogra rule, the state would become part of independent India. In his speech to the National Conference, Nehru sketched out Kashmir's future in no uncertain terms:

> Kashmir has to become independent. But when? The answer is when Hindustan attains independence. The question of the independence of Kashmir is linked to the independence of India. Kashmir cannot make its one-half inch mosque by staying independent. It can, if it so wishes, remain independent, but in the present world situation, that would be a very dangerous step. For this reason, inevitably this mulk will have to stay connected to Hindustan . . . You are fortunate that you live in a mulk like Kashmir, but you will be congratulated when Kashmir gains independence, the whole of Hindustan gains independence.[99]

Once again the shrewd political commentator, P.N. Bazaz argued that Nehru wanted the National Conference to follow in the footsteps of the Indian National Congress, which was unwilling to share power with its rival, the Muslim League, in India. Pointing out the inherent contradiction in Nehru's speeches, Bazaz stated that if indeed the National Conference was the majority-representative organization in Kashmir, why did Nehru have to make speeches threatening those who did not support it? Warning Kashmiri Pandits, he further pointed out that Nehru and the leaders of the National Conference would be only too willing to sacrifice the interests of the minority for the sake of the larger struggle that would culminate with their takeover of power. Unless Kashmiri Pandits found a true leader, their future was doomed, declared Bazaz.[100]

Other Kashmiri Muslim leaders too resented the intervention of the Congress in Kashmiri affairs, particularly after the failure of the

[97] *Hamdard*, Srinagar, August 4, 1945.
[98] *Hamdard*, Srinagar, August 9, 1945.
[99] *Hamdard*, Srinagar, August 6, 1945.
[100] *Hamdard*, Srinagar, August 10, 1945.

Simla Conference in the summer of 1945. The fact that the Congress was unwilling to come to terms with the Muslim League had become apparent even to those Kashmiri leaders who were not necessarily part of the Muslim Conference. According to them, the Congress was an anti-Muslim organization that had clearly lost its popularity in the Muslim-majority provinces after the Simla Conference and had begun to assert its influence among Kashmiri Muslims in the Valley in an attempt to appear pro-Muslim. In a speech during the conference of the Dar-a-sul Islam, Pirzada Tayyab Shah explained that, whatever the political orientation of the Kashmiri Muslims, they did not like to criticize Jinnah and the Muslim League. For that reason, an anti-League party such as the Congress should not be allowed to function within the state. He went so far as to appeal to the government to prohibit the entry of Congress members into the state, for fear of breach of peace.[101]

It would be too simplistic to assume that Kashmiri Muslims were somehow pro-Pakistan in this period. However, it is important to note that, not unlike many Muslims in India, they were becoming increasingly disillusioned with the Congress, which in Kashmir translated into an antipathy toward the Congress' political ally, the National Conference. Furthermore, also like many Indian Muslims, they may have thought their best security lay in supporting the party that was making the strongest case for Muslims in India, the Muslim League, and in the Kashmiri case, the Muslim Conference. The League's ostensible successes during the 1945–6 elections drove this fact further home to Kashmiri Muslims. Again, some Kashmiri leaders felt that they wanted no part of the Congress and League's discussions on the future of India. At the congress of the Kashmir Kisan Conference held in Kabamarg in May 1946, the President of the organization, Ahad Ullah, declared that upper-class Hindus and Muslims were engaged in disputes over "Akhand Hindustan" (United India) with a view to preserve their vested interests. "But we stand neither for one nor the other," he said. "We believe that so long as it is not decided who the future rulers are to be we can neither support Akhand Hindustan nor side with the demand for Pakistan." The most important objective for

[101] *Hamdard*, Srinagar, July 28, 1945.

Kashmiris, according to the Kisan Conference, was to "do away with the prevailing social and economic inequality and injustice and lay the foundations of a new and just order of society."[102]

The National Conference was besieged on all fronts. In an ostentatious move, Abdullah withdrew the National Conference minister, Afzal Beg, from the government in 1946. Unfortunately for him, Mian Ahmad Yar, the senior National Conference member of the Assembly, defected to the government's side after being offered Beg's portfolio.[103] In yet another grandiose step in May 1946 designed to regain popularity, Abdullah declared the 1846 Treaty of Amritsar, under which Kashmir had been sold to the Dogra by the British, as invalid, and asked the Dogra Maharaja, Hari Singh, to "Quit Kashmir" and transfer sovereignty to the people. The vehemently anti-Dogra and anti-Hindu speeches made by National Conference members resulted in the dissociation of Dogra and Hindu members from the movement. The Kashmiri Pandit National Conference leader, Kashyap Bandhu, lamented that Abdullah had not consulted the members of the National Conference working committee before launching the movement.[104] Moreover, the Kisan Mazdoor Conference issued a statement advising its followers not to participate in the agitation. Most significantly, the Muslim Conference declared that "the agitation had been started at the behest of Congress leaders," and its "object was to restore the lost prestige of the Nationalists."[105]

The worst blow to the National Conference came when the Congress offered only lukewarm support to the agitation, since it so directly challenged the policy of the All India States Peoples' Conference, which was to achieve popular governments in the states under the aegis of the maharajas of the states. Needless to say, far from dethroning Maharaja Hari Singh, the movement only propelled the government to take severe action against the agitators. Abdullah was sentenced to three and a half years rigorous imprisonment, and several other National Conference members associated with the agitation received

---

[102] Quoted in Bazaz, *The Struggle for Freedom in Kashmir*, 239.

[103] *Khidmat*, Srinagar, April 19, 1946.

[104] *Hamdard*, Srinagar, May 15, 1946.

[105] *Hamdard*, Srinagar, May 16, 1946.

similar sentences. Despite Nehru's interventions in support of the National Conference, the organization was in disarray by mid-1946.[106] Not only had its trump card—the Quit Kashmir agitation—failed, but, more importantly, most of its leadership had ended up in jail during the most crucial period of Kashmir's modern history. Recognizing this reality, the National Conference withdrew from the 1946 assembly elections, alleging that the government would not allow free and fair elections.

The Muslim Conference, in the meantime, stood poised to fill the void left by the National Conference. However, dissension within party ranks left the organization in no position to do this effectively. The President of the Muslim Conference, Ghulam Abbas, was arrested by the government for agitating against an order banning a party meeting in Srinagar in October 1946. In the wake of his arrest, a dispute broke out between Mirwaiz Yusuf Shah and the Muslim Conference member in the legislative assembly, Chaudhuri Hamidullah, both of whom laid claim to the presidency. The impending January 1947 elections to the Praja Sabha exacerbated the factionalism within the party over the selection of candidates. By early 1947, newspaper articles were lamenting the fractiousness in the party's upper echelons. The articles blamed the regional differences between the Jammu and Kashmir leaders as the root cause behind these disputes. Whatever the reasons for the contentiousness within Muslim Conference ranks, the party had lost its opportunity to capitalize on the mistakes committed by the National Conference, particularly in the Kashmir Valley. However, it is important to note that the Muslim Conference reigned supreme in Poonch and Jammu in 1946.[107]

The political climate of Jammu and Kashmir was in a state of flux by the time the year of independence and partition rolled around. The National Conference's many blunders had resulted in its virtual withdrawal from the political scene. However, the Muslim Conference failed to provide a viable alternative to the National Conference, particularly to Muslims of the Kashmir Valley. It would be safe to say

---

[106] Nehru marched into Jammu and Kashmir to meet with Abdullah in spite of the Dogra government's order that banned his entry into the state, which ultimately resulted in his arrest. *Hamdard*, Srinagar, May 22, 1946.

[107] *Millat*, Srinagar, April 8, 1947.

that the political loyalties of Valley Kashmiris were divided in 1947. Although they may not have enthusiastically supported the National Conference, they had no choice but to support the party in the wake of the Muslim Conference's failure to provide a political program distinct from its rival. Furthermore, despite the good intentions of parties such as the Kisan Mazdoor (Peasant-Labor) Conference, these proved unable to present a political agenda that would clarify Kashmir's status in the increasingly lopsided negotiations between the British, the Congress, and the League leadership. Would the National Conference be able to provide the leadership expected of it and stand up for the rights of Kashmiris during the tumultuous years of independence and partition?

India, Pakistan, or Independence? Kashmir in 1947

Kashmir entered 1947 an exceedingly discordant entity, beleaguered by political dissension, a government unwilling to stand behind the interests of the Kashmiri people, and surrounded by a national movement determined to gain independence for India at any cost. I look at 1947 not so much as a turning point in the history of Kashmir, but instead as a significant year in the evolving narrative of Kashmiri political culture. During this year, in the context of the momentous changes taking place, the debates over regionalism, religious affiliations, sovereignty, and the legitimacy of both the Dogra state and the National Conference were articulated even more vigorously than in earlier years.

The British attitude toward princely states had undergone a startling shift in 1946, leaving the people of these states largely at the mercy of their rulers. The Cabinet Mission, which came to India to persuade Indian political leaders to accept some scheme for Indian self-rule that would preserve a semblance of unity in the subcontinent, also left the native states without recourse to any British protection once that self-rule had been achieved. The Cripps Mission's assurances to the native rulers in 1942—that their treaties with the British would be protected after the lapse of paramountcy, even if it required the use of British force—no longer seemed probable. The Cabinet Mission made this clear to the Chamber of Princes in a memorandum that stated:

When a new fully self-governing or independent Government or Governments come into being in British India . . . His Majesty's Government's influence with those Governments will not be such as to enable them to carry out the obligations of paramountcy. Moreover, they cannot contemplate that British troops would be retained in India for this purpose. Thus, as a logical sequence . . . His Majesty's Government will cease to exercise the powers of paramountcy. This means that the rights of the States which flow from their relationship to the Crown will no longer exist and that all the rights surrendered by the States to the paramount power will return to the States . . . The void will have to be filled either by the States entering into a federal relationship with the successor Government or Governments in British India, or failing this, entering into particular political arrangements with it or them.[108]

It was easy enough for the British to devolve all responsibility to the rulers of princely states and successor governments. This did not, however, mean that the question of what would happen to these states became any easier to resolve, particularly since the British had, in theory, made it possible for these states to choose to remain independent. At the same time, they were basically handing over the powers for this choice not to the people of the states but to their autocratic rulers.

It is important to note the enormity of the Cabinet Mission's declaration for the future of princely states, particularly Kashmir, which was neither able to enter into a federal relationship with successor governments, nor negotiate a political arrangement with them. Clearly, whatever political arrangement did come about in Kashmir has not satisfied the various political interests in that region, and has certainly not addressed the issue of Kashmiri people's rights, particularly as citizens. After all, none of the princely states had ever been a fully sovereign entity, and by their silence on the necessity of a constitutional structure within which such entities could become more viable after their withdrawal, the British had in effect left those decisions up to the regimes that would succeed them.[109] This is not to suggest that the responsibility for the Kashmir problem rests only with the British because of their policy shift toward princely states. The fact is that most princely states acceded to India or Pakistan without much crisis. However,

[108] Quoted in Lamb, *Incomplete Partition*, 13.

[109] For a detailed analysis of the implications of the potential of native states as sovereign entities, see Lamb, *Incomplete Partition*.

there is also no denying that the sudden withdrawal of the British from the affairs of the princely states had severe consequences for Jammu and Kashmir, which bordered on both India and Pakistan and could, in theory, accede to either dominion, or choose to remain independent. While the British were busy reneging on their promises with regard to the native states, the Kashmiri leadership remained ambiguous on the issue of the states' relationship with successor regimes in the subcontinent. In a long article on the impact of the Cabinet Mission Plan on the independence of India, Sheikh Abdullah appeared undecided on the status of Kashmir in the future constitutional set-up envisaged by the plan. Abdullah recognized that there was a "cleavage in the approach of the political parties towards the nature of the future federation," and that no attempt was being made by the parties to reach an understanding on this issue. According to him, the Jammu and Kashmir National Conference had suggested the most rational solution to the problem under the circumstances: "We are convinced that the right of self-determination to all the Nationalities inhabiting India will eliminate the possibility of a constitutional solution on communal lines." This was to be achieved through a territorial redivision of provinces with reference to the linguistic and cultural homogeneity of the units. These units would then become sovereign and the future constitution-making body would be composed of representatives of all the units chosen by the unit assemblies. In this proposed federation, each of the units would have the "unfettered right to self-determination" and be given the option of joining or not joining the proposed Indian union.[110]

Despite its flaws, the fact that Abdullah did propose a scheme for the status of Indian provinces in the future political structure of independent India is in itself significant, since he was ambiguous when it came to the position of the states in this make-up. As far as the princely states were concerned, he noted that the British seemed determined to "perpetuate the slavery" of states' people, since the Cabinet Mission Plan had ignored their fate. He then went on to say that states' people had declared they would "resist active encroachment on their sovereign rights." However, in the very next sentence he linked the freedom of states' people to the freedom of people in India: "If all the major

[110] *Khidmat,* Srinagar, April 24, 1946.

political parties do not agree on a constitutional solution, it leaves the people in Indian States in the clutches of their autocratic rulers. Freedom of Princely India will be meaningless without the freedom of Indian India."[111] Needless to say, this was not a declaration in favor of either India or Pakistan. Moreover, it did not chalk out a plan for the inclusion of states' people in the political structures of successor regime(s) in case the political parties did come to an agreement that would bring India independence.

At a press conference in May 1946, Sheikh Abdullah dismissed as premature a reporter's question on the nature of Kashmir's relationship with Pakistan. When pressed to answer whether Kashmir would join Pakistan if it did come into existence, Abdullah again replied that this was a "hypothetical question." He then went on to say, "it will be entirely for the people of Kashmir to decide. They may either choose to remain absolutely independent or join Pakistan," or, more significantly, considering its similarity to Jinnah's demand, "ask for a corridor in order to join the Government of Hindustan." According to Abdullah, he could not "commit my people prematurely to any arrangement," since the future situation still remained unclear.[112] He did not seem to recognize that he had no authority to either commit or not commit Kashmiris, since the British had handed over this authority to the maharajas who would, when paramountcy lapsed, make the decision for their subjects. It is evident that the National Conference and its leader, like Jinnah, did not believe that the British withdrawal would take place as swiftly as it did, and therefore felt he could bide his time and make a decision when independence was imminent. The time came sooner than Abdullah expected. What is more, soon after he made the above comments, Abdullah's Quit Kashmir movement failed miserably and the government incarcerated him until after the moment of Independence and Partition had come and gone.

The Muslim Conference had perhaps the clearest vision for the future state. In September 1946 it announced its blueprint for the future of the "Musalmans of Jammu and Kashmir" entitled "Azad Kashmir." According to this document, the organization wanted Kashmiris

---

[111] Ibid.
[112] *Khidmat*, Srinagar, May 6, 1946.

to achieve their goal of responsible government under the aegis of the Maharaja Bahadur, without association with either India or Pakistan. The minorities had nothing to fear from this new state, since their rights would be legally guaranteed by its constitution. In his speech to the people of Srinagar announcing the plan, the Mirwaiz stated that the minorities would be better protected in Azad Kashmir than in a government under Sheikh Abdullah, who did not take well to challenges to his authority.[113] Moreover, as Ian Copland has noted, in May 1947 the acting president of the Muslim Conference, Chaudhuri Hamidullah, "told the Praja Sabha that if Hari Singh conceded the principle of majority rule the Muslims would 'readily lay down their lives' for him," and by the end of May his deputy Ghulam Ahmad "urged the Maharaja to declare Kashmir an independent state."[114] It is important to note that the Muslim Conference, the pro-Muslim League political party in Kashmir, did not want the state to join Pakistan, but remain independent.

The people of the state, particularly the Kashmir Valley, were probably as divided as their leaders, given the uncertainty of the situation during these tumultuous years. Several Kashmiris remember that in the 1940s, even the National Conference followers in Srinagar accepted Jinnah's leadership beyond the Valley.[115] As we saw earlier, the Kashmiri poet Ghulam Ahmad Mahjoor, the most articulate member of the National Conference, wrote a poem in October 1947 that began, "though I would like to sacrifice my life and body for India, yet my heart is in Pakistan."[116] Not only did the National Conference government put him behind bars for this poem, the poem itself cannot be located in the Indian part of Kashmir. Furthermore, according to those who lived through those years, it was a common sight for followers of both the Muslim Conference and National Conference, and other parties in Srinagar, to have photographs of Sheikh Abdullah, Jinnah and Mohammad Iqbal hang side by side on the walls of their shops or homes.[117] The lines of division between the various political

---

[113] *Khidmat*, Srinagar, September 23, 1946.

[114] Copland, "The Abdullah Factor," 240.

[115] Interview with Fidah Mohammad Hassnain, September 22, 1997, Srinagar, Kashmir.

[116] Quoted in Bazaz, *The Struggle for Freedom in Kashmir*, 298.

[117] Interview with Fidah Mohammad Hassnain, September 22, 1997, Srinagar.

groupings were not as sharp as the leadership would make them out to be. Unfortunately, indecision was not about to be rewarded in the atmosphere of India's independence and the creation of Pakistan, when leaders on both sides wanted a swift solution to the problem of the native states.

Thus the action, or inaction, of the Kashmiri political leadership in conjunction with the Congress leadership had as much to do with future events in Kashmir, as did the machinations of the British to speed their withdrawal. With the June 1947 announcement of the Mountbatten Plan regarding the impending independence of India and the prospect of Pakistan, and with the specter of communal riots in India where Hindus had been massacred in Muslim-majority areas, Hindus of Jammu and Kashmir recognized that their salvation lay in following the National Conference.[118] This was not necessarily because the National Conference was unequivocally in favor of Kashmir's association with India in any future political arrangements between the Maharaja and successor governments in the subcontinent, but because, due to its Congress leanings, it was the political party most likely to become so.

The Congress leadership, while expecting the secession of Kashmir to India, was not willing to take any chances and had dispatched Acharya Kripalani in May and Gandhi in August to ensure Kashmir's accession to India. Whether either Kripalani or Gandhi had any impact on the Maharaja's future decision to sign the document of accession to India is unclear. What is clear is that Kashmiri Muslims were suspicious of Congress attempts at deciding their future. In a Kashmiri editorial on the subject, the author lamented that the fate of Kashmiris had been auctioned off once before in history: "Attempts are again being made to extend the period of the contract. So there may be another auction for Kashmiris in Delhi."[119] To the Congress leadership, of course, Kashmir was a potential anti-Pakistani buffer zone in the north of the Punjab.[120]

Perhaps this was the reason why the British returned the Gilgit Agency to the Maharaja in August 1947. The significance of the Gilgit

[118] *Hamdard,* Srinagar, July 17, 1947.

[119] *Khidmat,* Srinagar, May 6, 1947.

[120] Lamb, *Incomplete Partition,* 101.

tracts to future events in Jammu and Kashmir cannot be emphasized enough. The agency had been established in 1889 in order to stave off threats from Russia, and as a matter of convenience attached to Jammu and Kashmir, while in reality it was directly administered by the British. After 1925, when the British relaxed their hold over the administration of Jammu and Kashmir, the myth of the Gilgit region as part of the Maharaja's territory continued.[121] In 1935, the British took over the administration of Gilgit through what came to be known as the Gilgit Lease. In 1947, with independence looming, the question of where the Gilgit areas belonged re-emerged. Mountbatten's decision to "return" the territories to the Maharaja of Jammu and Kashmir may have had to do with the fact that Congress envisaged Jammu and Kashmir as part of India and considered the northern areas of Gilgit, a key access to Central Asia, vital for the defense of its frontier.[122] It did not seem to have occurred to the British or the Congress leadership that Gilgit had a tradition of rebellion against the Dogra Maharaja, a rebellion which had emerged as an organized political movement by the 1920s.

In the meantime, India became independent and Pakistan came into existence on August 14–15, 1947. The Maharaja, who had cherished dreams for an independent Kashmir under his own authority, entered the era of independence for all intents and purposes as the ruler of a sovereign territory, since he had not acceded to either India or Pakistan. His offer of "standstill agreements" with both India and Pakistan at the lapse of British paramountcy in the state of Jammu and Kashmir was accepted by Pakistan and rejected by India.[123] Alongside communal carnage in the Punjab, the restlessness of the Gilgit Scouts (a locally recruited Muslim army that controlled the Gilgit areas) was becoming apparent to the Maharaja. In an attempt to negotiate some settlement with the National Conference leadership in this uncertain atmosphere, the Maharaja released Sheikh Abdullah in September 1947. Even at this time, Abdullah remained undecided on whether

[121] Ibid., 105.

[122] Ibid.

[123] A standstill agreement, provided for by the Government of India Act of 1935, ensured the continuation of essential relations, in communications, posts, trade and so on, between a princely state that remained undecided on its future status, and one or both dominions. See Lamb, *Incomplete Partition*, 112–13.

Kashmir should join India or Pakistan. In a public meeting after his release, he stated that although he was a friend of Nehru and the Congress had supported their cause, the "question of accession will be decided in the best interests of the people of Kashmir." "Freedom before Accession," according to him, would have to be the slogan of the people of the state.[124]

While Sheikh Abdullah equivocated, the residents of Poonch began a revolt against the Maharaja, which soon spread to areas of Mirpur and Jammu. In full swing by the time of the transfer of power, this revolt became thoroughly imbricated with the question of the future of the whole state: to be independent or to exist in association with either India or Pakistan. The ferocity of the Dogra regime's repression of this revolt further stimulated doubts on the state's political future under the authority of the Maharaja.[125] In late October, the Poonch rebels announced the existence of an Azad Kashmir, or Independent Kashmir, to which state forces reacted by creating a three-mile deep depopulated zone along the state's border with Pakistan: this entailed the evacuation of Hindus and the massacre of Muslims. In reaction to these atrocities, tribesmen from the North West Frontier Province, who had close tribal alliances with the people of Poonch, began to filter into the state's boundaries, most likely not on the direct orders of the Pakistani high command. Significantly, thus, it was the revolt of the Poonchis against the authority of the Maharaja—not a Pakistani movement against the Indian state, as the latter claims—that laid the foundation for the de facto division of the princely state of Jammu and Kashmir in the coming months.

The role of India and Pakistan in the Kashmir crisis has to be viewed from the perspective of their relative political and economic positions at the moment of decolonization. Pakistan was still in the process of establishing itself as a viable political entity in this period and could not have initiated a planned military intervention in Kashmir, however much public opinion in the newly established state may have pressed for such action. However, the Pakistani high command did take advantage of a rapidly evolving situation on the Kashmir border to channel Pakistani military energies into the Valley. India, on the other hand, which had inherited its military and bureaucratic structures

[124] Abdullah, *Flames of the Chinar*, 85–6.
[125] Lamb, *Incomplete Partition*, 120–5.

from the British, was not only in a position to do so, but regarded such an action as imperative to its national security and protection of its sovereign territories. It is important to note here that neither the Pakistani nor Indian government recognized the possibility of Kashmir as a semi-autonomous state or a confederal entity that would have some type of relationship with both nation-states.

Sardar Vallabhbhai Patel, deputy to the Prime Minister of India, regarded the settlement of the status of princely states as a necessary prelude to the establishment of a stable, centralized government in India. The accession of Kashmir to India was a particular necessity given its border with Pakistan and its potential as a weapon against India. In any case, the extension of Indian military help to the Maharaja of Jammu and Kashmir in October 1947 is well documented. As for the controversy over whether the Maharaja signed the Document of Accession to India before or after its direct military intervention in Kashmir,[126] suffice it to say that the answer to this question is unclear and only mires the Kashmir question in the political wrangles of these nation-states, while the people of Kashmir continue to suffer from the failures of their leadership to arrive at a reasonable solution for the status of Kashmir in the post-independence period.

As late as October 22, 1947, Abdullah was speaking in terms of "Freedom before Accession," thus circumventing the question of the state's future status. Since Abdullah seemed unable to come to terms with the partition of India and the existence of two separate dominion states, there was no question of his playing a leadership role in negotiations about the state's future. In an article, he suggested that the Dominions of India and Pakistan "come to terms with each other as two sovereign and independent states and try to evolve a common centre with defence, communications, and foreign affairs."[127] Other articles from pro-National Conference newspapers argued against Kashmir's accession to India or Pakistan, instead advocating socialist revolution in the state: "What the present moment demands and demands urgently is not accession to Pakistan or India but power to the people. Are we going to sell ourselves to the Indian capitalists or

---

[126] See Lamb, *Incomplete Partition*, for a detailed analysis of this issue. According to official Indian sources, Hari Singh signed the document of accession to India on October 26, 1947.

[127] *Khidmat*, Srinagar, October 22, 1947.

the Pakistani nawabs?" The article further presaged events in Kashmir, stating that if Kashmir was "hustled into warfare" by the border raids, "all power will slip from the people into the hands of the Rulers, and if Pakistan is involved in the fray, India will be involved too, willy nilly."[128] Despite the thoughtful commentary on the subject, which was clearly not in favor of the direct accession of Kashmir to either India or Pakistan, the military intervention of India in Kashmir on October 27, 1947, as the article had predicted, foreclosed any possibility of Kashmir as an independent state.

Recognizing this eventuality, Sheikh Abdullah welcomed the arrival of the Indian army into Kashmir. Others, such as the Mirwaiz Yusuf Shah, left for the Azad Kashmir that had been declared by the Poonch rebels on October 24, 1947. Instead of labeling these choices as the outcome of pro-Indian and pro-Pakistani politics, it is necessary to view them in the context of the political atmosphere at the time. As has been amply demonstrated, Kashmiri political and public opinion was not in favor of either India or Pakistan, even among those who may have sympathized with one or the other. However, given the political situation in late October 1947, a choice had to be made by followers of the two camps, since the independence option had been effectively ruled out by the Indian military intervention. Sheikh Abdullah's pro-Congress leanings made him a likely candidate for political power in any arrangement that would be worked out between Kashmir and India, while the Mirwaiz's declarations for independence would not be tolerated within such an arrangement.

It was in this context that Sheikh Abdullah made his impassioned speech to the Security Council of the United Nations in February 1948, in which he clearly came out on the Indian side while lambasting Pakistan for encouraging tribesmen to invade Kashmir. This speech is sometimes seen as evidence of Sheikh Abdullah's enthusiastic support for the Maharaja's decision to accede to India. In fact, Abdullah's decision to support India should be seen in terms of political pragmatism rather than an unequivocal acceptance of, or undying gratitude toward, India. It is also important to note that Abdullah began the speech by glorifying the national service rendered by his own party, the National Conference, during the moment of Kashmir's crisis, a glorification meant no doubt to reinvigorate the dwindling support for his

[128] Ibid.

organization in 1948. Parts of the speech are worth quoting, for they illustrate Abdullah's unctuousness toward India quite startlingly:

> When the [Pakistani] raiders came to our land, massacred thousands of people . . . and almost reached the gates of our summer capital, Sri Nagar, the result was that the civil, military and police administration failed . . . In that hour of crisis, the National Conference came forward with its 10,000 volunteers . . . They started guarding the banks, the offices and houses of every person in the capital . . . I had thought all along that the world had got rid of Hitlers . . . , but from what is happening in my poor country, I am convinced they have transmigrated their souls into Pakistan . . . The [plebiscite] offer [was] made by the Prime Minister of India when, I think, he had not the slightest need for making it, for Kashmir was in distress . . . I refuse to accept Pakistan as a party in the affairs of Jammu and Kashmir; I refuse this point blank . . . We have seen enough of Pakistan.[129]

Not surprisingly, the Indian government appointed Abdullah as the Director-General, Administration, of the State of Jammu and Kashmir, which had just acceded to its Dominion.[130]

Far from being a unified entity, the state Abdullah inherited from the Dogra Maharaja was only half the area of the princely state of Jammu and Kashmir, a fact made clearer as war dragged on in the region. However, it is important to note that the division of the state was not simply the result of hostilities between India and Pakistan, but of regional movements against the authority of the Maharaja that began in various parts of the state in 1947. The significance of Poonch in this regard cannot be overemphasized. The Gilgit region, which the British returned to the Dogra state in 1947, had been seething with discontent against the Dogra regime ever since the 1920s. In November 1947 the Gilgit Scouts, the locally recruited army from the region, rebelled against the flotsam of Dogra rule and declared themselves for Pakistan, thereby laying the foundation for what would become the northern areas of Pakistan.

While the people of Gilgit and Poonch may have had a say in determining their futures, the individual Kashmiri, as always, was lost in the

---

[129] Quoted in Ashutosh Varshney, "Three Compromised Nationalisms," in Thomas, ed., *Perspectives on Kashmir*, 194–5. Varshney reads this speech as Abdullah's enthusiasm for Hari Singh's decision to accede to India.

[130] Abdullah, *Flames of the Chinar*, 96–7.

process. A case in point, from the perspective of the impact of the political happenings of 1947–8 on the common Kashmiri, is that of Bahar Shahabadi, a low-level National Conference worker from a pir family of Srinagar. Shahabadi, who prefers to be addressed as Bahar Kashmiri, was in charge of the distribution of grain to the district of Baramulla, which was at the frontline of the war between the Azad Kashmiri forces, the tribals, and the Indian army. Disgusted with the attitude of the National Conference leadership, which even at this moment of crisis was indulging in corrupt activities—such as hoarding grain while advising Kashmiris to subsist on potatoes and apples—Kashmiri resigned from the organization. In the winter of 1947–8 he retreated to the countryside and lived in a hut where he composed the poem, "Our Sweet Kashmir."[131] Kashmiri admitted that the horror of the events in Kashmir during these months propelled him to put his feelings in words, since politics had proven to be unsuccessful in redressing the situation. The poem, a long narrative lament on the impending fate of Kashmir, is a poignant articulation of the disempowerment felt by Kashmiris during a period that was supposed to bring them their long-awaited freedom and which, instead, ushered in perennial conflict.

The poem is an eulogy to Kashmir, encapsulating the culmination of the struggles undergone by Kashmir to rid itself of the ravage of its body and soul by successive rulers. The hopelessness of the poem stems from the fact that it puts forth no savior for Kashmir, no prophet, no revolutionary. Only darkness, terror and injustice lie in its future. The revolutionary is dead, as is the prophet, and there can be no end to Kashmir's sufferings:

> From all sides I am assaulted,
> The English, the Indians, the Afghans, the Pakistanis.
> To whom should I complain, to whom should I tell my fate?
> Capitalists, tyrants, oppressors, and friends, all want me to become their
>   accomplice,
> With whom should I agree, whom should I disagree with?
> To whom should I complain, to whom should I tell my fate?
> I am poor and downtrodden, whose side should I go to?

---

[131] Bahar Kashmiri, "Our Sweet Kashmir" (1947–8). My knowledge of this poem is based on an interview with Bahar Kashmiri, September 23–4, 1997, Srinagar, Kashmir.

If I agree with one, the second will be angry, the third will impale me on
the sword, and the fourth and fifth strangle me.
To whom should I complain, to whom should I tell my fate?[132]

All Kashmir could do, according to the poet, was complain to God,
but even God did not seem to care any longer about the fate of this
paradise on earth. Instead, Kashmir had been reduced to an example
of conflict in the world, looked on by the Chinese, Turks, British and
the rest. Needless to say, Kashmiri's poem proved prophetic and his
sweet Kashmir continues to provide the world with a case study in
conflict. Despite its ostensible finality, 1947 was not the end, but
rather the beginning of Kashmir's travails.

"Truth about Kashmir": Kashmiri Politics in Postcolonial India, 1947–1953

By 1948 Kashmir had become an "issue," a piece of territory that the
Indian and Pakistani states would fight over for the rest of the century
and into the next millenium. The first Prime Minister of independent
India, Jawaharlal Nehru, referred Pakistan's "aggression" in Kashmir
to the United Nations, with a view to garnering world public opinion
in favor of Indian military intervention in the Valley. Suffice it to say
that the United Nations failed to bring the two sides to the negotiating
table to smooth over their increasingly acrimonious relations. In the
Indian part of the now partitioned state of Jammu and Kashmir, in the
meantime, Sheikh Abdullah took over as head of the National Conference regime, with the blessing of the Indian government, as the rightful representative of the inhabitants of the state. But the extent to
which this new regime, under the ultimate sovereignty of the Indian
state, ensured Kashmiris' political, economic and social rights is debatable.

Sheikh Abdullah noted in his autobiography, "United Nations
agents and their reports could not slow the tempo of events in the
Valley. We continued to mould our country according to our own
principles and ideologies."[133] Despite its good intentions, and Nehru's
claims that "the present government of Kashmir was not put down

---

[132] Ibid.
[133] Abdullah, *Flames of the Chinar*, 107.

Map 3: The Disputed Area of Kashmir and Neighboring Regions.
(This is a sketch map; its intention is to provide a picture of the disputed area, not to give authentic political demarcations from either the Indian or Pakistani perspectives.)

there from the air; they represented the popular organisation and remained there because of their own strength and not because of legal sanctions alone,"[134] the National Conference regime was without doubt an installation of the Indian government, a fact made apparent by the presence of a vast number of Indian troops in the state. Not only had the National Conference lost its popular mandate with the Kashmiris—both Muslims and Hindus—but, as significantly, it had never commanded the support of Muslims, Hindus and Sikhs of the Jammu region, a region that now effectively came under its control. The regime was caught between preserving its own power in the face of multifarious challenges to its authority, pressure from the Indian government to maintain the security of the newly-founded Indian state by suppressing dissident elements within the territory, and its own ideological platform that had promised far-reaching reforms in the political and economic structures of the state.

Ironically, and perhaps predictably, the organization that had first demanded political and social rights on behalf of Kashmiris became their greatest repressor. The National Conference regime systematically suppressed papers and periodicals that did not agree with Sheikh Abdullah, particularly in the matter of Kashmir's accession to India. The state government promulgated an ordinance entitled the Enemy Agents Ordinance allowing for the arrest and summary trials of those suspected of pro-Pakistan leanings.[135] Prem Nath Bazaz, who had spoken out during the 1947–8 crisis in favor of Kashmir's accession to Pakistan, was expelled from state territories and his organization, the Kashmir Socialist Party, banned within the state. In a pamphlet entitled *Truth about Kashmir*, published in 1950, Bazaz launched a scathing critique of the complicity of the Indian and National Conference governments in denying political rights to the Kashmiri people:

> Never before even in the reign of the hated Dogras were Kashmiris victimised and ruled so despotically as is done now under Shaikh Abdullah as the Chief Minister of the Maharaja. All vestiges of freedom earned by manifold sacrifices during the last 19 years have disappeared. Nationalist

[134] Quoted in P.N. Bazaz, *Truth About Kashmir* (Delhi: Kashmir Democratic Union, 1950), 7.

[135] P.N. Bazaz, *The Shape of Things in Kashmir* (Delhi: Pamposh Publications, 1965), 12.

rule stands on the strength of Indian bayonets and not on its own strength or efficiency. That is the naked truth about Kashmir. They [people in India] know that Kashmir people are not with Abdullah but they argue: since we have occupied the territory why should we leave it?[136]

With characteristic prescience, Bazaz noted that in future the regime would not be able to sustain its rule under the onslaught of enraged Kashmiris, not even with the support and strength of Indian bayonets.

It is important to examine the increasing disillusionment of Kashmiris in the context of the denial of citizenship rights to them within the larger Indian framework, in order to dispel popular notions of the Kashmiri movement over the last decade as being the result of irreconcilable differences between "Muslim-majority" Kashmir and "Hindu-majority" India. Such superficial explanations of the movement not only obscure historical fact, they also fail to take into account the role of the state, both Indian and Kashmiri, in excluding Kashmiris from political and economic structures, resulting in their eventual alienation. In fact, most Kashmiri Muslims who had stayed behind in Indian Kashmir were still debating the relative value of the state's association with India and Pakistan in the late 1940s. By the 1950s, however, the openly repressive policies of the National Conference government and the attitude of the Indian state, which seemed determined to settle the issue of the state's accession to India without reference to the opinions of the people, had driven Kashmiri Muslims toward extolling the virtues of Pakistan and condemning India's high-handedness in occupying the territory. Even ardent nationalists who had been in India's favor had begun to speak in terms of the state's association with Pakistan.[137]

The issue that occupied the people of the state, regardless of their religious affiliation, was the unsettled fact of Kashmir's accession to India. While both the National Conference regime and the Indian government preferred to elide over the events around which a part of the princely state had joined the Indian Union, for the inhabitants of the state these events indicated that the state remained outside the ambit of Indian political structures. The unsettled fact of the state's position in independent India was further exacerbated by the special position accorded to it by the Indian constitution. Article 370 of the

---

[136] Bazaz, *Truth About Kashmir*, 8.
[137] Ibid., 9.

constitution, adopted in October 1949, addressed the case of Kashmir alone, "in view of the special problem with which the Jammu and Kashmir government is faced, we have made special provisions for the continuance of the State with the Union on the existing basis."[138] According to this article, the power of the Indian parliament to make laws for the state would be limited to defense, external affairs, and communications, while the government of Jammu and Kashmir had complete jurisdiction over other areas of governance, including its own flag, legislative assembly and constitution. For all intents and purposes, then, the government of Jammu and Kashmir did not adopt the constitution of India as the constitution of the state.[139] Who, then, would guarantee the rights due to Kashmiris as citizens of a sovereign, democratic state—the Jammu and Kashmir regime or the Indian state? As it turned out, neither was up to the challenge.

Although Article 370 was intended by its framers to be a temporary provision that would eventually bring the state into the ambit of the Indian union, its existence indicated the special status of the Jammu and Kashmir state within the Indian framework, the result of a politically expedient arrangement between the Indian state and the regime of Jammu and Kashmir. In the early 1950s, Jammu Dogra Hindus founded the Praja Parishad with a view to demanding the final and irrevocable settlement of the issue of Kashmir's accession to India. The Praja Parishad was against the use of a plebiscite to decide the issue, instead arguing for the passage of a resolution by the Jammu Assembly. It is important to note that the Praja Parishad did not recognize the National Conference as the representative body of the Jammu Hindus, and moreover did not consider the interests of the inhabitants of Jammu to be similar to those of Kashmiris. The Praja Parishad put forth the question: "If the ultimate accession of the State to India continues to be undecided and if decision will have to be based on a general plebiscite of the people, what will be the fate of Jammu in case the majority of the people, consisting of Muslims, vote against India?"[140]

---

[138] Quoted in Justice A. S. Anand, *The Constitution of Jammu and Kashmir: Its Development and Comments* (Delhi: Universal Book Traders, 1995), 128.

[139] Ibid., 121.

[140] "Mookerjee's letter to Jawaharlal Nehru," January 9, 1953, in *Nehru–Mookerjee–Abdullah Correspondence* (New Delhi: Information Officer, Kashmir Bureau of Information, 1953), 4.

To dismiss the claims of the Praja Parishad simply as the bigoted grumblings of a right-wing organization, as was too often done by the National Conference and Indian governments, obscures the widespread alienation of the people of the state from the National Conference regime. In the case of Jammu, this resulted as much from the regional factor as the religious one, both of which had divided the politics of Jammu from Kashmir for decades.[141] While repression by the National Conference regime drove Kashmiri Muslims toward Pakistan, it led Jammu Hindus to demand that the state be governed by the constitution of India. In a letter to Nehru, Shyama Prasad Mookerjee, a Mahasabhaite and ardent supporter of the Praja Parishad, wrote:

> Repression will be no answer to the fundamental question which the people of Jammu are asking today—namely, have they not the right to demand that they should be governed by the same Constitution as has been made applicable to the rest of India? If the people of the Kashmir Valley think otherwise, must Jammu also suffer because of such unwillingness to merge completely with India?[142]

Additionally, most of the policies of the National Conference were geared toward redressing the grievances of Kashmiris, particularly Muslims, who were ensured a major share of key gazetted posts in the government. The regime founded the National Militia of Kashmir, which allowed Kashmiris to carry firearms. On the educational front, the first university was established in Kashmir and Kashmiri was installed as the medium of instruction in primary schools,[143] a move abandoned shortly thereafter.

The National Conference regime also attempted to implement the economic reforms laid out in its 1944 Naya Kashmir Manifesto. In 1948 the state resumed all assignments of government revenue known as jagirs and muafis and the fixed cash grants known as *mukarraris*, while leaving religious assignments and grants intact. In the case of such assignments, the practice of recovery of revenue in cash alone was

---

[141] For a discussion of Jammu politics in this period, see Balraj Puri, *Kashmir: Towards Insurgency* (New Delhi: Orient Longman, 1993), particularly chapters 2, 3, and 4.

[142] "Mookerjee's letter to Jawaharlal Nehru," 5.

[143] Abdullah, *Flames of the Chinar*, 110.

recognized as lawful.[144] The reforms also amended the State Tenancy Act, 1924, providing for a maximum rental payment by a tenant to his landlord and restrictions against arbitrary ejections. The tenant was now liable to pay not more than a quarter of the produce in case of wet land and not more than a third of the produce in case of dry land in respect of tenancy holdings exceeding 12½ acres, while in the case of holdings not exceeding 12½ acres, the landlord was entitled to no more than half of the produce.[145] In 1950 the government passed the Big Landed Estates Abolition Act, under which each proprietor could only retain only 22¾ acres of land and the right of ownership in land in excess of this unit was transferred to the tillers to the extent of their actual cultivating possession.[146]

Undoubtedly, these reforms were revolutionary, at least on paper. However, in practice they were not as effective as the government may have intended, for several reasons. Most importantly, the weakness of the reforms was built into the machinery for their implementation. By retaining the old revenue administration to carry out the reforms, the government had ensured that corruption would be rampant. As Daniel Thorner observed during his visit to the Valley in 1953, those who benefited the most from the reforms were the individuals who had close ties to the revenue administration. He summed it up well:

> Land reform in Kashmir has clearly done away with the jagirs, and has weakened the position of all the great landlords. It has distinctly benefited those individuals who, at the village level, were already the more important and substantial people. It has done the least for petty tenants and landless laborers, these two categories being the largest in the country-side.[147]

Furthermore, by deciding not to compensate landlords for the expropriation of their lands through the reforms, the Jammu and

[144] *Land Reforms (A Review of the Land Reforms with Special Reference to Big Landed Estates Abolition Act for the Period Ending July, 1952, in the Jammu and Kashmir State)* (Land Reforms Officer, J&K State, 1953), 3–4.

[145] Ibid., 5.

[146] Ibid., 7–10.

[147] Daniel Thorner, "The Kashmir Land Reforms: Some Personal Impressions," *The Economic Weekly*, September 12, 1953: 1002.

Kashmir constituent assembly may have saved the state from a huge financial burden, but in the process it alienated a large section of the landlord population. Since a majority of landlords were Hindu, the reforms led to a mass exodus of Hindus from the state. Additionally, the land reforms notwithstanding, the problems of acute scarcity of grain, high food prices, widespread unemployment, and starvation continued to beset the state during this period.[148] The unsettled nature of Kashmir's accession to India, coupled with the threat of economic and social decline in the face of the land reforms, led to increasing insecurity among Hindus in Jammu, and among Kashmiri Pandits, 20 per cent of whom had emigrated from the Valley by 1950.[149]

Along with the regime's ostensibly pro-Kashmir policies, its discourse was geared toward articulating a nationalist vision for the state in terms of a specifically Kashmiri identity. During its brief reign, Abdullah's regime devoted much time and resources to the propagation of its mantra—*Kashmiriyat*.[150] As I suggested earlier, this secular discourse elided over the increasingly visible religious, regional, and linguistic cleavages in the state. Many Kashmiri Pandits were clearly in no mood to be mollified by ideas of a tolerant Kashmiri culture when it seemed to them that the state had done very little to ensure their economic and political rights as a minority.[151] As a disillusioned Kashmiri Pandit, Jia Lal Kaul Jalali, who had retired from government service, observed in 1950, "I am a Kashmiri to whom Kashmir has always been the dearest of treasures, and suffered for it. To me the nationalism of today is nothing but a garbled version of majority-communalism directed towards a definite end."[152]

[148] Bazaz, *Truth About Kashmir*, 8.

[149] Ibid., 10.

[150] As we saw, the regime adopted poet Ghulam Ahmad Mahjoor as the main votary of this idea.

[151] This is not to suggest that *all* Kashmiri Pandits condemned *Kashmiriyat*. There are several examples of Pandit poets, authors, and officials who gave voice to this shared Kashmiri culture and identity, the most significant among them being the poet Dina Nath Nadim, who held the position of General Secretary of the Hindu–Muslim Amity Council, Srinagar. Other notable Kashmiri Pandit votaries of *Kashmiriyat* included Zinda Kaul and Moti Lal Saqi. See Raina, ed. and trans., *An Anthology of Modern Kashmiri Verse*.

[152] "Jia Lal Kaul Jalali's letter to Kashyap Bandhu," June 3, 1950, Private Collection of Jia Lal Kaul Jalali, Srinagar State Archives.

Jalali was pointing to a profound schism between the National Conference's discourse and practice, implicit since the 1930s, which pervaded and vitiated its narrative on *Kashmiriyat.* While the Conference propounded a secular philosophy, its regime unabashedly used religion as a tool of legitimacy. This is amply illustrated by the language policies of the successive National Conference regimes. The Abdullah regime declared Urdu as the official language of the state in 1948 with a view to facilitating administrative tasks in a language that had been the language of government for close to sixty years.[153] At the same time, the state attempted to address the demands of Kashmiris and Jammu Dogras by installing Kashmiri and Dogri as media of instruction in regional primary schools.

In 1953 the Bakhshi regime rejected this policy for the ostensible reason that both Kashmiri and Dogri did not have uniform scripts and that the adoption of different regional languages within the state thwarted "national integration."[154] Instead, the state now adopted Urdu as the only official language of the state, obviously pandering to the increasingly vocal elements in Kashmir that were articulating the Kashmiri identity in Muslim terms. While mother-tongues were thus given short shrift, Asaan Urdu, or Hindustani in Persian and Devnagari scripts, became the medium of instruction at the primary level. At the middle-school level, students had to choose between Hindi, Urdu, and Punjabi as their first language, while English was taught as a compulsory second language. In addition, Sanskrit or Persian or Arabic could be taken as the third language. The same scheme continued at the high-school stage.[155] Interestingly, the National Conference regime adopted the same language policy as the Dogra state, a policy that it had so roundly denounced in 1941.

By ignoring mother-tongues, and promoting languages that had by this time become associated with different religious groups—Hindi with Hindus, Urdu with Muslims, and Punjabi with Sikhs—the Jammu and Kashmir regimes succeeded, inadvertently perhaps, in

[153] Nishat Ansaari, "Urdu in Jammu and Kashmir," in P.N. Pushp and K. Warikoo, eds., *Jammu, Kashmir, and Ladakh: Linguistic Predicament* (Delhi: Har-Anand Publications, 1996), 172–3.

[154] P.N. Pushp, "Kashmiri and the Linguistic Predicament of the State," in Pushp and Warikoo, eds., *Jammu, Kashmir and Ladakh*, 23–6.

[155] Sheetal Gupta, *Trilingual Aspects of Language Learning and Teaching in Jammu and Kashmir* (Jammu: Jay Kay Book House, 1986), 21–2.

emphasizing the congruence between regional and religious interests within the state. Thus, Urdu and the Persian script were ignored in Jammu schools, while Hindi and the Devnagari script were ignored in Kashmir schools. Furthermore, the fact that Urdu, the language of the Muslims and the enemy state of Pakistan, was the official language of the state was not lost on Jammu Hindus and Ladakhi Buddhists. Urdu may have continued as the official language of the state, but its status existed merely on paper. As a result, English has come to act as the de facto official language of the post-1947 state of Jammu and Kashmir.[156] As for Kashmiri, it is ironic that the votaries of *Kashmiriyat* have consistently failed to promote the language of the people as a possible medium of instruction in educational institutions and the language of state administration.[157] At the same time, the more vocal elements of the insurgency in the Valley have emphasized their relationship to Urdu, Persian, and Arabic as the languages of the Muslim ummat, rather than to their regional language.

The overt propagation of a secular Kashmiri identity, while acceptable in principle to the Indian nation-state—since it was so closely related to its own majoritarianism—nevertheless threatened its sacrosanct territorial integrity. After all, if taken to its logical conclusion, *Kashmiriyat*, which emphasized Kashmir's uniqueness in India, implied some kind of autonomy for Kashmir. This, coupled with the uncertain question of the state's accession to India, ensured an increasingly strained relationship between the Jammu and Kashmir government and the Indian Union by the early 1950s. The Dixon Commission, sent by the United Nations to find a solution to the Kashmir problem in 1950, failed after both India and Pakistan rejected its proposals for "regional plebiscites."[158] The National Conference regime began to

---

[156] Ansaari, "Urdu in Jammu and Kashmir," 172–3.

[157] According to the Kashmiri leadership, the reason they overlooked Kashmiri was to deflect any charges by the Indian state that they were promoting a dissident Kashmiri regional identity. K. Warikoo, "Language and Politics in Jammu and Kashmir: Issues and Perspectives," in Pushp and Warikoo, eds., *Jammu, Kashmir and Ladakh*, 195–203. There were other reasons for this, however, such as the fact that the adoption of Kashmiri would inevitably have raised the issue of the script it should be written in—Persian or Devnagari—a debate the government probably wanted to avoid in the already seething atmosphere in the state.

[158] The Dixon Commission's concept of regional plebiscites was either "a plan for taking the plebiscite by sections or areas and the allocation of each section or

press for the election of a constituent assembly for Kashmir, "which should include the representatives of every section and class of the people of the state, as well as every unit." In 1951, when the assembly was convened and Abdullah was elected Prime Minister, he categorically ruled out the central government's demand that the assembly should adopt a resolution reiterating its accession to India.[159] Abdullah went a step further in 1953, when his regime set up a working group to study the Kashmir problem and put forth four proposals for its solution: a plebiscite would be held, autonomy would be obtained for the entire state, foreign affairs and defense would be placed under the joint control of India and Pakistan, and the Dixon Plan would be implemented along with the autonomy of the region where plebiscite was to be held.[160]

It was clear that Sheikh Abdullah was in favor of the settlement of the Kashmir issue through a plebiscite, an idea anathema to the Indian government. At the same time, the Praja Parishad movement had begun to put pressure on the Indian government to force the complete accession of Jammu and Kashmir to India through means other than a plebiscite. The Indian state found the pretext it needed to depose Abdullah when leaders of the Parishad movement were arrested and imprisoned in Srinagar. Soon after, Sheikh Abdullah made fiery speeches denouncing the Indian state and proclaiming his personal commitment to Kashmiri self-determination.[161] On Nehru's orders, Abdullah was arrested and imprisoned in August 1953, for a period of eleven years, until his release in 1964. His second-in-command, Bakhshi Ghulam Mohammad, became the state's next Prime Minister, under whose regime political repression and economic deprivation reached their acme in the state.

The first National Conference government, as well as successive Jammu and Kashmir regimes, far from creating the socialist utopia

---

area according to the result of the vote therein," or "a plan by which it was conceded that some areas were certain to vote for accession to Pakistan and some for accession to India and by which, without taking a vote therein, they should be allotted accordingly and the plebiscite should be confined only to the uncertain area, which . . . appeared to be the Valley of Kashmir and perhaps some adjacent country." Quoted in Lamb, *Kashmir: A Disputed Legacy*, 171–2.

[159] Abdullah, *Flames of the Chinar*, 115–16.

[160] Ibid., 117.

[161] Ibid., 118–21 and Bazaz, *The Shape of Things*, 14.

they had promised the people, left an unfortunate legacy of political repression and economic underdevelopment in the state of Jammu and Kashmir.[162] The contradictions within the organization's narrative on united nationalism and citizenship rights were readily apparent in the post-independence period, when its regime was unable to translate the discourse on *Kashmiriyat* into policies that would satisfy the disparate regional, religious and class interests of the state people. As significantly, while its rhetoric emphasized its independence from the Indian state, the National Conference relied heavily on that same Indian state to bolster its flagging authority in Jammu and Kashmir. This disjunction between the discourse and practice of the National Conference in its relationship with the Indian state was key in determining the state's political future.

* * *

The political culture of Kashmir in the 1940s was far more ambiguous and complex than has been portrayed by scholarship on this decade. Furthermore, it was merely an aspect, albeit an important one, of the ongoing dialogue between religious identities, community definitions, and a deep longing for a homeland with just rulers that continues in Kashmir to this day. The outcome of 1947 and its aftermath was determined not only by a complex negotiation between religious and regional identities, but as much by the inability of the main Kashmiri political organizations to successfully incorporate ideas of national identity and citizenship rights into the political fabric of the Kashmir Valley, and their unwillingness to allow for articulations of dissent on these issues. Naya Kashmir, it would seem, had turned out to be yet another version of the old.

---

[162] For a political economy perspective on the Kashmir insurgency, see Siddhartha Prakash, "The Political Economy of Kashmir since 1947," *Contemporary South Asia* (2000) 9(3): 315–37. Prakash argues that the post-1947 state in Kashmir has been in effect a "failed state," where "agricultural growth benefited only a small section of the population. In addition, industrial development was minimal. As a result, the supply of job opportunities in the administration, public and private sectors lagged behind the growing demand. Coupled with a high level of economic mismanagement and political nepotism over the years, this conspired to alienate the youth. For many, militancy proved to be a way out of what in effect grew into a 'failed state'." Ibid., 316.

Conclusion

Kashmir has had many appellations, all flattering, most undeserved: Paradise on Earth, Solomon's Garden, Happy Valley, Supremely Beautiful Woman, Switzerland of India, to name but a few. In the popular imagination, Kashmir has no history or people. This is not surprising, given the pride of place Kashmir occupies in both Indian and Pakistani nationalist narratives. For the Indian state, Kashmir is a prime example of its claim that India's religious communities lived together in harmony until the divisive policies of the colonial state wreaked havoc and brought about the partition of the nation. Equally significantly, the presence of Kashmir within the Union of India legitimizes the state's cherished ideal of secularism. For Pakistan, Kashmir continues to be a blot on the two-nation theory. After all, if the Muslims of the Indian subcontinent do indeed form a distinct nation, then how can one explain the presence of a Muslim-majority region in India?

One need only give the public discourse in the two countries a cursory glance to recognize the extent to which these ideas on Kashmir have withstood the test of time. The omnipresent "Kashmir problem" has been so intractable and foiled Indo–Pakistan relations for more than half a century because Kashmir is inextricably wrapped up in the very fabric of Indian and Pakistani nationalist imaginations. Perhaps the first step toward renegotiating the Kashmir imbroglio is to disentangle the rhetoric and polemics on the region from its history. Unless the two states fundamentally rethink their narratives of nationalism with respect to Kashmir, they will continue to churn out, as an *Indian Express* editorial put it, "the same tired old statements and shibboleths which have only led them to go around in never-ending circles like blinded bulls yoked together by violence."[1]

---

[1] "Bombastic Bombardments," *Indian Express*, Delhi, October 24, 2001. It is important to note that while the *Indian Express* supports continued dialogue

This book takes the initial step of questioning and transcending polemical and teleological interpretations of Kashmiri history. In the process, it seeks to rescue the region's history from its contemporary political discourse—which is so overshadowed by the imperatives of the nation-states involved in the regional conflict. It argues that Kashmir, in many ways, was not much different from other regions in South Asia, where the discourse on religious identities and regional affiliations interacted in significant ways with political and economic formations, in both pre-colonial and colonial periods, to produce a dissimilar, although not unique, political culture. Kashmir has never been isolated, insular, or exhibited an exceptional culture where religious communities have necessarily lived in mutual harmony since the beginning of time. In fact, Kashmir has had intimate relationships with several political entities outside its borders, and the relationships between religious communities within its borders have been determined by a complex set of issues, including the nature of the state, the perception and demands of local leadership, socio-economic changes, and the evolving attitudes of the colonial state.

Pre-colonial Kashmiri political culture was formulated through an engagement between the particular and the universal, that is, between the vernacularization of Kashmiri culture—which led to the emergence of a discourse on regional belonging—and the propagation of a universal religion with its concomitant discourse on religious identities. As a result, the narrative on regional identities transcended, but did not obscure, religious differences, which were not necessarily perceived as being antithetical to expressions of longing for a homeland. The concept of *Mulk-i-Kashmir*, redolent with a sense of belonging to the homeland of Kashmir—which was in a state of unmitigated decline due to the rapacious rule of outsiders—emerged in the late eighteenth and early nineteenth centuries. In their long narrative poems in Persian, Kashmiri writers displayed an ability to glorify their regional affiliation while remaining faithful to their religious identities. While clear religious affiliations existed in Kashmir, and may even have been antithetical to each other in certain contexts, the discourse on regional belonging quite effortlessly harnessed them for the greater good of the homeland.

---

between India and Pakistan, it does not question either the Indian nationalist narrative or the Indian state's stance on Kashmir.

The transformation of the Valley's political and economic structures with its incorporation into the princely state of Jammu and Kashmir in 1846 shifted the balance in the public discourse toward the religious component of identities. Not only did the British create the state of Jammu and Kashmir from a disparate group of territories shorn from the Sikh kingdom and place it under the rule of a Dogra raja, but more significantly by the late nineteenth century they directly intervened in the administration of the state. The consequent land settlement of the region led to the breakdown of the state monopoly on grain distribution, the emergence of a class of grain dealers, the creation of a recognizable peasant class, and the decline of the indigenous landed elite. Additionally, the slump in the shawl trade beginning in the 1870s meant that shawl traders were in a state of financial and social decline by the late nineteenth century. At the same time, the Dogra state became more interventionist, centralized, and the "Hindu" idiom of its rule became increasingly apparent.

In this context, while the discourse on the oppressions suffered by the homeland continued, Kashmiris increasingly began to identify with their religious affiliation in an attempt to locate themselves, socially, politically, and economically, within the rapidly changing structures of the state of Jammu and Kashmir. The intervention of the British in the Valley, ostensibly on behalf of Kashmiri Muslims, added significance to this movement toward defining the contours of an identifiable Kashmiri Muslim community. This did not, however, lead to the articulation of a rigidly defined and unified Kashmiri Muslim identity antagonistic to other religions or the regional identity. Instead, the Kashmiri Muslim religious leadership in the late-nineteenth and early-twentieth centuries engaged in fierce battles over the meaning of Islam and the rights to preach these definitions at the sacred spaces of the Valley. At the same time, this leadership petitioned the Dogra state to officially recognize Kashmiri Muslims as a community with specific needs, particularly in the educational arena.

By the 1920s, as a new Kashmiri Muslim leadership, educated in British India, came to replace the religious leadership, the discourse on economic, political and social rights and freedoms for Kashmiris as citizens became a central aspect of Kashmiri political culture. This narrative on citizenship, particularly in the 1930s, depended on the articulation of a coherent nationalism that accommodated the diverse local, religious, and sectarian interests of the princely state's inhabitants.

Although the Jammu and Kashmir Muslim Conference changed its appellation to the Jammu and Kashmir National Conference, and its primary leader, Sheikh Abdullah, claimed the title of sole spokesman of all residents of Jammu and Kashmir, the organization's politics tended to be majoritarian. Even at the level of discourse, the National Conference was unable to reconcile the interests of its primary constituency—namely Kashmiri Muslims of the Valley, themselves not a homogeneous group—with the disparate interests of social groups in other parts of the state.

The disjunction between the politics of the National Conference and Kashmiri demands became increasingly apparent in the 1940s, as the organization insisted on glorifying national identity at the expense of religious and other local affiliations. As support for the organization dwindled, even in the Valley, its identification with the Indian National Congress became increasingly apparent. Meanwhile, the British had begun their moves to withdraw from the subcontinent, leaving the inhabitants of princely states at the mercy of their rulers and of the independent entities that would succeed the colonial state. In the absence of a popular political organization that could effectively direct Kashmiri politics, local and regional movements and organizations against the authority of the Dogra ruler—such as in Poonch, Gilgit and the Kashmir Valley—determined the course of Kashmir's immediate future. As the troops of the independent states of India and Pakistan clashed over Kashmir and eventually led to its partition, Sheikh Abdullah became the head of the newly acceded state of Jammu and Kashmir in India, all without reference to the aspirations of the Kashmiri people.

The Kashmiri people's struggle for political, economic, and social rights continued into the postcolonial period, which has been characterized by political repression and economic underdevelopment. Such negligence is particularly egregious given the fact that the people of the state were unequivocally in favor of neither India nor Pakistan in 1947, and since then have not been allowed the right to decide their own future. While India and Pakistan continue to blame each other for real or imagined "aggressions," the aspirations of the people of Kashmir on both sides of the "line of control" hang in the balance. Clearly, the dispute and the more recent insurgency that have riddled the region were neither inevitable nor the result of the clash between a Muslim-majority region and a Hindu-majority nation-state. Instead, their causes can be located in the failure of the mechanisms of decolonization, the vastly different aspirations of the various regions in the state of Jammu and Kashmir, the inability of the leadership to harness differences into a consensual political ideology, and the actions of a centralized Indian nation-state which has perpetuated the myth of the special status of Jammu and Kashmir while denying its population even a semblance of democracy.

* * *

One of the more pernicious consequences of the conflation of polemics and history in the case of Kashmir has been the denial of citizenship rights to Kashmiris by the postcolonial nation-states of South Asia. Both states had loudly proclaimed at their inception that their first order of business was the conferral of citizenship rights on their inhabitants. If, however, your loyalties as a citizen were suspect, as was the case with Kashmiris, some of whom had become citizens of India and others of Pakistan, both under dubious circumstances, then your constitutional rights were not necessarily guaranteed. If Indian Muslims in general were suspect in their loyalties toward the newly formed Indian nation-state, the Muslims of Kashmir were even more so. In an irony of history, the successive postcolonial regimes of the Jammu and Kashmir state rode roughshod over the political rights of the state's citizens to ensure loyalty and placate the doubts of the Indian nation-state.

The citizenship rights of Kashmiris, both Hindu and Muslim, were obfuscated in the narrative of united nationalism generated by the postcolonial nation-states, alongside the policies of the regional governments of Kashmir as they strove to establish their own legitimacy within the national framework. In an atmosphere where India's government was unwilling to countenance the existence of more than one nation within its territorial confines, it was imperative for successive regimes of the Jammu and Kashmir state to curb any appearance of Kashmiri nationalism. While the National Conference regime under Sheikh Abdullah had alternatively stoked the fires of religious, regional, and national belonging in the state, successive National Conference regimes were unable to disentangle this religion–region–nation conflation and draw a necessary bridge, for Kashmiris, between the discourses of Kashmiri regional identity and the nationalist narratives of the Indian state. It was much easier, instead, to simply curb any opinions that might appear anti-national.

Successive governments at the center tacitly accepted the policies of regional governments. Not surprisingly, these policies alienated a significant proportion of the Valley's population from the regional regimes, while also raising questions about the Indian government's complicity in anti-democratic activities. From the Kashmiri perspective, Indian independence and the concomitant development of democratic political institutions held very little meaning. Much as in the Dogra period, Kashmiri Muslims were still suspect, still disenfranchised, and still poor. While being denied citizenship rights by the Indian nation-state, Kashmiris were expected to proclaim an unquestioning allegiance to that very nation-state, while eschewing their individual loyalties to their religious and regional communities. In this context, the symbols and idioms of the public discourse of the Kashmir Valley from the colonial period were quite easily translated into the postcolonial era.

Most works on the contemporary movement in the region study it solely as a product of the postcolonial era, emphasizing the sudden emergence of political consciousness among Kashmiris in the 1980s and 1990s. While these studies disagree on the timing of the insurgency and the reasons behind it, they concur that an earlier generation of Kashmiris had been politically quiescent and that the current movement is a product of the peculiarities of postcolonial politics.[2] There is no doubt that the postcolonial context is crucial in understanding the development of the nature and contours of the movement in the region. At the same time, however, there is some merit in recognizing the

[2] See, for instance, Sumit Ganguly, *The Crisis in Kashmir* and Robert Wirsing, *India, Pakistan and the Kashmir Dispute: On Regional Conflict and its Resolution* (Delhi: Rupa & Co., 1994). Both these and other works on the current conflict in the region deal with the historical context and its relevance for the postcolonial period in perfunctory fashion, going only as far back as the 1930s and 1940s. It is understood that while the historical context is important, the roots of the conflict are located in the postcolonial period. It is important to reiterate that Kashmiri Muslims were hardly politically quiescent in the colonial period or even the early postcolonial period. Simply because their voices were successfully repressed until the early 1990s does not imply that there was no political engagement in the Valley prior to this decade. Unfortunately, it is beyond the scope of this book to examine the political culture of Kashmiri Muslims in the post-1953 period.

transcendence of themes, issues, and concerns across the 1947 divide, particularly since the present movement is, in many ways, a continuation of Kashmiri regionalist movements of the early twentieth century, albeit in a dramatically altered political scenario.

Given the events surrounding Kashmir's accession to India, the subsequent partition of the state, and the realignment of Kashmiri identities required in the new political scenario, it is not surprising that issues of religious affiliation, regional belonging, and nationalism continued to inform the public discourse of the Valley in the post-colonial period. The National Conference, with its avowedly secular and nationalist stance, resorted to the homogenizing discourse of *Kashmiriyat* to paper over the widespread discontent within Kashmiri society, particularly among Muslims of the Valley. The concept of *Kashmiriyat* was a neat way to propagate the idea of a peaceful co-existence of religious communities while obscuring the question of economic, material and social differences between them. This Kashmiri exceptionalist discourse, moreover, was squarely located within the narrative and agenda of the Indian nation-state, and did not allow for an expression of Kashmiri regional or religious aspirations. Much like its Dogra predecessor, the National Conference laid claim to religious neutrality while overtly using religion as a tool to establish its own legitimacy.[3] It is not surprising, then, that the movements that have arisen in the Valley in the postcolonial period seek to address Kashmiri regional, political, and economic aspirations through an appeal to people's religious identities.

The situation in Pakistani Kashmir has not been much better. Despite its misnomer, Azad Kashmir does not afford its inhabitants

---

[3] The National Conference, as much as its so-called "fundamentalist" rivals in the Valley, seized upon the theft of the strand of the Prophet's hair from the Haz-ratbal mosque in Srinagar in December 1963 to present themselves as protectors of Islam, in the process whipping up communitarian antagonisms in the Valley. It should also be noted that the demonstrations against the theft provided Kashmiri Muslims with a forum for the expression of deep discontent against the regional and national governments, much as the insult to the Holy *Quran* incident in 1931 had provided the context for their articulation of political, economic, and social grievances against the Dogra state. See P.N. Bazaz, *The Dialogue between Mirwaiz Farooq and Sheikh Abdullah* (Delhi: Pamposh Publications, 1964) and Victoria Schofield, *Kashmir in the Crossfire* (London and New York: I.B. Tauris, 1996), 197–200.

even basic freedoms, having come under Pakistani military occupation soon after its establishment in 1948. Maintaining a tenuous relationship with the Pakistani state, which does not recognize it as a province of Pakistan, Azad Kashmir has never been integrated into Pakistani politics.[4] More recently, Pakistani military control has given way to an ever-increasing arms and drugs economy tying the Pakistani and Indian portions of Kashmir into a criminal web that has shifted attention from the genuine grievances of Kashmiris on both sides of the de facto border. Equally significantly, it has led to the subversion, to an extent, of the popularly backed insurgency in the Valley by an array of reactionary groups in Pakistan and Afghanistan, providing Indian authorities with a legitimate excuse to crack down on the human rights of the inhabitants.

Even Indian nationalist observers cannot deny that Kashmiris have been the victims of the continuing imbroglio between India and Pakistan, and the more than decade-old insurgency in the Valley. The extent of Kashmiri disillusionment, not only with Indian rule but also about the possibility of an Indo-Pak rapprochement, was apparent during the much-heralded Agra summit between the two countries in July 2001.[5] A reporter from the Valley lamented that Kashmiris' engagement with the summit did not go beyond superficial discussions of Musharraf's sartorial savvy.[6] Despite the controversy generated around the role of the All Parties Hurriyat Conference[7] during the

[4] Schofield, *Kashmir in the Crossfire*, 181–3.

[5] This disillusionment is rooted in reality, as became clear from India's insistence during the talks that Kashmir was not the central issue between India and Pakistan, while Pakistani President Musharraf took the opportunity to voice his support for the Kashmiri movement for self-determination in the Valley. The talks, inevitably, failed.

[6] Muzamil Jameel, "Chronicle of a Failed Dialogue Foretold," *Indian Express*, Delhi, July 19, 2001.

[7] The All Parties Hurriyat Conference, or the APHC, is a political coalition of 23 parties, including the Jamaat-i-Islami, Muslim Conference, Awami Action Committee, People's Conference, Ittehad-ul-Muslimeen, J&K Democratic Freedom Party, Jammu and Kashmir Liberation Front, People's League, Communist Party of India (Marxist) and People's Political Front. The APHC is the self-proclaimed sole representative of the people of Jammu and Kashmir, which might well be the case since it incorporates a dizzying array of the political spectrum. The organization has declared that it favors tripartite talks between India, Pakistan, and the people of Kashmir as the only means to resolve the Kashmir issue. For a

talks, with the Pakistani delegation making overtures to the organization while the Indian state decried this as an act of sabotage, it is clear that Kashmiris were without representation, yet again, as the dialogue between the two countries unfolded. The summit did, however, bring to light the widespread feeling among Kashmiris that they were not consulted, even by their own political leaders. As an editorial in the Kashmiri Urdu daily, *Aftab*, noted: "Of late, it has become fashionable for political parties here to cry hoarse that people's wishes be respected at every step. However, everybody here knows how well the leaders, both the pro-India and secessionist ones, have shown utter disregard for eliciting mass-based opinion on any development."[8]

Kashmir once again emerged as a point of contention between the two nation-states as South Asia became the center of America's effort against Afghanistan. Pakistan, now key to America's "campaign against terrorism," has used this opportunity to reiterate the oft-repeated idea that Kashmiris are engaged in a freedom struggle that needs to be differentiated from terrorism. India, in its turn, has been insisting that due to its support of terrorist groups in Kashmir, Pakistan is part of the problem of terrorism, and therefore cannot be part of the solution. Far from uniting South Asia, the war in Afghanistan has brought forth schisms along familiar lines within Indian and Pakistani societies. Most significantly, it has served to strengthen the agendas of the two nation-states in relation to Kashmir, once again at the expense of Kashmiris.

At the same time, the support expressed by some groups of Indian Muslims for Osama Bin Laden has led to questions about the loyalty of Indian Muslims as a whole toward the Indian state.[9] Since Kashmiris

---

detailed discussion of the political stances of the APHC in the Valley until 1997, see Sumantra Bose, *The Challenge in Kashmir*, especially chapter 7.

[8] *Aftab*, Srinagar, July 17, 2001.

[9] In his article "The Indian Muslim and the Loyalty Test: Did I Pass or Fail?" Mushirul Hasan laments the fact that America's war against terrorism has prompted "self-proclaimed patriots" to once again question the loyalty of Indian Muslims. Since all Indian Muslims are suspect, regardless of regional, class, political or linguistic affiliation, they all have to take the loyalty test by condemning Pakistan's actions in Kargil and terrorism in Kashmir and America, lest their silence be construed as acquiescence in terrorism, or worse, disloyalty to India. When Muslims do condemn these actions, they are told that "liberal" Muslims hardly represent the community, instead, it is the "fanatics" supporting Osama

form a significant proportion of Indian Muslims who have been, moreover, articulating their anti-Indian feelings for a decade or more, this situation merely provides the Indian state with yet another ostensibly legitimate excuse for curbing insurgent movements in the Valley. Pakistan's current President, General Musharraf, beleaguered due to his regime's support for America, needs to stand firm on Kashmir as evidence that he has not deserted the cause of Islam or the Kashmiris. Not surprisingly, nationalist narratives from both sides of the border have reappeared faithfully in the public sphere of late, reiterating their irreconcilable stances on Kashmir.

Ultimately, the Kashmir question has been so problematic because it does not fit the one state–one nation–one religion trope that has defined South Asia in the postcolonial era. This does not stem so much from its uniqueness, or its legacy of *Kashmiriyat*, with its teleological acceptance of autonomy, but rather from its complex history as an indirectly ruled region within British India, where the evolving relationship between the state and communitarian identities led to the articulation of a variety of regional nationalisms in the early twentieth century. Had the Indian and Pakistani nation-states been more willing to accommodate Kashmir's regional aspirations, instead of transforming it into a symbol of the contest between their competing nationalist visions, it is likely that Kashmir would have remained quiescent in the postcolonial period. At the same time, it is important to point out that as much responsibility for the present imbroglio in the region rests with a particular brand of Kashmiri nationalism represented by the Kashmiri nationalist organization that inherited state structures in this region. Exhibiting similar deformities to the unitary nationalisms of India and Pakistan, this Kashmiri nationalism has been as reluctant to accommodate regional and religious differences, and multiple visions of nationalism within Kashmir, as its Indian and Pakistani counterparts.

Clearly, political solutions to the "Kashmir problem" will be abortive until nationalist narratives—Indian, Pakistani, and Kashmiri—that are primarily responsible for its intractability, are dismantled. Perhaps only a poet can capture the nexus of memory, history, narration, and conflict that defines Kashmir's position in postcolonial South Asia in a poem entitled, appropriately, "Farewell":

Bin Laden who in reality represent the true feelings of the 12 million Indian Muslims. See *Indian Express*, Delhi, November 14, 2001.

At a certain point I lost track of you.
They make a desolation and call it peace.
When you left even the stones were buried:
The defenceless would have no weapons.

When the ibex rubs itself against the rocks, who collects
    its fallen fleece from the slopes?
O Weaver whose seams perfectly vanished, who weighs the
    hairs on the jeweler's balance?
They make a desolation and call it peace.
Who is the guardian tonight of the Gates of Paradise?

My memory is again in the way of your history.
Army convoys all night like desert caravans:
In the smoking oil of dimmed headlights, time dissolved—all
    winter—its crushed fennel.
We can't ask them: *Are you done with the world?*
In the lake the arms of temples and mosques are locked
    in each other's reflections.
Have you soaked saffron to pour on them when they are
    found like this centuries later in this country
        I have stitched to your shadow?

In this country we step out with doors in our arms.
Children run out with windows in their arms.
You drag it behind you in lit corridors.
If the switch is pulled you will be torn from everything.

I'm everything you lost. You won't forgive me.
My memory keeps getting in the way of your history.
There is nothing to forgive. You won't forgive me.

I hid my pain even from myself; I revealed my pain only to
    myself.
There is everything to forgive. You can't forgive me.
If only somehow you could have been mine,
what would not have been possible in the world?[10]

---

[10] Agha Shahid Ali, "Farewell", in Agha Shahid Ali, *The Country Without a Post Office, Poems* (New York: W.W. Norton & Company, 1997), 21–3. These are selections from the poem, which has not been quoted here in its entirety. The format, including italics and spacing, is faithful to the original.

Bibliography

Primary Sources

A. Manuscripts

Anonymous. "Che-Bakra." Unpublished manuscript in Kashmiri. Private Collection of Peerzada Mohammad Ashraf, Srinagar, Kashmir, July 9, 1999.

Anonymous. "A Short History of Chinese Turkistan." Unpublished manuscript in Persian. Srinagar: Central Asian Studies Department, University of Kashmir, 1981.

Anonymous. "Untitled." Unpublished manuscript in Persian. Acc. # 1376, Arabic and Persian Manuscript Section, Research and Publications Department, University of Kashmir, Srinagar.

Dhar, Pandit Ramju. "Kaifiyat Intezame Mulk-i-Kashmir (1760–1880)." Unpublished manuscript in Persian. Acc # 1913, Arabic and Persian Manuscript Section, Research and Publications Department, University of Kashmir, Srinagar.

Furahi, Sayyid Nizamuddin, "Mulhemaat." Unpublished manuscript in Persian. Private Collection of Peerzada Mohammad Ashraf, Bemina, Kashmir, November 20, 1997.

Hakkani, Azizullah. "Tamhide Hadisaye Kashmir." Manuscript # 623, Srinagar State Archives, Srinagar, Kashmir.

"Kashmiri Shawl with Map of Srinagar," Sri Pratap Singh Museum, Srinagar, Kashmir.

Khoiyami, Ali Shah. "Akhir Zamaan." Unpublished manuscript in Kashmiri. Private Collection of Shafi Shauq, Srinagar, Kashmir, September 25, 1997.

Pandit, Nath. "Gulshan Dastoor." Unpublished manuscript in Persian. Acc # 2314, Persian and Arabic Manuscript Section, Research and Publications Department, University of Kashmir, Srinagar.

Saifuddin, Mirza. "Mirza Saifuddin Papers." 12 vols. Manuscript # 1420, Arabic and Persian Manuscript section, Research and Publications Department, University of Kashmir, Srinagar.

Shahabadi, Mullah Hamidullah. "Babujnama." Unpublished manuscript in

Persian. Acc. # 866, Persian and Arabic Manuscript Section, Research and Publications Department, University of Kashmir, Srinagar.

———. "Shaher-i-Ashob." Manuscript # 585, Srinagar State Archives, Srinagar, Kashmir.

Tarabali, Sheikh Ahmad. "Tarabali's Letter to Yahya Shah." Unpublished manuscript in Persian. Private Collection of Mufti Mohammad Maqbool, Srinagar, Kashmir, August 25, 1997.

Traali, Sheikh Ahmad. "Tarikh-u sadad fi tayidi ziaratil kaboor wal istimdad." Unpublished manuscript in Persian. Private Collection of Peerzada Mohammad Ashraf, Bemina, Kashmir, April 18, 1998.

B. *Archival Documents*

JAMMU STATE ARCHIVES, JAMMU

Old English Records
General Department Records
Political Department Records
Vernacular Department Records
Education Department Records
Private Records of His Highness
State Department Records
Proceedings of the State Council of Jammu and Kashmir

SRINAGAR STATE ARCHIVES, SRINAGAR

Ex-Governor's Records
District Magistrate's Records

NATIONAL ARCHIVES OF INDIA, NEW DELHI

Foreign Department Secretariat Records
Foreign and Political Department Records

INDIA OFFICE LIBRARY AND RECORDS, LONDON (Microfilm)

Foreign Department Records
Foreign and Political Department Records
Crown Representative Papers of India

C. *Official Reports*

Administration Reports of the Jammu and Kashmir State, 1873–1941.

Administration Reports of the Education Department of the Jammu and Kashmir State, 1912–1916.

All Jammu Kashmir Muslim Auqaf Trust. *Trust Deed.* Srinagar, 1973.

Bates, Charles Ellison. *A Gazetteer of Kashmir and the Adjacent Districts of Kishtwar, Badrawar, Jamu, Naoshera, Punch, and the Valley of the Kishenganga.* Calcutta: Office of the Superintendent of Government Printing, 1873. Reprint, New Delhi: Light and Life, 1980.

Board of Grain Control. *Grain Control in Kashmir.* Jammu and Kashmir State, August 1923.

Dalal, Barjor. *Report of the Srinagar Riot Enquiry Committee S.1988 (1931).* Srinagar: Pratap Government Press, S.1988 (1932).

First Annual Report of the Working of Cooperative Societies Act of 1914 in the State of His Highness the Maharaja Sahib Bahadur of Jammu and Kashmir up till 16 Sept., 1923. Lahore: Civil and Military Press, 1923.

Gazetteer of Jammu and Kashmir State, 1890–1945.

Girdlestone, Charles. *Memorandum on Cashmere and Adjacent Territories.* Calcutta: Foreign Department Press, 1874.

Glancy, B.J. *Report of the Commission appointed under the order of His Highness, the Maharaja Bahadur dated 12th November, 1931 to enquire into Grievances and Complaints.* Jammu: Ranbir Government Press, 1933.

Gulab Bhawan Research Series. 12 vols. Jammu, 1979.

The Imperial Gazetteer of India Vol.XV Karachi to Kotayam. Calcutta: Superintendent of Government Printing, 1908. Reprint, New Delhi: Today and Tomorrow's Printers, 1993.

Interim Report of the Educational Reorganization Committee. Reports/192, 1932. Srinagar State Archives.

Kaye, J.L. *Note on the Assessment Report on the Minor Jagir Villages situated in the Valley of Kashmir.* Lahore: Civil and Military Gazette Press, 1897.

Khan, Bahadur Munshi Ghulam Ahmed. *Census of India, 1901, Vol. XXIII, Kashmir, Part I, Report.* Lahore: Civil and Military Gazette Press, 1902.

Land Reforms (A review of the land reforms with special reference to Big Landed Estates Abolition Act for the period ending July, 1952, in the Jammu and Kashmir State). J&K State: Land Reforms Officer, 1953.

Lawrence, Walter R. *Assessment Report of Baramulla Tehsil.* Jammu, 1905.

Laws of Jammu and Kashmir. 5 vols. 3rd ed. Srinagar: Jammu and Kashmir Government Press, 1972.

Khan, Mohammad Matin-uz-Zaman. *Census of India 1911, Vol. XX, Kashmir, Part I Report.* Lucknow: Newul Kishore Press, 1912.

Mohammad, Khan Bahadur Chaudhri Khushi. *Census of India, 1921, Vol. XXII, Kashmir, Part I Report.* Lahore: Mufid-i-Am Press, 1922.

Nath, Shri Ganga. *Commission Report on Administration of Jammu and Kashmir State.* Jammu, 1944.

Proceedings of the Christian Missionary Society in Africa and Asia for the year 1884–85. London, 1885.

Ram, Rai Bahadur Pandit Bhag. *Census of India, 1891, Vol. XXVIII, The Kashmir State.* Lahore: Mufid-i-Am Press, 1893.

Ram, Rai Bahadur Pandit Anant and Pandit Hira Nand Raina. *Census of India, 1931, Vol. XXIV, Jammu and Kashmir State, Part I Report.* Jammu: Ranbir Government Press, 1933.

Report of the Indian States Committee 1928–1929. His Majesty's Stationary Office: London, 1929.

Rivett, H.L. *Assessment Report on the Minor Jagir Villages situated in the Valley of Kashmir, 1896–97.* Lahore: Civil and Military Gazette Press, 1897.

Rules Regarding Grant of Waste Land for Cultivation as Sanctioned by His Highness the Maharaja Sahib Bahadur. Jammu, 1917.

"Sharp Committee Report." In Rasool, Ghulam. *Education in Jammu and Kashmir: Issues and Documents.* Jammu: Jay Kay Book House, 1986.

Terms of Reference for the Committee appointed to define the term 'State Subject.' Srinagar: K.M. Press, 1923.

Trade Report of the Jammu and Kashmir State, (1935–38). Jammu: Ranbir Government Press, 1940.

Wingate, A. *Preliminary Report of Settlement Operations in Kashmir and Jammu.* Lahore: W. Ball & Co., 1888.

———. *Proposed Settlement Rules for Kashmir.* Lahore: W. Ball & Co., 1889.

Wreford, R.G. *Census of India, 1941, Vol. XXII, Jammu and Kashmir.* Jammu: Ranbir Government Press, 1943.

D. Books

Abdullah, Sheikh Mohammad. *Flames of the Chinar: An Autobiography.* New Delhi: Viking, 1993.

———. "Presidential Address by Sheikh Mohammad Abdullah at First Session of All Jammu and Kashmir Muslim Conference, 15–17 October, 1932, Srinagar." In Mirza Shafiq Hussain, ed. *The Political Struggle of Kashmiri Muslims, 1931–1939: Selected Documents.* Srinagar: Gulshan Publishers, 1991.

———. "Sheikh Mohammad Abdullah's Presidential Address at the Fifth Annual Session of the Muslim Conference at Poonch, 13–15 May, 1937," in Mirza Shafiq Hussain, ed. *The Political Struggle of Kashmiri Muslims, 1931–1939: Selected Documents.* Srinagar: Gulshan Publishers, 1991.

Aitchison, C.U. *A Collection of Treaties, Engagements and Sanads relating to India and Neighboring Countries (revised and continued up to 1929). Vol. XII: Jammu & Kashmir, Sikkim, Assam & Burma.* Calcutta: Government of India Central Publications Branch, 1929. Reprint, Delhi: Mittal Publications, 1983.

338   Bibliography

Bazaz, P.N. *Inside Kashmir*. Srinagar: Kashmir Publishing Co., 1941. Reprint, Azad Kashmir: Verinag Publishers, 1987.

Bhande, Khwaja Abdul Rahim. "Reception Address by Khwaja Abdul Rahim Bhande at First Session of Jammu and Kashmir Azad Party Conference, December 3, 1933, Srinagar." In Mirza Shafiq Hussain, ed. *The Political Struggle of Kashmiri Muslims, 1931–1939: Selected Documents*. Srinagar: Gulshan Publishers, 1991.

Bernier, Francois. *Travels in the Mughal Empire, A.D. 1656–1668*. London: W. Pickering, 1826. Reprint, New Delhi: Munshiram Manoharlal, 1992.

Biscoe, C.E. Tyndale. *Kashmir in Sunlight and Shade; A Description of the Beauties of the Country, the Life, Habits, and Humor of its Inhabitants and an Account of the Gradual but Steady Rebuilding of a Once Down–trodden People*. London: Seeley, Service & Co. Limited, 1922.

Dogra, Sant Ram. *Code of Tribal Custom in Kashmir*. Jammu, 1930.

Gadru, S.N. ed. *Kashmir Papers: British Intervention in Kashmir, including Arthur Brinckman's 'Wrongs of Cashmere', Robert Thorpe's 'Kashmir Misgovernment', and Sir William Digby's Condemned Unheard*. Srinagar: Freethought Literature, 1973.

Hamdaani, Mirwaiz Ghulam Nabi. "Reception address by Mirwaiz Ghulam Nabi Hamdaani at Fourth Annual Session of the All Jammu and Kashmir Muslim Conference, Srinagar, October 25, 1935." In Mirza Shafiq Hussain, ed. *The Political Struggle of Kashmiri Muslims, 1931–1939: Selected Documents*. Srinagar: Gulshan Publishers, 1991.

Hugel, Baron Charles. *Travels in Kashmir and the Punjab*. London: John Petheran, 1845.

Ireland, John B. *From Wall Street to Cashmere, Five Years in Asia, Africa and Europe*. New York: Rollo, 1859.

Jalali, Jia Lal Kaul. *Economics of Food Grains in Kashmir*. Lahore: Mercantile Press, 1931.

Jinnah, Mohammad Ali, "Address by M.A. Jinnah, June 3, 1936." In Mirza Shafiq Hussain, ed. *The Political Struggle of Kashmiri Muslims, 1931–1939: Selected Documents*. Srinagar: Gulshan Publishers, 1991.

Khasta, Pandit Hargopal. *Tawarikh-i-Guldasta Kashmir* [A History of Kashmir]. Reprint, Srinagar: City Book Center, 1994.

Khoiyami, Pir Hassan Shah. *Tarikh-i-Hassan*. 3 vols. Reprint, Srinagar: Ghulam Mohammad Noor Mohammad, 1989.

Lawrence, Walter R. *The Valley of Kashmir*. London: H. Frowde, 1895. Reprint, Jammu: Kashmir Kitab Ghar, 1996.

Mookerjee, Shyama Prasad. "Mookerjee's letter to Jawaharlal Nehru, January 9, 1953." In *Nehru-Mookerjee-Abdullah Correspondence*. New Delhi: Information Officer, Kashmir Bureau of Information, 1953.

Saadat, Mufti Mohammad Shah. *Tarikh-i-Kashmir ki Rozana Diary 1846–1947.* [Daily Diary of the History of Kashmir]. Srinagar: Noor Mohammad Ghulam Mohammad, 1997.

Saifuddin, Mirza. *Khulasatul-Tawarikh.* [Summary of the History]. Reprint, Srinagar: Gulshan Publishers, 1984.

"Samad Makri versus the State." In *The Punjab Law Reporter, Jammu and Kashmir High Court Rulings, s. 1979–1991.* Lahore: Punjab Law Reporter Press, 1935.

Shah, Mirwaiz Mohammd Yusuf. "Presidential Address by Mirwaiz Mohammad Yusuf at First Session of Jammu and Kashmir Azad Party Conference, December 3, 1933, Srinagar." In Mirza Shafiq Hussain, ed. *The Political Struggle of Kashmiri Muslims, 1931–1939: Selected Documents.* Srinagar: Gulshan Publishers, 1991.

Sharma, D.C. *Documentation on Kashmir: Documentation of English Language Newspapers of India.* Jammu: Jay Kay Book House, 1985.

Stein, Aurel. *Catalogue of the Sanskrit Manuscripts in the Raghu Natha Temple Library of His Highness, the Maharaja of Jammu and Kashmir.* London: Luzac, 1900. Reprint, Bombay: Nirnaya-Sagara Press, 1983.

Teng, M.Y. *Talaash: Tahkiki te Tabkidi Majmoonan Hinz Sombran* [Quest: A Collection of Essays on Research and Critical Studies]. New Delhi: Jammu and Kashmir Offset Prints, 1988.

Torrens, Lt. Col. *Travels in Ladak, Tartary, and Kashmir.* London: Saunders, Otley, and Co., 1862.

Vigne, G.T. *Travels in Kashmir, Ladak, Iskardo.* 2 vols. London: Henry Colburn, 1842.

Wardle, Sir Thomas. *Kashmir: Its New Silk Industry, with Some Account of its Natural History, Geology, Sport, etc.* London: Simpkin, Marshall, Hamilton, Kent and Co., 1904.

E. Pamphlets

ENGLISH

Bazaz, P.N. *The Shape of Things in Kashmir.* Delhi: Pamposh Publications, 1965.

———. *The Dialogue between Mirwaiz Farooq and Sheikh Abdullah.* Delhi: Pamposh Publications, 1964.

———. *Truth About Kashmir.* Delhi: Kashmir Democratic Union, 1950.

Sanatan Dharma Youngmen's Association, Srinagar. *Kashmir Hindus and the Recent Disturbances.* Lahore: Bharat Printing Works, 1931.

KASHMIRI

Ahmed, Pir Ghulam. *Hablullah* [The Rope of God]. Srinagar, 1912.

Ahmed, Abu Abdul Hai Pir Hanafi Kashmiri. *Shamsher-i-Birhana bar Dushmanani* [Naked Sword]. Amritsar, 1906.

Gami, Mahmood. *Yak Hikayat* [A Story]. Srinagar, 1913.

Hundu, Ghulam Mohiuddin. *Takrir Dilpazir Dar Islahe Quom* [Speech for the Good of the Quom]. Amritsar, 1906.

Kraalwari, Maqbool Shah. *Greeznama* [The Story of the Peasant]. Srinagar: Privately Printed, 1912.

———. *Pirnama* [Story of the Pir]. Srinagar, 1913.

Qari, Moulvi Mohammad Nooruddin. *Hayat-ul-Nabi* [The Life of the Prophet]. Srinagar: Privately Printed, 1921.

———. *Kashur Haar Baghe.* Lahore: Karimi Press, 1926.

———. *Kashur Masal Kitab* [Book of Juristic Verdicts]. Lahore: Rafiq-i-Am Press, 1929.

———. *Dard-i-Dil wa Haquiqat-i-Haal* [The Aching Heart and the Reality of the Situation]. Srinagar: Privately Printed, 1922.

Shah, Khalil. *Malnama* [Story of the Mullah]. Srinagar, 1913.

Shah, Moulvi Mohammad Yusuf. *Kashur Tafsir.* Amritsar: Sana-i-Barki Press, 1935.

URDU

Bazaz, Prem Nath. *Gandhism, Jinnahism, Socialism.* Srinagar: Nishat Electric Press, 1944.

Halat wa Rouidad. Annual Report of the Convocation of the Madrasa Anjuman Nusrat-ul-Islam. Srinagar: Privately Printed, 1900.

Halat wa Rouidad. Annual Report of the Convocation of the Madrasa Anjuman Nusrat-ul-Islam. Srinagar: Salgram Press, 1912.

Halat wa Rouidad. Annual Report of the Convocation of the Madrasa Anjuman Nusrat-ul-Islam. Lahore: Hindustan Steam Press, 1913.

Halat wa Rouidad. Annual Report of the Convocation of the Madrasa Anjuman Nusrat-ul-Islam. Srinagar: Privately Printed, 1915.

Khan, Babu Fakirullah. *Safinaye Nooh, Almaroof Sach Aawaaz.* Amritsar: Ahmadiyya Press, 1932.

Mousiki Kashmiri ka Nava Hissa [The Ninth Part of Kashmiri Music]. Lahore: Inqilab Steam Press, 1932.

Mousiki Kashmiri ka Dassva Hissa [The Tenth Part of Kashmiri Music]. Lahore: Inqilab Steam Press, 1933.

Sadaat, Mohammad Shah. *Jannat-ul-Duniya*. Lahore: Mahir Electric Press, 1936.

PERSIAN

Ashai, Hajji Mukhtar Shah, *Tract on the Art of Shawl Weaving*. Lahore: Kohinoor Press, 1887.

Waiz, Sheikh Ahmad. *Rajumul Wahabbiya Najumul al-Shahbiyya*. [Throwing Stones at the Wahabbis]. Lahore: Kohitoor Press, 1912.

F. Private Collections

Ashraf, Peerzada Mohammad. *Private Collection including Pamphlets, Letters, Manuscripts and Newspaper Cuttings*. Bemina, Kashmir.

Bazaz, Bhushan. *Private Collection of Prem Nath Bazaz*. New Delhi.

Jalali, Jia Lal Kaul. *Private Collection of Jia Lal Kaul Jalali*. Srinagar State Archives, Srinagar, Kashmir.

Jalali, Syed Iftekar. *Private Collection including Newspaper Cuttings and Pamphlets*. Srinagar, Kashmir.

Kondoo, Abdul Rahman. *Private Collection including Letters and Diaries*. Srinagar, Kashmir.

Hassnain, Fidah Mohammad. *Private Collection including Pamphlets and Manuscripts*. Srinagar, Kashmir.

Qari, Moulvi Mohammad Shafi. *Private Collection of Moulvi Mohammad Nooruddin Qari Kashmiri*. Srinagar, Kashmir.

Wafai, A.R. *Private Collection including Pamphlets and Letters*. Srinagar, Kashmir.

Zahid, Nooruddin. *Private Collection including Pamphlets and Published Sources*. Badgaam, Kashmir.

G. Interviews

Ashraf, Peerzada Mohammad. Bemina, Kashmir. April 18, 1998.

Hassnain, Fidah Mohammad. Srinagar, Kashmir. September 22, 1997.

Kashmiri, Bahar. Srinagar, Kashmir. September 23 and 24, 1997.

Qari, Moulana Mohammad Shafi. Srinagar, Kashmir. November 26, 1997.

Zahid, Nooruddin. Badgaam, Kashmir. April 23 and 29, 1998 and May 5, 1998.

H. Newspapers

Aftab, Srinagar. 2001. Author's Personal Collection.

Amar, Jammu. 1940. Jammu State Archives.

Civil and Military Gazette, Lahore. 1885–1932. Private Collections.

Hamdard, Srinagar. 1933–48. Government Press Department, Srinagar, and Private Collections.

Indian Express, New Delhi and Bombay. 2000–1. Author's Personal Collection.

Inquilab, Srinagar. 1933. Jammu State Archives.

Jammu and Kashmir State Gazette, Jammu. 1900–43. Jammu State Archives.

Khalid-i-Kashmir, Srinagar. 1940–7. Government Press Department, Srinagar.

Khidmat, Srinagar. 1940–7. Government Press Department, Srinagar.

Martand, Srinagar. 1937. Jammu State Archives.

Rahnuma, Srinagar. 1940–3. Jammu State Archives.

Sadaqat, Srinagar. 1933. Jammu State Archives.

The Times, London. 1870–80. Earl Gregg Swem Library, The College of William and Mary.

Secondary Sources

A. Books

ENGLISH

Ahangar, Mohammed Altaf Hussain. *Customary Succession Among Muslims (A Critical Appraisal of Judicial Interpretation in Kashmir)*. New Delhi: Uppal Publishing House, 1986.

Ahmad, Aziz. *Islamic Modernism in India and Pakistan 1857–1964*. London: Oxford University Press, 1967.

Ahmed, Rafiuddin. *The Bengal Muslims 1871–1906: A Quest for Identity*. Delhi: Oxford University Press, 1981.

Akbar, M.J. *India: The Siege Within*. England: Penguin Books, 1985.

Alam, Muzaffar. *The Crisis of Empire in Mughal North India, Awadh and the Punjab, 1707–48*. Delhi: Oxford University Press, 1986.

Ali, Agha Shahid. "Farewell." In *The Country Without a Post Office, Poems*. New York: W.W. Norton & Company, 1997.

Alston, Leonard. *Education and Citizenship in India*. London: Longmans, Green, And Co., 1910.

Ames, Frank. *The Kashmir Shawl and its Indo-French Influence*. England: Antique Collector's Club, 1986.

Anand, Justice A.S. *The Constitution of Jammu and Kashmir: Its Development and Comments*. Delhi: Universal Book Traders, 1995.

Anderson, Benedict. *Imagined Communities: Reflections on the Origins and Spread of Nationalism*. Revised Edition, London and New York: Verso, 1995.

Anderson, Michael R. "Islamic Law and the Colonial Encounter in British-India." In David Arnold and Peter Robb, eds. *Institutions and Ideologies: A SOAS South Asia Reader*. Richmond, Surrey: Curzon Press, 1993.

Ansaari, Nishat. "Urdu in Jammu and Kashmir." In P.N. Pushp and K. Warikoo, eds. *Jammu, Kashmir, and Ladakh: Linguistic Predicament.* Delhi: Har-Anand Publications, 1996.

Ansari, Sarah F.D. *Sufi Saints and State Power: The Pirs of Sind, 1843–1947.* Cambridge: Cambridge University Press, 1992.

Bamzai, P.N.K. *Culture and Political History of Kashmir.* 3 vols. New Delhi: MD Publications, 1994.

———. *A History of Kashmir, Political, Social, Cultural From the Earliest Times to the Present Day.* New Delhi: Metropolitan Book Company, 1973.

Basu, Aparna. *The Growth of Education and Political Development in India, 1898–1920.* Delhi: Oxford University Press, 1974.

Bazaz, Prem Nath. *The History of the Struggle for Freedom in Kashmir, Cultural and Political, From the Earliest Times to the Present Day.* New Delhi: Kashmir Publishing Company, 1954.

Bayly, C.A. *The New Cambridge History of India, II., 1, Indian Society and the Making of the British Empire.* Cambridge: Cambridge University Press, 1990.

———. *Rulers, Townsmen and Bazaars: North Indian Society in the Age of British Expansion.* 1st Indian edn: Delhi: Oxford University Press, 1992.

———. *Empire and Information: Intelligence Gathering and Social Communication in India 1780–1870.* Cambridge: Cambridge University Press, 1996.

———. *Origins of Nationality in South Asia: Patriotism and Ethical Government in the Making of Modern India.* Delhi: Oxford University Press, 1998.

Bayly, Susan. *Saints, Goddesses, and Kings: Muslims and Christians in South Indian Society 1700–1900.* Cambridge: Cambridge University Press, 1989.

Bhatia, B.M. *Famines in India: A Study in Some Aspects of the Economic History of India (1860–1965).* New Delhi: Asia Publishing House, 1967.

Bose, Sugata. *Agrarian Bengal: Economy, Social Structure and Politics, 1919–1947.* Cambridge: Cambridge University Press, 1986.

———. "A Doubtful Inheritance: The Partition of Bengal in 1947." In D.A. Low, ed. *The Political Inheritance of Pakistan.* New York: St Martin's Press, 1991.

Bose, Sumantra. *The Challenge in Kashmir: Democracy, Self Determination and a Just Peace.* New Delhi: Sage, 1997.

Brass, Paul R. *Language, Religion and Politics in North India.* London: Cambridge University Press, 1974.

Chatterjee, Partha. *Nationalist Thought and the Colonial World: A Derivative Discourse.* Minneapolis: University of Minnesota Press, 1993.

Copland, Ian. "The Abdullah Factor: Kashmiri Muslims and the Crisis of 1947." In D.A. Low, ed. *The Political Inheritance of Pakistan.* New York: St. Martin's Press, 1991.

————. *The Princes of India in the Endgame of Empire, 1917–1947.* Cambridge: Cambridge University Press, 1997

Dhar, D.N. *Socio-Economic History of the Kashmir Peasantry, From Ancient Times to the Present Day.* Srinagar: Centre for Kashmir Studies, 1989.

Dhar, K.N. "Mysticism in Kashmiri Poetry." In M. Amin Pandit, ed. *Alamdar-i-Kashmir: Standard Bearer, Patron-Saint of Kashmir.* Srinagar: Gulshan Publishers, 1997.

Dhar, S.N. "Glimpses of Rural Kashmir." In Suresh K. Sharma and Usha Sharma, eds. *Kashmir through the Ages: Society, Economy and Culture.* 3 vols. New Delhi: Deep and Deep Publications, 1998.

Dirks, Nicholas B. *The Hollow Crown: Ethnohistory of an Indian Kingdom.* Ann Arbor: University of Michigan Press, 1996.

Eaton, Richard. *The Rise of Islam and the Bengal Frontier, 1201–1760.* Berkeley: California University Press, 1993.

Eickelman, Dale. *Moroccan Islam: Tradition and Society in a Pilgrimage Center.* Austin: University of Texas Press, 1976.

———— and James Piscatori, eds. *Muslim Travelers: Pilgrimage, Migration and the Religious Imagination.* Berkeley: University of California Press, 1990.

Fisher, Michael H. *Indirect Rule in India: Residents and the Residency System, 1764–1858.* Delhi: Oxford University Press, 1991.

Freitag, Sandria B. *Collective Action and Community: Public Arenas and the Emergence of Communalism in North India.* Berkeley: University of California Press, 1989.

Ganguly, Sumit. *The Crisis in Kashmir: Portents of War, Hopes of Peace.* Cambridge: Woodrow Wilson Center Press and Cambridge University Press, 1997.

Ganju, M. *Textile Industries in Kashmir.* Delhi: Premier Publishing Company, 1945.

Gauhar, G.N. *Sheikh Noor-ud-Din Wali (Nund Rishi).* New Delhi: Sahitya Akademi, 1988.

Ghosh, Suresh Chandra. *Indian Nationalism: A Case Study for the First University Reform by the British Raj.* New Delhi: Vikas Publishing House, 1985.

Gilmartin, David. "Shrines, Succession, and Sources of Moral Authority." In Barbara Daly Metcalf, ed. *Moral Conduct and Authority: The Place of Adab in South Asian Islam.* Berkeley: University of California Press, 1984.

————. *Empire and Islam: Punjab and the Making of Pakistan.* Berkeley: University of California Press, 1988.

Gommans, Jos J.L. *The Rise of the Indo-Afghan Empire c. 1710–1780.* Leiden: E.J. Brill, 1994.

Gorra, Michael. "Response to *Identities.*" In Kwame Anthony Appiah and Henry Louis Gates, Jr., eds. *Identities.* Chicago: Chicago University Press, 1995.

Grover, Verinder. ed. *The Story of Kashmir, Yesterday and Today.* 3 vols. Delhi: Deep and Deep Publications, 1995.

Gupta, Narayani. *Delhi Between Two Empires, 1803–1931: Society, Government, and Urban Growth.* Delhi: Oxford University Press, 1981.

Gupta, Sheetal. *Trilingual Aspects of Language Learning and Teaching in Jammu and Kashmir.* Jammu: Jay Kay Book House, 1986.

Habib, Irfan. *Agrarian System of Mughal India, 1556–1707.* Bombay: Asia Publishing House, 1963.

Hangloo, R.L. *Agrarian System of Kashmir (1846–1889).* New Delhi: Commonwealth Publishers, 1995.

Hardiman, David. "Baroda: The Structure of a 'Progressive' State." In Robin Jeffrey, ed. *People, Princes and Paramount Power: Society and Politics in the Indian Princely States.* Delhi: Oxford University Press, 1978.

Hardy, Peter. *The Muslims of British India.* Cambridge: Cambridge University Press, 1972.

Hassnain, F.M. *British Policy towards Kashmir (1846–1921) (Kashmir in Anglo-Russian Politics).* New Delhi: Sterling Publishers, 1974.

————. *Freedom Struggle in Kashmir.* New Delhi: Rima Publishing House, 1988.

Hunter, W.W. *The Indian Musalmans.* First published in 1871. Reprint, Delhi: Indological Book House, 1969.

Hussain, Imtiyaz. *Muslim Law and Customs (With a special reference to the law as applied in Jammu and Kashmir).* Kashmir: Srinagar Law Journal, 1989.

Hussain, Syed Tassadque. *Customary Law and the Indian Constitution.* New Delhi: Rima Publishing House, 1987.

Ibrahim, Sardar Mohammad. *The Kashmir Saga.* 2nd ed. Azad Kashmir: Verinag Publishers, 1990.

Jaisingh, Hari. *Kashmir: A Tale of Shame.* Delhi: UBS Publishers, 1996.

Jha, Prem Shankar. *Kashmir 1947: Rival Versions of History.* Delhi: Oxford University Press, 1996.

Jalal, Ayesha. *Self and Sovereignty: Individual and Community in South Asian Islam since 1850.* London and New York: Routledge, 2000.

————. "Exploding Communalism: The Politics of Muslim Identity in South Asia." In Sugata Bose and Ayesha Jalal, eds. *Nationalism, Democracy and Development: State and Politics in India.* Delhi: Oxford University Press, 1997.

———. *Democracy and Authoritarianism in South Asia.* Cambridge: Cambridge University Press, 1995.

Jeffrey, Robin, ed. *People, Princes and Paramount Power: Society and Politics in the Indian Princely States.* Delhi: Oxford University Press, 1978.

Kaul, J.L. "Kashmiri Poetry: Some Forms and Themes." In Kalla, ed. *Literary Heritage of Kashmir.* Delhi: Mittal Publications, 1985.

———. "Parmanand: A Kashmiri Poet." In Kalla, ed. *Literary Heritage of Kashmir.* Delhi: Mittal Publications, 1985.

——— and Motilal Saqi. *Parmanand.* Srinagar: Cultural Academy, 1972.

Kessinger, Tom. "Regional Economy (1757–1857) North India." In Dharma Kumar, ed. *The Cambridge Economic History of India, vol. 2: c. 1757–c. 1970.* Cambridge: Cambridge University Press, 1983.

Kessler, Clive. *Islam and Politics in a Malay State: Kelantan 1838–1969.* Ithaca: Cornell University Press, 1978.

Khan, G.H. *Freedom Movement in Kashmir 1931–40.* Delhi: Light and Life Publishers, 1980.

Khan, Mohammad Ishaq. *History of Srinagar 1846–1947: A Study in Socio-Cultural Change.* Srinagar: Aamir Publications, 1978.

———. *Kashmir's Transition to Islam: The Role of Muslim Rishis (Fifteenth to Eighteenth Century).* Delhi: Manohar Publications, 1994.

———. "The Significance of the Dargah of Hazratbal in the Socio-Religious and Political Life of Kashmiri Muslims." In Christian W. Troll, ed. *Muslim Shrines in India: Their Character, History and Significance.* Delhi: Oxford University Press, 1992.

Khuhro, Hamida. *The Making of Modern Sindh: British Policy and Social Change in the Nineteenth Century.* 2nd edn Karachi: Oxford University Press, 1999.

Kilam, Jia Lal. *A History of Kashmiri Pandits.* Srinagar: Gandhi Memorial College Managing Committee, 1955.

Kishwar, Madhu. *Religion at the Service of Nationalism and Other Essays.* Delhi: Oxford University Press, 1998.

Kotru, Nil Kanth. *Lal Ded: Her Life and Sayings.* Srinagar: Utpal Publications, 1989.

Koul, Pandit Anand. *Lalla Yogishwari: Her Life and Sayings.* Lahore: Mercantile Press, 1900.

———. *Geography of Jammu and Kashmir State.* Reprint, Delhi: Light and Life Publishers, 1978.

———. *The Kashmiri Pandit.* Reprint, Delhi: Utpal Publications, 1991.

Kozlowski, Gregory C. *Muslim Endowments and Society in British India.* Cambridge: Cambridge University Press, 1985.

Kumar, Krishna. *Political Agenda of Education: A Study of Colonialist and Nationalist Ideas.* New Delhi: Sage Press, 1991.

Kumar, Nita. *Lessons from Schools: The History of Education in Banaras.* New Delhi: Sage Publications, 1991.

Lamb, Alastair. *Kashmir: A Disputed Legacy, 1846–1990.* Karachi: Oxford University Press, 1993.

———. *Incomplete Partition: The Genesis of the Kashmir Dispute 1947–48.* Hertingfordbury: Roxford Books, 1997.

Lavan, Spencer. *The Ahmadiyah Movement: A History and Perspective.* New Delhi: Manohar Book Service, 1977.

Leonard, Karen. "Hyderabad: The Mulki–Non-Mulki Conflict." In Robin Jeffrey, ed. *People, Princes and Paramount Power: Society and Politics in the Indian Princely States.* Delhi: Oxford University Press, 1978.

Lewis, Martin W. and Karen Wigen. *The Myth of Continents: A Critique of Metageography.* Berkeley: University of California Press, 1997.

Madan, T.N. *Family and Kinship: A Study of the Pandits of Rural Kashmir.* Delhi: Oxford University Press, 1989.

Malik, G.R. "Sheikh Noor-ud-Din Noorani—The Mystic Poet of Kashmir." In K.N. Kalla, ed. *Literary Heritage of Kashmir.* New Delhi: Mittal Publications, 1985.

Marshall, T.H. *Class, Citizenship and Social Development, Essays by T.H. Marshall.* Connecticut: Greenwood Press, 1973.

Mazumder, Rajit K. *The Indian Army and the Making of Punjab.* New Delhi: Permanent Black, 2003.

Metcalf, Barbara. *Islamic Revival in British India: Deoband, 1860–1900.* Princeton: Princeton University Press, 1982.

Mujeeb, M. *The Indian Muslims.* Montreal: McGill University Press, 1967.

Mukherji, S.N. *History of Education in India (Modern Period).* Baroda: Acharya Book Depot, 1957.

Murphy, Veronica. *Kashmir Shawls: Woven Art and Cultural Document.* London: Kyburg Limited, 1988.

Neve, Ernest F. *Beyond the Pir Panjal: Life among the Mountains and Valleys of Kashmir.* London: T.F. Unwin, 1912.

Om, Hari. *Muslims of Jammu and Kashmir: A Study in the Spread of Education and Consciousness, 1857–1925.* New Delhi: Archives Publishers, 1986.

Pappas, Paul C. *Jesus' Tomb in India: Debate on his Death and Resurrection.* Berkeley: Asian Humanities Press, 1991.

Parmu, R.K. *A History of Muslim Rule in Kashmir 1320–1819.* New Delhi: People's Publishing House, 1969.

Pasha, Mustapha Kamal. "Beyond the Two-Nation Divide: Kashmir and Resurgent Islam." In Raju G.C. Thomas, ed. *Perspectives on Kashmir: The Roots of Conflict in South Asia*. Boulder: Westview Press, 1992.

Punjabi, Riyaz. "Kashmir: The Bruised Identity." In Raju G.C. Thomas, ed. *Perspectives on Kashmir: The Roots of Conflict in South Asia*. Boulder: Westview Press, 1992.

Puri, Balraj. *Kashmir: Towards Insurgency*. New Delhi: Orient Longman, 1993.

Pushp, P.N. "Kashmiri and the Linguistic Predicament of the State." In P.N. Pushp and K. Warikoo, eds. *Jammu, Kashmir, and Ladakh: Linguistic Predicament*. Delhi: Har-Anand Publications, 1996.

Rai, Mridu. *Hindu Rulers, Muslim Subjects: Islam, Rights, and the History of Kashmir*. New Delhi: Permanent Black, Forthcoming.

Raina, A.N. *Geography of Jammu and Kashmir*. 3rd rev. edn. New Delhi: National Book Trust, 1981.

Raina, N.N. *Kashmir Politics and Imperialist Maneuvers, 1846–1980*. New Delhi: Patriot Publishers, 1988.

Raina, Trilokinath. *An Anthology of Modern Kashmiri Verse*. Poona: Sangam Press, 1972.

———. ed. *The Best of Mahjoor*. Srinagar: Cultural Academy, 1989.

Rangarajan, Mahesh. *India's Wildlife History: An Introduction*. New Delhi: Permanent Black, 2001.

Rasool, Ghulam. *Education in Jammu and Kashmir: Issues and Documents*. Jammu: Jay Kay Book House, 1986.

Rawlley, Ratan C. *Economics of the Silk Industry: A Study in Industrial Organization*. London: P.S. King & Son, 1919.

———. *The Silk Industry and Trade: A Study in the Economic Organization of the Export Trade of Kashmir and Indian Silks, with Special Reference to their Utilization in the British and French Markets*. England: P.S. King & Son, 1919.

Raychaudhuri, Tapan. "The Agrarian System of Mughal India: A Review Essay." In Muzaffar Alam and Sanjay Subrahmanyam, eds. *The Mughal State, 1526–1750*. Delhi: Oxford University Press, 1998.

Robb, Peter. "Ideas in Agrarian History: Some Observations on the British and Nineteenth-Century Bihar." In David Arnold and Peter Robb, eds. *Institutions and Ideologies: A SOAS South Asia Reader*. Richmond, Surrey: Curzon Press, 1993.

Robinson, Francis. *Islam and Muslim Society in South Asia*. New Delhi: Oxford University Press, 2000.

Roy, Asim. *The Islamic Syncretistic Tradition in Bengal*. Princeton: Princeton University Press, 1983.

Rudolph, Suzanne Hoeber and Lloyd L. Rudolph. *Education and Politics in India: Studies in Organization, Society, and Policy.* Cambridge: Harvard University Press, 1972.

Saberwal, Vasant, Mahesh Rangarajan, and Ashish Kothari. *People, Parks, and Wildlife: Towards Coexistence.* New Delhi: Orient Longman, 2001.

Schofield, Victoria. *Kashmir in the Crossfire.* London and New York: I.B. Tauris Publishers, 1996.

Scott, James C. *Domination and the Arts of Resistance: Hidden Transcripts.* New Haven: Yale University Press, 1990.

———. *Weapons of the Weak: Everyday Forms of Peasant Resistance.* New Haven: Yale University Press, 1985.

Sen, Amartya. "On Interpreting India's Past." In Sugata Bose and Ayesha Jalal, eds. *Nationalism, Democracy and Development: State and Politics in India.* Delhi: Oxford University Press, 1997.

Sender, Henriette. *The Kashmiri Pandits: A Study of Cultural Choice in North India.* Delhi: Oxford University Press, 1988.

Shaikh, Farzana. *Community and Consensus in Islam: Muslim Representation in Colonial India, 1860–1947.* Cambridge: Cambridge University Press, 1989.

Sharma, D.C. *Kashmir Agriculture and Land Revenue System under the Sikh Rule (1819–1846).* Delhi: Rima Publishing House, 1986.

Singh, Tavleen. *Kashmir: A Tragedy of Errors.* Delhi: Viking, 1995.

Stokes, Eric. *The Peasant and the Raj: Studies in Agrarian Society and Peasant Rebellion in Colonial India.* Cambridge: Cambridge University Press, 1978.

Sufi, G.M.D. *Kashir: Being a History of Kashmir From Earliest Times to Our Own.* 2 vols. New Delhi: Light and Life Publishers, 1974.

———. *Islamic Culture in Kashmir.* New Delhi: Light and Life Publishers, 1979.

Swarup, Devendra and Sushil Aggarwal, eds. *The Roots of the Kashmir Problem: The Continuing Battle between Secularism and Communal Separatism.* Delhi: Manthan Prakashan, 1992.

Talbot, Ian. "The Unionist Party and Punjabi Politics, 1937–1947." In D.A. Low, ed. *The Political Inheritance of Pakistan.* New York: St Martin's Press, 1991.

Thomas, Raju G.C., ed. *Perspectives on Kashmir: The Roots of Conflict in South Asia.* Boulder: Westview Press, 1992.

Tikku, G.L. *Persian Poetry in Kashmir 1339–1846: An Introduction.* Los Angeles: University of California Press, 1971.

Tomlinson, B.R. *The New Cambridge History of India, III. 3, The Economy of*

Modern India, 1860–1970. Cambridge: Cambridge University Press, 1993.

Varshney, Ashutosh. "Three Compromised Nationalisms: Why Kashmir has been a Problem." In Raju G.C. Thomas, ed. *Perspectives on Kashmir: The Roots of Conflict in South Asia.* Boulder: Westview Press, 1992.

Veer, Peter van der. *Religious Nationalism: Hindus and Muslims in India.* Berkeley: University of California Press, 1994.

Viswanathan, Gauri. *Masks of Conquest: Literary Study and British Rule in India.* New York: Columbia University Press, 1989.

Wakefield, W. *History of Kashmir and the Kashmiris: The Happy Valley.* Reprint, Delhi: Seema Publications, 1975.

Wakhlu, S.N. *Habba Khatoon: Nightingale of Kashmir.* Delhi: South Asia Publications, 1994.

Warikoo, K. "Language and Politics in Jammu and Kashmir: Issues and Perspectives." In P.N. Pushp and K. Warikoo, eds. *Jammu, Kashmir and Ladakh: Linguistic Predicament.* Delhi: Har-Anand Publications, 1996.

Wirsing, Robert G. *India, Pakistan, and the Kashmir Dispute: On Regional Conflict and its Resolution.* Delhi: Rupa & Co., 1994.

Yasin, Madhavi. *British Paramountcy in Kashmir 1876–1894.* New Delhi: Atlantic Publishers and Distributors, 1984.

———. "Kalhana and his *Rajatarangini.*" In K.N. Kalla, ed. *The Literary Heritage of Kashmir.* Delhi: Mittal Publications: 1985.

Younghusband, Francis. *Kashmir.* London: Adam and Charles Black, 1911.

Zutshi, U.K. *Emergence of Political Awakening in Kashmir.* Delhi: Manohar, 1986.

KASHMIRI

Inayatullah, Hafiz Mohammed. *Lalla Arifa barzabane Kashmiri* [Lal Ded in Kashmiri]. Lahore: Din Mohammad Electric Press, undated.

Munawwar, Naji and Shafi Shauq. *Kashur Adbuk Tawarikh* [History of Kashmiri Literature]. Srinagar: Department of Kashmiri, University of Kashmir, 1992.

PERSIAN

Jaan, Zubeida. *Mullah Hamidullah Shahabadi: Hayat aur Karname* [Mullah Hamidullah Shahabadi: Life and Works]. Srinagar: Maqdomi Press, 1996.

URDU

Bukhari, Sayyid Mohammad Farooq. *Kashmir me Arbi Sher wa Adab ki Tarikh* [History of Arabic Poetry and Literature in Kashmir]. Srinagar: Cultural Academy, 1993.

Ibrahim, Moulvi Mohammad. "Mirwaiz Moulana Rasul Shah." In M.Y. Teng, ed. *Hamara Adab Shaksiyat Number 2*. Srinagar: Cultural Academy, 1986.

Sarvari, Abdul Qadir. *Kashmir me Farsi Adab ki Tarikh* [History of Persian Literature in Kashmir]. Srinagar: Majlis-i-Takhikat-e-Urdu, 1968.

B. Dissertations and Theses

Dar, Ali Mohammad. "Trade and Commerce During Dogra Rule in Kashmir (1846-1947)." Ph.D. Thesis, University of Kashmir, 1991.

Deshpande, Prachi. "Narratives of Pride: History and Regional Identity in Maharashtra, India, c. 1870–1960." Ph.D. Dissertation, Tufts University, 2002.

Ghosh, Semanti. "Nationalism and the Problem of Difference: Bengal, 1905–1947." Ph.D. Dissertation, Tufts University, 2000.

Khan, Bashir Ahmed. "Ahl-i-Hadith Movement in Kashmir 1901–1981." M. Phil Thesis, University of Kashmir, 1984.

Mir, Farina. "The Social Space of Language: Punjabi Popular Narratives in Colonial India, c. 1850–1900." Ph.D. Dissertation, Columbia University, 2002.

Mir, Ghulam Hassan. "Muslim Shrines of Srinagar (Kashmir) and their Role (1857–1925)." M. Phil Thesis, University of Kashmir, 1986.

Rai, Mridu. "The Question of Religion in Kashmir: Sovereignty, Legitimacy, and Rights, c. 1846–1947." Ph.D. Dissertation, Columbia University, 2000.

C. Journal Articles

Ahmad, Aziz. "Conversions to Islam in the Valley of Kashmir." *Central Asiatic Journal*, xxiii (1–2) (1979): 3–18.

Bose, Sugata. "Nation, Reason, and Religion: India's Partition in International Perspective." *Economic and Political Weekly*. August 1, 1998: 2090–7.

Chakrabarty, Dipesh. "Postcoloniality and the Artifice of History: Who Speaks for Indian Pasts?" *Representations* 37 (Winter 1992): 1–25.

Eickelman, Dale F. "The Art of Memory: Islamic Education and its Social Reproduction." *Comparative Studies in Society and History* 20 (October 1978): 485–516.

Ghose, Ajit Kumar. "Food Supply and Starvation: A Study of Famines with Reference to the Indian Sub-continent." *Oxford Economic Papers* 34(2) (July 1982): 368–89.

Jalal, Ayesha. "Nation, Reason and Religion: Punjab's Role in the Partition of India." *Economic and Political Weekly*. August 8, 1998: 2183–90.

Khan, Mohammad Ishaq. "The Impact of Islam on Kashmir in the Sultanate

Period (1320–1586)." *Indian Economic and Social History Review* 23 (2) (1986): 187–205.

Pollock, Sheldon. "India in the Vernacular Millennium: Literary Culture and Polity, 1000–1500." *Daedalus* 127 (Summer 1998): 41–74.

Prakash, Gyan. "Subaltern Studies as Postcolonial Criticism." *American Historical Review* (December 1994): 1475–90.

Prakash, Siddhartha. "The Political Economy of Kashmir since 1947." *Contemporary South Asia* (2000) 9(3): 315–37.

Roff, William R. "Islam Obscured? Some Reflections on Studies of Islam and Society in Southeast Asia." *Archipel* 29 (1982): 7–34.

Tareen, K.A. "The Great Ahmadiyya Mosque at Srinagar (A Brief Historical Survey)." *Basharaat-E-Ahmadiyya, A Biannual International News Magazine of Ahmadiyya Anjuman Ishaat Islam, Lahore.* December 1996: 19–23.

Thorner, Daniel "The Kashmir Land Reforms: Some Personal Impressions." *The Economic Weekly.* September 12, 1953: 1000–4.

Tikku, G.L. "Mysticism in Kashmir: In the Fourteenth and Fifteenth Centuries." *Muslim World* LIII (July 1963): 226–33.

Index